England
The Complete One-Day International Record

Jason Woolgar

Eric Dobby Publishing

© Jason Woolgar 1995

Published by Eric Dobby Publishing Ltd,
12 Warnford Road, Orpington, Kent BR6 6LW

All rights reserved. No part of this book may be
reproduced, stored in a retrieval system now known
or yet to be invented, or transmitted in any form
or by any means, mechanical or electrical, photocopied
or recorded without the express written permission of
the publishers except by a reviewer wishing to quote
brief passages in a review either written or
broadcast.

A catalogue record of this book is available from
the British Library.

ISBN 1-85882-044 8

Typeset by Kevin O'Connor, Poole
Printed and bound in Great Britain by
Ipswich Book Co. Ltd., Ipswich, Suffolk.

This book is dedicated to Kim Sykes

Whose support and hard work made it possible

ACKNOWLEDGEMENTS

This book has involved a great deal of research and I would like to acknowledge the kind assistance I have received from the following:

Philip Bailey, Bill Frindall, Victor H. Isaacs, Richard Lockwood, Gordon Vince, the officials at the Cricket Boards' of Australia, India, New Zealand and Sri Lanka, The International Cricket Council, The Test and County Cricket Board and The Association of Cricket Statisticians and Historians.

The following publications were also consulted and I am most grateful to the authors and publishers of each.

The Wisden Book of One-Day International Cricket 1971-1985: Bill Frindall and Victor H. Isaacs
One-Day International Cricket Records: V.H. Isaacs and R.K. Whitham
Who's Who of Cricketers: Philip Bailey, Philip Thorn and Peter Wynne-Thomas
ACS International Cricket Year Book 1994-1995
The Cricketer Quarterly Facts and Figures

I am also indebted to Robin Smith for providing the foreword, and to Denis Bundy for his generous assistance.

Finally, I would like to thank Paul Gregorowski for both his practical assistance and initial encouragement.

CONTENTS

Dedication	3
Acknowledgements	4
Contents	5
Foreword by Robin Smith	6
Introduction	8
One-Day International Matches 1971-1995	11
Player Profiles	243
One-Day International Records 1971-1995	323
Venues	324
Results per Venue	325
Results	326
Summary of Results	332
World Cup 1975-1992	333
Prudential/Texaco Trophy 1972-1994	336
Benson & Hedges World Series Cup 1979-1995	337
Highest Totals	338
Lowest Completed Innings	338
Highest Totals against England	370
Lowest Completed Innings against England	339
Greatest Victories	340
Narrowest Victories	341
Heaviest Defeats	342
Narrowest Defeats	342
Total Appearances	343
Leading Run Scorers	346
Highest Individual Scores	347
Highest Partnerships for each wicket	352
Total Highest Partnerships	352
Leading Wicket Takers	354
Best Bowling	355
Most Career Dismissals	359
Most Dismissals in a Match	359
Most Career Catches	360
Most Catches in a Match	360
Best All-Round Performances in a Match	360
Best Career All-Round Performances	361
Captaincy Records	362
World One-Day International Records 1971-1995	363
Most appearances	364
Leading Run Scorers	364
Highest Individual Scores	365
Highest Partnerships for each Wicket	365
Total Highest Partnerships	365
Leading Wicket Takers	366
Best Bowling	366
Most Career Dismissals	367
Most Career Catches	367

FOREWORD

I am delighted to be associated with a book that thoroughly examines a part of English cricket which has been largely overlooked. Especially as one-day cricket has such an important role to play in the game's future, generating vital income at both county and international level.

Unfortunately, some still believe that too much limited-overs cricket has had a damaging effect on our Test match teams. While it is true we do definitely play too much cricket it is the first-class game that needs to be reduced and not the one-day matches that keep our counties financially solvent.

I sincerely believe that the introduction of a second league in this country, and the subsequent reduction in first-class matches, would see a tremendous improvement in the standard of our cricket, and enable England's players to be both physically and mentally stronger for the demands of international cricket. Until the number of matches we play is brought into line with other countries we will never be able to compete on an equal footing.

Contrary to popular opinion, one-day internationals are very demanding and every match played is at least the equivalent of a domestic one-day final. Each game commands a high level of concentration and a players approach to his innings should not alter simply because he is playing a limited-overs match. When you go out to bat, whatever the situation, you have to score runs and to do so you need a very sound technique. At most you have to try to be a little more positive, but in the right way. Playing the correct shots and changing your game only to the extent that you might hit over the top slightly earlier in an innings and possibly take a few more chances. When you see a player modify his game and begin to play unorthodox shots it is usually at a time when the run rate is increasing and the pressure begins to rise. This is when you have to be mentally strong and remember that pressure is something you put on yourself. If you do succumb to the tension you will become anxious and begin to play the loose shots that will probably get you out.

Personally I enjoy playing in one-day internationals just as much as Test matches and regard them as equally important. Playing for your country, whether you pull on the one lion or three, is always special and I do cherish my English badge whatever the occasion.

So much so, the biggest disappointment of my career remains a limited-overs match that I was not fortunate enough to play in, the 1992 World Cup Final. Although I had recovered from injury and declared myself fit for this game I was not selected and have always regretted missing a match played in such a fabulous atmosphere and marvellous stadium. Particularly as we lost a final that we could, and perhaps should, have won.

Of the 64 one-day internationals that I have played, I have many fond memories, particulary my first century, against New Zealand in 1990. This was a most enjoyable innings as not only was it scored against an attack featuring Sir Richard Hadlee, whom I regard as one of the all time great bowlers, but also because it was recorded at Headingley, a ground where I have not always excelled.

My 167 against Australia in 1993 was also another career highlight.
This was one of those rare innings where everything instantly clicks and although the ball was swinging fiercely I felt very rhythmical and knew that I would do well. It was also nice to succeed against Australia and in particular Merv Hughes!

It is also very satisfying for me to score runs against India and Pakistan, especially as I am not rated as a great player against spin bowling. A strange accusation considering that I have spent my entire career batting in the middle order against which the spinners predominantly bowl, and I actually have a better average (49.25) against Pakistan, India and Sri Lanka, than the other countries. I still consider that I have a lot to offer and my international record is comparable with most other players in world cricket.

Although I obviously regret not being selected for the recent Ashes series, I have been able to recover from a shoulder operation and have worked harder than ever to prepare myself for the challenge ahead and hopefully regain my England place. I am determined to do so, particularly with a series in South Africa looming and also the World Cup. A chance for me to perhaps erase the disappointment of the 1992 final.

INTRODUCTION

*If you can meet with Triumph and Disaster
And treat those two impostors just the same*

The sentiments are Kipling's, but equally you may have heard them uttered by any of England's numerous cricket captains during the last decade. For "Triumph" read one-day internationals and for "Disaster" simply insert Test matches.

Since they defeated Australia in 1985, England have played 95 Test matches, winning just 17 and losing 43. During this time a paltry 5 series have been won, with the West Indies and India inflicting humiliating whitewashes and Australia triumphing heavily in four consecutive Ashes series.

To call this record poor would be a considerable understatement; indeed it compares unfavourably with almost every other Test- playing nation.

The picture is very different however when it comes to the limited-overs game. During the same ten-year period England have played a total of 122 one-day internationals, 65 of which they have won. Of these victories 9 were achieved against Australia, with a further 16 against the mighty West Indies, who were whitewashed in consecutive Texaco Trophy series.

Despite never actually lifting the World Cup, England have contested the last 2 finals and have won more World Cup matches than any other nation. They have also been the most consistent, reaching 3 finals and 2 semi-finals (the only team to have done so) as well as winning the prestigious Benson and Hedges World Series Cup.

Why do we continue to produce such competitive teams at one-day level without being able to reproduce that form in the Test arena? Unfortunately, England's Test problems are acute, and the paradox will not be resolved until long-term deficiencies are overcome.

The main concern remains the lack of adequate facilities and coaching at grassroots level, particularly in inner-city comprehensive schools. It is imperative that younger players, from as early as 9 or 10 years of age, are given the encouragement and tuition that will enable them to compete at the highest level.

Coaching, although vital, is not the only answer; the situation needs to be taken one step further, with the players of the future exposed to competitive cricket at a much earlier age, allowing them time to develop the technique and determination that are essential for success.

An increase in the number of young players should also go a long way to resolving the conspicuous and alarming lack of variety in the English game. The seemingly endless production line of medium pace bowlers is all too seldom interspersed with any top quality spin bowlers. This not only propagates unimaginative, one-paced bowling attacks, but also produces batsmen not technically equipped to cope effectively with, for example, a top quality leg spinner's variations.

Added to all this is the poor state of English pitches with too many flat tracks allowing mediocre batsmen to prosper against even the best bowlers. Good wickets are an essential ingredient in top class cricket, and until we produce better wickets that allow a fast bowler pace and bounce, such batsmen will continue to thrive and give a false impression of quality.

Although there is no doubt that the English domestic season is a very hard one, the emphasis has for far too long been on quantity at the expense of quality. Most of our cricket is simply not competitive enough, with only a handful of teams challenging realistically for honours each season.

This could be obviated by creating a two-tier league that would introduce the fighting qualities that overseas crowds take for granted in their players. Making the threat of relegation, or the prospect of promotion, a substantial incentive for the players to respond to other than their own averages.

It would also enable us to overcome another significant problem that continues to debilitate our top players: too much cricket. The 18-20 first-class matches that each county plays are significantly more than for any other nation, and three domestic limited-overs tournaments are at least one too many. This amount of cricket is absurd, making it impossible for our players to maintain consistently high standards and inducing the stress-related injuries and exhaustion that have so ravaged our Test teams.

There is also little doubt that foreign players benefit from playing in English conditions, with most of them having a spell in this country to hone the techniques that will be needed when they later tour with their national sides.

Although this is detrimental to the English Test team, partially negating the home advantage that every other nation enjoys, a complete ban on foreign stars is probably not the answer, especially in a commercial world where it would be unrealistic to shun the much needed revenue that one overseas player can bring to a county. Their presence also provides English cricket with an essential quality, a quality that must have a beneficial effect on both their team-mates and younger, inexperienced players.

A possible solution would perhaps see the situation modified to the extent that overseas players would be allowed full participation in limited-overs tournaments but were restricted in the amount of first-class cricket they could play. Even if this compromise did not benefit our national side to any great degree it would at least dilute the extent to which overseas stars thrive at the expense of county cricketers.

In the short term, the easiest problem to rectify is the inconsistent selection policy that we continue to adopt. In the case of the England team many are called of whom almost all are chosen; in fact so bad has the situation become that anyone with a county cap not to have played for England in the past few years can count himself decidedly unfortunate! For the last 95 Test matches England have picked over 80 players, a large number of whom have been dropped and reselected with alarming regularity. Unlike other countries, most notably the all-conquering West Indies who allow their players to develop, England generally discard those, Graeme Hick apart, who do not instantly excel.

If this sounds like an exaggeration you need look no further than the recent treatment of Graham Thorpe and Robin Smith.

Picked to tour the West Indies after an excellent debut series against Australia, Thorpe returned from the Caribbean having acquitted himself well on a very difficult tour, only to be promptly dropped. Why? Ask the selectors.

The case of Robin Smith is even more perplexing. Although he had not reached his own very high standard in the previous year, he is probably the best middle order batsman in the country, and his overall record, approaching 4000 Test runs at an average of over 44, is still better than any other established English batsman.

Despite this world class record, Smith was axed 3 Test matches after making his highest test score, 175 against the West Indies in Antigua, on the grounds that he could not play spin bowling. This prior to a series against South Africa who did not have a single spin bowler worthy of the name in their entire squad!

Instead of inventing reasons to drop Smith, and this goes for the majority of other established players casually discarded, the selectors would have been better employed reviewing his previous record. In the 1990 series against India, for example, he averaged over 180 against a predominantly spin attack, and his many impressive innings have been scored against the world's greatest exponents of both fast and slow bowling.

Most other Test countries keep faith with their players, recognising that if they are of sufficient calibre to warrant selection they will generally recover from any slight lapse in form. Thorpe and Smith are but two in a long line of players who have been discarded in the hope of an overnight solution to England's problems. There are, however, no instant remedies and a consistent selection policy and long-term investment in players would go a long way to providing better international results. The knee-jerk reactions to which the English selectors constantly succumb rarely pay long-term dividends.

If all these factors have between them contributed to England's regular failures at Test match level, and all do produce powerful arguments for drastic and immediate change, they do not explain why these failures have not been transferred to the one-day arena.

It has been suggested that England's Test match deficiencies are inextricably linked to their limited-overs successes and that the saturation of the latter has bred careless shots into our cricketers. However, England have played 231 limited-overs matches since the inaugural game in 1971, compared to more than 300 contested by Australia and 280 featuring the West Indies. These two teams, despite playing so much one-day cricket, still manage to produce strong Test match sides.

Although it is therefore doubtful, fatigue apart, whether this abundance of domestic limited-overs cricket has had a detrimental effect on our Test team, it has certainly enhanced our prospects at one-day level, enabling players rapidly to develop the skills required for this form of cricket.

For the majority of our bowlers, accuarate line and length is a particular strength, with most perfectly capable of producing 10 economical overs but few able to take the high number of wickets needed to win Test matches with sufficient regularity.

We have also produced a plethora of attacking batsmen in the last ten years, stroke-makers who revel in the freedom that one-day cricket allows but who have been found wanting when required to exercise the mental application and tenacity so vital in Test matches.

We seem to have lost the fight and determination that were once a great strength, instantly capitulating when the odds are stacked against us and unable to produce consistently good cricket for more than one or two matches in a series or one or two days in a match.

While these weaknesses are regularly exposed in Test matches, they are not as apparent in the shortened game, where flashes of ability are often enough to win matches and sustained good performances are not necessarily a requirement. Even our fragile batting line-ups (and England's recent collapses have been witnessed in almost majestic proportions) would struggle to falter in the 50 overs that a one-day game provides.

The only way we will ever be able to produce a more competitive team, one capable not only of surviving but of excelling in the high-pressure atmosphere of top international cricket, will be to inculcate the kind of resolve shown by so many of our foreign counterparts.

Although this needs to be done at an early age, with the younger players having to fight for their places in a competitive system, a short-term solution may perversely be to play more international cricket during our own summers, taking our elite players out of the heavy war of attrition that is county cricket, as the Australians do with their players in the Sheffield Shield, a competition of a considerably higher standard than our own.

Some of our Antipodean counterparts may go for a year or more without actually playing for their state sides; instead they are constantly playing international cricket against opponents of the highest calibre. County cricket could then be used as a nursery to produce the Test players of the future.

This would be of particular importance if, as seems likely, the traditionalists resist the move to a two-divisional league and our cricketers are forced to continue playing the exhausting number of games currently expected of them.

The introduction of four-day cricket is at least a step in the right direction. Unfortunately English cricket officials are reluctant innovators and, despite our continued exposure at Test level, they seem unable to endorse the drastic changes that urgently need to be made.

There are no easy answers, and until the administrators accept that the one-day game presents financial security and that county cricket should be used purely as a breeding ground to produce top quality Test match cricketers, I fear that many experts will be marvelling at our one-day triumphs and pondering our Test disasters for a very long time to come.

Jason Woolgar

ONE-DAY INTERNATIONAL MATCHES

1971-1995

Match No: 1/1

AUSTRALIA v ENGLAND

Played at Melbourne Cricket Ground on 05/01/1971
Toss: Australia   Result: Australia won by 5 wickets
Umpires: T.F. Brooks and L.P. Rowan
Man of the match: J.H. Edrich
Debuts: Eng - All   Aus - All

ENGLAND
G. Boycott	c Lawry b Thomson	8
J.H. Edrich	c Walters b Mallett	82
K.W.R. Fletcher	c G.S. Chappell b Mallett	24
B.L. D'Oliveira	run out	17
J.H. Hampshire	c McKenzie b Mallett	10
M.C. Cowdrey	c Marsh b Stackpole	1
R. Illingworth*	b Stackpole	1
A.P.E. Knott+	b McKenzie	24
J.A. Snow	b Stackpole	2
K. Shuttleworth	c Redpath b McKenzie	7
P. Lever	not out	4
Extras	(B 1, LB 9)	10
TOTAL	(39.4 overs)	**190**

						Fall	
McKenzie	7.4	0	22	2	1st	21
Thomson	8	2	22	1	2nd	87
Connolly	8	0	62	0	3rd	124
Mallett	8	1	34	3	4th	144
Stackpole	8	0	40	3	5th	148
					6th	152
					7th	156
					8th	171
					9th	183
					10th	190

AUSTRALIA
W.M. Lawry*	c Knott b Illingworth	27
K.R. Stackpole	c & b Shuttleworth	13
I.M. Chappell	st Knott b Illingworth	60
K.D. Walters	c Knott b D'Oliveira	41
I.R. Redpath	b Illingworth	12
G.S. Chappell	not out	22
R.W. Marsh+	not out	10
A.A. Mallett		
G.D. McKenzie		
A.N. Connolly		
A.L. Thomson		
Extras	(LB 4, W 1, NB 1)	6
TOTAL	(34.6 overs) (for 5 wkts)	**191**

						Fall	
Snow	8	0	38	0	1st	19
Shuttleworth	7	0	29	1	2nd	51
Lever	5.6	0	30	0	3rd	117
Illingworth	8	1	50	3	4th	158
D'Oliveira	6	1	38	1	5th	165

Match No: 2/2

ENGLAND v AUSTRALIA

Prudential Trophy
Played at Old Trafford, Manchester on 24/08/1972
Toss: Australia   **Result:** England won by 6 wickets
Umpires: C.S. Elliott and A.E.G. Rhodes
Man of the match: D.L. Amiss
Debuts: Eng - D.L. Amiss, G.G. Arnold, D.B. Close, A.W. Greig, R.A. Woolmer
Aus - R. Edwards, D.K. Lillee, R.A.L. Massie, A.P. Sheahan, G.D. Watson

AUSTRALIA
K.R. Stackpole	c D'Oliveira b Greig	37
G.D. Watson	b Arnold	0
I.M. Chappell	b Woolmer	53
G.S. Chappell	b Woolmer	40
R. Edwards	run out	57
A.P. Sheahan	b Arnold	6
K.D. Walters	lbw b Woolmer	2
R.W. Marsh+	c Close b Snow	11
A.A. Mallett	not out	6
D.K. Lillee		
R.A.L. Massie		
Extras	(B 2, LB 3, NB 5)	10
TOTAL	(55 overs) (for 8 wkts)	**222**

						Fall	
Snow	11	1	33	1	1st	4
Arnold	11	0	38	2	2nd	66
Greig	11	0	50	1	3rd	125
Woolmer	10	1	33	3	4th	156
D'Oliveira	9	1	37	0	5th	167
Close	3	0	21	0	6th	170
					7th	205
					8th	222

ENGLAND
G. Boycott	c Marsh b Watson	25
D.L. Amiss	b Watson	103
K.W.R. Fletcher	b Massie	60
D.B. Close*	run out	1
J.H. Hampshire	not out	25
B.L. D'Oliveira	not out	5
A.W. Greig		
A.P.E. Knott+		
R.A. Woolmer		
J.A. Snow		
G.G. Arnold		
Extras	(B 1, LB 6)	7
TOTAL	(49.1 overs) (for 4 wkts)	**226**

						Fall	
Lillee	11	2	49	0	1st	48
Massie	11	1	49	1	2nd	173
Watson	8	1	28	2	3rd	174
Mallett	11	1	43	0	4th	215
G.S. Chappell	3	0	20	0		
Walters	3	1	16	0		
Stacjpole	2.1	0	14	0		

Match No: 3/3

ENGLAND v AUSTRALIA

Prudential Trophy
Played at Lord's, London on 26/08/1972
Toss: Australia
Result: Australia won by 5 wickets
Umpires: A.E. Fagg and T.W. Spencer
Man of the match: G.S. Chappell
Debuts: Aus - D.J. Colley

ENGLAND
G. Boycott	b Lillee	8
D.L. Amiss	b Mallett	25
D.B. Close*	run out	43
K.W.R. Fletcher	c Stackpole b G.S. Chappell	20
J.H. Hampshire	st Marsh b Mallett	13
B.L. D'Oliveira	c I.M. Chappell b Lillee	6
A.W. Greig	b Massie	31
A.P.E. Knott+	c Mallett b Massie	50
R.A. Woolmer	run out	9
J.A. Snow	not out	5
G.G Arnold	not out	11
Extras	(B 1, LB 10, W 1, NB 3)	15
TOTAL	(55 overs) (for 9 wkts)	**236**

	O	M	R	W		Fall
Lillee	11	0	56	2	1st	11
Massie	11	1	35	2	2nd	65
Colley	11	1	72	0	3rd	87
Mallett	11	2	24	2	4th	114
G.S. Chappell	11	0	34	1	5th	121
					6th	121
					7th	198
					8th	217
					9th	218

AUSTRALIA
K.R. Stackpole	lbw b D'Oliveira	52
R. Edwards	c Knott b Snow	6
I.M. Chappell*	c Knott b Woolmer	31
G.S. Chappell	lbw b Snow	48
A.P. Sheahan	c Knott b Snow	50
G.D. Watson	not out	11
R.W. Marsh+	not out	6
D.J. Colley		
A.A. Mallett		
D.K. Lillee		
R.A.L. Massie		
Extras	(B 6, LB 14, W 12, NB 4)	36
TOTAL	(51.3 overs) (for 5 wkts)	**240**

	O	M	R	W		Fall
Snow	11	2	35	3	1st	44
Arnold	11	0	47	0	2nd	112
D'Oliveira	11	0	46	1	3rd	116
Greig	9	1	29	0	4th	219
Woolmer	9.3	1	47	1	5th	224

Match No: 4/4

ENGLAND v AUSTRALIA

Prudential Trophy
Played at Edgbaston, Birmingham on 28/08/1972
Toss: England   **Result:** England won by 2 wickets
Umpires: D.J. Constant and A.S.M. Oakman
Man of the match: B. Wood
Debuts: Eng - B. Wood   Aus - J.R. Hammond

AUSTRALIA

K.R. Stackpole	b Woolmer	61
R. Edwards	b Arnold	6
I.M. Chappell*	run out	3
G.S. Chappell	c Wood b D'Oliveira	13
A.P. Sheahan	c Woolmer b Wood	19
K.D. Walters	b Wood	15
R.W. Marsh+	lbw b Arnold	0
A.A. Mallett	b Arnold	8
J.R. Hammond	not out	15
D.K. Lillee	c Wood b Arnold	13
R.A.L. Massie	not out	16
Extras	(LB 6, NB 4)	10
TOTAL	(55 overs) (for 9 wkts)	**179**

						Fall	
Snow	11	0	29	0	1st		8
Arnold	11	3	27	4	2nd		15
Greig	10	3	24	0	3rd		40
D'Oliveira	6	1	19	1	4th		87
Woolmer	11	1	50	1	5th		111
Wood	6	0	20	2	6th		112
					7th		127
					8th		136
					9th		158

ENGLAND

G. Boycott	c Massie b Lillee	41
D.L. Amiss	c Marsh b G.S. Chappell	40
D.B. Close*	c Marsh b Lillee	5
K.W.R. Fletcher	c Marsh b Hammond	34
B.L. D'Oliveira	run out	2
B. Wood	lbw b Lillee	19
A.W. Greig	not out	24
A.P.E. Knott+	c Mallett b Walters	6
R.A. Woolmer	c Marsh b Walters	0
J.A. Snow	not out	0
G.G. Arnold		
Extras	(LB 5, W 4)	9
TOTAL	(51.3 overs) (for 8 wkts)	**180**

						Fall	
Lillee	11	2	25	3	1st		76
Massie	8.3	3	45	0	2nd		89
Mallett	4	0	16	0	3rd		94
Hammond	9	1	41	1	4th		104
G.S. Chappell	11	3	20	1	5th		143
Walters	8	1	24	2	6th		154
					7th		172
					8th		172

Match No: 5/1

ENGLAND v NEW ZEALAND

Prudential Trophy
Played at St Helen's, Swansea on 18/07/1973
Toss: New Zealand   **Result:** England won by 7 wickets
Umpires: D.J. Constant and C.S. Elliott
Man of the match: D.L. Amiss
Debuts: Eng - F.C. Hayes, G.R.J. Roope, D.L. Underwood
NZ - V. Pollard, R.E. Redmond, B.R. Taylor

NEW ZEALAND

G.M. Turner	c & b Illingworth	26
R.E. Redmond	lbw b Arnold	3
B.E. Congdon*	c Knott b Snow	2
B.F. Hastings	c Roope b Snow	0
M.G. Burgess	c Knott b Arnold	1
V. Pollard	c Knott b Arnold	55
K.J. Wadsworth+	lbw b Underwood	3
B.R. Taylor	c Fletcher b Snow	22
R.J. Hadlee	c Snow b Greig	28
R.O. Collinge	c Knott b Snow	4
H.J. Howarth	not out	5
Extras	(LB 2, W 7)	9
TOTAL	**(52.5 overs)**	**158**

						Fall	
Snow	10	0	32	4	1st	4
Arnold	11	2	28	3	2nd	9
Greig	9.5	2	26	1	3rd	14
Underwood	11	3	29	1	4th	15
Illingworth	11	1	34	1	5th	70
					6th	81
					7th	108
					8th	133
					9th	144
					10th	158

ENGLAND

G. Boycott	c Turner b Congdon	20
D.L. Amiss	c Pollard b Taylor	100
G.R.J. Roope	b Howarth	0
F.C. Hayes	not out	20
K.W.R. Fletcher	not out	16
A.W. Greig		
R. Illingworth*		
A.P.E. Knott+		
J.A. Snow		
G.G. Arnold		
D.L. Underwood		
Extras	(B 1, LB 1, W 1)	3
TOTAL	**(45.3 overs) (for 3 wkts)**	**159**

						Fall	
Collinge	6	2	18	0	1st	96
Hadlee	11	1	35	0	2nd	97
Taylor	8.3	1	37	1	3rd	135
Howarth	11	3	34	1		
Congdon	9	2	32	1		

Match No: 6/2

ENGLAND v NEW ZEALAND

Prudential Trophy
Played at Old Trafford, Manchester on 20/07/1973
Toss: New Zealand   **Result:** Match Abandoned
Umpires: H.D. Bird and A.E.G. Rhodes
Man of the match: None
Debuts: None

ENGLAND
G. Boycott	lbw b Taylor	15
D.L. Amiss	c Wadsworth b Congdon	34
G.R.J. Roope	c Wadsworth b Hadlee	44
F.C. Hayes	b Congdon	9
K.W.R. Fletcher	c Hadlee b Taylor	25
A.W. Greig	c Taylor b Collinge	14
R. Illingworth*	c Turner b Hadlee	4
A.P.E. Knott+	c Wadsworth b Taylor	12
G.G. Arnold	not out	0
J.A. Snow		
P. Lever		
Extras	(LB 6, W 4)	10
TOTAL	(48.3 overs) (for 8 wkts)	**167**

						Fall	
Collinge	11	0	52	1	1st	23
Taylor	10.3	3	25	3	2nd	57
Hadlee	8	1	23	2	3rd	75
Congdon	8	1	24	2	4th	112
Howarth	11	1	33	0	5th	150
					6th	153
					7th	160
					8th	167

NEW ZEALAND
G.M. Turner
R.E. Redmond
B.E. Congdon*
B.F. Hastings
M.G. Burgess
V. Pollard
K.J. Wadsworth+
B.R. Taylor
R.J. Hadlee
R.O. Collinge
H.J. Howarth

18 England - The Complete One-Day International Record

Match No: 7/1

ENGLAND v WEST INDIES

Prudential Trophy
Played at Headingley, Leeds on 05/09/1973
Toss: West Indies   **Result:** England won by 1 wicket
Umpires: C.S. Elliott and A.E. Fagg
Man of the match: M.H. Denness
Debuts: Eng - M.H. Denness, M. Hendrick, C.M. Old, M.J. Smith, R.W. Taylor, R.G.D. Willis
WI - All

WEST INDIES		
R.C. Fredericks	c Greig b Willis	4
M.L.C. Foster	c Greig b Old	25
R.B. Kanhai*	c Greig b Underwood	55
C.H. Lloyd	b Willis	31
A.I. Kallicharran	st Taylor b Underwood	26
G. St A. Sobers	c Taylor b Old	0
B.D. Julien	c Taylor b Old	0
K.D. Boyce	b Underwood	7
D.L. Murray+	run out	11
V.A. Holder	c Old b Hendrick	10
L.R. Gibbs	not out	0
Extras	(LB 12)	12
TOTAL	**(54 overs)**	**181**

						Fall	
Willis	10	2	29	2	1st	4
Hendrick	11	4	27	1	2nd	65
Old	11	1	43	3	3rd	115
Underwood	11	2	30	3	4th	132
Greig	11	0	40	0	5th	133
					6th	133
					7th	158
					8th	159
					9th	181
					10th	181

ENGLAND		
G. Boycott	c Kanhai b Holder	0
M.J. Smith	lbw b Julien	31
M.H. Denness*	b Gibbs	66
F.C. Hayes	c Murray b Julien	9
K.W.R. Fletcher	lbw b Holder	2
A.W. Greig	c Sobers b Boyce	48
C.M. Old	b Sobers	4
R.W. Taylor+	run out	8
M. Hendrick	b Boyce	1
R.G.D. Willis	not out	5
D.L. Underwood	not out	1
Extras	(B 1, LB 3, NB 3)	7
TOTAL	**(54.3 overs) (for 9 wkts)**	**182**

						Fall	
Sobers	10.3	3	31	1	1st	3
Holder	11	1	34	2	2nd	74
Boyce	11	1	40	2	3rd	93
Julien	11	1	40	2	4th	95
Gibbs	11	0	30	1	5th	143
					6th	157
					7th	171
					8th	176
					9th	176

Match No: 8/2

ENGLAND v WEST INDIES

Prudential Trophy
Played at The Oval, London on 07/09/1973
Toss: England   **Result:** West Indies won by 8 wickets
Umpires: A.E.G. Rhodes and T.W. Spencer
Man of the match: R.C. Fredericks
Debuts: Eng - J.A. Jameson, D. Lloyd   WI - R.G.A. Headley, D.A. Murray

ENGLAND
M.J. Smith	b Lloyd	19
J.A. Jameson	c Holder b Gibbs	28
M.H. Denness*	lbw b Lloyd	0
D. Lloyd	run out	8
K.W.R. Fletcher	b Julien	63
A.W. Greig	c Lloyd b Foster	17
C.M. Old	c Murray b Holder	21
R.W. Taylor+	run out	3
G.G. Arnold	c Julien b Foster	17
R.G.D. Willis	not out	4
D.L. Underwood	not out	1
Extras	(B 2, LB 3, NB 3)	8
TOTAL	(55 overs) (for 9 wkts)	**189**

						Fall	
Holder	11	0	40	1	1st	38
Julien	11	2	35	1	2nd	39
Lloyd	11	2	25	2	3rd	59
Gibbs	11	4	12	1	4th	59
Boyce	6	0	47	0	5th	100
Foster	5	0	22	2	6th	135
					7th	142
					8th	177
					9th	184

WEST INDIES
R.C. Fredericks	b Arnold	105
R.G.A. Headley	c Taylor b Arnold	19
A.I. Kallicharran	not out	53
D.A. Murray+	not out	1
R.B. Kanhai*		
C.H. Lloyd		
M.L.C. Foster		
B.D. Julien		
K.D. Boyce		
V.A. Holder		
L.R. Gibbs		
Extras	(B 1, LB 6, NB 5)	12
TOTAL	(42.2 overs) (for 2 wkts)	**190**

						Fall	
Willis	10.2	0	55	0	1st	43
Arnold	9	1	24	2	2nd	186
Old	10	0	52	0		
Underwood	7	0	26	0		
Greig	6	2	21	0		

Match No: 9/1

ENGLAND v INDIA

Prudential Trophy
Played at Headingley, Leeds on 13/07/1974
Toss: England   Result: England won by 4 wickets
Umpires: W.E. Alley and H.D. Bird
Man of the match: J.H. Edrich
Debuts: Eng - R.D. Jackman   Ind- All

INDIA

S.M. Gavaskar	b Arnold	28
S.S. Naik	lbw b Jackman	18
A.L. Wadekar*	b Jackman	67
G.R. Viswanath	b Woolmer	4
F.M. Engineer+	lbw b Old	32
B.P. Patel	c Fletcher b Greig	82
E.D. Solkar	lbw b Arnold	3
S. Abid Ali	c & b Woolmer	17
Madan Lal	b Old	2
S. Venkataraghavan	not out	1
B.S. Bedi	c Lloyd b Old	0
Extras	(LB 8, NB 3)	11
TOTAL	(53.5 overs)	**265**

						Fall	
Arnold	10	1	42	2	1st	44
Old	10.5	0	43	3	2nd	50
Jackman	11	0	44	2	3rd	60
Woolmer	11	0	62	2	4th	130
Greig	11	0	63	1	5th	181
					6th	194
					7th	246
					8th	264
					9th	265
					10th	265

ENGLAND

D.L. Amiss	lbw b Solkar	20
D. Lloyd	st Engineer b Solkar	34
J.H. Edrich	c Bedi b Venkataraghavan	90
M.H. Denness*	c Venkataraghavan b Madan Lal	8
K.W.R. Fletcher	c & b Bedi	39
A.W. Greig	c & b Bedi	40
A.P.E. Knott+	not out	15
C.M. Old	not out	5
R.A. Woolmer		
R.D. Jackman		
G.G. Arnold		
Extras	(LB 12, NB 3)	15
TOTAL	(51.1 overs) (for 6 wkts)	**266**

						Fall	
Abid Ali	9	0	51	0	1st	37
Solkar	11	1	31	2	2nd	84
Madan Lal	9.1	1	43	1	3rd	96
Venkataraghavan	11	0	58	1	4th	179
Bedi	11	0	68	2	5th	212
					6th	254

Match No: 10/2

INDIA v ENGLAND

Prudential Trophy
Played at The Oval, London on 15/07/1974
Toss: India   **Result:** England won by 6 wickets
Umpires: C.S. Elliott and A. Jepson
Man of the match: K.W.R. Fletcher
Debuts: Ind - G. Bose, A.V. Mankad

INDIA

S.M. Gavaskar	c Arnold b Jackman	20
S.S. Naik	c Greig b Old	20
G. Bose	c Denness b Jackman	13
A.L. Wadekar*	c Lloyd b Underwood	6
G.R. Viswanath	c Knott b Old	32
F.M. Engineer+	lbw b Jackman	4
B.P. Patel	run out	12
A.V. Mankad	b Old	44
E.D. Solkar	c Knott b Greig	0
S. Abid Ali	c Smith b Greig	6
Madan Lal	not out	3
Extras	(LB 9, W 1, NB 1)	11
TOTAL	(47.3 overs)	**171**

						Fall	
Arnold	7	0	20	0	1st	40
Old	9.3	0	36	3	2nd	48
Jackman	11	1	41	3	3rd	60
Underwood	11	0	36	1	4th	64
Greig	9	0	27	2	5th	75
					6th	94
					7th	139
					8th	142
					9th	156
					10th	171

ENGLAND

M.J. Smith	c Engineer b Abid Ali	6
D. Lloyd	c sub (S.M.H. Kirmani) b Bose	39
J.H. Edrich	c Patel b Madan Lal	19
M.H. Denness*	c Wadekar b Mankad	24
K.W.R. Fletcher	not out	55
A.W. Greig	not out	24
A.P.E. Knott+		
C.M. Old		
R.D. Jackman		
G.G. Arnold		
D.L. Underwood		
Extras	(LB 4, W 1)	5
TOTAL	(48.5 overs) (for 4 wkts)	**172**

						Fall	
Abid Ali	11	3	21	1	1st	19
Solkar	11	3	37	0	2nd	65
Madan Lal	10	0	23	1	3rd	71
Bose	11	2	39	1	4th	113
Mankad	5.5	0	47	1		

Match No: 11/1

ENGLAND v PAKISTAN

Prudential Trophy
Played at Trent Bridge, Nottingham on 31/08/1974
Toss: England **Result:** Pakistan won by 7 wickets
Umpires: W.L. Budd and D.J. Constant
Man of the match: Majid Khan
Debuts: Pak - Imran Khan, Zaheer Abbas

ENGLAND
D. Lloyd	not out	116
M.J. Smith	c Sadiq Mohammad b Sarfraz Nawaz	14
J.H. Edrich	c Wasim Bari b Asif Iqbal	18
M.H. Denness*	st Wasim Bari b Intikhab Alam	32
C.M. Old	st Wasim Bari b Majid Khan	39
A.W. Greig	not out	7
K.W.R. Fletcher		
A.P.E. Knott+		
P. Lever		
D.L. Underwood		
R.G.D. Willis		
Extras	(B 5, LB 11, NB 2)	18
TOTAL	(50 overs) (for 4 wkts)	**244**

					Fall	
Asif Masood	10	2	31	0	1st	17
Sarfraz Nawaz	10	0	46	1	2nd	59
Asif Iqbal	10	1	40	1	3rd	162
Imran Khan	10	0	36	0	4th	226
Intikhab Alam	7	0	58	1		
Majid Khan	3	0	15	1		

PAKISTAN
Sadiq Mohammad	b Lever	41
Majid Khan	c Old b Underwood	109
Zaheer Abbas	c & b Willis	31
Asif Iqbal	not out	24
Mushtaq Mohammad	not out	24
Wasim Raja		
Intikhab Alam*		
Imran Khan		
Sarfraz Nawaz		
Wasim Bari+		
Asif Masood		
Extras	(B 1, LB 11, NB 5)	17
TOTAL	(42.5 overs) (for 3 wkts)	**246**

					Fall	
Willis	10	2	34	1	1st	113
Lever	10	0	58	1	2nd	187
Old	10	0	65	0	3rd	199
Underwood	8	1	32	1		
Greig	4.5	0	40	0		

Match No: 12/2

ENGLAND v PAKISTAN

Prudential Trophy
Played at Edgbaston, Birmingham on 03/09/1974
Toss: Pakistan   **Result:** Pakistan won by 8 wickets
Umpires: H.D. Bird and C.S. Elliott
Man of the match: Asif Masood
Debuts: None

ENGLAND
D. Lloyd	b Sarfraz Nawaz	4
M.J. Smith	lbw b Asif Masood	0
J.H. Edrich	b Sarfraz Nawaz	6
M.H. Denness*	b Imran Khan	9
K.W.R Fletcher	c Wasim Bari b Asif Masood	2
A.W. Greig	run out	1
C.M. Old	c Wasim Raja b Asif Iqbal	0
R.W. Taylor+	not out	26
G.G. Arnold	b Imran Khan	2
D.L. Underwood	b Asif Iqbal	17
P. Lever	not out	8
Extras	(LB 6)	6
TOTAL	(35 overs) (for 9 wkts)	**81**

						Fall	
Asif Masood	7	2	9	2	1st	1
Sarfraz Nawaz	7	0	15	2	2nd	12
Imran Khan	7	2	16	2	3rd	13
Asif Iqbal	7	1	17	2	4th	20
Intikhab Alam	6	1	12	0	5th	24
Majid Khan	1	0	6	0	6th	25
					7th	25
					8th	28
					9th	68

PAKISTAN
Sadiq Mohammad	c Lloyd b Underwood	12
Majid Khan	lbw b Arnold	0
Zaheer Abbas	not out	57
Mushtaq Mohammad	not out	1
Asif Iqbal		
Wasim Raja		
Intikhab Alam*		
Sarfraz Nawaz		
Wasim Bari+		
Imran Khan		
Asif Masood		
Extras	(B 1, LB 7, NB 6)	14
TOTAL	(18 overs) (for 2 wkts)	**84**

						Fall	
Arnold	6	3	7	1	1st	1
Lever	4	0	22	0	2nd	60
Old	5	0	25	0		
Underwood	3	0	16	1		

Match No: 13/5

AUSTRALIA v ENGLAND

Played at Melbourne Cricket Ground on 01/01/1975
Toss: England   **Result:** England won by 3 wickets
Umpires: R.C. Bailhache and T.F. Brooks
Man of the match: Aus: I.M. Chappell   Eng: D.L. Amiss
Debuts: Eng - B.W. Luckhurst
Aus - W.J. Edwards, A.G. Hurst, T.J. Jenner, J.R. Thomson

AUSTRALIA

I.R. Redpath	c Greig b Lever	2
W.J. Edwards	b Arnold	2
I.M. Chappell*	c Lever b Old	42
G.S. Chappell	b Old	44
R. Edwards	b Old	20
K.D. Walters	b Old	18
R.W. Marsh+	run out	14
T.J. Jenner	c Fletcher b Greig	12
M.H.N. Walker	b Greig	20
J.R. Thomson	b Arnold	4
A.G. Hurst	not out	1
Extras	(B 7, W 1, NB 3)	11
TOTAL	(34.5 overs)	**190**

					Fall	
Lever	5	0	24	1	1st	5
Arnold	8	2	30	2	2nd	11
Greig	7.5	0	48	2	3rd	65
Old	8	0	57	4	4th	105
Underwood	6	0	20	0	5th	122
					6th	139
					7th	159
					8th	173
					9th	183
					10th	190

ENGLAND

D.L. Amiss	b Walker	47
D. Lloyd	run out	49
B.W. Luckhurst	run out	14
K.W.R. Fletcher	c Redpath b Thomson	31
C.M. Old	b Hurst	12
A.W. Greig	run out	3
M.H. Denness*	c Walker b Hurst	12
A.P.E. Knott+	not out	2
D.L. Underwood	not out	1
G.G. Arnold		
P. Lever		
Extras	(B 5, LB 11, NB 4)	20
TOTAL	(37.1 overs) (for 7 wkts)	**191**

					Fall	
Thomson	7	1	33	1	1st	70
Hurst	8	0	27	2	2nd	117
Jenner	8	1	28	0	3rd	124
Walters	3	0	32	0	4th	154
Walker	8	0	27	1	5th	157
G.S. Chappell	3	0	24	0	6th	182
W.J. Edwards	0.1	0	0	0	7th	182

Match No: 14/3

NEW ZEALAND v ENGLAND

Played at Carisbrook, Dunedin on 08/03/1975
Toss: New Zealand   **Result:** Match abandoned
Umpires: E.W. Dempster and E.G. Wainscott
Man of the match: None
Debuts: Eng - F.J. Titmus   NZ - G.P. Howarth, B.G. Hadlee

ENGLAND
D.L. Amiss	c Wadsworth b R.J. Hadlee	3
B. Wood	b H.J. Howarth	33
B.W. Luckhurst	c G.P. Howarth b Collinge	0
K.W.R. Fletcher	c Turner b Congdon	11
J.H. Edrich*	c R.J. Hadlee b H.J. Howarth	8
C.M. Old	c Parker b H.J. Howarth	27
R.W. Taylor+	not out	23
F.J. Titmus	b D.R. Hadlee	11
G.G. Arnold	b D.R. Hadlee	0
D.L. Underwood	c Parker b R.J. Hadlee	2
M. Hendrick	b Collinge	1
Extras	(LB 12, NB 5)	17
TOTAL	**(34.1 overs)**	**136**

Collinge	6.1	0	17	2	1st	14
R.J. Hadlee	7	0	21	2	2nd	17
H.J. Howarth	7	0	35	3	3rd	36
Congdon	7	0	25	1	4th	51
D.R. Hadlee	7	1	21	2	5th	90
					6th	90
					7th	122
					8th	122
					9th	132
					10th	136

NEW ZEALAND
G.M. Turner	not out	8
B.G. Hadlee	not out	7
J.M. Parker		
G.P. Howarth		
B.E. Congdon*		
K.J. Wadsworth+		
B.F. Hastings		
R.J. Hadlee		
D.R. Hadlee		
R.O. Collinge		
H.J. Howarth		
Extras		0
TOTAL	**(4 overs) (for 0 wkts)**	**15**

Arnold	2	0	6	0
Hendrick	2	0	9	0

Match No: 15/4

NEW ZEALAND v ENGLAND

Played at Basin Reserve, Wellington on 09/03/1975
Toss: New Zealand   **Result:** Match abandoned
Umpires: J.B.R. Hastie and R.L. Monteith
Man of the match: None
Debuts: NZ - J.F.M. Morrison

NEW ZEALAND

G.M. Turner	b Hendrick	18
J.F.M. Morrison	c Taylor b Lever	5
B.E. Congdon*	lbw b Lever	101
B.F. Hastings	c Greig b Titmus	37
K.J. Wadsworth+	lbw b Titmus	0
J.M. Parker	c Wood b Titmus	25
G.P. Howarth	c sub (D.L. Amiss) b Old	13
R.J. Hadlee	not out	6
D.R. Hadlee	run out	0
R.O. Collinge	c Titmus b Lever	0
H.J. Howarth	b Lever	11
Extras	(B 6, LB 2, NB 3)	11
TOTAL	**(34.6 overs)**	**227**

					Fall	
Lever	6.6	0	35	4	1st	13
Old	6	0	32	1	2nd	46
Hendrick	4	0	21	1	3rd	130
Greig	5	0	34	0	4th	130
Titmus	7	0	53	3	5th	178
Wood	6	0	41	0	6th	206
					7th	209
					8th	209
					9th	210
					10th	227

ENGLAND

B. Wood	not out	14
B.W. Luckhurst	c Wadsworth b Collinge	1
K.W.R. Fletcher	not out	18
J.H. Edrich		
M.H. Denness*		
A.W. Greig		
C.M. Old		
R.W. Taylor+		
F.J. Titmus		
P. Lever		
M. Hendrick		
Extras	(B 1, LB 1)	2
TOTAL	**(10 overs) (for 1 wkt)**	**35**

					Fall	
Collinge	4	1	9	1	1st	3
D.R. Hadlee	3	0	6	0		
Congdon	2	0	14	0		
R.J. Hadlee	1	0	4	0		

Match No: 16/3

ENGLAND v INDIA

Prudential World Cup
Played at Lord's, London on 07/06/1975
Toss: England   **Result:** England won by 202 runs
Umpires: D.J. Constant and J.G. Langridge
Man of the match: D.L. Amiss
Debuts: Ind - M. Amarnath, A.D. Gaekwad, K.D. Ghavri

ENGLAND
J.A. Jameson	c Venkataraghavan b Amarnath	21
D.L. Amiss	b Madan Lal	137
K.W.R. Fletcher	b Abid Ali	68
A.W. Greig	lbw b Abid Ali	4
M.H. Denness*	not out	37
C.M. Old	not out	51
B. Wood		
A.P.E. Knott+		
J.A. Snow		
P. Lever		
G.G. Arnold		
Extras	(LB 12, W 2, NB 2)	16
TOTAL	(60 overs) (for 4 wkts)	**334**

						Fall	
Madan Lal	12	1	64	1	1st	54
Amarnath	12	2	60	1	2nd	230
Abid Ali	12	0	58	2	3rd	237
Ghavri	11	1	83	0	4th	245
Venkataraghavan	12	0	41	0		
Solkar	1	0	12	0		

INDIA
S.M. Gavaskar	not out	36
E.D. Solkar	c Lever b Arnold	8
A.D. Gaekwad	c Knott b Lever	22
G.R. Viswanath	c Fletcher b Old	37
B.P. Patel	not out	16
M. Amarnath		
F.M. Engineer+		
S. Abid Ali		
Madan Lal		
S. Venkataraghavan*		
K.D. Ghavri		
Extras	(LB 3, W 1, NB 9)	13
TOTAL	(60 overs) (for 3 wkts)	**132**

						Fall	
Snow	12	2	24	0	1st	21
Arnold	10	2	20	1	2nd	50
Old	12	4	26	1	3rd	108
Greig	9	1	26	0		
Wood	5	2	4	0		
Lever	10	0	16	1		
Jameson	2	1	3	0		

Match No: 17/5

ENGLAND v NEW ZEALAND

Prudential World Cup
Played at Trent Bridge, Nottingham on 11/06/1975
Toss: New Zealand					**Result:** England won by 80 runs
Umpires: W.E. Alley and T.W. Spencer
Man of the match: K.W.R. Fletcher
Debuts: None

ENGLAND
D.L. Amiss	b Collinge	16
J.A. Jameson	c Wadsworth b Collinge	11
K.W.R. Fletcher	run out	131
F.C. Hayes	lbw b R.J. Hadlee	34
M.H. Denness*	c Morrison b D.R. Hadlee	37
A.W. Greig	b D.R. Hadlee	9
C.M. Old	not out	20
A.P.E. Knott+		
D.L. Underwood		
G.G. Arnold		
P. Lever		
Extras	(LB 6, W 1, NB 1)	8
TOTAL	(60 overs) (for 6 wkts)	**266**

						Fall	
Collinge	12	2	43	2	1st	27
R.J. Hadlee	12	2	66	1	2nd	28
D.R. Hadlee	12	1	55	2	3rd	111
McKechnie	12	2	38	0	4th	177
Howarth	12	2	56	0	5th	200
					6th	266

NEW ZEALAND
J.F.M. Morrison	c Old b Underwood	55
G.M. Turner*	b Lever	12
B.G. Hadlee	b Greig	19
J.M. Parker	b Greig	1
B.F. Hastings	c Underwood b Old	10
K.J. Wadsworth+	b Arnold	25
R.J. Hadlee	b Old	0
B.J. McKechnie	c Underwood b Greig	27
D.R. Hadlee	c Arnold b Greig	20
H.J. Howarth	not out	1
R.O. Collinge	b Underwood	6
Extras	(B 1, LB 4, W 1, NB 4)	10
TOTAL	(60 overs)	**186**

						Fall	
Arnold	12	3	35	1	1st	30
Lever	12	0	37	1	2nd	83
Old	12	2	29	2	3rd	91
Greig	12	0	45	4	4th	95
Underwood	12	2	30	2	5th	129
						6th	129
						7th	129
						8th	177
						9th	180
						10th	186

Match No: 18/1

ENGLAND v EAST AFRICA

Prudential World Cup
Played at Edgbaston, Birmingham on 14/06/1975
Toss: East Africa **Result:** England won by 196 runs
Umpires: W.E. Alley and J.G. Langridge
Man of the match: J.A. Snow
Debuts: None

ENGLAND
B. Wood	b Mehmood Quaraishy	77
D.L. Amiss	c Nana b Zulfiqar Ali	88
F.C. Hayes	b Zulfiqar Ali	52
A.W. Greig	lbw b Zulfiqar Ali	9
A.P.E. Knott+	not out	18
C.M. Old	b Mehmood Quaraishy	18
M.H. Denness*	not out	12
K.W.R. Fletcher		
J.A. Snow		
P. Lever		
D.L. Underwood		
Extras	(B 7, LB 7, W 1, NB 1)	16
TOTAL	(60 overs) (for 5 wkts)	**290**

					Fall	
Frasat Ali	9	0	40	0	1st	158
Pringle	12	0	41	0	2nd	192
Nana	12	2	46	0	3rd	234
Ramesh Sethi	5	0	29	0	4th	244
Zulfiqar Ali	12	0	63	3	5th	277
Mehmood Quaraishy	10	0	55	2		

EAST AFRICA
Frasat Ali	b Snow	0
S. Walusimba	lbw b Snow	7
Yunus Badat	b Snow	0
Jawahir Shah	lbw b Snow	4
Ramesh Sethi	b Lever	30
Harilal Shah*	b Greig	6
Mehmood Quaraishy	c Amiss b Greig	19
Zulfiqar Ali	b Lever	7
H. McLeod+	b Lever	0
P.G. Nana	not out	8
D. Pringle	b Old	3
Extras	(LB 6, W 1, NB 3)	10
TOTAL	(52.3 overs)	**94**

					Fall	
Snow	12	6	11	4	1st	7
Lever	12	3	32	3	2nd	7
Underwood	10	5	11	0	3rd	15
Wood	7	3	10	0	4th	21
Greig	10	1	18	2	5th	42
Old	1.3	0	2	1	6th	72
					7th	76
					8th	79
					9th	88
					10th	94

Match No: 19/6

ENGLAND v AUSTRALIA

Prudential World Cup Semi-Final
Played at Headingley, Leeds on 18/06/1975
Toss: Australia   Result: Australia won by 4 wickets
Umpires: W.E. Alley and D.J. Constant
Man of the match: G.J. Gilmour
Debuts: None

ENGLAND

D.L. Amiss	lbw b Gilmour	2
B. Wood	b Gilmour	6
K.W.R. Fletcher	lbw b Gilmour	8
A.W. Greig	c Marsh b Gilmour	7
F.C. Hayes	lbw b Gilmour	4
M.H. Denness*	b Walker	27
A.P.E. Knott+	lbw b Gilmour	0
C.M. Old	c G.S. Chappell b Walker	0
J.A. Snow	c Marsh b Lillee	2
G.G. Arnold	not out	18
P. Lever	lbw b Walker	5
Extras	(LB 5, W 7, NB 2)	14
TOTAL	(36.2 overs)	**93**

						Fall	
Lillee	9	3	26	1	1st	2
Gilmour	12	6	14	6	2nd	11
Walker	9.2	3	22	3	3rd	26
Thomson	6	0	17	0	4th	33
					5th	35
					6th	36
					7th	37
					8th	52
					9th	73
					10th	93

AUSTRALIA

A. Turner	lbw b Arnold	7
R.B. McCosker	b Old	15
I.M. Chappell*	lbw b Snow	2
G.S. Chappell	lbw b Snow	4
K.D. Walters	not out	20
R. Edwards	b Old	0
R.W. Marsh+	b Old	5
G.J. Gilmour	not out	28
M.H.N. Walker		
D.K. Lillee		
J.R. Thomson		
Extras	(B 1, LB 6, NB 6)	13
TOTAL	(28.4 overs) (for 6 wkts)	**94**

						Fall	
Arnold	7.4	2	15	1	1st	17
Snow	12	0	30	2	2nd	24
Old	7	2	29	3	3rd	32
Lever	2	0	7	0	4th	32
					5th	32
					6th	39

Match No: 20/3

ENGLAND v WEST INDIES

Prudential Trophy
Played at Scarborough on 26/08/1976
Toss: West Indies   **Result:** West Indies won by 6 wickets
Umpires: D.J. Constant and A. Jepson
Man of the match: I.V.A. Richards
Debuts: Eng - G.D. Barlow, I.T. Botham, G.A. Gooch, J.K. Lever, D.S. Steele WI - M.A. Holding, C.L. King

ENGLAND
B. Wood	b Roberts	0
D.L. Amiss	b Julien	34
D.S. Steele	c King b Roberts	8
R.A. Woolmer	c Murray b Holding	3
G.D. Barlow	not out	80
G.A. Gooch	c Holder b Roberts	32
I.T. Botham	c Fredericks b Holding	1
A.P.E. Knott*+	run out	16
D.L. Underwood	c Julien b Roberts	14
J.K. Lever		
M. Hendrick		
Extras	(LB 11, W 1, NB 2)	14
TOTAL	(55 overs) (for 8 wkts)	**202**

						Fall	
Roberts	11	0	32	4	1st	0
Holding	11	1	38	2	2nd	18
Holder	11	3	30	0	3rd	23
Julien	11	2	37	1	4th	72
King	6	0	25	0	5th	136
Lloyd	5	1	26	0	6th	145
					7th	181
					8th	202

WEST INDIES
R.C. Fredericks	b Hendrick	1
C.G. Greenidge	b Wood	27
I.V.A. Richards	not out	119
C.H. Lloyd*	b Underwood	20
L.G. Rowe	c Hendrick b Botham	10
C.L. King	not out	14
D.L. Murray+		
B.D. Julien		
V.A. Holder		
M.A. Holding		
A.M.E. Roberts		
Extras	(B 8, LB 8)	16
TOTAL	(41 overs) (for 4 wkts)	**207**

						Fall	
Lever	9	1	38	0	1st	3
Hendrick	9	3	38	1	2nd	77
Wood	8	2	29	1	3rd	116
Underwood	9	1	35	1	4th	176
Botham	3	0	26	1		
Woolmer	2	0	16	0		
Steele	1	0	9	0		

Match No: 21/4

ENGLAND v WEST INDIES

Prudential Trophy
Played at Lord's, London on 28/08/1976
Toss: England
Umpires: W.E. Alley and A.E. Fagg
Man of the match: I.V.A. Richards
Debuts: Eng - D.W. Randall

Result: West Indies won by 36 runs

WEST INDIES

R.C. Fredericks	c Randall b Hendrick	19
C.G. Greenidge	b Hendrick	29
I.V.A. Richards	c Woolmer b Greig	97
C.H. Lloyd*	c Barlow b Woolmer	27
C.L. King	c Wood b Woolmer	1
L.G. Rowe	b Underwood	4
D.L. Murray+	c & b Underwood	1
B.D. Julien	c Randall b Underwood	4
M.A. Holding	c Barlow b Wood	16
V.A. Holder	b Greig	2
A.M.E. Roberts	not out	7
Extras	(B 5, LB 5, W 1, NB 3)	14
TOTAL	(47.5 overs)	221

						Fall	
Hendrick	9	2	34	2		1st	51
Jackman	10	1	50	0		2nd	53
Woolmer	10	0	52	2		3rd	121
Underwood	10	0	27	3		4th	124
Greig	5.5	0	31	2		5th	135
Wood	3	0	13	1		6th	143
						7th	154
						8th	193
						9th	201
						10th	221

ENGLAND

B. Wood	c & b Roberts	4
D.L. Amiss	c Murray b Roberts	12
R.A. Woolmer	b Roberts	9
G.D. Barlow	c Holder b Roberts	0
G.A. Gooch	c Murray b Holder	5
D.W. Randall	c King b Lloyd	88
A.W. Greig*	c Richards b Julien	3
A.P.E. Knott+	run out	22
R.D. Jackman	b Holder	14
D.L. Underwood	c Greenidge b Lloyd	2
M. Hendrick	not out	0
Extras	(LB 14, W 4, NB 8)	26
TOTAL	(45.3 overs)	185

						Fall	
Roberts	8	1	27	4		1st	4
Holding	8	0	26	0		2nd	25
Julien	10	4	22	1		3rd	30
Holder	10	0	35	2		4th	31
King	8	0	45	0		5th	48
Lloyd	1.3	0	4	2		6th	62
						7th	125
						8th	180
						9th	185
						10th	185

Match No: 22/5

ENGLAND v WEST INDIES

Prudential Trophy
Played at Edgbaston, Birmingham on 30 & 31/08/1976
Toss: England **Result:** West Indies won by 50 runs
Umpires: H.D. Bird and W.L. Budd
Man of the match: C.H. Lloyd
Debuts: None

WEST INDIES
R.C. Fredericks	c Barlow b Lever	1
C.G. Greenidge	c Hendrick b Underwood	42
I.V.A. Richards	c Wood b Lever	0
C.H. Lloyd*	b Greig	79
L.G. Rowe	run out	45
C.L. King	lbw b Hendrick	7
B.D. Julien	b Hendrick	5
D.L. Murray+	run out	27
M.A. Holding	b Botham	3
A.M.E. Roberts	not out	0
V.A. Holder		
Extras	(LB 12, NB 2)	14
TOTAL	(32 overs) (for 9 wkts)	**223**

						Fall	
Hendrick	10	0	45	2	1st	7
Lever	10	1	57	2	2nd	7
Botham	3	0	31	1	3rd	95
Underwood	3	0	28	1	4th	145
Greig	6	0	48	1	5th	162
					6th	174
					7th	209
					8th	223
					9th	223

ENGLAND
B. Wood	b Julien	34
D.L. Amiss	b Julien	47
G.D. Barlow	lbw b Holder	0
G.A. Gooch	c Murray b Holder	3
D.W. Randall	c Murray b Holder	39
A.W. Greig*	b Holder	2
I.T. Botham	c Julien b Fredericks	20
A.P.E. Knott+	c Greenidge b Holder	10
D.L. Underwood	st Murray b Richards	6
J.K. Lever	b Fredericks	1
M. Hendrick	not out	1
Extras	(B 2, LB 6, NB 2)	10
TOTAL	(31.4 overs)	**173**

						Fall	
Roberts	5	1	9	0	1st	54
Holding	7	1	34	0	2nd	59
Holder	10	0	50	5	3rd	73
Julien	7	0	56	2	4th	89
Fredericks	1.4	0	10	2	5th	111
Richards	1	0	4	1	6th	138
					7th	151
					8th	171
					9th	171
					10th	173

Match No: 23/7

ENGLAND v AUSTRALIA

Prudential Trophy
Played at Old Trafford, Manchester on 02/06/1977
Toss: Australia   **Result:** England won by 2 wickets
Umpires: D.J. Constant and B.J. Meyer
Man of the match: R.W. Marsh
Debuts: Eng - J.M. Brearley, P. Willey
Aus - D.W. Hookes, M.F. Malone, K.J. O'Keeffe, L.S. Pascoe, C.S. Serjeant

AUSTRALIA

R.B. McCosker	c Knott b Willis	1
I.C. Davis	c Greig b Lever	1
G.S. Chappell*	lbw b Underwood	30
C.S. Serjeant	c Randall b Greig	46
K.D. Walters	c Amiss b Old	0
D.W. Hookes	c Knott b Greig	11
R.W. Marsh+	b Lever	42
K.J. O'Keeffe	not out	16
M.H.N. Walker	c Barlow b Underwood	5
M.F. Malone	c Brearley b Underwood	4
L.S. Pascoe	not out	4
Extras	(B 4, LB 4, NB 1)	9
TOTAL	(55 overs) (for 9 wkts)	169

						Fall	
Willis	8	2	16	1		1st	2
Lever	10	1	45	2		2nd	2
Underwood	11	1	29	3		3rd	55
Old	11	3	30	1		4th	62
Willey	11	1	29	0		5th	93
Greig	4	0	11	2		6th	94
						7th	145
						8th	152
						9th	156

ENGLAND

D.L. Amiss	c Serjeant b Walker	8
J.M. Brearley*	lbw b Malone	29
D.W. Randall	c McCosker b Malone	19
G.D. Barlow	run out	42
P. Willey	c Walker b O'Keeffe	1
A.W. Greig	run out	22
A.P.E. Knott+	not out	21
C.M. Old	c Hookes b Walker	25
J.K. Lever	c Walters b Walker	1
D.L. Underwood	not out	0
R.G.D. Willis		
Extras	(B 1, LB 3, W 1)	5
TOTAL	(45.2 overs) (for 8 wkts)	173

						Fall	
Pascoe	10.2	1	44	0		1st	17
Walker	7	3	20	3		2nd	51
Malone	11	1	37	2		3rd	70
O'Keeffe	11	3	36	1		4th	71
Chappell	6	1	31	0		5th	123
						6th	125
						7th	160
						8th	168

Match No: 24/8

ENGLAND v AUSTRALIA

Prudential Trophy
Played at Edgbaston, Birmingham on 04/06/1977
Toss: Australia   **Result:** England won by 101 runs
Umpires: W.E. Alley and W.L. Budd
Man of the match: J.K.Lever
Debuts: Aus - K.J. Hughes, R.D. Robinson

ENGLAND
D.L. Amiss	c Marsh b Chappell	35
J.M. Brearley*	lbw b Chappell	10
D.W. Randall	c Marsh b Chappell	0
G.D. Barlow	c Hughes b Chappell	25
P. Willey	c Marsh b Cosier	6
A.W. Greig	c Chappell b Cosier	0
A.P.E. Knott+	lbw b Cosier	0
C.M. Old	c Hughes b Chappell	35
J.K. Lever	not out	27
D.L. Underwood	b Cosier	0
R.G.D. Willis	c Marsh b Cosier	7
Extras	(LB 15, W 4, NB 7)	26
TOTAL	(53.5 overs)	**171**

						Fall	
Thomson	9	0	46	0		1st	19
Malone	11	2	27	0		2nd	19
Chappell	11	5	20	5		3rd	67
Walker	11	3	29	0		4th	84
Cosier	8.5	3	18	5		5th	84
Bright	3	0	5	0		6th	84
						7th	90
						8th	145
						9th	160
						10th	171

AUSTRALIA
I.C. Davis	c Old b Willis	0
C.S. Serjeant	c Willis	2
G.S. Chappell*	b Lever	19
G.J. Cosier	lbw b Lever	3
K.J. Hughes	c Knott b Lever	2
R.D. Robinson	b Old	12
R.W. Marsh+	c Old b Lever	1
R.J. Bright	not out	17
M.H.N. Walker	run out	0
M.F. Malone	run out	1
J.R. Thomson	b Greig	3
Extras	(B 4, LB 5, NB 1)	10
TOTAL	(25.2 overs)	**70**

						Fall	
Willis	6	1	14	2		1st	0
Lever	11	2	29	4		2nd	27
Old	7	2	15	1		3rd	31
Greig	1.2	0	2	1		4th	34
						5th	35
						6th	38
						7th	58
						8th	58
						9th	60
						10th	70

Match No: 25/9

ENGLAND v AUSTRALIA

Prudential Trophy
Played at The Oval, London on 06/06/1977
Toss: Australia   **Result:** Australia won by 2 wickets
Umpires: H.D. Bird and K.E. Palmer
Man of the match: G.S. Chappell
Debuts: Eng - G. Miller

ENGLAND

J.M. Brearley*	st Robinson b O'Keeffe	78
D.L. Amiss	b Pascoe	108
D.W. Randall	c & b Bright	6
G.D. Barlow	run out	2
A.W. Greig	c Robinson b Thomson	4
A.P.E. Knott+	c Robinson b Pascoe	4
G. Miller	c Robinson b Pascoe	4
C.M. Old	c Thomson b Chappell	20
J.K. Lever	b Thomson	2
D.L. Underwood	c Pascoe b Dymock	5
R.G.D. Willis	not out	0
Extras	(LB 1, W 2, NB 6)	9
TOTAL	(54.2 overs)	**242**

						Fall	
Thomson	11	2	51	2		1st	161
Dymock	10	0	39	1		2nd	168
Pascoe	11	0	44	3		3rd	179
O'Keeffe	11	0	43	1		4th	196
Bright	11	1	56	1		5th	203
Chappell	0.2	0	0	1		6th	207
						7th	217
						8th	227
						9th	241
						10th	242

AUSTRALIA

R.B. McCosker	lbw b Old	11
R.D. Robinson+	c Brearley b Willis	70
G.S. Chappell*	not out	125
K.J. Hughes	lbw b Willis	3
K.D. Walters	c Brearley b Underwood	12
D.W. Hookes	b Lever	3
R.J. Bright	c Randall b Old	0
K.J. O'Keeffe	run out	0
J.R. Thomson	run out	3
G. Dymock	not out	2
L.S. Pascoe		
Extras	(B 1, LB 14, W 1, NB 1)	17
TOTAL	(53.2 overs) (for 8 wkts)	**246**

						Fall	
Willis	11	0	49	2		1st	33
Lever	10	0	43	1		2nd	181
Old	10.2	0	56	2		3rd	186
Underwood	11	2	21	1		4th	209
Miller	5	0	24	0		5th	225
Greig	6	0	36	0		6th	228
						7th	228
						8th	237

Match No: 26/3

PAKISTAN v ENGLAND

Played at Sahiwal Stadium on 23/12/1977
Toss: Pakistan   **Result:** England won by 3 wickets
Umpires: Azhar Hussain and Shakoor Rana
Man of the match: Batting: Javed Miandad, Bowling: I.T. Botham, Fielding: I.T. Botham
Debuts: Eng - P.R. Downton, P.H. Edmonds, M.W. Gatting, B.C. Rose
Pak - Aamer Hameed, Hasan Jamil, Liaqat Ali, Mudassar Nazar, Shafiq Ahmed

PAKISTAN

Mudassar Nazar	run out	20
Sadiq Mohammad	b Botham	2
Shafiq Ahmed	b Miller	29
Javed Miandad	not out	77
Wasim Raja	c Randall b Botham	36
Parvez Mir	lbw b Hendrick	18
Hasan Jamil	c Downton b Botham	20
Wasim Bari*+	not out	1
Salim Altaf		
Aamer Hameed		
Liaqat Ali		
Extras	(LB 3, NB 2)	5
TOTAL	(35 overs) (for 6 wkts)	**208**

	O	M	R	W	Fall	
Hendrick	7	0	50	1	1st	4
Botham	7	0	39	3	2nd	46
Old	7	0	49	0	3rd	63
Edmonds	7	0	19	0	4th	114
Miller	7	0	46	1	5th	167
					6th	201

ENGLAND

J.M. Brearley*	c Parvez Mir b Aamer Hameed	30
B.C. Rose	c & b Wasim Raja	54
M.W. Gatting	run out	17
D.W. Randall	c Wasim Bari b Salim Altaf	35
C.M. Old	lbw b Parvez Mir	1
G.R.J. Roope	b Liaqat Ali	29
I.T. Botham	not out	15
P.H. Edmonds	run out	5
G. Miller	not out	0
P.R. Downton+		
M. Hendrick		
Extras	(B 5, LB 14, NB 7)	26
TOTAL	(35 overs) (for 7 wkts)	**212**

	O	M	R	W	Fall	
Salim Altaf	7	0	34	1	1st	66
Liaqat Ali	7	0	50	1	2nd	111
Aamer Hameed	7	1	32	1	3rd	127
Parvez Mir	4	0	18	1	4th	134
Javed Miandad	7	1	29	0	5th	181
Wasim Raja	2	0	11	1	6th	193
Mudassar Nazar	1	0	12	0	7th	205

Match No: 27/4

PAKISTAN v ENGLAND

Played at Jinnah Park, Sialkot on 30/12/1977
Toss: England   **Result:** England won by 6 wickets
Umpires: Javed Akhtar and Khalid Aziz
Man of the match: Batting: Wasim Raja, Bowling: J.K. Lever, Fielding: D.W. Randall
Debuts: Eng - G.A. Cope
Pak - Haroon Rashid, Iqbal Qasim, Sikander Bakht

PAKISTAN

Sadiq Mohammad	c Taylor b Lever	13
Mudassar Nazar	c Randall b Cope	33
Shafiq Ahmed	c & b Edmonds	9
Haroon Rashid	c Rose b Miller	5
Javed Miandad	run out	8
Wasim Raja	b Botham	43
Wasim Bari*+	b Edmonds	1
Hasan Jamil	c Taylor b Lever	28
Salim Altaf	not out	4
Iqbal Qasim	c & b Lever	0
Sikander Bakht	run out	0
Extras	(B 4, LB 2, NB 1)	7
TOTAL	(33.7 overs)	**151**

						Fall	
Lever	6	1	18	3	1st	20
Botham	6.7	0	21	1	2nd	55
Cope	7	0	19	1	3rd	57
Miller	6	1	43	1	4th	65
Edmonds	7	0	28	2	5th	74
Gatting	1	0	15	0	6th	76
					7th	140
					8th	150
					9th	150
					10th	151

ENGLAND

B.C. Rose	b Iqbal Qasim	45
G.R.J. Roope	c Haroon Rashid b Sikander Bakht	7
G. Miller	c Sikander Bakht b Iqbal Qasim	16
D.W. Randall	not out	51
M.W. Gatting	run out	5
I.T. Botham	not out	17
G. Boycott*		
R.W. Taylor+		
P.H. Edmonds		
J.K. Lever		
G.A. Cope		
Extras	(LB 4, W 1, NB 6)	11
TOTAL	(32.7 overs) (for 4 wkts)	**152**

						Fall	
Salim Altaf	5.7	0	20	0	1st	17
Sikander Bakht	6	0	25	1	2nd	43
Javed Miandad	7	0	32	0	3rd	104
Iqbal Qasim	7	2	16	2	4th	112
Hasan Jamil	6	0	39	0		
Wasim Raja	1	0	9	0		

Match No: 28/5

PAKISTAN v ENGLAND

Played at Gaddafi Stadium, Lahore on 13/01/1978
Toss: England   **Result:** Pakistan won by 36 runs
Umpires: Khalid Aziz and Shakoor Rana
Man of the match: Wasim Raja
Debuts: Pak - Arshad Pervez

PAKISTAN

Mudassar Nazar	b Edmonds	30
Arshad Pervez	b Lever	8
Shafiq Ahmed	st Taylor b Edmonds	3
Javed Miandad	c Boycott b Lever	31
Wasim Raja	c Boycott b Cope	0
Mohsin Khan	not out	51
Hasan Jamil	c Boycott b Old	21
Sarfraz Nawaz	not out	1
Wasim Bari*+		
Aamer Hameed		
Iqbal Qasim		
Extras	(LB 11, NB 2)	13
TOTAL	(35 overs) (for 6 wkts)	**158**

						Fall	
Old	7	0	35	1	1st	22
Lever	7	1	25	2	2nd	41
Botham	7	0	41	0	3rd	52
Edmonds	7	1	28	2	4th	53
Cope	7	0	16	1	5th	112
					6th	148

ENGLAND

G. Boycott	lbw b Sarfraz Nawaz	6
J.M. Brearley*	c Shafiq Ahmed b Sarfraz Nawaz	1
D.W. Randall	c Mudassar Nazar b Wasim Raja	32
M.W. Gatting	c & b Hasan Jamil	3
I.T. Botham	c Wasim Bari b Iqbal Qasim	11
C.M. Old	c Wasim Raja b Hasan Jamil	4
G.R.J. Roope	run out	37
R.W. Taylor+	b Wasim Raja	12
P.H. Edmonds	run out	0
J.K. Lever	c Aamer Hameed b Wasim Raja	0
G.A. Cope	not out	1
Extras	(B 2, LB 6, W 1, NB 6)	15
TOTAL	(31.6 overs)	**122**

						Fall	
Sarfraz Nawaz	5	2	7	2	1st	11
Aamer Hameed	4	1	6	0	2nd	15
Hasan Jamil	5	0	20	2	3rd	25
Iqbal Qasim	7	2	25	1	4th	42
Javed Miandad	6	0	26	0	5th	49
Wasim Raja	4.6	0	23	3	6th	97
					7th	118
					8th	119
					9th	121
					10th	122

Match No: 29/6
ENGLAND v PAKISTAN

Prudential Trophy
Played at Old Trafford, Manchester on 24 & 25/05/1978
Toss: England   Result: England won by 132 runs
Umpires: D.J. Constant and K.E. Palmer
Man of the match: R.G.D. Willis
Debuts: Eng - D.I. Gower, C.T. Radley

ENGLAND
G. Boycott*	c Wasim Bari b Sarfraz Nawaz	3
B. Wood	c Javed Miandad b Wasim Raja	26
C.T. Radley	c & b Mudassar Nazar	79
D.I. Gower	c Javed Miandad b Mudassar Nazar	33
G.R.J. Roope	c Wasim Bari b Sikander Bakht	10
I.T. Botham	c Haroon Rashid b Sikander Bakht	31
G. Miller	b Sikander Bakht	0
C.M. Old	not out	6
P.H. Edmonds	not out	4
R.W. Taylor+		
R.G.D. Willis		
Extras	(B 2, LB 15, W 3, NB 5)	25
TOTAL	(55 overs) (for 7 wkts)	217

						Fall	
Sarfraz Nawaz	11	6	13	1		1st	3
Liaqat Ali	11	3	20	0		2nd	86
Sikander Bakht	11	0	56	3		3rd	157
Mudassar Nazar	11	1	52	2		4th	158
Iqbal Qasim	4	1	24	0		5th	176
Wasim Raja	7	1	27	1		6th	185
						7th	209

PAKISTAN
Mudassar Nazar	c Wood b Botham	8
Sadiq Mohammad	b Willis	3
Haroon Rashid	b Old	1
Javed Miandad	lbw b Willis	9
Mohsin Khan	c Roope b Willis	1
Wasim Raja	lbw b Willis	0
Sarfraz Nawaz	c Taylor b Botham	7
Wasim Bari*+	b Wood	19
Iqbal Qasim	b Wood	9
Sikander Bakht	not out	16
Liaqat Ali	b Old	7
Extras	(LB 3, W 1, NB 1)	5
TOTAL	(47 overs)	85

						Fall	
Willis	11	5	15	4		1st	3
Old	7	4	6	2		2nd	7
Botham	8	1	17	2		3rd	20
Wood	11	3	25	2		4th	21
Edmonds	10	4	17	0		5th	21
						6th	31
						7th	31
						8th	60
						9th	61
						10th	85

Match No: 30/7

ENGLAND v PAKISTAN

Prudential Trophy
Played at The Oval, London on 26/05/1978
Toss: Pakistan   **Result:** England won by 94 runs
Umpires: H.D. Bird and W.L. Budd
Man of the match: D.I. Gower
Debuts: Pak - Naeem Ahmed

ENGLAND

D. Lloyd	b Wasim Raja	34
B. Wood	b Sarfraz Nawaz	8
C.T. Radley	b Liaqat Ali	13
D.I. Gower	not out	114
G.R.J. Roope	c Naeem Ahmed b Mudassar Nazar	35
I.T. Botham	b Mudassar Nazar	1
G. Miller	lbw b Sikander Bakht	0
C.M. Old	not out	25
R.W. Taylor+		
J.K. Lever		
R.G.D. Willis*		
Extras	(B 5, LB 9, NB 4)	18
TOTAL	(55 overs) (for 6 wkts)	**248**

						Fall	
Sarfraz Nawaz	11	2	48	1	1st	27
Liaqat Ali	11	1	41	1	2nd	60
Sikander Bakht	11	0	53	1	3rd	83
Wasim Raja	6	0	14	1	4th	188
Naeem Ahmed	10	0	43	0	5th	194
Mudassar Nazar	6	0	31	2	6th	195

PAKISTAN

Mudassar Nazar	c Willis b Botham	56
Sadiq Mohammad	c & b Old	9
Arshad Pervez	lbw b Miller	3
Javed Miandad	b Old	0
Haroon Rashid	st Taylor b Miller	20
Wasim Raja	c sub (P.H. Edmonds) b Lloyd	44
Wasim Bari*+	c Taylor b Wood	1
Sarfraz Nawaz	c Gower b Wood	12
Naeem Ahmed	not out	0
Sikander Bakht	not out	0
Liaqat Ali		
Extras	(B 1, LB 7, W 1)	9
TOTAL	(55 overs) (for 8 wkts)	**154**

						Fall	
Willis	9	1	25	0	1st	27
Old	11	1	26	2	2nd	38
Miller	11	3	24	2	3rd	39
Botham	11	2	36	1	4th	80
Lever	7	1	17	0	5th	117
Wood	4	0	14	2	6th	130
Lloyd	2	1	3	1	7th	154
					8th	154

Match No: 31/6

ENGLAND v NEW ZEALAND

Prudential Trophy
Played at Scarborough on 15/07/1978
Toss: New Zealand   **Result:** England won by 19 runs
Umpires: D.J. Constant and J.G. Langridge
Man of the match: G.A. Gooch
Debuts: NZ - S.L. Boock, J.G. Wright

ENGLAND
J.M. Brearley*	c Burgess b Boock	31
G.A. Gooch	c Parker b Cairns	94
C.T. Radley	c Parker b Cairns	41
D.I. Gower	c Burgess b Cairns	4
I.T. Botham	c Anderson b Cairns	3
G.R.J. Roope	b Cairns	11
G. Miller	c Edwards b Hadlee	2
R.W. Taylor+	lbw b Hadlee	0
J.K. Lever	not out	5
M. Hendrick	not out	2
R.G.D. Willis		
Extras	(B 2, LB 10, W 1)	13
TOTAL	(55 overs) (for 8 wkts)	**206**

					Fall	
Hadlee	11	3	22	2	1st	67
Collinge	11	0	46	0	2nd	178
Cairns	11	3	28	5	3rd	181
Congdon	11	2	25	0	4th	185
Boock	9	1	57	1	5th	185
Howarth	2	0	15	0	6th	198
					7th	198
					8th	198

NEW ZEALAND
J.G. Wright	run out	18
R.W. Anderson	c Taylor b Hendrick	12
G.P. Howarth	c Taylor b Hendrick	42
M.G. Burgess*	b Botham	1
J.M. Parker	b Willis	7
G.N. Edwards+	c Gower b Gooch	12
R.J. Hadlee	st Taylor b Gooch	1
B.E. Congdon	not out	52
B.L. Cairns	run out	23
R.O. Collinge	not out	5
S.L. Boock		
Extras	(LB 13, W 1)	14
TOTAL	(55 overs) (for 8 wkts)	**187**

					Fall	
Willis	11	1	35	1	1st	28
Hendrick	11	1	35	2	2nd	43
Lever	11	2	25	0	3rd	51
Botham	11	1	43	1	4th	62
Miller	1	0	6	0	5th	91
Gooch	10	1	29	2	6th	97
					7th	105
					8th	173

Match No: 32/7

ENGLAND v NEW ZEALAND

Prudential Trophy
Played at Old Trafford, Manchester on 17/07/1978
Toss: England   **Result:** England won by 126 runs
Umpires: H.D. Bird and B.J. Meyer
Man of the match: C.T. Radley
Debuts: NZ - B.P. Bracewell, B.A. Edgar

ENGLAND
J.M. Brearley*	c Edwards b Bracewell	27
G.A. Gooch	run out	0
C.T. Radley	not out	117
D.I. Gower	run out	50
D.W. Randall	run out	41
I.T. Botham	c Edgar b Hadlee	34
G. Miller		
R.W. Taylor+		
P.H. Edmonds		
J.K. Lever		
R.G.D. Willis		
Extras	(LB 6, W 1, NB 2)	9
TOTAL	(55 overs) (for 5 wkts)	**278**

						Fall	
Hadlee	11	1	70	1		1st	0
Collinge	11	0	48	0		2nd	44
Bracewell	11	0	41	1		3rd	149
Congdon	11	2	26	0		4th	238
Cairns	11	0	84	0		5th	278

NEW ZEALAND
J.G. Wright	b Botham	30
B.A. Edgar	run out	31
G.P. Howarth	st Taylor b Edmonds	12
G.N. Edwards+	c Randall b Miller	0
M.G. Burgess*	c Taylor b Willis	0
B.E. Congdon	c Randall b Edmonds	2
R.J. Hadlee	c Gower b Miller	1
B.L. Cairns	c Botham b Edmonds	60
R.O. Collinge	c Gooch c Lever	3
B.P. Bracewell	not out	0
J.M. Parker	absent hurt	
Extras	(B 7, LB 6,)	13
TOTAL	(41.2 overs)	**152**

						Fall	
Willis	9	5	21	1		1st	44
Lever	7	0	28	1		2nd	80
Miller	11	4	27	2		3rd	80
Botham	7	0	24	1		4th	84
Edmonds	7.2	1	39	3		5th	84
						6th	85
						7th	88
						8th	133
						9th	152

Match No: 33/10

AUSTRALIA v ENGLAND

Benson & Hedges Cup
Played at Sydney Cricket Ground on 13/01/1979
Toss: England   **Result:** Match Abandoned
Umpires: A.R. Crafter and C.E. Harvey
Man of the match: None
Debuts: Eng - R.W. Tolchard
Aus - A.R. Border, P.H. Carlson, J.A. Maclean

AUSTRALIA
G.M. Wood	c Tolchard b Old	6
W.M. Darling	not out	7
K.J. Hughes	not out	0
G.N. Yallop*		
G.J. Cosier		
P.M. Toohey		
A.R. Border		
P.H. Carlson		
J.A. Maclean+		
G. Dymock		
A.G. Hurst		
Extras	(LB 4)	4
TOTAL	(7.2 overs) (for 1 wkt)	17

                                                        Fall
Lever	3	0	8	0	1st	17
Old	3.2	1	5	1		
Hendrick	1	1	0	0		

ENGLAND
J.M. Brearley*
G. Boycott
D.W. Randall
D.I. Gower
G.A. Gooch
I.T. Botham
R.W. Tolchard+
P.H. Edmonds
C.M. Old
M. Hendrick
J.K. Lever

Match No: 34/11

AUSTRALIA v ENGLAND

Benson & Hedges Cup
Played at Melbourne Cricket Ground on 24/01/1979
Toss: Australia   **Result:** England won by 7 wickets
Umpires: A.R. Crafter and C.E. Harvey
Man of the match: M. Hendrick
Debuts: Eng - D.L. Bairstow   Aus - A.M.J. Hilditch, R.M. Hogg

AUSTRALIA
G.M. Wood	c Gower b Edmonds	28
A.M.J. Hilditch	c Bairstow b Botham	10
A.R. Border	c Willis b Hendrick	11
G.N. Yallop*	run out	9
K.J. Hughes	lbw b Hendrick	0
P.H. Carlson	c Randall b Willis	11
T.J. Laughlin	c Willis b Hendrick	6
J.A. Maclean+	c Edmonds b Botham	11
R.M. Hogg	c Botham b Hendrick	4
G. Dymock	c & b Botham	1
A.G. Hurst	not out	0
Extras	(B 4, LB 2, NB 4)	10
TOTAL	(33.5 overs)	**101**

						Fall	
Willis	8	4	15	1	1st	27
Lever	5	2	7	0	2nd	52
Hendrick	8	1	25	4	3rd	54
Botham	4.5	2	16	3	4th	55
Edmonds	7	0	26	1	5th	76
Gooch	1	0	2	0	6th	78
					7th	94
					8th	99
					9th	101
					10th	101

ENGLAND
G. Boycott	not out	39
J.M. Brearley*	b Hogg	0
D.W. Randall	c Yallop b Dymock	12
G.A. Gooch	b Carlson	23
D.I. Gower	not out	19
I.T. Botham		
P.H. Edmonds		
D.L. Bairstow+		
J.K. Lever		
R.G.D. Willis		
M. Hendrick		
Extras	(LB 5, NB 4)	9
TOTAL	(28.2 overs) (for 3 wkts)	**102**

						Fall	
Hogg	6	1	20	1	1st	7
Dymock	6	1	16	1	2nd	29
Laughlin	5	1	13	0	3rd	69
Carlson	5	0	21	1		
Hurst	5.2	1	14	0		
Border	1	0	9	0		

Match No: 35/12

AUSTRALIA v ENGLAND

Benson & Hedges Cup
Played at Melbourne Cricket Ground on 04/02/1979
Toss: Australia   **Result:** Australia won by 4 wickets
Umpires: R.C. Bailhache and D.G. Weser
Man of the match: D.I. Gower
Debuts: Aus - K.J. Wright

ENGLAND

G. Boycott	lbw b Laughlin	33
J.M. Brearley*	c Wright b Dymock	0
D.W. Randall	lbw b Dymock	4
G.A. Gooch	c Hurst b Carlson	19
D.I. Gower	not out	101
I.T. Botham	c Wood b Hurst	31
D.L. Bairstow+	run out	1
C.M. Old	not out	16
R.G.D. Willis		
M. Hendrick		
J.K. Lever		
Extras	(B 3, LB 3, NB 1)	7
TOTAL	(40 overs) (for 6 wkts)	**212**

					Fall	
Hurst	8	1	36	1	1st	0
Dymock	8	1	31	2	2nd	7
Carlson	8	1	27	1	3rd	50
Cosier	8	0	48	0	4th	89
Laughlin	8	0	63	1	5th	153
					6th	158

AUSTRALIA

G.M. Wood	b Old	23
W.M. Darling	c Old b Willis	7
K.J. Hughes	c Boycott b Lever	50
G.N. Yallop*	c Gower b Hendrick	31
P.M. Toohey	not out	54
G.J. Cosier	b Lever	28
P.H. Carlson	c Boycott b Lever	0
T.J. Laughlin	not out	15
K.J. Wright+		
G. Dymock		
A.G. Hurst		
Extras	(LB 6, NB 1)	7
TOTAL	(38.6 overs) (for 6 wkts)	**215**

					Fall	
Willis	8	1	21	1	1st	7
Lever	7	1	51	3	2nd	55
Hendrick	8	0	47	1	3rd	90
Old	8	1	31	1	4th	145
Botham	7.6	0	58	0	5th	185
					6th	185

Match No: 36/13

AUSTRALIA v ENGLAND

Benson & Hedges Cup
Played at Melbourne Cricket Ground on 07/02/1979
Toss: Australia   **Result:** Australia won by 6 wickets
Umpires: R.C. Bailhache and D.G. Weser
Man of the match: G.Dymock
Debuts: None

ENGLAND
G. Boycott	c Cosier b Dymock	2
J.M. Brearley*	c Wright b Cosier	46
D.W. Randall	c Hughes b Dymock	0
G.A. Gooch	c Hughes b Hurst	4
D.I. Gower	c Wood b Hurst	3
I.T. Botham	b Cosier	13
D.L. Bairstow+	run out	3
P.H. Edmonds	lbw b Laughlin	15
J.K. Lever	b Laughlin	1
R.G.D. Willis	c Wright b Cosier	2
M. Hendrick	not out	0
Extras	(LB 2, NB 3)	5
TOTAL	(31.7 overs)	**94**

					Fall	
Hurst	5	3	7	2	1st	10
Dymock	6	1	21	2	2nd	10
Carlson	8	2	22	0	3rd	17
Cosier	7	1	22	3	4th	22
Laughlin	5.7	0	17	2	5th	42
					6th	56
					7th	91
					8th	91
					9th	94
					10th	94

AUSTRALIA
G.M. Wood	c Bairstow b Botham	30
W.M. Darling	c Brearley b Willis	14
K.J. Hughes	c Brearley b Willis	0
G.N. Yallop*	b Lever	25
P.M. Toohey	not out	16
G.J. Cosier	not out	8
P.H. Carlson		
T.J. Laughlin		
K.J. Wright+		
G. Dymock		
A.G. Hurst		
Extras	(NB 2)	2
TOTAL	(21.5 overs) (for 4 wkts)	**95**

					Fall	
Willis	5	2	16	2	1st	29
Hendrick	6	0	32	0	2nd	37
Botham	5.5	0	30	1	3rd	54
Lever	5	0	15	1	4th	87

Match No: 37/14

ENGLAND v AUSTRALIA

Prudential World Cup
Played at Lord's, London on 09/06/1979
Toss: England
Umpires: D.J. Constant and B.J. Meyer
Man of the match: G.A. Gooch
Debuts: None

Result: England won by 6 wickets

AUSTRALIA

A.M.J. Hilditch	b Boycott	47
W.M. Darling	lbw b Willis	25
A.R. Border	c Taylor b Edmonds	34
K.J. Hughes*	c Hendrick b Boycott	6
G.N. Yallop	run out	10
G.J. Cosier	run out	6
T.J. Laughlin	run out	8
K.J. Wright+	lbw b Old	6
R.M. Hogg	run out	0
A.G. Hurst	not out	3
G. Dymock	not out	4
Extras	(B 4, LB 5, W 1)	10
TOTAL	(60 overs) (for 9 wkts)	**159**

					Fall	
Willis	11	2	20	1	1st	56
Hendrick	12	2	24	0	2nd	97
Old	12	2	33	1	3rd	111
Botham	8	0	32	0	4th	131
Edmonds	11	1	25	1	5th	132
Boycott	6	0	15	2	6th	137
					7th	150
					8th	153
					9th	153

ENGLAND

J.M. Brearley*	c Wright b Laughlin	44
G. Boycott	lbw b Hogg	1
D.W. Randall	c Wright b Hurst	1
G.A. Gooch	lbw b Laughlin	53
D.I. Gower	not out	22
I.T. Botham	not out	18
P.H. Edmonds		
R.W. Taylor+		
C.M. Old		
M. Hendrick		
R.G.D. Willis		
Extras	(LB 10, NB 11)	21
TOTAL	(47.1 overs) (for 4 wkts)	**160**

					Fall	
Hogg	9	1	25	1	1st	4
Hurst	10	3	33	1	2nd	5
Dymock	11	2	19	0	3rd	113
Cosier	8	1	24	0	4th	124
Laughlin	9.1	0	38	2		

Match No: 38/1

ENGLAND v CANADA

Prudential World Cup
Played at Old Trafford, Manchester on 13 & 14/06/1979
Toss: Canada   **Result:** England won by 8 wickets
Umpires: J.G. Langridge and B.J. Meyer
Man of the match: C.M. Old
Debuts: Can - R.G. Callender

CANADA

C.J.D. Chappell	lbw b Botham	5
G.R. Sealy	c Botham b Hendrick	3
F.A. Dennis	hit wicket b Willis	21
Tariq Javed	lbw b Old	4
J.C.B. Vaughan	b Old	1
C.A. Marshall	b Old	2
B.M. Mauricette*+	b Willis	0
M.P. Stead	b Old	0
J.M. Patel	b Willis	1
R.G. Callender	b Willis	0
J.N. Valentine	not out	3
Extras	(LB 4, NB 1)	5
TOTAL	(40.3 overs)	**45**

						Fall	
Willis	10.3	3	11	4	1st	5
Hendrick	8	4	5	1	2nd	13
Botham	9	5	12	1	3rd	25
Miller	2	1	1	0	4th	29
Boycott	1	0	3	0	5th	37
Old	10	5	8	4	6th	38
					7th	41
					8th	41
					9th	42
					10th	45

ENGLAND

J.M. Brearley*	lbw b Valentine	0
G. Boycott	not out	14
D.W. Randall	b Callender	5
G.A. Gooch	not out	21
D.I. Gower		
I.T. Botham		
G. Miller		
R.W. Taylor+		
C.M. Old		
R.G.D. Willis		
M. Hendrick		
Extras	(W 3, NB 3)	6
TOTAL	(13.5 overs) (for 2 wkts)	**46**

						Fall	
Valentine	7	2	20	1	1st	3
Callender	6	1	14	1	2nd	11
Stead	0.5	0	6	0		

Match No: 39/8

ENGLAND v PAKISTAN

Prudential World Cup
Played at Headingley, Leeds on 16/06/1979
Toss: Pakistan   Result: England won by 14 runs
Umpires: W.L. Budd and D.G.L. Evans
Man of the match: M. Hendrick
Debuts: None

ENGLAND
J.M. Brearley*	c Wasim Bari b Imran Khan	0
G. Boycott	lbw b Majid Khan	18
D.W. Randall	c Wasim Bari b Sikander Bakht	1
G.A. Gooch	c Sadiq Mohammad b Sikander Bakht	33
D.I. Gower	b Majid Khan	27
I.T. Botham	b Majid Khan	22
P.H. Edmonds	c Wasim Raja b Asif Iqbal	2
R.W. Taylor+	not out	20
C.M. Old	c & b Asif Iqbal	2
R.G.D. Willis	b Sikander Bakht	24
M. Hendrick	not out	1
Extras	(LB 3, W 7, NB 5)	15
TOTAL	(60 overs) (for 9 wkts)	165

						Fall	
Imran Khan	12	3	24	1	1st	0
Sikander Bakht	12	3	32	3	2nd	4
Mudassar Nazar	12	4	30	0	3rd	51
Asif Iqbal	12	3	37	2	4th	70
Majid Khan	12	2	27	3	5th	99
					6th	115
					7th	115
					8th	118
					9th	161

PAKISTAN
Majid Khan	c Botham b Hendrick	7
Sadiq Mohammad	b Hendrick	18
Mudassar Nazar	lbw b Hendrick	0
Zaheer Abbas	c Taylor b Botham	3
Haroon Rashid	c Brearley b Hendrick	1
Javed Miandad	lbw b Botham	0
Asif Iqbal*	c Brearley b Willis	51
Wasim Raja	lbw b Old	21
Imran Khan	not out	21
Wasim Bari+	c Taylor b Boycott	17
Sikander Bakht	c Hendrick b Boycott	2
Extras	(LB 8, W 1, NB 1)	10
TOTAL	(56 overs)	151

						Fall	
Willis	11	2	37	1	1st	27
Hendrick	12	6	15	4	2nd	27
Botham	12	3	38	2	3rd	28
Old	12	2	28	1	4th	30
Edmonds	3	0	8	0	5th	31
Boycott	5	0	14	2	6th	34
Gooch	1	0	1	0	7th	86
					8th	115
					9th	145
					10th	151

Match No: 40/8

ENGLAND v NEW ZEALAND

Prudential World Cup Semi-Final
Played at Old Trafford, Manchester on 20/06/1979
Toss: New Zealand   **Result:** England won by 9 runs
Umpires: J.G. Langridge and K.E. Palmer
Man of the match: G.A. Gooch
Debuts: Eng - W. Larkins

ENGLAND
J.M. Brearley*	c Lees b Coney	53
G. Boycott	c Howarth b Hadlee	2
W. Larkins	c Coney b McKechnie	7
G.A. Gooch	b McKechnie	71
D.I. Gower	run out	1
I.T. Botham	lbw b Cairns	21
D.W. Randall	not out	42
C.M. Old	c Lees b Troup	0
R.W. Taylor+	run out	12
R.G.D. Willis	not out	1
M. Hendrick		
Extras	(LB 8, W 3)	11
TOTAL	(60 overs) (for 8 wkts)	**221**

						Fall	
Hadlee	12	4	32	1	1st	13
Troup	12	1	38	1	2nd	38
Cairns	12	2	47	1	3rd	96
Coney	12	0	47	1	4th	98
McKechnie	12	1	46	2	5th	145
					6th	177
					7th	178
					8th	219

NEW ZEALAND
J.G. Wright	run out	69
B.A. Edgar	lbw b Old	17
G.P. Howarth	lbw b Boycott	7
J.V. Coney	lbw b Hendrick	11
G.M. Turner	lbw b Willis	30
M.G. Burgess*	run out	10
R.J. Hadlee	b Botham	15
W.K. Lees+	b Hendrick	23
B.L. Cairns	c Brearley b Hendrick	14
B.J. McKechnie	not out	4
G.B. Troup	not out	3
Extras	(B 5, W 4)	9
TOTAL	(60 overs) (for 9 wkts)	**212**

						Fall	
Botham	12	3	42	1	1st	47
Hendrick	12	0	55	3	2nd	58
Old	12	1	33	1	3rd	104
Boycott	9	1	24	1	4th	112
Gooch	3	1	8	0	5th	132
Willis	12	1	41	1	6th	162
					7th	180
					8th	195
					9th	208

Match No: 41/6

ENGLAND v WEST INDIES

Prudential World Cup Final
Played at Lord's, London on 23/06/1979
Toss: England **Result:** West Indies won by 92 runs
Umpires: H.D. Bird and B.J. Meyer
Man of the match: I.V.A. Richards
Debuts: None

WEST INDIES

C.G. Greenidge	run out	9
D.L. Haynes	c Hendrick b Old	20
I.V.A. Richards	not out	138
A.I. Kallicharran	b Hendrick	4
C.H. Lloyd*	c & b Old	13
C.L. King	c Randall b Edmonds	86
D.L. Murray+	c Gower b Edmonds	5
A.M.E. Roberts	c Brearley b Hendrick	0
J. Garner	c Taylor b Botham	0
M.A. Holding	b Botham	0
C.E.H. Croft	not out	0
Extras	(B 1, LB 10)	11
TOTAL	(60 overs) (for 9 wkts)	**286**

						Fall	
Botham	12	2	44	2	1st	22
Hendrick	12	2	50	2	2nd	36
Old	12	0	55	2	3rd	55
Boycott	6	0	38	0	4th	99
Edmonds	12	2	40	2	5th	238
Gooch	4	0	27	0	6th	252
Larkins	2	0	21	0	7th	258
					8th	260
					9th	272

ENGLAND

J.M. Brearley*	c King b Holding	64
G. Boycott	c Kallicharran b Holding	57
D.W. Randall	b Croft	15
G.A. Gooch	b Garner	32
D.I. Gower	b Garner	0
I.T. Botham	c Richards b Croft	4
W. Larkins	b Garner	0
P.H. Edmonds	not out	5
C.M. Old	b Garner	0
R.W. Taylor+	c Murray b Garner	0
M. Hendrick	b Croft	0
Extras	(LB 12, W 2, NB 3)	17
TOTAL	(51 overs)	**194**

						Fall	
Roberts	9	2	33	0	1st	129
Holding	8	1	16	2	2nd	135
Croft	10	1	42	3	3rd	183
Garner	11	0	38	5	4th	183
Richards	10	0	35	0	5th	186
King	3	0	13	0	6th	186
					7th	192
					8th	192
					9th	194
					10th	194

Match No: 42/7

ENGLAND v WEST INDIES

Benson & Hedges World Series Cup
Played at Sydney Cricket Ground on 28/11/1979
Toss: West Indies   **Result:** England won by 2 runs (revised target)
Umpires: C.E. Harvey and A.G. Watson
Man of the match: P. Willey
Debuts: Eng - G.R. Dilley

ENGLAND
D.W. Randall	c Parry b Garner	49
J.M. Brearley*	c Greenidge b Parry	25
D.I. Gower	b Croft	44
G.A. Gooch	c & b Parry	2
P. Willey	not out	58
I.T. Botham	b Garner	11
D.L. Bairstow+	c Murray b Garner	0
G. Miller	b Roberts	4
G.R. Dilley	run out	1
D.L. Underwood		
R.G.D. Willis		
Extras	(B 4, LB 13)	17
TOTAL	(50 overs) (for 8 wkts)	**211**

						Fall	
Roberts	9	0	37	1	1st	79
Holding	9	0	47	0	2nd	88
Croft	10	0	34	1	3rd	91
Garner	10	0	31	3	4th	160
Parry	10	0	35	2	5th	195
Kallicharran	2	0	10	0	6th	195
					7th	210
					8th	211

WEST INDIES
C.G. Greenidge	c Willis b Miller	42
D.L. Haynes	b Dilley	4
L.G. Rowe	lbw b Willis	60
A.I. Kallicharran	run out	44
C.H. Lloyd*	c Brearley b Willis	4
D.L. Murray+	c Gower b Underwood	3
D.R. Parry	b Underwood	4
A.M.E. Roberts	c Randall b Underwood	16
J. Garner	not out	8
M.A. Holding	c Gower b Underwood	0
C.E.H. Croft	b Botham	3
Extras	(B 1, LB 7)	8
TOTAL	(47 overs)	**196**

						Fall	
Dilley	6	2	21	1	1st	19
Botham	7	1	26	1	2nd	68
Underwood	10	0	44	4	3rd	132
Miller	10	0	33	1	4th	143
Willey	8	0	29	0	5th	144
Willis	6	0	35	2	6th	155
					7th	177
					8th	185
					9th	186
					10th	196

Match No: 43/15

AUSTRALIA v ENGLAND

Benson & Hedges World Series Cup
Played at Melbourne Cricket Ground on 08/12/1979
Toss: England   **Result:** England won by 3 wickets
Umpires: W.J. Copeland and R.A. French
Man of the match: G.S. Chappell
Debuts: Aus - J.M. Wiener

AUSTRALIA

J.M. Wiener	b Botham	7
B.M. Laird	lbw b Dilley	7
A.R. Border	c Willey b Dilley	29
G.S. Chappell*	c Gooch b Willey	92
K.J. Hughes	st Bairstow b Gooch	23
K.D. Walters	c Randall b Gooch	12
R.W. Marsh+	c Bairstow b Willey	14
R.J. Bright	c Gooch b Willey	1
D.K. Lillee	not out	13
R.M. Hogg	c Brearley b Underwood	1
J.R. Thomson		
Extras	(B 1, LB 5, NB 2)	8
TOTAL	(50 overs) (for 9 wkts)	**207**

	O	M	R	W		Fall	
Dilley	10	1	30	2	1st	15
Botham	9	2	27	1	2nd	15
Willis	7	0	28	0	3rd	73
Gooch	6	0	32	2	4th	114
Underwood	10	0	49	1	5th	145
Willey	8	0	33	3	6th	184
					7th	193
					8th	193
					9th	207

ENGLAND

D.W. Randall	lbw b Bright	28
G. Boycott	c Lillee b Hogg	68
P. Willey	c Marsh b Hogg	37
D.I. Gower	c Marsh b Lillee	17
G.A. Gooch	run out	1
I.T. Botham	c Walters b Hogg	10
J.M. Brearley*	c Marsh b Lillee	27
D.L. Bairstow+	not out	15
G.R. Dilley	not out	0
D.L. Underwood		
R.G.D. Willis		
Extras	(LB 3, NB 3)	6
TOTAL	(49 overs) (for 7 wkts)	**209**

	O	M	R	W		Fall	
Lillee	10	1	36	2	1st	71
Hogg	10	2	26	3	2nd	134
Thomson	10	1	49	0	3rd	137
Chappell	8	0	40	0	4th	138
Bright	9	1	40	1	5th	148
Walters	2	0	12	0	6th	183
					7th	205

Match No: 44/16

AUSTRALIA v ENGLAND

Benson & Hedges World Series Cup
Played at Sydney Cricket Ground on 11/12/1979
Toss: England **Result:** England won by 72 runs
Umpires: J.R. Collins and L.J. Stevens
Man of the match: G. Boycott
Debuts: None

ENGLAND

D.W. Randall	run out	42
G. Boycott	b Lillee	105
P. Willey	c Walker b Chappell	64
D.I. Gower	c Wiener b Lillee	7
G.A. Gooch	b Thomson	11
I.T. Botham	c Walters b Lillee	5
D.L. Bairstow+	c sub (D.W. Hookes) b Lillee	18
J.M. Brearley*	not out	2
G.R. Dilley		
D.L. Underwood		
R.G.D. Willis		
Extras	(LB 6, W 1, NB 3)	10
TOTAL	(49 overs) (for 7 wkts)	**264**

						Fall	
Lillee	10	0	56	4	1st	78
Thomson	9	0	53	1	2nd	196
Walker	10	1	30	0	3rd	220
Laughlin	8	0	39	0	4th	236
Border	4	0	24	0	5th	242
Chappell	5	0	28	1	6th	245
Walters	3	0	24	0	7th	264

AUSTRALIA

J.M. Wiener	st Bairstow b Willey	14
W.M. Darling	c Randall b Willis	20
A.R. Border	b Willey	1
G.S. Chappell*	run out	0
K.J. Hughes	c Bairstow b Willis	1
K.D. Walters	c Bairstow b Botham	34
R.W. Marsh+	b Dilley	12
T.J. Laughlin	c Gooch b Randall	74
D.K. Lillee	b Botham	14
J.R. Thomson	run out	0
M.H.N. Walker	not out	9
Extras	(LB 10, W 2, NB 1)	13
TOTAL	(47.2 overs)	**192**

						Fall	
Dilley	9	0	29	1	1st	33
Botham	10	1	36	2	2nd	36
Willis	10	1	32	2	3rd	36
Willey	5	0	18	2	4th	38
Underwood	6	1	29	0	5th	39
Gooch	7	0	33	0	6th	63
Randall	0.2	0	2	1	7th	115
						8th	146
						9th	147
						10th	192

Match No: 45/8

ENGLAND v WEST INDIES

Benson & Hedges World Series Cup
Played at Woolloongabba, Brisbane on 23/12/1979
Toss: West Indies   **Result:** West Indies won by 9 wickets
Umpires: C.E. Harvey and M.W. Johnson
Man of the match: C.G. Greenidge
Debuts: None

ENGLAND
D.W. Randall	c Lloyd b Roberts	0
G. Boycott	c sub (M.D. Marshall) b Holding	68
P. Willey	run out	34
D.I. Gower	c Holding b Roberts	59
G.A. Gooch	b Garner	17
I.T. Botham	lbw b Holding	4
D.L. Bairstow+	c Lloyd b Roberts	12
J.M. Brearley*	not out	9
G.R. Dilley	b Garner	0
D.L. Underwood		
R.G.D. Willis		
Extras	(LB 8, W 5, NB 1)	14
TOTAL	(50 overs) (for 8 wkts)	**217**

						Fall	
Roberts	10	3	26	3	1st	0
Holding	10	1	44	2	2nd	70
Garner	10	0	37	2	3rd	167
Richards	10	0	44	0	4th	174
King	10	0	52	0	5th	191
					6th	205
					7th	209
					8th	217

WEST INDIES
C.G. Greenidge	not out	85
D.L. Haynes	c Underwood b Gooch	41
I.V.A. Richards	not out	85
A.I. Kallicharran		
L.G. Rowe		
C.H. Lloyd*		
C.L. King		
D.L. Murray+		
A.M.E. Roberts		
J. Garner		
M.A. Holding		
Extras	(LB 4, NB 3)	7
TOTAL	(46.5 overs) (for 1 wkt)	**218**

						Fall	
Botham	10	1	39	0	1st	109
Dilley	8	1	25	0		
Willis	10	2	27	0		
Underwood	9	0	43	0		
Willey	6	0	39	0		
Gooch	3.5	0	38	1		

Match No: 46/17

AUSTRALIA v ENGLAND

Benson & Hedges World Series Cup
Played at Sydney Cricket Ground on 26/12/1979
Toss: Australia **Result:** England won by 4 wickets
Umpires: P.M. Cronin and R.C. Isherwood
Man of the match: G. Boycott
Debuts: None

AUSTRALIA
B.M. Laird	b Botham	6
J.M. Wiener	c Bairstow b Botham	2
A.R. Border	c Gower b Gooch	22
G.S. Chappell*	run out	52
K.J. Hughes	b Willis	23
I.M. Chappell	not out	60
R.W. Marsh+	c Bairstow b Dilley	10
D.K. Lillee	not out	2
R.M. Hogg		
G. Dymock		
L.S. Pascoe		
Extras	(B 3, LB 10, NB 4)	17
TOTAL	(47 overs) (for 6 wkts)	**194**

						Fall	
Dilley	10	1	32	1		1st	5
Botham	9	1	33	2		2nd	21
Willis	10	1	38	1		3rd	50
Underwood	10	2	36	0		4th	109
Gooch	8	0	38	1		5th	135
						6th	179

ENGLAND
G.A. Gooch	lbw b Hogg	29
G. Boycott	not out	86
P. Willey	b Pascoe	51
D.I. Gower	c Marsh b Hogg	2
D.W. Randall	c G.S. Chappell b Pascoe	1
I.T. Botham	lbw b Hogg	6
J.M. Brearley*	c Marsh b Hogg	0
D.L. Bairstow+	not out	7
G.R. Dilley		
D.L. Underwood		
R.G.D. Willis		
Extras	(LB 1, W 1, NB 11)	13
TOTAL	(45.1 overs) (for 6 wkts)	**195**

						Fall	
Lillee	10	0	47	0		1st	41
Pascoe	10	2	28	2		2nd	152
Hogg	10	0	46	4		3rd	157
Dymock	10	1	38	0		4th	170
G.S. Chappell	5.1	0	23	0		5th	179
						6th	179

58   England - The Complete One-Day International Record

Match No: 47/18

AUSTRALIA v ENGLAND

Benson & Hedges World Series Cup
Played at Sydney Cricket Ground on 14/01/1980
Toss: England   **Result:** England won by 2 wickets
Umpires: R.C. Isherwood and R.V. Whitehead
Man of the match: D.K. Lillee
Debuts: Eng - J.E. Emburey, G.B. Stevenson

AUSTRALIA

J.M. Wiener	st Bairstow b Emburey	33
R.B. McCosker	c Brearley b Willey	41
I.M. Chappell	c Randall b Emburey	8
G.S. Chappell*	c Randall b Stevenson	34
K.J. Hughes	c Larkins b Lever	34
A.R. Border	c Bairstow b Lever	0
R.W. Marsh+	c Bairstow b Stevenson	0
D.K. Lillee	lbw b Stevenson	0
G. Dymock	run out	0
J.R. Thomson	not out	3
L.S. Pascoe	b Stevenson	5
Extras	(LB 1, W 3, NB 1)	5
TOTAL	(48.4 overs)	**163**

						Fall	
Lever	9	1	11	2	1st	74
Botham	7	0	33	0	2nd	82
Gooch	3	0	13	0	3rd	89
Stevenson	9.4	0	33	4	4th	148
Emburey	10	1	33	2	5th	149
Willey	10	0	35	1	6th	150
					7th	150
					8th	152
					9th	155
					10th	163

ENGLAND

G.A. Gooch	c McCosker b Pascoe	69
W. Larkins	c Thomson b Lillee	5
P. Willey	lbw b Lillee	0
D.I. Gower	c Marsh b Lillee	3
J.M. Brearley*	b G.S Chappell	5
D.W. Randall	c Pascoe b G.S Chappell	0
I.T. Botham	b Lillee	0
D.L. Bairstow+	not out	21
J.E. Emburey	c G.S Chappell b Dymock	18
G.B. Stevenson	not out	28
J.K. Lever		
Extras	(LB 5, W 1, NB 9)	15
TOTAL	(48.5 overs) (for 8 wkts)	**164**

						Fall	
Thomson	9.5	0	46	0	1st	31
Dymock	9	1	30	1	2nd	31
Lillee	10	6	12	4	3rd	40
Pascoe	10	0	38	1	4th	51
G.S. Chappell	10	3	23	2	5th	56
					6th	61
					7th	105
					8th	129

Matches 59

Match No: 48/9

ENGLAND v WEST INDIES

Benson & Hedges World Series Cup
Played at Adelaide Oval on 16/01/1980
Toss: England **Result:** West Indies won by 107 runs
Umpires: P.M. Cronin and G. Duperouzel
Man of the match: A.M.E. Roberts
Debuts: None

WEST INDIES
C.G. Greenidge	c Emburey b Willey	50
D.L. Haynes	c Gooch b Stevenson	26
I.V.A. Richards	b Botham	88
A.I. Kallicharran	c & b Botham	57
C.L. King	run out	12
J. Garner	not out	7
A.M.E. Roberts	not out	0
C.H. Lloyd*		
L.G. Rowe		
D.L. Murray+		
M.A. Holding		
Extras	(B 1, LB 4, NB 1)	6
TOTAL	(50 overs) (for 5 wkts)	**246**

						Fall	
Lever	10	1	54	0	1st	58
Botham	10	0	35	2	2nd	115
Gooch	2	0	22	0	3rd	224
Stevenson	8	1	53	1	4th	227
Emburey	10	0	39	0	5th	245
Willey	10	1	37	1		

ENGLAND
G.A. Gooch	b King	20
J.M. Brearley*	c Murray b Roberts	0
P. Willey	c Lloyd b King	5
W. Larkins	c Lloyd b King	24
D.I. Gower	c sub (D.R. Parry) b King	12
D.W. Randall	b Roberts	16
I.T. Botham	c Haynes b Roberts	22
D.L. Bairstow+	not out	23
G.B. Stevenson	b Roberts	1
J.E. Emburey	c Murray b Roberts	1
J.K. Lever	b Garner	11
Extras	(LB 2, W 1, NB 1)	4
TOTAL	(42.5 overs)	**139**

						Fall	
Roberts	10	5	22	5	1st	5
Holding	7	0	16	0	2nd	24
King	9	3	23	4	3rd	31
Garner	7.5	3	9	1	4th	52
Richards	7	0	46	0	5th	68
Kallicharran	2	0	19	0	6th	98
					7th	100
					8th	105
					9th	109
					10th	139

Match No: 49/10

ENGLAND v WEST INDIES

Benson & Hedges World Series Cup 1st Final
Played at Melbourne Cricket Ground on 20/01/1980
Toss: England   **Result:** West Indies won by 2 runs
Umpires: R.C. Bailhache and C.E. Harvey
Man of the match: None
Debuts: None

WEST INDIES
C.G. Greenidge	c Larkins b Botham	80
D.L. Haynes	c Bairstow b Willis	9
I.V.A. Richards	c Bairstow b Dilley	23
A.I. Kallicharran	b Botham	42
C.H. Lloyd*	b Botham	4
C.L. King	not out	31
D.L. Murray+	c Bairstow b Dilley	4
A.M.E. Roberts	run out	1
J. Garner	run out	3
M.A. Holding	not out	5
C.E.H. Croft		
Extras	(LB 11, W 1, NB 1)	13
TOTAL	(50 overs) (for 8 wkts)	**215**

						Fall	
Willis	10	1	51	1		1st	17
Botham	10	2	33	3		2nd	66
Emburey	10	0	31	0		3rd	161
Dilley	10	0	39	2		4th	168
Willey	10	0	48	0		5th	168
						6th	181
						7th	183
						8th	197

ENGLAND
G.A. Gooch	c King b Holding	9
G. Boycott	c Greenidge b Roberts	35
P. Willey	run out	51
D.I. Gower	c Holding b Roberts	10
W. Larkins	run out	34
I.T. Botham	c Lloyd b Roberts	19
J.M. Brearley*	not out	25
D.L. Bairstow+	run out	4
J.E. Emburey		
G.R. Dilley		
R.G.D. Willis		
Extras	(B 12, LB 12, W 1, NB 1)	26
TOTAL	(50 overs) (for 7 wkts)	**213**

						Fall	
Roberts	10	1	30	3		1st	13
Holding	10	1	43	1		2nd	74
Garner	10	1	27	0		3rd	96
Croft	10	1	23	0		4th	152
King	4	0	30	0		5th	164
Richards	6	1	34	0		6th	190
						7th	213

Match No: 50/11

ENGLAND v WEST INDIES

Benson & Hedges World Series Cup 2nd Final
Played at Sydney Cricket Ground on 22/01/1980
Toss: England   **Result:** West Indies won by 8 wickets
Umpires: A.R. Crafter and M.G. O'Connell
Man of the finals: C.G. Greenidge
Debuts: None

ENGLAND
G.A. Gooch	lbw b Garner	23
G. Boycott	c Greenidge b Roberts	63
P. Willey	b Garner	3
D.I. Gower	c Murray b Holding	27
W. Larkins	b Croft	14
I.T. Botham	c King b Roberts	37
D.L. Bairstow+	not out	18
J.M. Brearley*	run out	4
J.E. Emburey	run out	6
G.R. Dilley		
R.G.D. Willis		
Extras	(B 1, LB 11, NB 1)	13
TOTAL	(50 overs) (for 8 wkts)	**208**

						Fall	
Roberts	10	3	31	2	1st	40
Holding	10	1	34	1	2nd	54
Croft	10	3	29	1	3rd	118
Garner	10	0	44	2	4th	126
Richards	3	0	19	0	5th	155
King	7	1	38	0	6th	188
					7th	194
					8th	208

WEST INDIES
C.G. Greenidge	not out	98
D.L. Haynes	lbw b Botham	17
I.V.A. Richards	c Botham b Willey	65
A.I. Kallicharran	not out	8
C.H. Lloyd*		
C.L. King		
D.L. Murray+		
A.M.E. Roberts		
J. Garner		
M.A. Holding		
C.E.H. Croft		
Extras	(B 5, LB 10, W 5, NB 1)	21
TOTAL	(47.3 overs) (for 2 wkts)	**209**

						Fall	
Willis	10	0	35	0	1st	61
Dilley	7	0	37	0	2nd	180
Botham	10	1	28	1		
Emburey	9.3	0	48	0		
Willey	10	2	35	1		
Gooch	1	0	5	0		

Match No: 51/12

ENGLAND v WEST INDIES

Prudential Trophy
Played at Headingley, Leeds on 28 & 29/05/1980
Toss: England   **Result:** West Indies won by 24 runs
Umpires: B.J. Meyer and K.E. Palmer
Man of the match: C.J. Tavare
Debuts: Eng - C.J. Tavare   WI - M.D. Marshall

WEST INDIES

C.G. Greenidge	b Botham	78
D.L. Haynes	c Tavare b Old	19
I.V.A. Richards	c Gower b Gooch	7
S.F.A.F. Bacchus	c Lever b Gooch	2
A.I. Kallicharran	c Botham b Old	10
C.H. Lloyd*	c & b Lever	21
M.D. Marshall	b Botham	6
D.L. Murray+	run out	9
A.M.E. Roberts	c Botham b Dilley	10
J. Garner	run out	14
M.A. Holding	not out	0
Extras	(B 5, LB 15, W 2)	22
TOTAL	**(55 overs)**	**198**

						Fall	
Dilley	11	3	41	1	1st	36
Lever	11	3	36	1	2nd	49
Botham	11	1	45	2	3rd	51
Old	11	4	12	2	4th	110
Gooch	7	2	30	2	5th	151
Willey	4	0	12	0	6th	161
					7th	163
					8th	178
					9th	197
					10th	198

ENGLAND

G. Boycott	c Kallicharran b Garner	5
P. Willey	c Richards b Marshall	7
C.J. Tavare	not out	82
G.A. Gooch	c Murray b Richards	2
D.I. Gower	c Murray b Holding	12
I.T. Botham*	c Murray b Marshall	30
D. Lloyd	b Greenidge	1
D.L. Bairstow+	c Garner b Holding	16
C.M. Old	b Marshall	4
G.R. Dilley	c Haynes b Roberts	0
J.K. Lever	run out	6
Extras	(B 3, LB 4, W 2)	9
TOTAL	**(51.2 overs)**	**174**

						Fall	
Holding	9	3	16	2	1st	11
Roberts	11	4	30	1	2nd	15
Garner	9.2	0	20	1	3rd	23
Marshall	11	2	28	3	4th	38
Richards	7	0	50	1	5th	81
Greenidge	4	0	21	1	6th	86
					7th	130
					8th	149
					9th	150
					10th	174

Match No: 52/13

ENGLAND v WEST INDIES

Prudential Trophy
Played at Lord's, London on 30/05/1980
Toss: England   **Result:** England won by 3 wickets
Umpires: D.J. Constant and D.G.L. Evans
Man of the match: G. Boycott
Debuts: Eng - V.J. Marks

WEST INDIES
C.G. Greenidge	c Lever b Marks	39
D.L. Haynes	c Willis b Marks	50
S.F.A.F. Bacchus	run out	40
I.V.A. Richards*	c Lever b Botham	26
A.I. Kallicharran	c Willis b Old	11
C.L. King	run out	33
A.M.E. Roberts	not out	25
J. Garner	run out	0
M.D. Marshall	b Willis	0
M.A. Holding	b Willis	0
D.L. Murray+		
Extras	(LB 9, NB 2)	11
TOTAL	(55 overs) (for 9 wkts)	**235**

						Fall	
Willis	10	1	25	2	1st	86
Lever	7	1	23	0	2nd	113
Botham	11	2	71	1	3rd	147
Old	11	1	43	1	4th	169
Marks	11	1	44	2	5th	186
Willey	5	0	18	0	6th	231
					7th	233
					8th	233
					9th	235

ENGLAND
P. Willey	c & b Holding	56
G. Boycott	run out	70
C.J. Tavare	c Murray b Holding	5
G.A. Gooch	c Bacchus b Marshall	12
D.I. Gower	c Bacchus b Roberts	12
I.T. Botham*	not out	42
V.J. Marks	b Holding	9
D.L. Bairstow+	run out	2
J.K. Lever	not out	0
C.M. Old		
R.G.D. Willis		
Extras	(LB 22, W 4, NB 2)	28
TOTAL	(54.3 overs) (for 7 wkts)	**236**

						Fall	
Roberts	11	3	42	1	1st	135
Holding	11	0	28	3	2nd	143
Garner	10.3	0	41	0	3rd	156
Marshall	11	1	45	1	4th	160
Richards	5	0	28	0	5th	176
Greenidge	6	0	24	0	6th	212
					7th	231

Match No: 53/19

ENGLAND v AUSTRALIA

Prudential Trophy
Played at The Oval, London on 20/08/1980
Toss: Australia   **Result:** England won by 23 runs
Umpires: W.E. Alley and D.G.L. Evans
Man of the match: M. Hendrick
Debuts: Eng - C.W.J. Athey, A.R. Butcher

ENGLAND

G.A. Gooch	b Border	54
G. Boycott	c Hughes b Lillee	99
A.R. Butcher	lbw b Dymock	14
C.W.J. Athey	c Chappell b Lillee	32
M.W. Gatting	not out	17
I.T. Botham*	c Yallop b Lillee	4
P. Willey	c Yallop b Lillee	2
D.L. Bairstow+	not out	9
R.D. Jackman		
C.M. Old		
M. Hendrick		
Extras	(B 2, LB 8, W 3, NB 4)	17
TOTAL	(55 overs) (for 6 wkts)	**248**

	O	M	R	W	Fall	
Lillee	11	1	35	4	1st	108
Thomson	11	3	25	0	2nd	140
Dymock	9	0	50	1	3rd	212
Pascoe	11	1	50	0	4th	221
Border	11	2	61	1	5th	225
Chappell	2	0	10	0	6th	232

AUSTRALIA

B.M. Laird	lbw b Gooch	15
G.M. Wood	c Athey b Jackman	4
G.S. Chappell*	c Bairstow b Hendrick	36
A.R. Border	b Hendrick	13
K.J. Hughes	not out	73
G.N. Yallop	b Hendrick	0
R.W. Marsh+	c Bairstow b Hendrick	41
D.K. Lillee	c Willey b Hendrick	0
J.R. Thomson	run out	15
G. Dymock	not out	14
L.S. Pascoe		
Extras	(B 3, LB 10, W 1)	14
TOTAL	(55 overs) (for 8 wkts)	**225**

	O	M	R	W	Fall	
Old	9	0	43	0	1st	11
Jackman	11	0	46	1	2nd	36
Botham	9	1	28	0	3rd	68
Gooch	7	0	29	1	4th	71
Hendrick	11	3	31	5	5th	75
Willey	8	0	34	0	6th	161
					7th	161
					8th	192

Match No: 54/20

ENGLAND v AUSTRALIA

Prudential Trophy
Played at Edgbaston, Birmingham on 22/08/1980
Toss: Australia **Result:** England won by 47 runs
Umpires: H.D. Bird and D.O. Oslear
Man of the match: G.A. Gooch
Debuts: Eng - R.O. Butcher   Aus - J. Dyson

ENGLAND

G.A. Gooch	b Thomson	108
G. Boycott	c Marsh b Border	78
C.W.J. Athey	b Pascoe	51
R.O. Butcher	c Dyson b Pascoe	52
M.W. Gatting	run out	2
I.T. Botham*	b Pascoe	2
D.L. Bairstow+	b Lillee	6
R.D. Jackman	c Marsh b Pascoe	6
J.E. Emburey	not out	1
C.M. Old	not out	2
M. Hendrick		
Extras	(B 4, LB 3, W 1, NB 4)	12
TOTAL	(55 overs) (for 8 wkts)	**320**

Fall

Bowler	O	M	R	W		
Thomson	11	1	69	1	1st	154
Lillee	11	0	43	1	2nd	215
Pascoe	11	0	69	4	3rd	292
Bright	8	0	48	0	4th	298
Chappell	11	0	65	0	5th	302
Border	3	0	14	1	6th	311
					7th	313
					8th	318

AUSTRALIA

B.M. Laird	c Emburey b Hendrick	36
J. Dyson	b Hendrick	24
K.J. Hughes	c & b Gooch	98
A.R. Border	run out	26
G.N. Yallop	not out	52
D.K. Lillee	b Hendrick	21
R.J. Bright	not out	5
G.S. Chappell*		
R.W. Marsh+		
J.R. Thomson		
L.S. Pascoe		
Extras	(B 1, LB 9, W 1)	11
TOTAL	(55 overs) (for 5 wkts)	**273**

Fall

Bowler	O	M	R	W		
Old	11	2	44	0	1st	53
Jackman	11	1	45	0	2nd	80
Botham	11	1	41	0	3rd	119
Hendrick	10	0	54	3	4th	222
Emburey	8	0	51	0	5th	229
Gooch	3	0	16	1		
Boycott	1	0	11	0		

Match No: 55/14

WEST INDIES v ENGLAND

Played at Arnos Vale, St Vincent on 04/02/1981
Toss: England   **Result:** West Indies won by 2 runs
Umpires: D.M. Archer and S. Mohammed
Man of the match: C.E.H. Croft
Debuts: WI - E.H. Mattis

WEST INDIES

D.L. Haynes	c Emburey b Stevenson	34
S.F.A.F. Bacchus	c Stevenson b Old	1
E.H. Mattis	run out	62
A.I. Kallicharran	b Emburey	2
C.H. Lloyd*	c Willey b Stevenson	2
H.A. Gomes	b Willey	8
D.A. Murray+	b Gooch	1
A.M.E. Roberts	st Bairstow b Gooch	2
J. Garner	run out	4
M.A. Holding	b Botham	1
C.E.H. Croft	not out	2
Extras	(LB 4, W 1, NB 3)	8
Total	(47.2 overs)	**127**

						Fall	
Old	5	4	8	1		1st	5
Botham	8	1	32	1		2nd	48
Stevenson	8.2	2	18	2		3rd	51
Emburey	10	4	20	1		4th	58
Willey	10	1	29	1		5th	89
Gooch	6	1	12	2		6th	90
						7th	102
						8th	110
						9th	120
						10th	127

ENGLAND

G. Boycott	c Mattis b Croft	2
G.A. Gooch	c Lloyd b Roberts	11
P. Willey	c Murray b Croft	0
D.I. Gower	c Haynes b Kallicharran	23
R.O. Butcher	c Murray b Croft	1
I.T. Botham*	c Murray b Croft	60
M.W. Gatting	b Croft	3
D.L. Bairstow+	b Croft	5
J.E. Emburey	b Holding	5
G.B. Stevenson	not out	6
C.M. Old	b Holding	1
Extras	(LB 8)	8
TOTAL	(48.2 overs)	**125**

						Fall	
Roberts	10	1	30	1		1st	14
Holding	9.2	2	30	2		2nd	14
Croft	9	4	15	6		3rd	14
Garner	10	2	17	0		4th	15
Kallicharran	10	3	25	1		5th	80
						6th	88
						7th	111
						8th	114
						9th	123
						10th	125

Match No: 56/15

WEST INDIES v ENGLAND

Played at Albion Sports Complex, Berbice, Guyana on 26/02/1981
Toss: West Indies **Result:** West Indies won by 6 wickets
Umpires: D.J. Narine and P.J. McConnell
Man of the match: H.A. Gomes
Debuts: None

ENGLAND
G. Boycott	b Richards	7
G.A. Gooch	c Murray b Roberts	11
M.W. Gatting	c Mattis b Gomes	29
D.I. Gower	b Gomes	3
R.O. Butcher	c Haynes b Gomes	5
I.T. Botham*	b Roberts	27
P. Willey	b Croft	21
D.L. Bairstow+	b Croft	16
J.E. Emburey	c Croft b Holding	0
G.B. Stevenson	not out	8
G.R. Dilley	b Croft	3
Extras	(B 4, LB 2, NB 1)	7
TOTAL	(47.2 overs)	**137**

						Fall	
Roberts	7	0	17	2		1st	16
Holding	7	1	13	1		2nd	27
Richards	10	0	26	1		3rd	34
Croft	6.2	1	9	3		4th	59
Gomes	10	2	30	3		5th	62
Garner	7	2	35	0		6th	108
						7th	112
						8th	119
						9th	132
						10th	137

WEST INDIES
C.G. Greenidge	run out	2
D.L. Haynes	c Gooch b Emburey	48
I.V.A. Richards	c Stevenson b Dilley	3
E.H. Mattis	b Emburey	24
H.A. Gomes	not out	22
C.H. Lloyd*	not out	25
D.A. Murray+		
A.M.E. Roberts		
M.A. Holding		
J. Garner		
C.E.H. Croft		
Extras	(B 4, LB 8, NB 2)	14
TOTAL	(39.3 overs) (for 4 wkts)	**138**

						Fall	
Dilley	5	0	21	1		1st	6
Botham	7	1	24	0		2nd	11
Stevenson	6	0	21	0		3rd	85
Emburey	10	4	22	2		4th	90
Gooch	2	0	8	0			
Willey	9	0	23	0			
Gower	0.3	0	5	0			

Match No: 57/21

ENGLAND v AUSTRALIA

Prudential Trophy
Played at Lord's, London on 04/06/1981
Toss: England   Result: England won by 6 wickets
Umpires: W.E. Alley and H.D. Bird
Man of the match: G. Boycott
Debuts: Eng - G.W. Humpage, J.D. Love

AUSTRALIA
J. Dyson	lbw b Willis	2
G.M. Wood	run out	22
T.M. Chappell	run out	16
K.J. Hughes*	lbw b Jackman	12
A.R. Border	not out	73
M.F. Kent	c Gooch b Botham	28
R.W. Marsh+	b Botham	18
R.J. Bright	b Willis	18
G.F. Lawson	not out	12
D.K. Lillee		
R.M. Hogg		
Extras	(B 1, LB 8)	9
TOTAL	(55 overs) (for 7 wkts)	**210**

					Fall	
Willis	11	0	56	2	1st	2
Botham	11	1	39	2	2nd	36
Hendrick	11	2	32	0	3rd	48
Jackman	11	1	27	1	4th	60
Willey	6	1	26	0	5th	134
Gooch	5	1	21	0	6th	162
					7th	189

ENGLAND
G.A. Gooch	c Kent b Lillee	53
G. Boycott	not out	75
M.W. Gatting	lbw b Lillee	0
D.I. Gower	c Kent b Chappell	47
J.D. Love	c Bright b Lawson	15
I.T. Botham*	not out	13
P. Willey		
G.W. Humpage+		
R.D. Jackman		
R.G.D. Willis		
M. Hendrick		
Extras	(B 5, LB 4)	9
TOTAL	(51.4 overs) (for 4 wkts)	**212**

					Fall	
Hogg	11	1	36	0	1st	86
Lillee	11	3	23	2	2nd	86
Lawson	9	0	51	1	3rd	172
Chappell	11	1	50	1	4th	199
Bright	9.4	0	43	0		

Match No: 58/22

ENGLAND v AUSTRALIA

Prudential Trophy
Played at Edgbaston, Birmingham on 06/06/1981
Toss: England   Result: Australia won by 2 runs
Umpires: D.J. Constant and A.G.T. Whitehead
Man of the match: M.W. Gatting
Debuts: Aus - T.M. Alderman

AUSTRALIA
G.M. Wood	c Willis b Jackman	55
T.M. Chappell	c Humpage b Botham	0
G.N. Yallop	b Hendrick	63
K.J. Hughes*	run out	34
A.R. Border	run out	17
R.W. Marsh+	c Love b Botham	20
M.F. Kent	lbw b Willis	1
G.F. Lawson	not out	29
D.K. Lillee	run out	8
R.M. Hogg	not out	0
T.M. Alderman		
Extras	(B 1, LB 18, W 1, NB 2)	22
TOTAL	(55 overs) (for 8 wkts)	249

						Fall	
Willis	11	3	41	1	1st	10
Botham	11	1	44	2	2nd	96
Hendrick	11	2	21	1	3rd	160
Jackman	11	0	47	1	4th	171
Willey	6	0	36	0	5th	183
Gooch	5	0	38	0	6th	193
					7th	213
					8th	248

ENGLAND
G.A. Gooch	b Hogg	11
G. Boycott	b Lawson	14
M.W. Gatting	c Lawson b Lillee	96
D.I. Gower	b Alderman	2
J.D. Love	b Lawson	43
P. Willey	c Wood b Chappell	37
I.T. Botham*	c Hughes b Lawson	24
G.W. Humpage+	b Lillee	5
R.D. Jackman	run out	2
R.G.D. Willis	not out	1
M. Hendrick	c Marsh b Lillee	0
Extras	(LB 12)	12
TOTAL	(54.5 overs)	247

						Fall	
Hogg	11	2	42	1	1st	20
Lillee	10.5	2	36	3	2nd	27
Alderman	11	1	46	1	3rd	36
Lawson	11	2	42	3	4th	111
Chappell	11	0	69	1	5th	177
					6th	224
					7th	232
					8th	244
					9th	244
					10th	247

Match No: 59/23

ENGLAND v AUSTRALIA

Prudential Trophy
Played at Headingley, Leeds on 08/06/1981
Toss: England **Result:** Australia won by 71 runs
Umpires: B.J. Meyer and K.E. Palmer
Man of the match: G.M. Wood
Debuts: None

AUSTRALIA

G.M. Wood	run out	108
J. Dyson	c Gooch b Hendrick	22
G.N. Yallop	run out	48
K.J. Hughes*	c Gatting b Jackman	0
A.R. Border	c Jackman b Willis	5
R.W. Marsh+	c Humpage b Botham	1
T.M. Chappell	c Gooch b Willis	14
G.F. Lawson	run out	8
D.K. Lillee	not out	0
R.M. Hogg		
T.M. Alderman		
Extras	(LB 27, W 1, NB 2)	30
TOTAL	(55 overs) (for 8 wkts)	**236**

						Fall	
Willis	11	1	35	2	1st	43
Botham	11	2	42	1	2nd	173
Hendrick	11	3	31	1	3rd	173
Gooch	11	0	50	0	4th	187
Jackman	11	1	48	1	5th	189
					6th	216
					7th	236
					8th	236

ENGLAND

G.A. Gooch	c Marsh b Lawson	37
G. Boycott	c Marsh b Hogg	4
M.W. Gatting	c Marsh b Hogg	32
D.I. Gower	b Alderman	5
J.D. Love	b Chappell	3
P. Willey	c Marsh b Hogg	42
I.T. Botham*	c Hughes b Chappell	5
G.W. Humpage+	c Border b Alderman	6
R.D. Jackman	b Chappell	14
R.G.D. Willis	not out	2
M. Hendrick	c Marsh b Hogg	0
Extras	(B 10, W 1, NB 4)	15
TOTAL	(46.5 overs)	**165**

						Fall	
Hogg	8.5	1	29	4	1st	5
Lillee	7	0	37	0	2nd	71
Lawson	11	3	34	1	3rd	80
Alderman	11	3	19	2	4th	89
Chappell	9	0	31	3	5th	95
					6th	106
					7th	133
					8th	160
					9th	164
					10th	165

Match No: 60/4

INDIA v ENGLAND

Wills Series
Played at Sardar Patel Stadium, Ahmedabad on 25/11/1981
Toss: England   **Result:** England won by 5 wickets
Umpires: M.V. Gothoskar and S.N. Hanumantha Rao
Man of the match: M.W. Gatting
Debuts: Eng - G. Cook, C.J. Richards
Ind - Randhir Singh, R.J. Shastri, K. Srikkanth

INDIA

S.M. Gavaskar*	c Gooch b Willis	0
K. Srikkanth	b Botham	0
D.B. Vengsarkar	c & b Underwood	46
G.R. Viswanath	c Cook b Gooch	8
K. Azad	b Botham	30
Madan Lal	c Lever b Underwood	6
S.M.H. Kirmani+	not out	18
R.J. Shastri	run out	19
R.M.H. Binny	not out	2
D.R. Doshi		
Randhir Singh		
Extras	(B 4, LB 13, W 7, NB 3)	27
TOTAL	(46 overs) (for 7 wkts)	**156**

						Fall	
Willis	9	3	17	1	1st	2
Botham	10	4	20	2	2nd	8
Lever	10	0	46	0	3rd	39
Gooch	7	0	28	1	4th	91
Underwood	10	3	18	2	5th	113
					6th	119
					7th	154

ENGLAND

G.A. Gooch	c Kirmani b Binny	23
G. Boycott	lbw b Madan Lal	5
G. Cook	c Viswanath b Binny	13
D.I. Gower	c & b Binny	8
K.W.R. Fletcher*	b Doshi	26
M.W. Gatting	not out	47
I.T. Botham	not out	25
C.J. Richards+		
J.K. Lever		
D.L. Underwood		
R.G.D. Willis		
Extras	(LB 7, W 2, NB 4)	13
TOTAL	(43.5 overs) (for 5 wkts)	**160**

						Fall	
Madan Lal	10	2	30	1	1st	5
Randhir Singh	6	0	18	0	2nd	43
R.M.H. Binny	7.5	3	35	3	3rd	46
R.J. Shastri	10	1	24	0	4th	61
D.R. Doshi	10	1	40	1	5th	126

Match No: 61/5

INDIA v ENGLAND

Wills Series
Played at Burlton Park, Jullundur on 20/12/1981
Toss: India **Result:** India won by 6 wickets
Umpires: J.D. Ghosh and Swaroop Kishen
Man of the match: D.B. Vengsarkar
Debuts: Ind - S.V. Nayak

ENGLAND
G.A. Gooch	b Madan Lal	12
G. Boycott	run out	6
I.T. Botham	lbw b Madan Lal	5
K.W.R. Fletcher*	c Azad b Patil	5
D.I. Gower	run out	53
M.W. Gatting	not out	71
G. Cook	b Kapil Dev	1
C.J. Richards+	lbw b Kapil Dev	0
J.K. Lever		
D.L. Underwood		
R.G.D. Willis		
Extras	(B 2, LB 4, W 1, NB 1)	8
TOTAL	(36 overs) (for 7 wkts)	161

					Fall	
Kapil Dev	8	1	26	2	1st	18
Madan Lal	7	0	33	2	2nd	22
Nayak	7	2	25	0	3rd	25
Patil	7	0	16	1	4th	48
Shastri	7	0	53	0	5th	158
					6th	161
					7th	161

INDIA
K. Srikkanth	lbw b Botham	17
D.B. Vengsarkar	not out	88
K. Azad	c Gower b Gooch	14
S.M. Patil	b Gooch	3
Kapil Dev	c Willis b Underwood	6
Yashpal Sharma	not out	28
S.M. Gavaskar*		
S.V. Nayak		
Madan Lal		
S.M.H. Kirmani+		
R.J. Shastri		
Extras	(B 3, LB 3, W 0, NB 2)	8
TOTAL	(35.3 overs) (for 4 wkts)	164

					Fall	
Willis	7.3	2	41	0	1st	41
Lever	7	0	31	0	2nd	69
Gooch	7	0	25	2	3rd	78
Botham	7	0	33	1	4th	89
Underwood	7	1	26	1		

Match No: 62/6

INDIA v ENGLAND

Wills Series
Played at Barabati Stadium, Cuttack on 27/01/1982
Toss: India **Result:** India won by 5 wickets
Umpires: P.R. Punjabi and K.B. Ramaswami
Man of the match: S.M. Gavaskar
Debuts: Ind - Arun Lal, A. Malhotra

ENGLAND
G.A. Gooch	c Arun Lal b Madan Lal	3
G. Cook	c Nayak b Patil	30
C.J. Tavare	c Madan Lal b Shastri	11
D.I. Gower	c & b Patil	42
I.T. Botham	b Nayak	52
K.W.R. Fletcher*	b Madan Lal	69
M.W. Gatting	not out	8
R.W. Taylor+	not out	2
J.K. Lever		
D.L. Underwood		
R.G.D. Willis		
Extras	(LB 9, W 1, NB 3)	13
TOTAL	(46 overs) (for 6 wkts)	**230**

						Fall	
Kapil Dev	8	3	23	0	1st	13
Madan Lal	8	0	56	2	2nd	33
Nayak	10	1	51	1	3rd	86
Shastri	10	1	34	1	4th	101
Patil	10	0	53	2	5th	181
					6th	228

INDIA
S.M. Gavaskar*	st Taylor b Underwood	71
Arun Lal	c Gooch b Botham	9
D.B. Vengsarkar	c Willis b Gooch	13
S.M. Patil	b Underwood	64
Yashpal Sharma	not out	34
Kapil Dev	c Gooch b Underwood	0
A. Malhotra	not out	28
S.M.H. Kirmani+		
S.V. Nayak		
Madan Lal		
R.J. Shastri		
Extras	(LB 7, W 2, NB 3)	12
TOTAL	(42 overs) (for 5 wkts)	**231**

						Fall	
Willis	6	1	29	0	1st	16
Botham	8	0	48	1	2nd	59
Lever	10	0	55	0	3rd	135
Gooch	8	0	39	1	4th	184
Underwood	10	0	48	3	5th	184

Match No: 63/1

SRI LANKA v ENGLAND

Played at Sinhalese Sports Club, Colombo on 13/02/1982
Toss: Sri Lanka **Result:** England won by 5 runs
Umpires: C.E.B. Anthony and H.C. Felsinger
Man of the match: I.T. Botham
Debuts: Eng - P.J.W. Allott
SL - A.L.F. de Mel, R.S.A. Jayasekera, S. Wettimuny

ENGLAND

G.A. Gooch	b G.R.A. de Silva	64
G. Cook	c G.R.A. de Silva b Kaluperuma	28
D.I. Gower	run out	15
I.T. Botham	b de Mel	60
K.W.R. Fletcher*	b D.S. de Silva	12
M.W. Gatting	c Mendis b de Mel	3
C.J. Richards+	b G.R.A. de Silva	3
J.E. Emburey	lbw b de Mel	0
P.J.W. Allott	run out	0
D.L. Underwood	b de Mel	4
R.G.D. Willis	not out	2
Extras	(B 6, LB 2, W 2, NB 10)	20
TOTAL	(44.4 overs)	**211**

						Fall	
de Mel	8.4	1	34	4	1st	55
Ranasinghe	8	2	20	0	2nd	83
Kaluperuma	7	0	35	1	3rd	152
D.S. de Silva	9	0	31	1	4th	191
G.R.A. de Silva	9	0	56	2	5th	197
Wettimuny	3	0	15	0	6th	202
					7th	205
					8th	205
					9th	205
					10th	211

SRI LANKA

B. Warnapura*	c Gower b Allott	10
S. Wettimuny	c Richards b Allott	46
R.S.A. Jayasekera+	c Gooch b Willis	17
R.L. Dias	c & b Underwood	4
L.R.D. Mendis	c Gower b Underwood	2
R.S. Madugalle	b Willis	22
A. Ranasinghe	c Cook b Botham	51
D.S. de Silva	b Botham	8
A.L.F. de Mel	not out	13
L. Kaluperuma	not out	14
G.R.A. de Silva		
Extras	(B 5, LB 10, W 2, NB 2)	19
TOTAL	(45 overs) (for 8 wkts)	**206**

						Fall	
Willis	9	1	32	2	1st	34
Botham	9	0	45	2	2nd	75
Emburey	5	0	18	0	3rd	84
Allott	9	0	40	2	4th	92
Gooch	6	1	18	0	5th	92
Underwood	7	0	34	2	6th	160
					7th	175
					8th	187

Match No: 64/2

SRI LANKA v ENGLAND

Played at Sinhalese Sports Club, Colombo on 14/02/1982
Toss: England **Result:** Sri Lanka won by 3 runs
Umpires: K.T. Francis and P.W. Vidanagamage
Man of the match: S. Wettimuny
Debuts: SL - H.M. Goonatillake, A. Ranatunga

SRI LANKA

B. Warnapura*	c Taylor b Botham	4
S. Wettimuny	not out	86
L.R.D. Mendis	c & b Botham	0
R.L. Dias	hit wicket b Lever	26
A. Ranatunga	run out	42
A. Ranasinghe	c Gooch b Underwood	0
R.S. Madugalle	c Taylor b Lever	12
A.L.F. de Mel	run out	14
D.S. de Silva	not out	9
H.M. Goonatillake+		
G.R.A. de Silva		
Extras	(B 2, LB 18, W 1, NB 1)	22
TOTAL	(45 overs) (for 7 wkts)	**215**

	O	M	R	W	Fall	
Willis	9	1	26	0	1st	5
Botham	9	4	29	2	2nd	5
Lever	9	0	51	2	3rd	43
Gooch	9	0	50	0	4th	130
Underwood	9	0	37	1	5th	130
					6th	138
					7th	186

ENGLAND

G.A. Gooch	st Goonatillake b G.R.A. de Silva	74
G. Cook	st Goonatillake b G.R.A. de Silva	32
D.I. Gower	lbw b de Mel	6
I.T. Botham	c & b Warnapura	13
K.W.R. Fletcher*	run out	38
C.J. Tavare	b D.S. de Silva	5
M.W. Gatting	run out	18
R.W. Taylor+	run out	3
J.K. Lever	not out	2
D.L. Underwood	run out	0
R.G.D. Willis	c Madugalle b de Mel	0
Extras	(LB 19, W 1, NB 1)	21
TOTAL	(44.5 overs)	**212**

	O	M	R	W	Fall	
de Mel	8.5	0	14	2	1st	109
Ranasinghe	9	0	37	0	2nd	122
Warnapura	9	0	42	1	3rd	122
D.S. de Silva	9	0	54	1	4th	147
G.R.A. de Silva	9	1	44	2	5th	170
					6th	203
					7th	206
					8th	211
					9th	211
					10th	212

Match No: 65/7

ENGLAND v INDIA

Prudential Trophy
Played at Headingley, Leeds on 02/06/1982
Toss: England
Umpires: D.J. Constant and D.O. Oslear
Man of the match: B. Wood
Debuts: Eng - A.J. Lamb

Result: England won by 9 wickets

Ind - G.A. Parkar

INDIA

S.M. Gavaskar*	c Botham b Allott	38
G.A. Parkar	c Tavare b Willis	10
D.B. Vengsarkar	c Taylor b Botham	5
G.R. Viswanath	b Botham	9
S.M. Patil	c Taylor b Botham	0
Yashpal Sharma	c Taylor b Allott	20
R.J. Shastri	run out	18
Kapil Dev	run out	60
S.M.H. Kirmani+	c Taylor b Botham	11
S.V. Nayak	c Tavare b Willis	3
Madan Lal	not out	1
Extras	(B 4, LB 9, W 1, NB 4)	18
TOTAL	(55 overs)	**193**

						Fall	
Willis	11	0	32	2	1st	30
Dilley	5	1	20	0	2nd	54
Allott	11	4	21	2	3rd	58
Botham	11	0	56	4	4th	59
Wood	7	2	17	0	5th	68
Miller	10	0	29	0	6th	113
					7th	114
					8th	154
					9th	192
					10th	193

ENGLAND

B. Wood	not out	78
C.J. Tavare	lbw b Madan Lal	66
A.J. Lamb	not out	35
D.I. Gower		
I.T. Botham		
D.W. Randall		
G. Miller		
G.R. Dilley		
R.W. Taylor+		
P.J.W. Allott		
R.G.D. Willis*		
Extras	(B 1, LB 7, W 3, NB 4)	15
TOTAL	(50.1 overs) (for 1 wkt)	**194**

						Fall	
Kapil Dev	9	2	21	0	1st	133
Madan Lal	9	3	21	1		
Nayak	9	0	37	0		
Shastri	11	0	37	0		
Patil	7	0	29	0		
Yashpal Sharma	5.1	0	34	0		

Match No: 66/8

ENGLAND v INDIA

Prudential Trophy
Played at The Oval, London on 04/06/1982
Toss: India   **Result:** England won by 114 runs
Umpires: D.G.L. Evans and B.J. Meyer
Man of the match: A.J. Lamb
Debuts: None

ENGLAND
B. Wood	b Patil	15
C.J. Tavare	b Patil	27
A.J. Lamb	c & b Madan Lal	99
D.I. Gower	c Vengsarkar b Yashpal Sharma	76
I.T. Botham	run out	4
D.W. Randall	run out	24
G. Miller	run out	0
G.R. Dilley	c Yashpal Sharma b Madan Lal	1
R.W. Taylor+	not out	3
P.J.W. Allott	run out	5
R.G.D. Willis*		
Extras	(B 3, LB 10, W 6, NB 3)	22
TOTAL	(55 overs) (for 9 wkts)	276

						Fall	
Kapil Dev	11	1	39	0	1st	43
Madan Lal	11	0	50	2	2nd	53
Nayak	11	1	48	0	3rd	212
Patil	11	0	37	2	4th	218
Yashpal Sharma	3	0	27	1	5th	260
Shastri	8	0	53	0	6th	260
					7th	267
					8th	268
					9th	276

INDIA
S.M. Gavaskar*	c Willis b Miller	15
G.A. Parkar	c Botham b Willis	2
D.B. Vengsarkar	c Taylor b Dilley	15
Yashpal Sharma	lbw b Allott	2
A. Malhotra	b Botham	4
S.M. Patil	b Miller	1
Kapil Dev	c Gower b Wood	47
S.M.H. Kirmani+	c Botham b Miller	8
Madan Lal	not out	53
R.J. Shastri	not out	9
S.V. Nayak		
Extras	(B 1, LB 3, W 2)	6
TOTAL	(55 overs) (for 8 wkts)	162

						Fall	
Willis	7	2	10	1	1st	5
Dilley	7	1	19	1	2nd	28
Botham	9	2	22	1	3rd	36
Allott	8	3	24	1	4th	42
Miller	11	3	27	3	5th	42
Wood	11	0	51	1	6th	43
Tavare	2	0	3	0	7th	66
						8th	131

Match No: 67/9

ENGLAND v PAKISTAN

Prudential Trophy
Played at Trent Bridge, Nottingham on 17/07/1982
Toss: Pakistan   Result: England won by 7 wickets
Umpires: D.G.L. Evans and A.G.T. Whitehead
Man of the match: A.J. Lamb
Debuts: Eng - E.E. Hemmings, D.R. Pringle

PAKISTAN

Mudassar Nazar	run out	51
Mohsin Khan	b Botham	47
Zaheer Abbas	lbw b Pringle	53
Javed Miandad	c Willis b Pringle	28
Majid Khan	c Willis b Botham	23
Wasim Raja	c Hemmings b Botham	14
Imran Khan*	not out	16
Sarfraz Nawaz	not out	2
Wasim Bari+		
Iqbal Qasim		
Sikander Bakht		
Extras	(B 4, LB 4, W 6, NB 2)	16
TOTAL	(55 overs) (for 6 wkts)	250

						Fall	
Willis	11	1	46	0	1st	102
Botham	11	0	57	3	2nd	103
Pringle	11	1	50	2	3rd	175
Miller	11	1	36	0	4th	208
Hemmings	11	1	45	0	5th	222
					6th	238

ENGLAND

D.I. Gower	c Wasim Bari b Sikander Bakht	17
C.J. Tavare	b Imran Khan	48
A.J. Lamb	c Wasim Bari b Imran Khan	118
M.W. Gatting	not out	37
I.T. Botham	not out	10
D.W. Randall		
G. Miller		
D.R. Pringle		
E.E. Hemmings		
R.W. Taylor+		
R.G.D. Willis*		
Extras	(LB 12, W 5, NB 5)	22
TOTAL	(47.1 overs) (for 3 wkts)	252

						Fall	
Imran Khan	11	2	35	2	1st	25
Sarfraz Nawaz	11	3	43	0	2nd	132
Sikander Bakht	7	0	34	1	3rd	234
Iqbal Qasim	7	0	49	0		
Mudassar Nazar	5.1	0	26	0		
Majid Khan	4	0	25	0		
Wasim Raja	2	0	18	0		

Match No: 68/10

ENGLAND v PAKISTAN

Prudential Trophy
Played at Old Trafford, Manchester on 19/07/1982
Toss: Pakistan   **Result:** England won by 73 runs
Umpires: H.D. Bird and D.J. Constant
Man of the match: M.W. Gatting
Debuts: None

ENGLAND

Batsman	Dismissal	Runs
D.I. Gower	c Wasim Bari b Mudassar Nazar	33
C.J. Tavare	run out	16
A.J. Lamb	c Wasim Bari b Iqbal Qasim	27
M.W. Gatting	run out	76
I.T. Botham	c Wasim Raja b Imran Khan	49
D.W. Randall	run out	6
G. Miller	b Imran Khan	26
D.R. Pringle	not out	34
E.E. Hemmings	c Iqbal Qasim b Tahir Naqqash	1
R.W. Taylor+	not out	1
R.G.D. Willis*		
Extras	(LB 16, W 10)	26
TOTAL	(55 overs) (for 8 wkts)	**295**

Bowler	O	M	R	W		Fall	
Imran Khan	11	1	48	2		1st	32
Tahir Naqqash	10	0	37	1		2nd	54
Sikander Bakht	11	0	42	0		3rd	101
Mudassar Nazar	11	0	50	1		4th	185
Iqbal Qasim	8	0	76	1		5th	217
Majid Khan	4	1	16	0		6th	226
						7th	280
						8th	284

PAKISTAN

Batsman	Dismissal	Runs
Mudassar Nazar	run out	31
Mohsin Khan	b Pringle	17
Zaheer Abbas	c Randall b Pringle	13
Mansoor Akhtar	run out	28
Majid Khan	b Miller	5
Wasim Raja	c Botham b Willis	60
Imran Khan*	c Gower b Miller	31
Tahir Naqqash	run out	1
Wasim Bari+	b Hemmings	4
Iqbal Qasim	lbw b Botham	13
Sikander Bakht	not out	2
Extras	(LB 14, W 2, NB 1)	17
TOTAL	(49.4 overs)	**222**

Bowler	O	M	R	W		Fall	
Willis	8	0	36	1		1st	52
Botham	8.4	0	40	1		2nd	55
Miller	11	1	56	2		3rd	82
Pringle	11	0	43	2		4th	97
Hemmings	11	3	30	1		5th	123
						6th	183
						7th	200
						8th	201
						9th	213
						10th	222

80   England - The Complete One-Day International Record

Match No: 69/24

AUSTRALIA v ENGLAND

Benson & Hedges World Series Cup
Played at Sydney Cricket Ground on 11/01/1983
Toss: England   **Result:** Australia won by 31 runs
Umpires: R.A. French and M.W. Johnson
Man of the match: C.G. Rackemann
Debuts: Eng - N.G. Cowans, T.E. Jesty

AUSTRALIA
J. Dyson	c Randall b Marks	49
K.C. Wessels	b Cowans	18
G.S. Chappell	c Marks b Botham	3
K.J. Hughes*	c Taylor b Jesty	0
A.R. Border	b Miller	22
D.W. Hookes	b Marks	11
R.W. Marsh+	c Taylor b Miller	7
G.F. Lawson	not out	33
J.R. Thomson	b Miller	8
R.M. Hogg	c & b Cowans	8
C.G. Rackemann	b Willis	0
Extras	(LB 13, W 8)	21
TOTAL	**(46.4 overs)**	**180**

					Fall	
Willis	6.4	1	20	1	1st	26
Cowans	7	0	20	2	2nd	33
Botham	7	1	41	1	3rd	36
Jesty	6	0	23	1	4th	77
Marks	10	1	27	2	5th	118
Miller	10	0	28	3	6th	124
					7th	132
					8th	158
					9th	175
					10th	180

ENGLAND
D.I. Gower	c Hookes b Thomson	9
C.J. Tavare	c Border b Rackemann	6
A.J. Lamb	b Thomson	49
D.W. Randall	b Rackemann	5
I.T. Botham	b Rackemann	18
T.E. Jesty	run out	12
G. Miller	lbw b Hogg	2
V.J. Marks	not out	7
R.W. Taylor+	lbw b Chappell	2
R.G.D. Willis*	c Marsh b Chappell	0
N.G. Cowans	b Chappell	4
Extras	(LB 12, W 17, NB 6)	35
TOTAL	**(41.1 overs)**	**149**

					Fall	
Lawson	8	1	33	0	1st	11
Thomson	10	4	21	2	2nd	44
Hogg	10	1	15	1	3rd	53
Rackemann	8	1	28	3	4th	95
Chappell	5.1	0	17	3	5th	131
					6th	131
					7th	135
					8th	142
					9th	142
					10th	149

Match No: 70/9

ENGLAND v NEW ZEALAND

Benson & Hedges World Series Cup
Played at Melbourne Cricket Ground on 13/01/1983
Toss: England **Result:** New Zealand won by 2 runs
Umpires: M.W. Johnson and B.E. Martin
Man of the match: D.I. Gower
Debuts: None

NEW ZEALAND
J.G. Wright	run out	55
B.A. Edgar	c Randall b Marks	30
B.L. Cairns	c Miller b Botham	36
G.M. Turner	b Willis	38
G.P. Howarth*	c Willis b Botham	13
J.F.M. Morrison	c Randall b Botham	11
R.J. Hadlee	c Botham b Willis	24
J.V. Coney	not out	13
W.K. Lees+	run out	3
M.C. Snedden		
E.J. Chatfield		
Extras	(B 1, LB 10, W 5)	16
TOTAL	(50 overs) (for 8 wkts)	**239**

						Fall	
Willis	8	1	29	2	1st	87
Cowans	10	0	50	0	2nd	100
Jesty	3	0	11	0	3rd	137
Botham	10	0	40	3	4th	164
Marks	9	0	47	1	5th	188
Miller	10	0	46	0	6th	205
					7th	231
					8th	239

ENGLAND
D.I. Gower	c Turner b Hadlee	122
C.J. Tavare	run out	16
A.J. Lamb	st Lees b Coney	15
T.E. Jesty	c Wright b Coney	5
I.T. Botham	c Chatfield b Snedden	41
D.W. Randall	c Snedden b Coney	8
G. Miller	c Turner b Chatfield	2
V.J. Marks	b Snedden	5
R.W. Taylor+	not out	5
R.G.D. Willis*		
N.G. Cowans		
Extras	(LB 14, W 3, NB 1)	18
TOTAL	(50 overs) (for 8 wkts)	**237**

						Fall	
Snedden	10	0	34	2	1st	42
Chatfield	10	0	38	1	2nd	80
Cairns	10	1	64	0	3rd	92
Hadlee	10	1	37	1	4th	190
Coney	10	0	46	3	5th	205
					6th	221
					7th	223
					8th	237

Match No: 71/10

ENGLAND v NEW ZEALAND

Benson & Hedges World Series Cup
Played at Woolloongabba, Brisbane on 15/01/1983
Toss: New Zealand   **Result:** England won by 54 runs
Umpires: R.A. French and B.E. Martin
Man of the match: D.I. Gower
Debuts: Eng - I.J. Gould

ENGLAND
I.J. Gould+	c Howarth b Troup	15
C.J. Tavare	b Cairns	24
D.I. Gower	c sub (J.J. Crowe) b Snedden	158
A.J. Lamb	c Cairns b Hadlee	13
I.T. Botham	c Webb b Hadlee	0
D.W. Randall	run out	34
T.E. Jesty	not out	4
G. Miller		
V.J. Marks		
R.G.D. Willis*		
N.G. Cowans		
Extras	(LB 9, W 9, NB 1)	19
TOTAL	(50 overs) (for 6 wkts)	**267**

						Fall	
Hadlee	10	1	44	2		1st	26
Chatfield	10	3	44	0		2nd	89
Snedden	10	0	76	1		3rd	114
Troup	7	1	38	1		4th	116
Cairns	10	0	29	1		5th	229
Coney	3	0	17	0		6th	267

NEW ZEALAND
J.G. Wright	c Randall b Cowans	30
B.A. Edgar	c Gould b Botham	40
G.P. Howarth*	c Jesty b Marks	13
B.L. Cairns	c Gould b Marks	12
G.M. Turner	c Jesty b Botham	29
J.V. Coney	st Gould b Marks	13
P.N. Webb+	c Cowans b Botham	4
R.J. Hadlee	b Willis	21
M.C. Snedden	run out	0
G.B. Troup	c Botham b Willis	39
E.J. Chatfield	not out	0
Extras	(LB 6, W 6)	12
TOTAL	(48.2 overs)	**213**

						Fall	
Willis	9.2	1	30	2		1st	43
Cowans	10	0	52	1		2nd	75
Botham	9	2	47	3		3rd	100
Marks	10	2	30	3		4th	100
Miller	10	1	42	0		5th	148
						6th	148
						7th	150
						8th	150
						9th	213
						10th	213

Match No: 72/25

AUSTRALIA v ENGLAND

Benson & Hedges World Series Cup
Played at Woolloongabba, Brisbane on 16/01/1983
Toss: Australia   **Results:** Australia won by 7 wickets
Umpires: M.W. Johnson and P.J. McConnell
Man of the match: D.W. Hookes
Debuts: None

ENGLAND
G. Cook	c Hookes b Lawson	2
I.J. Gould+	run out	2
D.I. Gower	b Hogg	22
A.J. Lamb	c Marsh b Thomson	19
I.T. Botham	c Hookes b Rackemann	29
D.W. Randall	b Lawson	57
T.E. Jesty	c Marsh b Rackemann	0
G. Miller	run out	4
V.J. Marks	b Thomson	3
R.G.D. Willis*	not out	7
N.G. Cowans	c Lawson b Rackemann	0
Extras	(B 4, LB 12, W 13, NB 8)	37
TOTAL	(46.4 overs)	**182**

						Fall	
Lawson	10	2	23	2	1st	2
Thomson	10	0	32	2	2nd	10
Hogg	9	1	29	1	3rd	54
Rackemann	8.4	1	28	3	4th	71
Chappell	9	1	33	0	5th	128
					6th	138
					7th	143
					8th	165
					9th	178
					10th	182

AUSTRALIA
K.C. Wessels	c Gould b Botham	19
J. Dyson	c Marks b Botham	40
G.S. Chappell	c Jesty b Botham	30
D.W. Hookes	not out	54
A.R. Border	not out	30
K.J. Hughes*		
R.W. Marsh+		
G.F. Lawson		
J.R. Thomson		
R.M. Hogg		
C.G. Rackemann		
Extras	(LB 9, W 2)	11
TOTAL	(41 overs) (for 3 wkts)	**184**

						Fall	
Willis	7	1	31	0	1st	41
Cowans	9	1	35	0	2nd	95
Botham	8	1	29	3	3rd	98
Miller	6	0	25	0		
Marks	10	0	46	0		
Jesty	1	0	7	0		

Match No: 73/11

ENGLAND v NEW ZEALAND

Benson & Hedges World Series Cup
Played at Sydney Cricket Ground on 20/01/1983
Toss: New Zealand   **Result:** England won by 8 wickets
Umpires: A.R. Crafter and R.A. French
Man of the match: A.J. Lamb
Debuts: Eng - G. Fowler

NEW ZEALAND

J.G. Wright	c Randall b Willis	9
B.A. Edgar	c Willis b Cowans	74
G.P. Howarth*	c Miller b Willis	1
G.M. Turner	c Gower b Marks	37
B.L. Cairns	c Gower b Miller	11
W.K. Lees+	b Botham	12
J.J. Crowe	run out	12
R.J. Hadlee	c Lamb b Willis	15
J.V. Coney	c Miller b Willis	6
M.C. Snedden	not out	2
E.J. Chatfield	lbw b Botham	0
Extras	(LB 17, W 3)	20
TOTAL	(47.2 overs)	**199**

						Fall	
Willis	9	0	23	4	1st	14
Cowans	10	1	26	1	2nd	20
Botham	8.2	0	30	2	3rd	101
Marks	10	0	49	1	4th	118
Miller	10	0	51	1	5th	152
					6th	171
					7th	178
					8th	197
					9th	197
					10th	199

ENGLAND

C.J. Tavare	not out	83
G. Fowler	c sub (P.N. Webb) b Chatfield	0
D.I. Gower	b Hadlee	0
A.J. Lamb	not out	108
I.T. Botham		
D.W. Randall		
G. Miller		
I.J. Gould+		
V.J. Marks		
R.G.D. Willis*		
N.G. Cowans		
Extras	(B 1, LB 5, W 3)	9
TOTAL	(42.4 overs) (for 2 wkts)	**200**

						Fall	
Hadlee	9	2	37	1	1st	9
Chatfield	10	2	25	1	2nd	10
Cairns	8	2	31	0		
Snedden	8.4	0	61	0		
Coney	7	0	37	0		

Match No: 74/26

AUSTRALIA v ENGLAND

Benson & Hedges World Series Cup
Played at Melbourne Cricket Ground on 23/01/1983
Toss: Australia   **Result:** Australia won by 5 wickets
Umpires: A.R. Crafter and P.J. McConnell
Man of the match: A.J. Lamb
Debuts: Aus - J.N. Maguire

ENGLAND
C.J. Tavare	c Lillee b Rackemann	20
I.T. Botham	b Lillee	19
D.I. Gower	c Marsh b Rackemann	6
A.J. Lamb	c sub (K.H. MacLeay) b Lillee	94
D.W. Randall	not out	51
I.J. Gould+	b Hogg	3
T.E. Jesty	not out	1
D.R. Pringle		
G. Miller		
R.G.D. Willis*		
N.G. Cowans		
Extras	(LB 10, W 4, NB 5)	19
TOTAL	(37 overs) (for 5 wkts)	**213**

						Fall	
Hogg	7	0	36	1	1st	32
Lillee	8	2	50	2	2nd	50
Rackemann	8	0	41	2	3rd	66
Chappell	7	0	33	0	4th	205
Maguire	7	0	34	0	5th	209

AUSTRALIA
J. Dyson	run out	54
A.R. Border	run out	54
D.W. Hookes	c Gower b Cowans	50
K.J. Hughes*	c Miller b Cowans	6
G.S. Chappell	not out	32
R.W. Marsh+	run out	8
K.C. Wessels	not out	5
R.M. Hogg		
D.K. Lillee		
J.N. Maguire		
C.G. Rackemann		
Extras	(LB 5, W 2, NB 1)	8
TOTAL	(34.4 overs) (for 5 wkts)	**217**

						Fall	
Willis	6.4	1	29	0	1st	85
Cowans	6	0	46	2	2nd	157
Botham	7	1	45	0	3rd	167
Pringle	7	0	47	0	4th	176
Miller	8	0	42	0	5th	190

Match No: 75/27

AUSTRALIA v ENGLAND

Benson & Hedges World Series Cup
Played at Sydney Cricket Ground on 26/01/1983
Toss: England
Umpires: R.A. French and B.E. Martin
Man of the match: R.D. Jackman
Debuts: None

Result: England won by 98 runs

ENGLAND

C.J. Tavare	c Marsh b Thomson	14
I.T. Botham	c Wessels b Hogg	0
D.I. Gower	b Lillee	25
A.J. Lamb	lbw b Lillee	0
D.W. Randall	run out	47
T.E. Jesty	b Maguire	30
I.J. Gould+	c Wessels b Hogg	42
V.J. Marks	c & b Lillee	22
E.E. Hemmings	run out	3
R.D. Jackman	b Hogg	0
R.G.D. Willis*	not out	5
Extras	(B 2, LB 4, W 9, NB 4)	19
TOTAL	(41 overs)	**207**

					Fall	
Hogg	10	1	44	3	1st	8
Maguire	8	0	42	1	2nd	45
Lillee	8	0	34	3	3rd	47
Thomson	8	0	40	1	4th	47
Chappell	7	0	28	0	5th	101
					6th	157
					7th	197
					8th	201
					9th	201
					10th	207

AUSTRALIA

J. Dyson	c Randall b Botham	23
A.R. Border	c & b Willis	31
D.W. Hookes	b Marks	32
K.J. Hughes*	c Gould b Jackman	0
G.S. Chappell	b Jackman	0
K.C. Wessels	b Jackman	1
R.W. Marsh+	b Hemmings	1
D.K. Lillee	b Hemmings	3
J.R. Thomson	b Marks	7
R.M. Hogg	not out	0
J.N. Maguire	c Lamb b Hemmings	2
Extras	(B 2, LB 2, W 3, NB 2)	9
TOTAL	(27.3 overs)	**109**

					Fall	
Willis	6	1	23	1	1st	40
Jackman	10	1	41	3	2nd	72
Botham	2	0	13	1	3rd	73
Marks	6	0	12	2	4th	73
Hemmings	3.3	0	11	3	5th	77
					6th	96
					7th	99
					8th	106
					9th	106
					10th	109

Match No: 76/12

ENGLAND v NEW ZEALAND

Benson & Hedges World Series Cup
Played at Adelaide Oval on 29/01/1983
Toss: England   **Result:** New Zealand won by 4 wickets
Umpires: A.R. Crafter and R.A. French
Man of the match: R.J. Hadlee
Debuts: None

ENGLAND
C.J. Tavare	c Crowe b Chatfield	16
I.T. Botham	b Chatfield	65
D.I. Gower	c Coney b Troup	109
A.J. Lamb	run out	19
D.W. Randall	c Wright b Snedden	31
T.E. Jesty	not out	52
I.J. Gould+	not out	1
V.J. Marks		
E.E. Hemmings		
R.D. Jackman		
R.G.D. Willis*		
Extras	(LB 1, W 1, NB 1)	3
TOTAL	(50 overs) (for 5 wkts)	**296**

						Fall	
Hadlee	10	1	36	0	1st	75
Cairns	10	1	45	0	2nd	86
Snedden	10	0	72	1	3rd	121
Chatfield	10	2	64	2	4th	204
Troup	10	0	76	1	5th	278

NEW ZEALAND
G.M. Turner	b Willis	23
J.G. Wright	run out	30
G.P. Howarth*	b Jackman	3
J.J. Crowe	c Willis b Botham	50
B.L. Cairns	c Gower b Botham	49
J.V. Coney	not out	47
R.J. Hadlee	c Jesty b Jackman	79
W.K. Lees+	not out	1
M.C. Snedden		
E.J. Chatfield		
G.B. Troup		
Extras	(B 2, LB 7, NB 6)	15
TOTAL	(48.5 overs) (for 6 wkts)	**297**

						Fall	
Willis	9.5	2	43	1	1st	26
Jackman	10	1	49	2	2nd	33
Jesty	8	0	52	0	3rd	96
Hemmings	6	0	49	0	4th	166
Botham	8	0	61	2	5th	166
Marks	7	1	28	0	6th	287

Match No: 77/28

AUSTRALIA v ENGLAND

Benson & Hedges World Series Cup
Played at Adelaide Oval on 30/01/1983
Toss: England   **Result:** England won by 14 runs
Umpires: M.W. Johnson and P.J. McConnell
Man of the match: D.I. Gower
Debuts: None

ENGLAND
C.J. Tavare	b Hogg	18
I.T. Botham	b Lawson	14
D.I. Gower	c Lillee b Thomson	77
A.J. Lamb	b Hogg	2
D.W. Randall	c & b Lawson	49
T.E. Jesty	not out	22
I.J. Gould+	c Lillee b Lawson	9
V.J. Marks	not out	10
E.E. Hemmings		
R.D. Jackman		
R.G.D. Willis*		
Extras	(B 1, LB 14, W 6, NB 6)	27
TOTAL	(47 overs) (for 6 wkts)	**228**

					Fall	
Lawson	10	0	27	3	1st	25
Lillee	10	0	50	0	2nd	62
Hogg	9	1	25	2	3rd	70
Thomson	9	0	38	1	4th	176
Chappell	7	0	45	0	5th	178
Hookes	2	0	16	0	6th	200

AUSTRALIA
A.R. Border	c Randall b Willis	19
J. Dyson	c Lamb b Hemmings	17
K.J. Hughes*	c Gower b Marks	4
D.W. Hookes	c Jesty b Jackman	76
R.W. Marsh+	c Jackman b Botham	7
G.S. Chappell	c Gower b Jackman	33
K.C. Wessels	b Botham	7
G.F. Lawson	not out	28
J.R. Thomson	not out	12
D.K. Lillee		
R.M. Hogg		
Extras	(B 6, LB 5)	11
TOTAL	(47 overs) (for 7 wkts)	**214**

					Fall	
Willis	10	1	40	1	1st	27
Jackman	10	3	36	2	2nd	89
Botham	7	0	49	2	3rd	97
Hemmings	10	0	40	1	4th	149
Marks	10	1	38	1	5th	161
					6th	167
					7th	189

Matches 89

Match No: 78/13

ENGLAND v NEW ZEALAND

Benson & Hedges World Series Cup
Played at WACA Ground, Perth on 05/02/1983
Toss: New Zealand   **Result:** New Zealand won by 7 wickets
Umpires: R.A. French and P.J. McConnell
Man of the match: R.J. Hadlee
Debuts: None

ENGLAND		
C.J. Tavare	c Lees b Hadlee	0
I.T. Botham	c Lees b Hadlee	19
D.I. Gower	not out	35
A.J. Lamb	c Crowe b Snedden	7
D.W. Randall	c Howarth b Snedden	12
T.E. Jesty	run out	0
I.J. Gould+	b Snedden	0
V.J. Marks	b Hadlee	2
R.D. Jackman	not out	0
R.G.D. Willis*		
N.G. Cowans		
Extras	(B 3, LB 10)	13
TOTAL	(23 overs) (for 7 wkts)	**88**

					Fall	
Hadlee	8	2	15	3	1st	18
Cairns	5	0	21	0	2nd	23
Snedden	6	1	25	3	3rd	37
Chatfield	4	1	14	0	4th	66
					5th	66
					6th	82
					7th	87

NEW ZEALAND		
J.G. Wright	c Tavare b Willis	12
G.M. Turner	c Jackman b Willis	0
J.J. Crowe	c Botham b Cowans	18
J.V. Coney	not out	29
G.P. Howarth*	not out	26
J.F.M. Morrison		
W.K. Lees+		
R.J. Hadlee		
B.L. Cairns		
M.C. Snedden		
E.J. Chatfield		
Extras	(LB 1, W 3)	4
TOTAL	(20.3 overs) (for 3 wkts)	**89**

					Fall	
Willis	8.3	1	28	2	1st	5
Cowans	8	0	32	1	2nd	20
Jackman	2	0	16	0	3rd	47
Botham	2	0	9	0		

Match No: 79/14

NEW ZEALAND v ENGLAND

Rothmans Cup
Played at Eden Park, Auckland on 19/02/1983
Toss: England   Result: New Zealand won by 6 wickets
Umpires: F.R. Goodall and D.A. Kinsella
Man of the match: G.M. Turner
Debuts: None

ENGLAND
C.J. Tavare	b Cairns	11
I.T. Botham	c Morrison b Chatfield	12
D.I. Gower	c Morrison b Snedden	84
A.J. Lamb	run out	0
D.W. Randall	b Chatfield	30
T.E. Jesty	c Coney b Chatfield	1
I.J. Gould+	lbw b Cairns	3
G. Miller	lbw b Morrison	3
V.J. Marks	not out	23
R.D. Jackman	b Cairns	4
R.G.D. Willis*	not out	1
Extras	(LB 10, W 2)	12
TOTAL	(50 overs) (for 9 wkts)	**184**

						Fall	
Webb	10	0	30	0	1st	17
Cairns	10	2	28	3	2nd	40
Snedden	8	1	35	1	3rd	40
Chatfield	10	0	27	3	4th	104
Coney	2	0	17	0	5th	106
Morrison	10	1	35	1	6th	110
					7th	115
					8th	168
					9th	176

NEW ZEALAND
G.M. Turner	c sub (N.G. Cowans) b Willis	88
B.A. Edgar	c Jackman b Miller	35
B.L. Cairns	c Lamb b Botham	19
J.J. Crowe	lbw b Botham	15
J.V. Coney	not out	9
G.P. Howarth*	not out	14
J.F.M. Morrison		
W.K. Lees+		
M.C. Snedden		
E.J. Chatfield		
R.J. Webb		
Extras	(B 1, LB 4, NB 2)	7
TOTAL	(46.3 overs) (for 4 wkts)	**187**

						Fall	
Willis	10	1	39	1	1st	101
Jackman	8.3	0	38	0	2nd	129
Botham	8	0	40	2	3rd	164
Marks	10	1	30	0	4th	166
Miller	10	0	33	1		

Match No: 80/15

NEW ZEALAND v ENGLAND

Rothmans Cup
Played at Basin Reserve, Wellington on 23/02/1983
Toss: England **Result:** New Zealand won by 103 runs
Umpires: S.C. Cowman and S.J. Woodward
Man of the match: G.M. Turner
Debuts: None

NEW ZEALAND
G.M. Turner	b Willis	94
B.A. Edgar	run out	60
B.L. Cairns	b Willis	44
J.G. Wright	b Miller	30
J.V. Coney	not out	31
G.P. Howarth*	c Botham b Jackman	10
J.F.M. Morrison	b Botham	8
W.K. Lees+	not out	3
M.C. Snedden		
E.J. Chatfield		
R.J. Webb		
Extras	(LB 9, W 4, NB 2)	15
TOTAL	(50 overs) (for 6 wkts)	**295**

						Fall	
Willis	9	0	54	2	1st	152
Jackman	10	2	38	1	2nd	192
Pringle	7	0	57	0	3rd	214
Miller	10	0	51	1	4th	250
Marks	7	0	34	0	5th	275
Botham	7	0	46	1	6th	287

ENGLAND
C.J. Tavare	c Howarth b Chatfield	32
I.T. Botham	c Lees b Cairns	15
D.I. Gower	c & b Chatfield	2
A.J. Lamb	b Coney	7
D.W. Randall	c Howarth b Morrison	16
I.J. Gould+	c Wright b Coney	14
G. Miller	b Cairns	46
V.J. Marks	c Snedden b Webb	27
D.R. Pringle	b Webb	11
R.D. Jackman	b Cairns	9
R.G.D. Willis*	not out	2
Extras	(LB 6, W 5)	11
TOTAL	(44.5 overs)	**192**

						Fall	
Snedden	10	1	37	0	1st	20
Cairns	10	0	38	3	2nd	37
Webb	7.5	0	27	2	3rd	52
Chatfield	7	1	28	2	4th	60
Coney	5	0	17	2	5th	83
Morrison	5	0	34	1	6th	106
						7th	162
						8th	170
						9th	182
						10th	192

Match No: 81/16

NEW ZEALAND v ENGLAND

Rothmans Cup
Played at Lancaster Park, Christchurch on 26/02/1983
Toss: New Zealand   **Result:** New Zealand won by 84 runs
Umpires: F.R. Goodall and I.C. Higginson
Man of the match: M.C. Snedden
Debuts: None

NEW ZEALAND

G.M. Turner	lbw b Botham	34
B.A. Edgar	b Marks	32
J.G. Wright	st Gould b Marks	2
B.L. Cairns	c Marks b Jackman	21
J.J. Crowe	lbw b Jackman	18
J.V. Coney	run out	30
G.P. Howarth*	lbw b Miller	8
J.F.M. Morrison	not out	24
W.K. Lees+	c Botham b Cowans	2
M.C. Snedden	not out	31
E.J. Chatfield		
Extras	(LB 5, W 3, NB 1)	9
TOTAL	(50 overs) (for 8 wkts)	**211**

						Fall	
Cowans	10	3	55	1	1st	64
Willis	10	1	35	0	2nd	70
Botham	5	1	17	1	3rd	93
Marks	10	2	31	2	4th	103
Miller	7	1	32	1	5th	126
Jackman	8	1	32	2	6th	152
					7th	153
					8th	156

ENGLAND

I.J. Gould+	c Turner b Snedden	0
C.J. Tavare	b Snedden	4
D.I. Gower	c Wright b Chatfield	53
A.J. Lamb	c Chatfield b Morrison	37
I.T. Botham	c & b Morrison	3
D.W. Randall	b Coney	2
G. Miller	c & b Chatfield	7
V.J. Marks	b Cairns	1
R.D. Jackman	b Cairns	5
R.G.D. Willis*	c Coney b Morrison	6
N.G. Cowans	not out	1
Extras	(LB 6, W 1, NB 1)	8
TOTAL	(40.1 overs)	**127**

						Fall	
Snedden	7	3	14	2	1st	0
Cairns	7	0	13	2	2nd	8
Chatfield	8	2	26	2	3rd	94
Coney	10	0	42	1	4th	103
Morrison	8.1	0	24	3	5th	105
						6th	114
						7th	114
						8th	116
						9th	125
						10th	127

Match No: **82/17**

ENGLAND v NEW ZEALAND

Prudential World Cup
Played at The Oval, London on 09/06/1983
Toss: England   **Result:** England won by 106 runs
Umpires: B.J. Meyer and D.O. Oslear
Man of the match: A.J. Lamb
Debuts: None

ENGLAND

Batsman	Dismissal	Runs
G. Fowler	c Coney b Cairns	8
C.J. Tavare	c Edgar b Chatfield	45
D.I. Gower	c Edgar b Coney	39
A.J. Lamb	b Snedden	102
M.W. Gatting	b Snedden	43
I.T. Botham	c Lees b Hadlee	22
I.J. Gould+	not out	14
G.R. Dilley	not out	31
V.J. Marks		
P.J.W. Allott		
R.G.D. Willis*		
Extras	(LB 12, W 1, NB 5)	18
TOTAL	(60 overs) (for 6 wkts)	**322**

Bowler	O	M	R	W		Fall	
Hadlee	12	4	26	1	1st	13
Cairns	12	4	57	1	2nd	79
Snedden	12	1	105	2	3rd	117
Chatfield	12	1	45	1	4th	232
Coney	6	1	20	1	5th	271
Crowe	6	0	51	0	6th	278

NEW ZEALAND

Batsman	Dismissal	Runs
G.M. Turner	lbw b Willis	14
B.A. Edgar	c Gould b Willis	3
J.G. Wright	c Botham b Dilley	10
G.P. Howarth*	c Lamb b Marks	18
J.V. Coney	run out	23
M.D. Crowe	run out	97
W.K. Lees+	b Botham	8
R.J. Hadlee	c Lamb b Marks	1
B.L. Cairns	lbw b Botham	1
M.C. Snedden	c Gould b Gatting	21
E.J. Chatfield	not out	9
Extras	(B 2, LB 4, W 4, NB 1)	11
TOTAL	(59 overs)	**216**

Bowler	O	M	R	W		Fall	
Willis	7	2	9	2	1st	3
Dilley	8	0	33	1	2nd	28
Botham	12	0	42	2	3rd	31
Allott	12	1	47	0	4th	62
Marks	12	1	39	2	5th	85
Gatting	8	1	35	1	6th	123
					7th	136
					8th	138
					9th	190
					10th	216

Match No: 83/3

ENGLAND v SRI LANKA

Prudential World Cup
Played at County Ground, Taunton on 11/06/1983
Toss: England   **Result:** England won by 47 runs
Umpires: M.J. Kitchen and K.E. Palmer
Man of the match: D.I. Gower
Debuts: None

ENGLAND

G. Fowler	b John	22
C.J. Tavare	c de Alwis b Ranatunga	32
D.I. Gower	b de Mel	130
A.J. Lamb	b Ratnayake	53
M.W. Gatting	run out	7
I.T. Botham	run out	0
I.J. Gould+	c Ranatunga b Ratnayake	35
G.R. Dilley	b de Mel	29
V.J. Marks	run out	5
P.J.W. Allott	not out	0
R.G.D. Willis*		
Extras	(LB 11, W 9)	20
TOTAL	(60 overs) (for 9 wkts)	333

	O	M	R	W		Fall	
de Mel	12	3	62	2	1st	49
John	12	0	55	1	2nd	78
Ratnayake	12	0	66	2	3rd	174
Ranatunga	12	0	65	1	4th	193
de Silva	12	0	65	0	5th	194
					6th	292
					7th	298
					8th	333
					9th	333

SRI LANKA

S. Wettimuny	lbw b Marks	33
D.S.B.P. Kuruppu	c Gatting b Dilley	4
R.L. Dias	c Botham b Dilley	2
L.R.D. Mendis*	c Willis b Marks	56
R.S. Madugalle	c Tavare b Marks	12
A. Ranatunga	c Lamb b Marks	34
D.S. de Silva	st Gould b Marks	28
R.G. de Alwis+	not out	58
A.L.F. de Mel	c Dilley b Allott	27
R.J. Ratnayake	c Lamb b Dilley	15
V.B. John	b Dilley	0
Extras	(LB 12, W 2, NB 3)	17
TOTAL	(58 overs)	286

	O	M	R	W		Fall	
Willis	11	3	43	0	1st	11
Dilley	11	0	45	4	2nd	17
Allott	12	1	82	1	3rd	92
Botham	12	0	60	0	4th	108
Marks	12	3	39	5	5th	117
					6th	168
					7th	192
					8th	246
					9th	281
					10th	286

Match No: 84/11

ENGLAND v PAKISTAN

Prudential World Cup
Played at Lord's, London on 13/06/1983
Toss: Pakistan **Result:** England won by 8 wickets
Umpires: B.J. Meyer and A.G.T. Whitehead
Man of the match: Zaheer Abbas
Debuts: None

PAKISTAN
Mohsin Khan	c Tavare b Willis	3
Mudassar Nazar	c Gould b Allott	26
Mansoor Akhtar	c Gould b Willis	3
Javed Miandad	c Gould b Botham	14
Zaheer Abbas	not out	83
Imran Khan*	run out	7
Wasim Raja	c Botham b Marks	9
Abdul Qadir	run out	0
Sarfraz Nawaz	c & b Botham	11
Wasim Bari+	not out	18
Rashid Khan		
Extras	(B 5, LB 8, W 3, NB 3)	19
TOTAL	(60 overs) (for 8 wkts)	**193**

						Fall	
Willis	12	4	24	2	1st	29
Dilley	12	1	33	0	2nd	33
Allott	12	2	48	1	3rd	49
Botham	12	3	36	2	4th	67
Marks	12	1	33	1	5th	96
					6th	112
					7th	118
					8th	154

ENGLAND
G. Fowler	not out	78
C.J. Tavare	lbw b Rashid Khan	8
D.I. Gower	c Sarfraz Nawaz b Mansoor Akhtar	48
A.J. Lamb	not out	48
M.W. Gatting		
I.T. Botham		
I.J. Gould+		
V.J. Marks		
G.R. Dilley		
P.J.W. Allott		
R.G.D. Willis*		
Extras	(B 1, LB 12, W 2, NB 2)	17
TOTAL	(50.4 overs) (for 2 wkts)	**199**

						Fall	
Rashid Khan	7	2	19	1	1st	15
Sarfraz Nawaz	11	5	22	0	2nd	93
Wasim Raja	3	0	14	0		
Mudassar Nazar	8	0	30	0		
Abdul Qadir	9.4	0	53	0		
Mansoor Akhtar	12	2	44	1		

Match No: 85/18

ENGLAND v NEW ZEALAND

Prudential World Cup
Played at Edgbaston, Birmingham on 15/06/1983
Toss: England **Result:** New Zealand won by 2 wickets
Umpires: J. Birkenshaw and K.E. Palmer
Man of the match: J.V. Coney
Debuts: None

ENGLAND

G. Fowler	c J.J. Crowe b Chatfield	69
C.J. Tavare	c Cairns b Coney	18
I.T. Botham	c & b Bracewell	12
D.I. Gower	not out	92
A.J. Lamb	c J.J. Crowe b Cairns	8
M.W. Gatting	b Cairns	1
I.J. Gould+	lbw b Cairns	4
V.J. Marks	b Hadlee	5
G.R. Dilley	b Hadlee	10
P.J.W. Allott	c Smith b Hadlee	0
R.G.D. Willis*	lbw b Chatfield	0
Extras	(B 4, LB 10, W 1)	15
TOTAL	(55.2 overs)	**234**

					Fall	
Hadlee	10	3	32	3	1st	63
Cairns	11	0	44	3	2nd	77
Coney	12	2	27	1	3rd	117
Bracewell	12	0	66	1	4th	143
Chatfield	10.2	0	50	2	5th	154
					6th	162
					7th	203
					8th	233
					9th	233
					10th	234

NEW ZEALAND

G.M. Turner	lbw b Willis	2
B.A. Edgar	c Gould b Willis	1
G.P. Howarth*	run out	60
J.J. Crowe	b Allott	17
M.D. Crowe	b Marks	20
J.V. Coney	not out	66
I.D.S. Smith+	b Botham	4
R.J. Hadlee	b Willis	31
B.L. Cairns	lbw b Willis	5
J.G. Bracewell	not out	4
E.J. Chatfield		
Extras	(B 2, LB 22, W 1, NB 3)	28
TOTAL	(59.5 overs) (for 8 wkts)	**238**

					Fall	
Willis	12	1	42	4	1st	2
Dilley	12	1	43	0	2nd	3
Botham	12	1	47	1	3rd	47
Allott	11.5	2	44	1	4th	75
Marks	12	1	34	1	5th	146
					6th	151
					7th	221
					8th	231

Match No: 86/12

ENGLAND v PAKISTAN

Prudential World Cup
Played at Old Trafford, Manchester on 18/06/1983
Toss: Pakistan **Result:** England won by 7 wickets
Umpires: H.D. Bird and D.O. Oslear
Man of the match: G. Fowler
Debuts: None

PAKISTAN
Mohsin Khan	c Marks b Allott	32
Mudassar Nazar	c Gould b Dilley	18
Zaheer Abbas	c Gould b Dilley	0
Javed Miandad	run out	67
Imran Khan*	c Willis b Marks	13
Wasim Raja	c Willis b Marks	15
Ijaz Faqih	not out	42
Sarfraz Nawaz	b Willis	17
Abdul Qadir	run out	6
Wasim Bari+	not out	2
Rashid Khan		
Extras	(B 3, LB 14, W 2, NB 1)	20
TOTAL	(60 overs) (for 8 wkts)	**232**

						Fall	
Willis	12	3	37	1		1st	33
Dilley	12	2	46	2		2nd	34
Allott	12	1	33	1		3rd	87
Botham	12	1	51	0		4th	116
Marks	12	0	45	2		5th	144
						6th	169
						7th	204
						8th	221

ENGLAND
G. Fowler	c Javed Miandad b Mudassar Nazar	69
C.J. Tavare	c Wasim Raja b Zaheer Abbas	58
D.I. Gower	c Zaheer Abbas b Mudassar Nazar	31
A.J. Lamb	not out	38
M.W. Gatting	not out	14
I.T. Botham		
I.J. Gould+		
V.J. Marks		
G.R. Dilley		
P.J.W. Allott		
R.G.D. Willis*		
Extras	(B 1, LB 15, W 7)	23
TOTAL	(57.2 overs) (for 3 wkts)	**233**

						Fall	
Rashid Khan	11	1	58	0		1st	115
Sarfraz Nawaz	10.2	2	22	0		2nd	165
Abdul Qadir	11	0	51	0		3rd	181
Ijaz Faqih	6	0	19	0			
Mudassar Nazar	12	2	34	2			
Zaheer Abbas	7	0	26	1			

Match No: 87/4

ENGLAND v SRI LANKA

Prudential World Cup
Played at Headingley, Leeds on 20/06/1983
Toss: England **Result:** England won by 9 wickets
Umpires: B. Leadbeater and R. Palmer
Man of the match: R.G.D. Willis
Debuts: None

SRI LANKA

S. Wettimuny	lbw b Botham	22
D.S.B.P. Kuruppu	c Gatting b Willis	6
A. Ranatunga	c Lamb b Botham	0
R.L. Dias	c Gould b Cowans	7
L.R.D. Mendis*	b Allott	10
R.S. Madugalle	c Gould b Allott	0
D.S. de Silva	c Gower b Marks	15
R.G. de Alwis+	c Marks b Cowans	19
A.L.F. de Mel	c Lamb b Marks	10
R.J. Ratnayake	not out	20
V.B. John	c Cowans b Allott	15
Extras	(B 5, LB 2, W 3, NB 2)	12
TOTAL	(50.4 overs)	**136**

						Fall	
Willis	9	4	9	1	1st	25
Cowans	12	3	31	2	2nd	30
Botham	9	4	12	2	3rd	32
Allott	10.4	0	41	3	4th	40
Gatting	4	2	13	0	5th	43
Marks	6	2	18	2	6th	54
					7th	81
					8th	97
					9th	103
					10th	136

ENGLAND

G. Fowler	not out	81
C.J. Tavare	c de Alwis b de Mel	19
D.I. Gower	not out	27
A.J. Lamb		
M.W. Gatting		
I.T. Botham		
I.J. Gould+		
V.J. Marks		
P.J.W. Allott		
R.G.D. Willis*		
N.G. Cowans		
Extras	(B 1, LB 3, W 3, NB 3)	10
TOTAL	(24.1 overs) (for 1 wkt)	**137**

						Fall	
de Mel	10	1	33	1	1st	68
Ratnayake	5	0	23	0		
John	6	0	41	0		
de Silva	3	0	29	0		
Ranatunga	0.1	0	1	0		

Match No: 88/9

ENGLAND v INDIA

Prudential World Cup Semi-Final
Played at Old Trafford, Manchester on 22/06/1983
Toss: England   **Result:** India won by 6 wickets
Umpires: D.G.L. Evans and D.O. Oslear
Man of the match: M. Amarnath
Debuts: None

ENGLAND
G. Fowler	b Binny	33
C.J. Tavare	c Kirmani b Binny	32
D.I. Gower	c Kirmani b Amarnath	17
A.J. Lamb	run out	29
M.W. Gatting	b Amarnath	18
I.T. Botham	b Azad	6
I.J. Gould+	run out	13
V.J. Marks	b Kapil Dev	8
G.R. Dilley	not out	20
P.J.W. Allott	c Patil b Kapil Dev	8
R.G.D. Willis*	b Kapil Dev	0
Extras	(B 1, LB 17, W 7, NB 4)	29
TOTAL	(60 overs)	**213**

						Fall	
Kapil Dev	11	1	35	3	1st	69
Sandhu	8	1	36	0	2nd	84
Binny	12	1	43	2	3rd	107
Madan Lal	5	0	15	0	4th	141
Azad	12	1	28	1	5th	150
Amarnath	12	1	27	2	6th	160
					7th	175
					8th	177
					9th	202
					10th	213

INDIA
S.M. Gavaskar	c Gould b Allott	25
K. Srikkanth	c Willis b Botham	19
M. Amarnath	run out	46
Yashpal Sharma	c Allott b Willis	61
S.M. Patil	not out	51
Kapil Dev*	not out	1
K. Azad		
R.M.H. Binny		
Madan Lal		
S.M.H. Kirmani+		
B.S. Sandhu		
Extras	(B 5, LB 6, W 1, NB 2)	14
TOTAL	(54.4 overs) (for 4 wkts)	**217**

						Fall	
Willis	10.4	2	42	1	1st	46
Dilley	11	0	43	0	2nd	50
Allott	10	3	40	1	3rd	142
Botham	11	4	40	1	4th	205
Marks	12	1	38	0		

Match No: 89/19

NEW ZEALAND v ENGLAND

Rothmans Cup
Played at Lancaster Park, Christchurch on 18/02/1984
Toss: New Zealand　　　　　　　　　　**Result:** England won by 54 runs
Umpires: F.R. Goodall and I.C. Higginson
Man of the match: D.W. Randall
Debuts: Eng - N.A. Foster, C.L. Smith

ENGLAND

Batsman	Dismissal	Runs
D.I. Gower	c J.J. Crowe b Hadlee	3
C.L. Smith	run out	17
A.J. Lamb	c Robertson b Hadlee	43
D.W. Randall	c Cairns b Hadlee	70
I.T. Botham	c Smith b Hadlee	1
M.W. Gatting	b Hadlee	0
V.J. Marks	lbw b Cairns	28
R.W. Taylor+	run out	2
N.A. Foster	c Wright b Cairns	0
N.G. Cowans	not out	4
R.G.D. Willis*		
Extras	(B 8, LB 4, NB 8)	20
TOTAL	(50 overs) (for 9 wkts)	**188**

Fall

Bowler	O	M	R	W		
Hadlee	10	2	32	5	1st	9
Chatfield	10	4	20	0	2nd	59
Cairns	10	2	41	2	3rd	107
Coney	10	1	30	0	4th	109
Robertson	10	0	45	0	5th	109
					6th	177
					7th	184
					8th	184
					9th	188

NEW ZEALAND

Batsman	Dismissal	Runs
J.G. Wright	c Taylor b Willis	4
B.A. Edgar	c Taylor b Botham	10
G.P. Howarth*	run out	18
M.D. Crowe	run out	0
J.J. Crowe	b Botham	0
J.V. Coney	c Botham b Foster	19
B.L. Cairns	lbw b Marks	23
R.J. Hadlee	c Gower b Marks	23
I.D.S. Smith+	c Gower b Foster	7
G.K. Robertson	lbw b Willis	10
E.J. Chatfield	not out	0
Extras	(LB 9, W 6, NB 5)	20
TOTAL	(42.1 overs)	**134**

Fall

Bowler	O	M	R	W		
Willis	6.1	1	18	2	1st	7
Cowans	10	2	37	0	2nd	38
Botham	6	3	7	2	3rd	38
Foster	10	4	19	2	4th	38
Marks	10	1	33	2	5th	44
					6th	76
					7th	112
					8th	120
					9th	124
					10th	134

Match No: 90/20

NEW ZEALAND v ENGLAND

Rothmans Cup
Played at Basin Reserve, Wellington on 22/02/1984
Toss: New Zealand   **Result:** England won by 6 wickets
Umpires: G.C. Morris and S.J. Woodward
Man of the match: V.J. Marks
Debuts: NZ - T.J. Franklin

NEW ZEALAND

B.A. Edgar	b Marks	12
T.J. Franklin	c & b Marks	6
G.P. Howarth*	lbw b Marks	21
M.D. Crowe	c Foster b Marks	8
J.J. Crowe	c Foster b Marks	1
J.V. Coney	b Botham	44
R.J. Hadlee	c Randall b Foster	21
B.L. Cairns	c Gower b Foster	0
I.D.S. Smith+	lbw b Botham	0
G.K. Robertson	run out	11
E.J. Chatfield	not out	0
Extras	(LB 9, W 2)	11
TOTAL	(47.1 overs)	**135**

						Fall	
Willis	9	4	17	0	1st	23
Cowans	10	1	33	0	2nd	34
Marks	10	3	20	5	3rd	50
Botham	8.1	1	25	2	4th	52
Foster	10	3	29	2	5th	63
					6th	104
					7th	104
					8th	104
					9th	135
					10th	135

ENGLAND

D.I. Gower	c J.J. Crowe b Chatfield	21
C.L. Smith	b Hadlee	70
A.J. Lamb	c & b Chatfield	6
D.W. Randall	not out	25
I.T. Botham	b Hadlee	15
M.W. Gatting	not out	0
V.J. Marks		
R.W. Taylor+		
N.A. Foster		
N.G. Cowans		
R.G.D. Willis*		
Extras	(LB 2)	2
TOTAL	(45.1 overs) (for 4 wkts)	**139**

						Fall	
Hadlee	10	2	31	2	1st	36
Robertson	6	0	28	0	2nd	54
Coney	10	1	29	0	3rd	117
Chatfield	10	5	16	2	4th	135
Cairns	9.1	1	33	0		

Match No: 91/21

NEW ZEALAND v ENGLAND

Rothmans Cup
Played at Eden Park, Auckland on 25/02/1984
Toss: England **Result:** New Zealand won by 7 wickets
Umpires: D.A. Kinsella and G.C. Morris
Man of the match: M.D. Crowe
Debuts: None

ENGLAND

D.I. Gower	lbw b Chatfield	35
C.L. Smith	b Hadlee	5
A.J. Lamb	not out	97
D.W. Randall	b Boock	11
I.T. Botham	c Wright b Coney	18
M.W. Gatting	c Smith b Chatfield	4
V.J. Marks	b Chatfield	3
R.W. Taylor+	run out	8
N.A. Foster	run out	1
N.G. Cowans	run out	0
R.G.D. Willis*	not out	7
Extras	(B 4, LB 11, W 1, NB 4)	20
TOTAL	(50 overs) (for 9 wkts)	**209**

						Fall	
Cairns	10	2	31	0	1st	6
Hadlee	10	2	51	1	2nd	73
Boock	10	0	40	1	3rd	86
Coney	10	0	38	1	4th	130
Chatfield	10	2	29	3	5th	140
					6th	148
					7th	185
					8th	192
					9th	192

NEW ZEALAND

P.N. Webb	b Willis	8
J.G. Wright	c & b Marks	14
G.P. Howarth*	lbw b Botham	72
M.D. Crowe	not out	105
J.V. Coney	not out	2
J.J. Crowe		
R.J. Hadlee		
B.L. Cairns		
I.D.S. Smith+		
S.L. Boock		
E.J. Chatfield		
Extras	(LB 7, W 2)	9
TOTAL	(45.3 overs) (for 3 wkts)	**210**

						Fall	
Willis	10	1	36	1	1st	22
Cowans	9.3	0	59	0	2nd	34
Marks	10	1	27	1	3rd	194
Botham	7	1	22	1		
Foster	6	0	37	0		
Smith	3	0	20	0		

Match No: 92/13

PAKISTAN v ENGLAND

Wills Series
Played at Gaddafi Stadium, Lahore on 09/03/1984
Toss: Pakistan   **Result:** Pakistan won by 6 wickets
Umpires: Amanullah Khan and Shakil Khan
Man of the match: Zaheer Abbas
Debuts: Pak - Saadat Ali

ENGLAND
G. Fowler+	b Sarfraz Nawaz	43
C.J. Tavare	c Ashraf Ali b Rashid Khan	4
D.I. Gower	c Qasim Omar b Shahid Mahboob	7
A.J. Lamb	run out	57
D.W. Randall	run out	16
I.T. Botham	not out	18
M.W. Gatting	b Sarfraz Nawaz	9
G.R. Dilley	lbw b Sarfraz Nawaz	1
V.J. Marks	b Rashid Khan	2
N.A. Foster	not out	6
R.G.D. Willis*		
Extras	(LB 13, W 6, NB 2)	21
TOTAL	**(40 overs) (for 8 wkts)**	**184**

						Fall	
Rashid Khan	8	1	28	2	1st	11
Shahid Mahboob	8	2	28	1	2nd	24
Mudassar Nazar	8	1	34	0	3rd	94
Sarfraz Nawaz	8	0	33	3	4th	134
Wasim Raja	8	0	40	0	5th	147
					6th	160
					7th	164
					8th	173

PAKISTAN
Mohsin Khan	b Dilley	39
Saadat Ali	run out	44
Qasim Omar	c Fowler b Marks	11
Zaheer Abbas*	not out	59
Salim Malik	c Tavare b Willis	11
Mudassar Nazar	not out	8
Wasim Raja		
Shahid Mahboob		
Ashraf Ali+		
Sarfraz Nawaz		
Rashid Khan		
Extras	(B 1, LB 5, W 1, NB 8)	15
TOTAL	**(38.4 overs) (for 4 wkts)**	**187**

						Fall	
Willis	7.4	1	25	1	1st	79
Dilley	8	0	38	1	2nd	96
Botham	7	0	43	0	3rd	120
Marks	8	1	32	1	4th	156
Foster	8	0	34	0		

Match No: 93/14

PAKISTAN v ENGLAND

Wills Series
Played at National Stadium, Karachi on 26/03/1984
Toss: England   **Result:** England won by 6 wickets
Umpires: Mahboob Shah and Shakil Khan
Man of the match: M.W. Gatting
Debuts: Eng - N.G.B. Cook   Pak - Anil Dalpat, Naved Anjum

PAKISTAN

Batsman	Dismissal	Runs
Mohsin Khan	st Fowler b Cook	37
Saadat Ali	not out	78
Wasim Raja	c Fowler b Gatting	14
Salim Malik	c Foster b Gatting	2
Qasim Omar	c & b Gatting	7
Naved Anjum	st Fowler b Smith	2
Mudassar Nazar	run out	6
Abdul Qadir	c Cook b Smith	3
Sarfraz Nawaz*	c Gower b Cowans	3
Anil Dalpat+	not out	0
Rashid Khan		
Extras	(B 4, LB 4, NB 3)	11
TOTAL	(40 overs) (for 8 wkts)	**163**

Bowler	O	M	R	W	Fall	
Foster	8	0	36	0	1st	76
Cowans	5	0	20	1	2nd	102
Gatting	8	1	32	3	3rd	107
Marks	8	1	22	0	4th	123
Cook	8	0	34	1	5th	135
Smith	3	0	8	2	6th	146
					7th	155
					8th	160

ENGLAND

Batsman	Dismissal	Runs
G. Fowler+	c Anil Dalpat b Mudassar Nazar	25
C.L. Smith	lbw b Abdul Qadir	17
D.I. Gower*	b Mudassar Nazar	31
A.J. Lamb	c Salim Malik b Naved Anjum	19
M.W. Gatting	not out	38
D.W. Randall	not out	19
C.J. Tavare		
V.J. Marks		
N.A. Foster		
N.G.B. Cook		
N.G. Cowans		
Extras	(B 1, LB 8, W 3, NB 3)	15
TOTAL	(38.4 overs) (for 4 wkts)	**164**

Bowler	O	M	R	W	Fall	
Rashid Khan	8	0	31	0	1st	37
Sarfraz Nawaz	7.4	1	24	0	2nd	79
Mudassar Nazar	8	1	22	2	3rd	88
Abdul Qadir	8	0	33	1	4th	119
Wasim Raja	5	0	30	0		
Naved Anjum	2	0	9	1		

Match No: 94/16

ENGLAND v WEST INDIES

Texaco Trophy
Played at Old Trafford, Manchester on 31/05/1984
Toss: West Indies   **Result:** West Indies won by 104 runs
Umpires: D.J. Constant and D.R. Shepherd
Man of the match: I.V.A. Richards
Debuts: Eng - T.A. Lloyd

WEST INDIES
C.G. Greenidge	c Bairstow b Botham	9
D.L. Haynes	run out	1
R.B. Richardson	c & b Willis	6
I.V.A. Richards	not out	189
H.A. Gomes	b Miller	4
C.H. Lloyd*	c Pringle b Miller	8
P.J.L. Dujon+	c Gatting b Miller	0
M.D. Marshall	run out	4
E.A.E. Baptiste	c Bairstow b Botham	26
J. Garner	c & b Foster	3
M.A. Holding	not out	12
Extras	(B 4, LB 2, W 1, NB 3)	10
TOTAL	(55 overs) (for 9 wkts)	**272**

						Fall	
Willis	11	2	38	1		1st	5
Botham	11	0	67	2		2nd	11
Foster	11	0	61	1		3rd	43
Miller	11	1	32	3		4th	63
Pringle	11	0	64	0		5th	89
						6th	98
						7th	102
						8th	161
						9th	166

ENGLAND
G. Fowler	c Lloyd b Garner	1
T.A. Lloyd	c Dujon b Holding	15
M.W. Gatting	lbw b Garner	0
D.I. Gower*	c Greenidge b Marshall	15
A.J. Lamb	c Richardson b Gomes	75
I.T. Botham	c Richardson b Baptiste	2
D.L. Bairstow+	c Garner b Richards	13
G. Miller	b Richards	7
D.R. Pringle	c Garner b Holding	6
N.A. Foster	b Garner	24
R.G.D. Willis	not out	1
Extras	(LB 6, NB 3)	9
TOTAL	(50 overs)	**168**

						Fall	
Garner	8	1	18	3		1st	7
Holding	11	2	23	2		2nd	8
Baptiste	11	0	38	1		3rd	33
Marshall	6	1	20	1		4th	48
Richards	11	1	45	2		5th	51
Gomes	3	0	15	1		6th	80
						7th	100
						8th	115
						9th	162
						10th	168

Match No: 95/17

ENGLAND v WEST INDIES

Texaco Trophy
Played at Trent Bridge, Nottingham on 02/06/1984
Toss: England   **Result:** England won by 3 wickets
Umpires: H.D. Bird and D.O. Oslear
Man of the match: D.R. Pringle
Debuts: None

WEST INDIES

C.G. Greenidge	c Botham b Pringle	20
D.L. Haynes	lbw b Willis	4
R.B. Richardson	c Gower b Pringle	10
I.V.A. Richards	c Pringle b Miller	3
H.A. Gomes	b Pringle	15
C.H. Lloyd*	c Pringle b Miller	52
P.J.L. Dujon+	run out	21
M.D. Marshall	run out	20
E.A.E. Baptiste	lbw b Willis	19
M.A. Holding	b Botham	0
J. Garner	not out	6
Extras	(LB 7, NB 2)	9
TOTAL	(48.3 overs)	**179**

						Fall	
Willis	9.3	0	26	2	1st	24
Botham	9	1	33	1	2nd	38
Pringle	10	3	21	3	3rd	39
Miller	10	2	44	2	4th	43
Foster	10	0	46	0	5th	75
					6th	128
					7th	148
					8th	160
					9th	161
					10th	179

ENGLAND

G. Fowler	b Baptiste	25
T.A. Lloyd	c Dujon b Baptiste	49
D.I. Gower*	lbw b Marshall	36
A.J. Lamb	b Gomes	11
I.T. Botham	c Gomes b Holding	15
M.W. Gatting	b Garner	6
D.L. Bairstow+	b Holding	9
G.Miller	not out	3
D.R. Pringle	not out	2
N.A. Foster		
R.G.D. Willis		
Extras	(B 4, LB 14, NB 6)	24
TOTAL	(47.5 overs) (for 7 wkts)	**180**

						Fall	
Garner	9	1	22	1	1st	75
Holding	8.5	1	29	2	2nd	103
Marshall	10	1	30	1	3rd	131
Baptiste	10	2	31	2	4th	145
Richards	5	0	23	0	5th	157
Gomes	5	0	21	1	6th	173
						7th	177

Match No: 96/18

ENGLAND v WEST INDIES

Texaco Trophy
Played at Lord's, London on 04/06/1984
Toss: West Indies   **Result:** West Indies won by 8 wickets
Umpires: D.G.L. Evans and B.J. Meyer
Man of the match: R.A. Harper
Debuts: None

ENGLAND
G. Fowler	b Holding	34
T.A. Lloyd	b Harper	37
D.I. Gower*	b Marshall	29
A.J. Lamb	run out	0
I.T. Botham	c Harper b Baptiste	22
D.W. Randall	c Dujon b Marshall	8
D.L. Bairstow+	b Marshall	8
G. Miller	b Holding	10
D.R. Pringle	lbw b Garner	8
N.A. Foster	not out	4
R.G.D. Willis	not out	6
Extras	(B 1, LB 17, W 4, NB 8)	30
TOTAL	(55 overs) (for 9 wkts)	**196**

						Fall	
Garner	11	4	17	1	1st	60
Holding	11	0	33	2	2nd	91
Marshall	11	0	38	3	3rd	91
Baptiste	11	1	40	1	4th	128
Harper	11	0	38	1	5th	144
					6th	151
					7th	167
					8th	177
					9th	182

WEST INDIES
C.G. Greenidge	c Bairstow b Pringle	32
D.L. Haynes	c Randall b Miller	18
H.A. Gomes	not out	56
I.V.A. Richards	not out	84
C.H. Lloyd*		
P.J.L. Dujon+		
M.D. Marshall		
E.A.E. Baptiste		
R.A. Harper		
J. Garner		
M.A. Holding		
Extras	(B 1, W 1, NB 5)	7
TOTAL	(46.5 overs) (for 2 wkts)	**197**

						Fall	
Willis	10.5	2	52	0	1st	50
Botham	8	0	25	0	2nd	63
Miller	9	1	35	1		
Pringle	8	0	38	1		
Foster	11	1	40	0		

Match No: 97/10

INDIA v ENGLAND

Played at Nehru Stadium, Poona on 05/12/1984
Toss: England **Result:** England won by 4 wickets
Umpires: S. Banerjee and Mohammad Ghouse
Man of the match: M.W. Gatting and D.B. Vengsarkar
Debuts: Eng - R.M. Ellison, R.T. Robinson
Ind - R.S. Ghai, K.S. More

INDIA

K. Srikkanth	b Edmonds	50
S.M. Gavaskar*	b Foster	0
D.B. Vengsarkar	b Ellison	105
S.M. Patil	run out	2
Yashpal Sharma	c Ellison b Foster	37
R.J. Shastri	c Ellison b Foster	11
R.M.H. Binny	not out	0
K.S. More+		
M. Prabhakar		
Chetan Sharma		
R.S. Ghai		
Extras	(LB 2, W 7)	9
TOTAL	(45 overs) (for 6 wkts)	**214**

Bowler	O	M	R	W	Fall	
Cowans	8	0	32	0	1st	1
Foster	10	0	44	3	2nd	119
Ellison	7	0	45	1	3rd	126
Marks	10	0	48	0	4th	189
Edmonds	10	0	43	1	5th	212
					6th	214

ENGLAND

G. Fowler	c Yashpal Sharma b Chetan Sharma	5
R.T. Robinson	lbw b Ghai	15
M.W. Gatting	not out	115
A.J. Lamb	c & b Prabhakar	3
V.J. Marks	run out	31
D.I. Gower*	c Shastri b Binny	3
R.M. Ellison	run out	4
P.R. Downton+	not out	27
P.H. Edmonds		
N.A. Foster		
N.G. Cowans		
Extras	(LB 8, NB 4)	12
TOTAL	(43.2 overs) (for 6 wkts)	**215**

Bowler	O	M	R	W	Fall	
Chetan Sharma	8.2	0	50	1	1st	14
Prabhakar	10	1	27	1	2nd	43
Ghai	9	0	38	1	3rd	47
Shastri	8	0	49	0	4th	114
Binny	8	0	43	1	5th	117
					6th	129

Match No: 98/11

INDIA v ENGLAND

Played at Barabati Stadium, Cuttack on 27/12/1984
Toss: England **Result:** England won on faster scoring rate
Umpires: J.D. Ghosh and P.G. Pandit
Man of the match: R.J. Shastri
Debuts: None

INDIA

K. Srikkanth	lbw b Gatting	99
R.J. Shastri	b Gatting	102
D.B. Vengsarkar	c Gower b Marks	23
Yashpal Sharma	lbw b Marks	4
M. Amarnath	not out	1
R.M.H. Binny	b Marks	2
S.M. Gavaskar*	not out	6
K.S. More+		
M. Prabhakar		
R.S. Ghai		
A. Patel		
Extras	(B 5, LB 5, W 3, NB 2)	15
TOTAL	(49 overs) (for 5 wkts)	**252**

Bowler	O	M	R	W	Fall	
Foster	5	0	26	0	1st	188
Cowans	10	0	39	0	2nd	235
Ellison	6	0	31	0	3rd	243
Edmonds	10	0	47	0	4th	243
Marks	8	0	50	3	5th	246
Gatting	10	0	49	2		

ENGLAND

G. Fowler	c Shastri b Binny	15
R.T. Robinson	b Prabhakar	1
M.W. Gatting	b Patel	59
D.I. Gower*	c Prabhakar b Binny	21
A.J. Lamb	run out	28
V.J. Marks	run out	44
P.R. Downton+	not out	44
R.M. Ellison	not out	14
P.H. Edmonds		
N.A. Foster		
N.G. Cowans		
Extras	(LB 9, W 1, NB 5)	15
TOTAL	(46 overs) (for 6 wkts)	**241**

Bowler	O	M	R	W	Fall	
Ghai	8	0	40	0	1st	3
Prabhakar	10	1	34	1	2nd	50
Binny	7	0	48	2	3rd	93
Patel	10	0	53	1	4th	128
Shastri	10	0	48	0	5th	145
Amarnath	1	0	9	0	6th	203

Match No: 99/12

INDIA v ENGLAND

Played at Chinnaswamy Stadium, Bangalore on 20/01/1985
Toss: England **Result:** England won by 3 wickets
Umpires: S.K. Das and S.V. Ramani
Man of the match: A.J. Lamb
Debuts: Ind - M. Azharuddin, S. Viswanath

INDIA
S.M. Gavaskar*	c Gatting b Marks	40
K. Srikkanth	b Cowans	29
D.B. Vengsarkar	st Downton b Marks	23
Kapil Dev	c Gower b Marks	8
Yashpal Sharma	run out	8
R.J. Shastri	b Edmonds	33
M. Azharuddin	not out	47
S. Viswanath+	not out	6
A. Patel		
R.S. Ghai		
T.A.P. Sekar		
Extras	(B 4, LB 6, W 1)	11
TOTAL	(46 overs) (for 6 wkts)	**205**

						Fall	
Cowans	10	1	31	1	1st	70
Foster	6	0	33	0	2nd	70
Ellison	6	0	25	0	3rd	90
Marks	10	1	35	3	4th	108
Edmonds	10	0	44	1	5th	119
Gatting	4	0	27	0	6th	185

ENGLAND
G. Fowler	run out	45
R.T. Robinson	c Viswanath b Kapil Dev	2
M.W. Gatting	run out	3
D.I. Gower*	b Shastri	38
A.J. Lamb	not out	59
V.J. Marks	c Gavaskar b Patel	17
P.R. Downton+	c Shastri b Kapil Dev	12
P.H. Edmonds	c Viswanath b Kapil Dev	7
R.M. Ellison	not out	1
N.A. Foster		
N.G. Cowans		
Extras	(LB 10, W 7, NB 5)	22
TOTAL	(45 overs) (for 7 wkts)	**206**

						Fall	
Kapil Dev	10	0	38	3	1st	15
Sekar	9	0	36	0	2nd	21
Patel	10	1	42	1	3rd	91
Ghai	4	0	37	0	4th	103
Shastri	10	2	29	1	5th	144
Yashpal Sharma	2	0	14	0	6th	186
					7th	204

Match No: 100/13

INDIA v ENGLAND

Played at Vidarbha CA Ground, Nagpur on 23/01/1985
Toss: India   **Result:** India won by 3 wickets
Umpires: R. Mrithyunjayan and A.L. Narasimhan
Man of the match: Kapil Dev
Debuts: Eng - J.P. Agnew, C.S. Cowdrey, M.D. Moxon   Ind - L. Rajput

ENGLAND
G. Fowler	b Shastri	37
M.D. Moxon	c Srikkanth b Kapil Dev	70
M.W. Gatting	b Shastri	1
D.I. Gower*	c & b Shastri	11
A.J. Lamb	st Viswanath b Shastri	30
C.S. Cowdrey	not out	46
V.J. Marks	b Sekar	4
P.R. Downton+	c Rajput b Sekar	13
P.H. Edmonds	not out	8
J.P. Agnew		
N.G. Cowans		
Extras	(B 3, LB 15, W 1, NB 1)	20
TOTAL	(50 overs) (for 7 wkts)	**240**

Bowling	O	M	R	W	Fall	
Kapil Dev	10	1	42	1	1st	70
Prabhakar	10	1	36	0	2nd	78
Sekar	10	0	50	2	3rd	100
Patel	10	1	54	0	4th	154
Shastri	10	1	40	4	5th	176
					6th	199
					7th	221

INDIA
K. Srikkanth	b Cowans	6
L.S. Rajput	c Downton b Cowans	0
D.B. Vengsarkar	c Downton b Agnew	11
M. Azharuddin	b Cowdrey	47
S.M. Gavaskar*	b Agnew	52
Kapil Dev	c Gatting b Cowans	54
R.J. Shastri	not out	24
M. Prabhakar	b Agnew	4
S. Viswanath+	not out	23
T.A.P. Sekar		
A. Patel		
Extras	(B 3, LB 14, W 1, NB 2)	20
TOTAL	(47.4 overs) (for 7 wkts)	**241**

Bowling	O	M	R	W	Fall	
Cowans	10	0	44	3	1st	5
Agnew	10	0	38	3	2nd	11
Marks	6	0	32	0	3rd	31
Edmonds	10	0	44	0	4th	90
Cowdrey	7.4	0	52	1	5th	166
Gatting	4	0	14	0	6th	197
					7th	204

Match No: 101/14

INDIA v ENGLAND

Played at Sector 16 Stadium, Chandigarh on 27/01/1985
Toss: India   Result: England won by 7 runs
Umpires: R.B. Gupta and B. Nagaraja Rao
Man of the match: R.J. Shastri
Debuts: Eng - B.N. French

ENGLAND
G. Fowler	run out	17
M.W. Gatting	c Azharuddin b Sekar	31
D.I. Gower*	b Sekar	19
A.J. Lamb	not out	33
C.S. Cowdrey	c Rajput b Shastri	5
P.H. Edmonds	c Azharuddin b Sekar	5
V.J. Marks	run out	2
R.M. Ellison	not out	4
J.P. Agnew		
N.A. Foster		
B.N. French+		
Extras	(LB 5)	5
TOTAL	(15 overs) (for 6 wkts)	121

					Fall	
Kapil Dev	3	0	17	0	1st	31
Prabhakar	3	0	26	0	2nd	71
Chetan Sharma	3	0	20	0	3rd	74
Sekar	3	0	23	3	4th	86
Shastri	3	0	30	1	5th	93
					6th	104

INDIA
R.J. Shastri	run out	53
K. Srikkanth	run out	9
Kapil Dev	c Agnew b Edmonds	17
M. Azharuddin	c Gatting b Edmonds	10
Yashpal Sharma	b Cowdrey	6
S.M. Gavaskar*	not out	2
L.S. Rajput	not out	1
S. Viswanath+		
T.A.P. Sekar		
M. Prabhakar		
Chetan Sharma		
Extras	(LB 4, W 12)	16
TOTAL	(15 overs) (for 5 wkts)	114

					Fall	
Agnew	3	0	23	0	1st	22
Foster	3	0	17	0	2nd	49
Ellison	3	0	20	0	3rd	83
Edmonds	3	0	20	2	4th	111
Gatting	2	0	27	0	5th	112
Cowdrey	1	0	3	1		

Match No: 102/29

AUSTRALIA v ENGLAND

Benson & Hedges World Championship
Played at Melbourne Cricket Ground, on 17/02/1985
Toss: England   Result: Australia won by 7 wickets
Umpires: A.R. Crafter and R.C. Isherwood
Man of the match: R.B. Kerr
Debuts: None

ENGLAND
G. Fowler	c & b McDermott	26
P.R. Downton+	c McCurdy b McDermott	27
D.I. Gower*	c Alderman b McCurdy	6
A.J. Lamb	c Kerr b Lawson	53
M.W. Gatting	c Alderman b O'Donnell	34
C.S. Cowdrey	lbw b McDermott	0
V.J. Marks	b Lawson	24
P.H. Edmonds	b Lawson	20
R.M. Ellison	not out	2
J.P. Agnew	not out	2
N.G. Cowans		
Extras	(B 3, LB 12, NB 5)	20
TOTAL	(49 overs) (for 8 wkts)	**214**

						Fall	
Lawson	10	3	31	3	1st	61
Alderman	10	0	48	0	2nd	66
McDermott	10	0	39	3	3rd	76
McCurdy	10	1	42	1	4th	159
O'Donnell	9	0	39	1	5th	159
					6th	166
					7th	200
					8th	211

AUSTRALIA
K.C. Wessels	c Gatting b Ellison	39
R.B. Kerr	not out	87
K.J. Hughes	run out	0
A.R. Border*	c Cowans b Marks	1
D.M. Jones	not out	78
W.B. Phillips+		
S.P. O'Donnell		
G.F. Lawson		
C.J. McDermott		
R.J. McCurdy		
T.M. Alderman		
Extras	(B 1, LB 3, NB 6)	10
TOTAL	(45.2 overs) (for 3 wkts)	**215**

						Fall	
Cowans	10	0	52	0	1st	57
Ellison	10	4	34	1	2nd	57
Agnew	8	0	59	0	3rd	58
Marks	7.2	0	33	1		
Edmonds	10	0	33	0		

Match No: 103/15
ENGLAND v INDIA

Benson & Hedges World Championship
Played at Sydney Cricket Ground on 26/02/1985
Toss: England   **Result:** India won by 86 runs
Umpires: R.A. French and B.E. Martin
Man of the match: K. Srikkanth
Debuts: None

INDIA
R.J. Shastri	c Fowler b Ellison	13
K. Srikkanth	run out	57
M. Azharuddin	c & b Cowans	45
D.B. Vengsarkar	run out	43
Kapil Dev	c Downton b Cowans	29
S.M. Gavaskar*	not out	30
M. Amarnath	c Lamb b Cowans	6
R.M.H. Binny	c Marks b Foster	2
Madan Lal	c Downton b Foster	0
S. Viswanath+	run out	8
L. Sivaramakrishnan		
Extras	(LB 2)	2
TOTAL	(50 overs) (for 9 wkts)	**235**

					Fall	
Cowans	10	0	59	3	1st	67
Ellison	10	1	46	1	2nd	74
Foster	10	0	33	2	3rd	147
Edmonds	10	1	38	0	4th	183
Marks	10	0	57	0	5th	197
					6th	216
					7th	220
					8th	220
					9th	235

ENGLAND
G. Fowler	c Viswanath b Binny	26
M.D. Moxon	c & b Sivaramakrishnan	48
D.I. Gower*	c Vengsarkar b Sivaramakrishnan	25
A.J. Lamb	b Sivaramakrishnan	13
M.W. Gatting	c Viswanath b Shastri	7
P.R. Downton+	c Shastri b Kapil Dev	9
V.J. Marks	st Viswanath b Shastri	2
P.H. Edmonds	st Viswanath b Shastri	5
R.M. Ellison	c Viswanath b Madan Lal	1
N.A. Foster	c Srikkanth b Madan Lal	1
N.G. Cowans	not out	3
Extras	(B 3, LB 4, W 1, NB 1)	9
TOTAL	(41.4 overs)	**149**

					Fall	
Kapil Dev	7	0	21	1	1st	41
Binny	8	0	33	1	2nd	94
Madan Lal	6.4	0	19	2	3rd	113
Sivaramakrishnan	10	0	39	3	4th	126
Shastri	10	2	30	3	5th	126
					6th	130
					7th	142
					8th	144
					9th	146
					10th	149

Match No: 104/15

ENGLAND v PAKISTAN

Benson & Hedges World Championship
Played at Melbourne Cricket Ground on 02/03/1985
Toss: Pakistan   **Result:** Pakistan won by 67 runs
Umpires: R.C. Isherwood and M.W. Johnson
Man of the match: A.J. Lamb
Debuts: None

PAKISTAN

Mudassar Nazar	c Foster b Edmonds	77
Mohsin Khan	c Moxon b Ellison	9
Ramiz Raja	c Moxon b Marks	21
Javed Miandad*	c Downton b Foster	11
Imran Khan	b Ellison	35
Salim Malik	c Gatting b Foster	8
Qasim Omar	b Cowans	12
Tahir Naqqash	not out	21
Anil Dalpat+	b Ellison	8
Azeem Hafeez	not out	0
Wasim Akram		
Extras	(B 5, LB 4, W 2)	11
TOTAL	(50 overs) (for 8 wkts)	**213**

						Fall	
Cowans	10	0	52	1	1st	37
Ellison	10	0	42	3	2nd	93
Foster	10	0	56	2	3rd	114
Marks	10	2	25	1	4th	126
Edmonds	10	1	29	1	5th	144
					6th	181
					7th	183
					8th	212

ENGLAND

G. Fowler	c Anil Dalpat b Imran Khan	0
D.I. Gower*	c Tahir Naqqash b Imran Khan	27
A.J. Lamb	c Wasim Akram b Azeem Hafeez	81
M.W. Gatting	c Mudassar Nazar b Tahir Naqqash	11
P.R. Downton+	run out	6
R.M. Ellison	c Anil Dalpat b Tahir Naqqash	6
V.J. Marks	run out	1
M.D. Moxon	c Imran Khan b Azeem Hafeez	3
P.H. Edmonds	not out	0
N.A. Foster	run out	1
N.G. Cowans	b Tahir Naqqash	0
Extras	(B 1, LB 7, W 1, NB 1)	10
TOTAL	(24.2 overs)	**146**

						Fall	
Imran Khan	7	0	33	2	1st	0
Wasim Akram	10	0	59	0	2nd	56
Azeem Hafeez	3	0	22	2	3rd	102
Tahir Naqqash	4.2	0	24	3	4th	125
					5th	138
					6th	139
					7th	141
					8th	145
					9th	146
					10th	146

Match No: 105/30

ENGLAND v AUSTRALIA

Rothmans Four-Nations Trophy Semi-Final
Played at Sharjah CA Stadium, UAE on 24/03/1985
Toss: Australia   **Result:** Australia won by 2 wickets
Umpires: Khizar Hayat and Swaroop Kishen
Man of the match: G.R.J. Matthews
Debuts: Eng - N. Gifford, C.M. Wells

ENGLAND

G. Fowler	c Hughes b Alderman	26
R.T. Robinson	c Rixon b Matthews	37
M.D. Moxon	lbw b O'Donnell	0
D.W. Randall	st Rixon b Bennett	19
C.M. Wells	lbw b Bennett	17
D.R. Pringle	st Rixon b Border	4
P.H. Edmonds	not out	15
B.N. French+	c Rixon b Border	4
R.M. Ellison	c Wessels b Border	24
N.A. Foster	not out	5
N. Gifford*		
Extras	(B 9, LB 5, W 6, NB 6)	26
TOTAL	(50 overs) (for 8 wkts)	**177**

Bowler	O	M	R	W		Fall	
Alderman	7	1	36	1	1st	47
McCurdy	5	0	23	0	2nd	53
O'Donnell	8	2	26	1	3rd	95
Bennett	10	2	27	2	4th	109
Matthews	10	3	15	1	5th	123
Border	7	0	21	3	6th	128
Wessels	3	0	15	0	7th	134
					8th	169

AUSTRALIA

K.C. Wessels	b Edmonds	16
G.M. Wood	c French b Pringle	35
D.M. Jones	c Moxon b Edmonds	27
A.R. Border*	c & b Pringle	9
K.J. Hughes	c French b Foster	14
G.R.J. Matthews	c Foster b Ellison	24
S.P. O'Donnell	c Moxon b Ellison	19
S.J. Rixon+	not out	11
M.J. Bennett	run out	0
R.J. McCurdy	not out	6
T.M. Alderman		
Extras	(LB 9, W 8)	17
TOTAL	(50 overs) (for 8 wkts)	**178**

Bowler	O	M	R	W		Fall	
Foster	10	1	34	1	1st	54
Ellison	10	1	28	2	2nd	64
Pringle	10	0	49	2	3rd	82
Edmonds	10	2	31	2	4th	100
Gifford	10	1	27	0	5th	120
					6th	151
					7th	168
					8th	168

Match No: 106/16

ENGLAND v PAKISTAN

Rothmans Four-Nations Trophy Plate-Winner's Final
Played at Sharjah CA Stadium, UAE on 26/03/1985
Toss: England   **Result:** Pakistan won by 43 runs
Umpires: M.W. Johnson and Swaroop Kishen
Man of the match: Javed Miandad
Debuts: Eng - R.J. Bailey, P.I. Pocock

PAKISTAN

Mudassar Nazar	c French b Gifford	36
Mohsin Khan	c Robinson b Pringle	13
Ramiz Raja	c Robinson b Pringle	16
Javed Miandad*	c Gifford b Edmonds	71
Salim Malik	lbw b Gifford	2
Imran Khan	c Pringle b Gifford	0
Shoaib Mohammad	st French b Gifford	3
Ashraf Ali+	not out	19
Tahir Naqqash	not out	2
Tausif Ahmed		
Wasim Akram		
Extras	(B 1, LB 9, W 2, NB 1)	13
TOTAL	(50 overs) (for 7 wkts)	**175**

						Fall	
Ellison	7	1	18	0	1st	24
Pringle	7	1	32	2	2nd	43
Edmonds	10	0	47	1	3rd	107
Pocock	10	1	20	0	4th	113
Gifford	10	0	23	4	5th	113
Bailey	6	0	25	0	6th	125
					7th	172

ENGLAND

G. Fowler	c Javed Miandad b Tausif Ahmed	19
R.T. Robinson	b Tahir Naqqash	9
M.D. Moxon	b Shoaib Mohammad	11
C.M. Wells	b Shoaib Mohammad	5
R.J. Bailey	not out	41
D.R. Pringle	b Wasim Akram	13
P.H. Edmonds	c & b Shoaib Mohammad	3
R.M. Ellison	b Wasim Akram	3
B.N. French+	c Shoaib Mohammad b Tahir Naqqash	7
N. Gifford*	c Javed Miandad b Imran Khan	0
P.I. Pocock	run out	4
Extras	(B 1, LB 12, NB 4)	17
TOTAL	(48.2 overs)	**132**

						Fall	
Imran Khan	9	2	26	1	1st	19
Wasim Akram	10	0	28	2	2nd	35
Tahir Naqqash	9.2	1	20	2	3rd	48
Tausif Ahmed	10	1	25	1	4th	49
Shoaib Mohammad	10	1	20	3	5th	76
						6th	89
						7th	98
						8th	117
						9th	132
						10th	132

Match No: 107/31

ENGLAND v AUSTRALIA

Texaco Trophy
Played at Old Trafford, Manchester on 30/05/1985
Toss: England   **Result**: Australia won by 3 wickets
Umpires: D.G.L. Evans and K.E. Palmer
Man of the match: I.T. Botham
Debuts: None

ENGLAND

G.A. Gooch	c O'Donnell b Holland	57
G. Fowler	c Phillips b McDermott	10
D.I. Gower*	b Lawson	3
A.J. Lamb	c Phillips b Lawson	0
I.T. Botham	b Matthews	72
M.W. Gatting	not out	31
P. Willey	b Holland	12
P.R. Downton+	c Matthews b Lawson	11
P.H. Edmonds	c Border b Lawson	0
P.J.W. Allott	b McDermott	2
N.G. Cowans	c & b McDermott	1
Extras	(B 2, LB 7, W 2, NB 9)	20
TOTAL	(54 overs)	**219**

						Fall	
Lawson	10	1	26	4	1st	21
McDermott	11	0	46	3	2nd	27
O'Donnell	11	0	44	0	3rd	27
Matthews	11	1	45	1	4th	143
Holland	11	2	49	2	5th	160
					6th	181
					7th	203
					8th	203
					9th	213
					10th	219

AUSTRALIA

K.C. Wessels	c Botham b Willey	39
G.M. Wood	c Downton b Cowans	8
D.M. Wellham	c & b Edmonds	12
A.R. Border*	c & b Allott	59
D.C. Boon	c Botham b Gooch	12
W.B. Phillips+	c Gatting b Cowans	28
S.P. O'Donnell	b Botham	1
G.R.J. Matthews	not out	29
G.F. Lawson	not out	14
C.J. McDermott		
R.G. Holland		
Extras	(B 2, LB 12, W 4)	18
TOTAL	(54.1 overs) (for 7 wkts)	**220**

						Fall	
Cowans	10.1	1	44	2	1st	15
Botham	11	2	41	1	2nd	52
Allott	11	0	47	1	3rd	74
Edmonds	11	2	33	1	4th	118
Willey	9	1	31	1	5th	156
Gooch	2	0	10	1	6th	157
					7th	186

Match No: 108/32

ENGLAND v AUSTRALIA

Texaco Trophy
Played at Edgbaston, Birmingham on 01/06/1985
Toss: Australia   **Result:** Australia won by 4 wickets
Umpires: D.J. Constant and D.R. Shepherd
Man of the match: A.R. Border
Debuts: None

ENGLAND
G.A. Gooch	b McDermott	115
R.T. Robinson	c & b O'Donnell	26
D.I. Gower*	c Phillips b O'Donnell	0
A.J. Lamb	b Thomson	25
I.T. Botham	c Wellham b Lawson	29
M.W. Gatting	c Lawson b McDermott	6
P. Willey	c Phillips b Lawson	0
P.R. Downton+	not out	16
P.H. Edmonds	not out	6
P.J.W. Allott		
N.G. Cowans		
Extras	(LB 2, W 2, NB 4)	8
TOTAL	(55 overs) (for 7 wkts)	**231**

						Fall	
Lawson	11	0	53	2	1st	63
McDermott	11	0	56	2	2nd	69
O'Donnell	11	2	32	2	3rd	134
Thomson	11	0	47	1	4th	193
Matthews	10	0	38	0	5th	206
Border	1	0	3	0	6th	208
					7th	216

AUSTRALIA
K.C. Wessels	c & b Willey	57
G.M. Wood	lbw b Cowans	5
D.M. Wellham	lbw b Botham	7
A.R. Border*	not out	85
D.C. Boon	b Allott	13
W.B. Phillips+	c Gatting b Cowans	14
S.P. O'Donnell	b Botham	28
G.R.J. Matthews	not out	8
G.F. Lawson		
C.J. McDermott		
J.R. Thomson		
Extras	(LB 13, W 2, NB 1)	16
TOTAL	(54 overs) (for 6 wkts)	**233**

						Fall	
Botham	10	2	38	2	1st	10
Cowans	11	2	42	2	2nd	19
Allott	10	1	40	1	3rd	116
Willey	11	1	38	1	4th	137
Edmonds	10	0	48	0	5th	157
Gooch	2	0	14	0	6th	222

Match No: 109/33

ENGLAND v AUSTRALIA

Texaco Trophy
Played at Lord's, London on 03/06/1985
Toss: England   Result: England won by 8 wickets
Umpires: H.D. Bird and B.J. Meyer
Man of the match: D.I. Gower
Debuts: None

AUSTRALIA

G.M. Wood	not out	114
A.M.J. Hilditch	lbw b Foster	4
G.M. Ritchie	c Gooch b Botham	15
A.R. Border*	b Gooch	44
D.C. Boon	c Gower b Willey	45
W.B. Phillips+	run out	10
S.P. O'Donnell	not out	0
G.R.J. Matthews		
G.F. Lawson		
C.J. McDermott		
J.R. Thomson		
Extras	(B 2, LB 13, W 6, NB 1)	22
TOTAL	(55 overs) (for 5 wkts)	**254**

						Fall	
Cowans	8	2	22	0	1st	6
Foster	11	0	55	1	2nd	47
Botham	8	1	27	1	3rd	143
Allott	7	1	45	0	4th	228
Gooch	11	0	46	1	5th	252
Willey	10	1	44	1		

ENGLAND

G.A. Gooch	not out	117
R.T. Robinson	lbw b McDermott	7
D.I. Gower*	c Border b McDermott	102
A.J. Lamb	not out	9
I.T. Botham		
M.W. Gatting		
P. Willey		
P.R. Downton+		
N.A. Foster		
P.J.W. Allott		
N.G. Cowans		
Extras	(B 2, LB 9, W 2, NB 9)	22
TOTAL	(49 overs) (for 2 wkts)	**257**

						Fall	
Lawson	9	0	37	0	1st	25
McDermott	10	0	51	2	2nd	227
Thomson	8	1	50	0		
O'Donnell	11	0	54	0		
Matthews	10	0	49	0		
Border	1	0	5	0		

Match No: 110/19

WEST INDIES v ENGLAND

Played at Sabina Park, Kingston, Jamaica on 18/02/1986
Toss: West Indies **Result:** West Indies won by 6 wickets
Umpires: D.M. Archer and A. Gaynor
Man of the match: M.D. Marshall
Debuts: Eng - L.B. Taylor, J.G. Thomas   WI - B.P. Patterson

ENGLAND

Batsman	Dismissal	Runs
G.A. Gooch	b Marshall	36
R.T. Robinson	b Patterson	0
D.I. Gower*	c Richards b Patterson	0
M.W. Gatting	b Marshall	10
A.J. Lamb	c Greenidge b Marshall	30
P. Willey	c Richardson b Marshall	26
P.R. Downton+	lbw b Garner	8
J.E. Emburey	b Garner	5
N.A. Foster	not out	5
J.G. Thomas	not out	0
L.B. Taylor		
Extras	(B 8, LB 2, W 4, NB 11)	25
TOTAL	(46 overs) (for 8 wkts)	**145**

Bowler	O	M	R	W	Fall	
Garner	10	0	18	2	1st	2
Patterson	7	0	17	2	2nd	10
Walsh	9	0	42	0	3rd	47
Marshall	10	1	23	4	4th	63
Harper	10	0	35	0	5th	125
					6th	125
					7th	137
					8th	143

WEST INDIES

Batsman	Dismissal	Runs
C.G. Greenidge	c Downton b Thomas	45
D.L. Haynes	c Downton b Foster	35
R.B. Richardson	lbw b Gooch	32
H.A. Gomes	st Downton b Willey	19
P.J.L. Dujon+	not out	3
R.A. Harper	not out	1
I.V.A. Richards*		
M.D. Marshall		
J. Garner		
B.P. Patterson		
C.A. Walsh		
Extras	(B 4, LB 2, NB 5)	11
TOTAL	(43.5 overs) (for 4 wkts)	**146**

Bowler	O	M	R	W	Fall	
Taylor	7	2	17	0	1st	84
Thomas	8	1	35	1	2nd	89
Foster	10	1	44	1	3rd	142
Emburey	10	3	19	0	4th	142
Willey	6.5	0	25	1		
Gooch	2	2	0	1		

Match No: 111/20

WEST INDIES v ENGLAND

Played at Queens Park Oval, Port of Spain, Trinidad on 04/03/1986
Toss: England   **Result:** England won by 5 wickets
Umpires: C.E. Cumberbatch and S. Mohammed
Man of the match: G.A. Gooch
Debuts: Eng - W.N. Slack, D.M. Smith   WI - C.A. Best

WEST INDIES

D.L. Haynes	b Foster	53
C.A. Best	run out	10
R.B. Richardson	not out	79
I.V.A. Richards*	c Foster b Botham	82
R.A. Harper	not out	0
H.A. Gomes		
T.R.O. Payne+		
M.D. Marshall		
J. Garner		
C.A. Walsh		
B.P. Patterson		
Extras	(LB 4, NB 1)	5
TOTAL	(37 overs) (for 3 wkts)	**229**

Fall
1st 37
2nd 106
3rd 223

Botham	8	1	59	1	
Foster	10	1	42	1	
Ellison	8	0	57	0	
Emburey	8	2	48	0	
Willey	3	0	19	0	

ENGLAND

G.A. Gooch	not out	129
I.T. Botham	c Richards b Garner	8
W.N. Slack	c Payne b Walsh	34
A.J. Lamb	b Garner	16
D.I. Gower*	run out	9
P. Willey	c Richards b Garner	10
D.M. Smith	not out	10
P.R. Downton+		
R.M. Ellison		
J.E. Emburey		
N.A. Foster		
Extras	(B 1, LB 7, NB 6)	14
TOTAL	(37 overs) (for 5 wkts)	**230**

Fall
1st 9
2nd 98
3rd 143
4th 170
5th 183

Garner	9	1	62	3	
Patterson	6	0	30	0	
Walsh	9	0	49	1	
Marshall	10	1	59	0	
Harper	3	0	22	0	

Match No: 112/21

WEST INDIES v ENGLAND

Played at Kensington Oval, Bridgetown, Barbados on 19/03/1986
Toss: England   **Result:** West Indies won by 135 runs
Umpires: D.M. Archer and L.H. Barker
Man of the match: I.V.A. Richards
Debuts: None

WEST INDIES

C.G. Greenidge	c Downton b Foster	31
D.L. Haynes	b Foster	28
R.B. Richardson	b Botham	62
I.V.A. Richards*	c Foster b Emburey	62
P.J.L. Dujon+	c Lamb b Foster	23
R.A. Harper	not out	24
J. Garner	b Emburey	3
M.D. Marshall	c & b Botham	9
M.A. Holding	not out	0
H.A. Gomes		
B.P. Patterson		
Extras	(B 4, W 2, NB 1)	7
TOTAL	(46 overs) (for 7 wkts)	**249**

						Fall	
Botham	9	2	39	2		1st	61
Thomas	7	1	50	0		2nd	64
Foster	9	0	39	3		3rd	181
Willey	6	0	21	0		4th	195
Gooch	6	1	41	0		5th	225
Emburey	9	0	55	2		6th	239
						7th	248

ENGLAND

G.A. Gooch	c Dujon b Garner	6
R.T. Robinson	c Richardson b Marshall	23
W.N. Slack	c Dujon b Holding	9
D.I. Gower*	lbw b Marshall	0
A.J. Lamb	c Marshall b Holding	18
I.T. Botham	c Garner b Marshall	14
P. Willey	c Greenidge b Harper	9
P.R. Downton+	b Harper	0
J.E. Emburey	c Dujon b Patterson	15
N.A. Foster	not out	9
J.G. Thomas	c Richards b Patterson	0
Extras	(LB 3, W 3, NB 5)	11
TOTAL	(39 overs)	**114**

						Fall	
Garner	6	2	6	1		1st	18
Patterson	9	1	38	2		2nd	42
Marshall	6	2	14	3		3rd	42
Holding	10	1	29	2		4th	46
Harper	8	1	24	2		5th	69
						6th	81
						7th	82
						8th	85
						9th	113
						10th	114

Match No: 113/22

WEST INDIES v ENGLAND

Played at Queens Park Oval, Port of Spain, Trinidad on 31/03/1986
Toss: West Indies   **Result:** West Indies won by 8 wickets
Umpires: C.E. Cumberbatch and S. Mohammed
Man of the match: J. Garner
Debuts: None

ENGLAND
G.A. Gooch	c Richards b Marshall	10
R.T. Robinson	b Marshall	55
D.I. Gower*	b Walsh	20
A.J. Lamb	c Dujon b Walsh	16
I.T. Botham	c Harper b Garner	29
P. Willey	c Greenidge b Marshall	6
P.R. Downton+	c Greenidge b Marshall	12
R.M. Ellison	b Garner	5
J.E. Emburey	not out	2
P.H. Edmonds	b Garner	0
N.A. Foster		
Extras	(B 1, LB 4, W 2, NB 3)	10
TOTAL	(47 overs) (for 9 wkts)	**165**

						Fall	
Marshall	9	0	37	4		1st	15
Garner	9	1	22	3		2nd	49
Holding	9	1	32	0		3rd	88
Walsh	10	0	25	2		4th	126
Harper	10	0	44	0		5th	138
						6th	154
						7th	161
						8th	165
						9th	165

WEST INDIES
C.G. Greenidge	b Foster	0
D.L. Haynes	not out	77
R.B. Richardson	c Gooch b Emburey	31
I.V.A. Richards*	not out	50
H.A. Gomes		
P.J.L. Dujon+		
R.A. Harper		
M.D. Marshall		
M.A. Holding		
J. Garner		
C.A. Walsh		
Extras	(LB 7, W 1)	8
TOTAL	(38.2 overs) (for 2 wkts)	**166**

						Fall	
Foster	6	1	27	1		1st	0
Ellison	7	0	30	0		2nd	75
Botham	5	0	24	0			
Edmonds	10	1	38	0			
Emburey	10	2	31	1			
Gower	0.2	0	9	0			

Match No: 114/16

ENGLAND v INDIA

Texaco Trophy
Played at The Oval, London on 24/05/1986
Toss: India   Result: India won by 9 wickets
Umpires: D.R. Shepherd and A.G.T. Whitehead
Man of the match: M. Azharuddin
Debuts: None

ENGLAND

G.A. Gooch	c Azharuddin b Chetan Sharma	30
G. Fowler	run out	20
M.W. Gatting	c Kapil Dev b Shastri	27
D.I. Gower*	c Kapil Dev b Shastri	0
A.J. Lamb	c Kapil Dev b Maninder Singh	0
D.R. Pringle	c Azharuddin b Chetan Sharma	28
P.R. Downton+	c Azharuddin b Binny	4
R.M. Ellison	c & b Binny	10
J.E. Emburey	run out	20
G.R. Dilley	c Pandit b Chetan Sharma	6
L.B. Taylor	not out	1
Extras	(B 1, LB 10, W 3, NB 2)	16
TOTAL	(55 overs)	**162**

						Fall	
Kapil Dev	11	1	32	0	1st	54
Binny	11	2	38	2	2nd	67
Chetan Sharma	11	2	25	3	3rd	67
Maninder Singh	11	1	31	1	4th	70
Shastri	11	0	25	2	5th	102
					6th	115
					7th	131
					8th	138
					9th	151
					10th	162

INDIA

K. Srikkanth	c Downton b Dilley	0
S.M. Gavaskar	not out	65
M. Azharuddin	not out	83
D.B. Vengsarkar		
S.M. Patil		
R.J. Shastri		
Kapil Dev*		
C.S. Pandit+		
Chetan Sharma		
R.M.H. Binny		
Maninder Singh		
Extras	(LB 9, W 4, NB 2)	15
TOTAL	(47.2 overs) (for 1 wkt)	**163**

						Fall	
Dilley	11	0	53	1	1st	0
Taylor	7	1	30	0		
Pringle	8.2	4	20	0		
Ellison	10	1	36	0		
Emburey	11	2	15	0		

Match No: 115/17

ENGLAND v INDIA

Texaco Trophy
Played at Old Trafford, Manchester on 26/05/1986
Toss: England Result: England won by 5 wickets
Umpires: H.D. Bird and D.J. Constant
Man of the match: D.I. Gower
Debuts: None

INDIA

K. Srikkanth	c Fowler b Emburey	67
S.M. Gavaskar	c Gooch b Ellison	4
M. Azharuddin	c Gower b Edmonds	7
D.B. Vengsarkar	b Emburey	29
S.M. Patil	b Dilley	12
R.J. Shastri	not out	62
Kapil Dev*	c Downton b Dilley	51
Chetan Sharma	not out	8
C.S. Pandit+		
R.M.H. Binny		
Maninder Singh		
Extras	(B 5, LB 4, W 2, NB 3)	14
TOTAL	(55 overs) (for 6 wkts)	254

						Fall	
Dilley	11	2	46	2	1st	4
Ellison	11	0	55	1	2nd	49
Pringle	11	0	49	0	3rd	109
Edmonds	11	1	49	1	4th	117
Emburey	11	1	46	2	5th	130
					6th	234

ENGLAND

G.A. Gooch	lbw b Kapil Dev	10
G. Fowler	c & b Binny	10
D.I. Gower*	b Binny	81
A.J. Lamb	run out	45
M.W. Gatting	run out	39
D.R. Pringle	not out	49
P.R. Downton+	not out	4
P.H. Edmonds		
J.E. Emburey		
R.M. Ellison		
G.R. Dilley		
Extras	(LB 13, W 5)	18
TOTAL	(53.5 overs) (for 5 wkts)	256

						Fall	
Kapil Dev	10	0	41	1	1st	18
Binny	10	1	47	2	2nd	27
Chetan Sharma	9.5	0	49	0	3rd	142
Shastri	11	0	37	0	4th	157
Maninder Singh	11	0	55	0	5th	242
Azharuddin	2	0	14	0		

Match No: 116/22

ENGLAND v NEW ZEALAND

Texaco Trophy
Played at Headingley, Leeds on 16/07/1986
Toss: New Zealand **Result:** New Zealand won by 47 runs
Umpires: J. Birkenshaw and B.J. Meyer
Man of the match: J.J. Crowe
Debuts: Eng - M.R. Benson

NEW ZEALAND
B.A. Edgar	lbw b Foster	0
J.G. Wright	c Richards b Ellison	21
K.R. Rutherford	b Ellison	11
M.D. Crowe	b Ellison	9
J.V. Coney*	run out	27
J.J. Crowe	c & b Foster	66
R.J. Hadlee	lbw b Dilley	11
E.J. Gray	not out	30
I.D.S. Smith+	run out	4
J.G. Bracewell	not out	10
E.J. Chatfield		
Extras	(LB 18, W 7, NB 3)	28
TOTAL	(55 overs) (for 8 wkts)	**217**

						Fall	
Dilley	11	1	37	1	1st	9
Foster	9	1	27	2	2nd	36
Pringle	9	0	42	0	3rd	48
Ellison	11	1	43	3	4th	54
Emburey	11	0	30	0	5th	112
Gooch	4	0	20	0	6th	138
					7th	165
					8th	187

ENGLAND
G.A. Gooch	b Hadlee	18
M.R. Benson	c Chatfield b Bracewell	24
D.I. Gower	b Coney	18
A.J. Lamb	run out	33
M.W. Gatting*	b Gray	19
D.R. Pringle	c Rutherford b Gray	28
C.J. Richards+	run out	8
J.E. Emburey	lbw b Bracewell	0
R.M. Ellison	run out	12
N.A. Foster	b Hadlee	5
G.R. Dilley	not out	2
Extras	(LB 1, W 2)	3
TOTAL	(48.2 overs)	**170**

						Fall	
Hadlee	9.2	0	29	2	1st	38
Chatfield	8	2	24	0	2nd	48
Bracewell	11	2	27	2	3rd	83
M.D. Crowe	4	0	15	0	4th	103
Gray	11	1	55	2	5th	131
Coney	5	0	19	1	6th	143
					7th	144
					8th	162
					9th	165
					10th	170

Match No: 117/23

ENGLAND v NEW ZEALAND

Texaco Trophy
Played at Old Trafford, Manchester on 18/07/1986
Toss: England   **Result:** England won by 6 wickets
Umpires: K.E. Palmer and N.T. Plews
Man of the match: C.W.J. Athey
Debuts: None

NEW ZEALAND
J.G. Wright	c Pringle b Emburey	39
B.A. Edgar	lbw b Dilley	5
K.R. Rutherford	b Edmonds	63
M.D. Crowe	not out	93
J.V. Coney*	run out	1
J.J. Crowe	b Pringle	48
R.J. Hadlee	not out	18
E.J. Gray		
I.D.S. Smith+		
J.G. Bracewell		
W. Watson		
Extras	(LB 2, W 14, NB 1)	17
TOTAL	(55 overs) (for 5 wkts)	**284**

	O	M	R	W	Fall	
Dilley	9	0	55	1	1st	16
Foster	7	0	40	0	2nd	89
Pringle	10	2	63	1	3rd	133
Gooch	7	0	48	0	4th	136
Edmonds	11	1	42	1	5th	249
Emburey	11	1	34	1		

ENGLAND
G.A. Gooch	c & b Coney	91
C.W.J. Athey	not out	142
D.I. Gower	c Wright b Coney	9
A.J. Lamb	b Bracewell	28
M.W. Gatting*	b M.D. Crowe	7
D.R. Pringle	not out	0
C.J. Richards+		
J.E. Emburey		
P.H. Edmonds		
N.A. Foster		
G.R. Dilley		
Extras	(LB 5, W 3, NB 1)	9
TOTAL	(53.4 overs) (for 4 wkts)	**286**

	O	M	R	W	Fall	
Hadlee	11	1	34	0	1st	193
Watson	11	1	46	0	2nd	219
Crowe M.D.	6	0	36	1	3rd	265
Bracewell	10.4	0	67	1	4th	274
Gray	4	0	39	0		
Coney	11	0	59	2		

Match No: 118/34

AUSTRALIA v ENGLAND

Benson & Hedges Perth Challenge
Played at WACA Ground, Perth on 01/01/1987
Toss: England   Result: England won by 37 runs
Umpires: R.A. French and P.J. McConnell
Man of the match: I.T. Botham
Debuts: Eng - B.C. Broad, P.A.J. DeFreitas, G.C. Small

ENGLAND
B.C. Broad	run out	76
C.W.J. Athey	c Zoehrer b O'Donnell	34
D.I. Gower	c Zoehrer b Whitney	6
A.J. Lamb	c Zoehrer b Reid	66
I.T. Botham	c Zoehrer b Waugh	68
M.W. Gatting*	not out	5
C.J. Richards+	c Border b Reid	4
P.A.J. DeFreitas	not out	0
J.E. Embury		
G.C. Small		
G.R. Dilley		
Extras	(B 2, LB 6, W 4, NB 1)	13
TOTAL	(49 overs) (for 6 wkts)	272

						Fall	
Davis	8	1	48	0	1st	86
Whitney	10	0	56	1	2nd	95
MacLeay	9	0	51	0	3rd	150
Reid	10	1	46	2	4th	256
O'Donnell	7	0	39	1	5th	262
Waugh	5	0	24	1	6th	271

AUSTRALIA
G.R. Marsh	b Botham	28
D.C. Boon	c Emburey b DeFreitas	1
D.M. Jones	c Gower b Dilley	104
A.R. Border*	b Emburey	26
S.R. Waugh	c Richards b Small	16
S.P. O'Donnell	run out	0
K.H. MacLeay	c Emburey b Dilley	21
T.J. Zoehrer+	c Botham b DeFreitas	1
M.R. Whitney	run out	6
B.A. Reid	b DeFreitas	10
S.P. Davis	not out	1
Extras	(LB 7, W 10, NB 4)	21
TOTAL	(48.2 overs)	235

						Fall	
DeFreitas	9.2	0	42	3	1st	7
Dilley	10	1	31	2	2nd	50
Botham	10	0	52	1	3rd	125
Small	9	0	62	1	4th	149
Emburey	10	0	41	1	5th	158
					6th	210
					7th	214
					8th	217
					9th	233
					10th	235

Match No: 119/23
ENGLAND v WEST INDIES

Benson & Hedges Perth Challenge
Played at WACA Ground, Perth on 03/01/1987
Toss: West Indies   Result: England won by 19 runs
Umpires: R.A. French and P.J. McConnell
Man of the match: G.R. Dilley
Debuts: None

ENGLAND
B.C. Broad	c Garner b Marshall	0
C.W.J. Athey	c Richardson b Garner	1
D.I. Gower	c Dujon b Garner	11
A.J. Lamb	c Harper b Marshall	71
M.W. Gatting*	c Garner b Walsh	15
I.T. Botham	c Greenidge b Harper	11
C.J. Richards+	c Dujon b Garner	50
J.E. Emburey	c Harper b Garner	18
P.H. Edmonds	not out	16
G.R. Dilley	c & b Garner	1
G.C. Small	not out	8
Extras	(LB 10, W 8, NB 8)	26
TOTAL	(50 overs) (for 9 wkts)	**228**

						Fall	
Marshall	10	1	30	2	1st	3
Garner	10	0	47	5	2nd	10
Holding	10	0	33	0	3rd	35
Walsh	9	0	40	1	4th	67
Harper	10	0	63	1	5th	96
Richards	1	0	5	0	6th	156
					7th	194
					8th	209
					9th	211

WEST INDIES
C.G. Greenidge	b Small	20
D.L. Haynes	lbw b Small	4
R.B. Richardson	c Gatting b Botham	12
I.V.A. Richards*	c Broad b Emburey	45
A.L. Logie	c Richards b Dilley	51
P.J.L. Dujon+	b Dilley	36
R.A.. Harper	run out	4
M.D. Marshall	b Dilley	7
M.A. Holding	c Edmonds b Dilley	7
J. Garner	not out	4
C.A. Walsh	lbw b Emburey	0
Extras	(B 4, LB 9, W 4, NB 2)	19
TOTAL	(48.2 overs)	**209**

						Fall	
Dilley	10	0	46	4	1st	9
Small	10	1	37	2	2nd	39
Botham	10	1	29	1	3rd	51
Edmonds	9	1	53	0	4th	104
Emburey	9.2	0	31	2	5th	178
					6th	187
					7th	187
					8th	201
					9th	208
					10th	209

Match No: 120/17

ENGLAND v PAKISTAN

Benson & Hedges Perth Challenge
Played at WACA Ground, Perth on 05/01/1987
Toss: Pakistan   **Result:** England won by 3 wickets
Umpires: A.R. Crafter and R.A. French
Man of the match: B.C. Broad
Debuts: None

PAKISTAN
Qasim Omar	b Botham	32
Shoaib Mohammad	c DeFreitas b Emburey	66
Ramiz Raja	run out	15
Javed Miandad	c Athey b Emburey	59
Imran Khan*	c Gower b DeFreitas	23
Manzoor Elahi	not out	9
Wasim Akram	not out	1
Asif Mujtaba		
Salim Yousuf+		
Mudassar Nazar		
Salim Jaffer		
Extras	(LB 15, W 1, NB 8)	24
TOTAL	(50 overs) (for 5 wkts)	**229**

						Fall	
DeFreitas	9	1	24	1	1st	61
Small	10	0	41	0	2nd	98
Foster	4	0	23	0	3rd	156
Botham	10	1	37	1	4th	198
Gatting	7	0	24	0	5th	225
Emburey	10	0	65	2		

ENGLAND
B.C. Broad	c Salim Yousuf b Imran Khan	97
C.W.J. Athey	b Manzoor Elahi	42
D.I. Gower	c Shoaib Mohammad b Mudassar Nazar	2
A.J. Lamb	c Javed Miandad b Shoaib Mohammad	32
I.T. Botham	c Ramiz Raja b Wasim Akram	10
M.W. Gatting*	run out	7
C.J. Richards+	run out	0
P.A.J. DeFreitas	not out	13
J.E. Emburey	not out	11
N.A. Foster		
G.C. Small		
Extras	(B 1, LB 13, W 3, NB 1)	18
TOTAL	(49.4 overs) (for 7 wkts)	**232**

						Fall	
Wasim Akram	9.4	1	28	1	1st	104
Salim Jaffer	10	2	43	0	2nd	108
Imran Khan	9	0	41	1	3rd	156
Mudassar Nazar	10	0	39	1	4th	184
Asif Mujtaba	3	0	19	0	5th	199
Manzoor Elahi	3	0	24	1	6th	204
Shoaib Mohammad	5	0	24	1	7th	208

Match No: 121/18

ENGLAND v PAKISTAN

Benson & Hedges Perth Challenge Final
Played at WACA Ground, Perth on 07/01/1987
Toss: England   **Result:** England won by 5 wickets
Umpires: A.R. Crafter and R.A. French
Man of the match: Javed Miandad
Debuts: None

PAKISTAN
Qasim Omar	c Broad b Botham	21
Shoaib Mohammad	b Dilley	0
Ramiz Raja	c Athey b Botham	22
Javed Miandad	not out	77
Asif Mujtaba	c Gower b Botham	7
Imran Khan*	c Richards b Gatting	5
Manzoor Elahi	c Gower b Small	20
Salim Yousuf+	c Athey b Small	0
Mudassar Nazar	c Gower b Emburey	0
Wasim Akram	c Gatting b Small	2
Salim Jaffer	not out	3
Extras	(LB 5, W 1, NB 3)	9
TOTAL	(50 overs) (for 9 wkts)	**166**

						Fall	
DeFreitas	10	1	33	0	1st	2
Dilley	10	0	23	1	2nd	36
Botham	10	2	29	3	3rd	58
Small	10	0	28	3	4th	76
Emburey	8	0	34	1	5th	89
Gatting	2	0	14	1	6th	127
					7th	127
					8th	128
					9th	131

ENGLAND
B.C. Broad	c Salim Yousuf b Wasim Akram	0
C.W.J. Athey	c Salim Yousuf b Imran Khan	1
D.I. Gower	c Shoaib Mohammad b Imran Khan	31
A.J. Lamb	c Salim Yousuf b Wasim Akram	47
M.W. Gatting*	b Wasim Akram	49
I.T. Botham	not out	23
C.J. Richards+	not out	7
P.A.J. DeFreitas		
J.E. Emburey		
G.R. Dilley		
G.C. Small		
Extras	(LB 8, W 1)	9
TOTAL	(40.1 overs) (for 5 wkts)	**167**

						Fall	
Imran Khan	8	2	30	2	1st	1
Wasim Akram	10	2	27	3	2nd	7
Salim Jaffer	10	1	43	0	3rd	47
Mudassar Nazar	5.1	0	22	0	4th	136
Shoaib Mohammad	2	0	11	0	5th	145
Manzoor Elahi	5	0	26	0		

Matches 133

Match No: 122/24

ENGLAND v WEST INDIES

Benson & Hedges World Series Cup
Played at Woolloongabba, Brisbane on 17/01/1987
Toss: England   **Result:** England won by 6 wickets
Umpires: M.W. Johnson and P.J. McConnell
Man of the match: G.R. Dilley
Debuts: None

WEST INDIES
C.G. Greenidge	lbw b DeFreitas	0
D.L. Haynes	c DeFreitas b Emburey	48
R.B. Richardson	c Botham b Dilley	15
I.V.A. Richards*	b Dilley	0
A.L. Logie	c Lamb b Emburey	46
P.J.L. Dujon+	b DeFreitas	22
R.A. Harper	lbw b Small	2
M.D. Marshall	b Dilley	13
M.A. Holding	c Richards b Emburey	0
J. Garner	c Richards b Dilley	1
C.A. Walsh	not out	3
Extras	(LB 4)	4
TOTAL	(46.3 overs)	**154**

						Fall	
Dilley	8.3	1	23	4	1st	1
DeFreitas	9	2	17	2	2nd	26
Botham	10	1	46	0	3rd	26
Small	10	1	29	1	4th	112
Emburey	9	0	35	3	5th	120
					6th	122
					7th	147
					8th	148
					9th	151
					10th	154

ENGLAND
B.C. Broad	b Richards	49
C.W.J. Athey	c Dujon b Holding	14
D.I. Gower	c Garner b Harper	42
A.J. Lamb	c sub (W.K.M. Benjamin) b Harper	22
M.W. Gatting*	not out	3
I.T. Botham	not out	14
C.J. Richards+		
P.A.J. DeFreitas		
J.E. Emburey		
G.C. Small		
G.R. Dilley		
Extras	(LB 2, W 2, NB 8)	12
TOTAL	(43.1 overs) (for 4 wkts)	**156**

						Fall	
Marshall	5	1	11	0	1st	30
Garner	4	0	17	0	2nd	91
Holding	6	0	33	1	3rd	134
Walsh	7.1	0	19	0	4th	140
Harper	10	0	43	2		
Richards	10	1	27	1		
Richardson	1	0	4	0		

Match No: 123/35

AUSTRALIA v ENGLAND

Benson & Hedges World Series Cup
Played at Woolloongabba, Brisbane on 18/01/1987
Toss: Australia   Result: Australia won by 11 runs
Umpires: M.W. Johnson and P.J. McConnell
Man of the match: D.M. Jones
Debuts: Aus - P.L. Taylor

AUSTRALIA
G.R. Marsh	lbw b Dilley	93
D.M. Wellham	c Emburey b Small	26
D.M. Jones	b Emburey	101
A.R. Border*	b Dilley	11
S.R. Waugh	not out	14
S.P. O'Donnell	not out	3
G.R.J. Matthews		
K.H. MacLeay		
T.J. Zoehrer+		
P.L. Taylor		
B.A. Reid		
Extras	(LB 9, W 3, NB 1)	13
TOTAL	(50 overs) (for 4 wkts)	261

						Fall	
Dilley	10	2	40	2	1st	48
DeFreitas	10	2	41	0	2nd	226
Small	10	0	57	1	3rd	234
Botham	10	0	54	0	4th	246
Emburey	10	0	60	1		

ENGLAND
B.C. Broad	c Matthews b O'Donnell	15
C.W.J. Athey	c O'Donnell b Reid	111
D.I. Gower	b Waugh	15
A.J. Lamb	c Marsh b Matthews	6
I.T. Botham	b O'Donnell	22
M.W. Gatting*	b Taylor	30
C.J. Richards+	c O'Donnell b Reid	7
P.A.J. DeFreitas	c Border b Waugh	6
J.E. Emburey	not out	24
G.C. Small	run out	2
G.R. Dilley	not out	0
Extras	(B 1, LB 10, NB 1)	12
TOTAL	(50 overs) (for 9 wkts)	250

						Fall	
MacLeay	8	0	39	0	1st	48
Reid	10	1	34	2	2nd	73
O'Donnell	10	0	59	2	3rd	92
Waugh	9	0	56	2	4th	149
Matthews	10	0	34	1	5th	197
Taylor	3	0	17	1	6th	210
					7th	218
					8th	225
					9th	250

Match No: 124/36

AUSTRALIA v ENGLAND

Benson & Hedges World Series Cup
Played at Sydney Cricket Ground on 22/01/1987
Toss: Australia   **Result:** England won by 3 wickets
Umpires: A.R. Crafter and R.A. French
Man of the match: A.J.Lamb
Debuts: None

AUSTRALIA

G.R. Marsh	c Richards b Edmonds	47
D.M. Wellham	c Athey b Emburey	97
D.M. Jones	c Athey b DeFreitas	34
A.R. Border*	c Dilley b Edmonds	13
S.R. Waugh	c Athey b Dilley	10
G.R.J. Matthews	c DeFreitas b Emburey	2
K.H. MacLeay	b Dilley	12
T.J. Zoehrer+	not out	9
P.L. Taylor	st Richards b Emburey	0
S.P. O'Donnell		
B.A. Reid		
Extras	(B 2, LB 5, NB 2)	9
TOTAL	(50 overs) (for 8 wkts)	**233**

						Fall	
Dilley	9	2	28	2	1st	109
DeFreitas	10	0	46	1	2nd	156
Gatting	2	0	11	0	3rd	189
Botham	10	0	51	0	4th	205
Emburey	9	0	42	3	5th	208
Edmonds	10	0	48	2	6th	208
					7th	230
					8th	233

ENGLAND

B.C. Broad	c Matthews b Taylor	45
C.W.J. Athey	c Zoehrer b Reid	2
D.I. Gower	c Wellham b O'Donnell	50
A.J. Lamb	not out	77
M.W. Gatting*	b O'Donnell	1
I.T. Botham	b Waugh	27
J.E. Emburey	run out	4
C.J. Richards+	c Waugh b O'Donnell	3
P.A.J. DeFreitas	not out	6
P.H. Edmonds		
G.R. Dilley		
Extras	(LB 16, W 2, NB 1)	19
TOTAL	(49.5 overs) (for 7 wkts)	**234**

						Fall	
MacLeay	4	0	22	0	1st	33
Reid	9.5	3	44	1	2nd	51
Taylor	10	0	42	1	3rd	137
Waugh	5	0	22	1	4th	143
Matthews	10	1	36	0	5th	186
Border	3	0	13	0	6th	191
O'Donnell	8	0	39	3	7th	202

Match No: 125/25

ENGLAND v WEST INDIES

Benson & Hedges World Series Cup
Played at Adelaide Oval on 24/01/1987
Toss: West Indies**Result:** England won by 89 runs
Umpires: B.E. Martin and S.G. Randell
Man of the match: B.C. Broad
Debuts: None

ENGLAND

B.C. Broad	st Dujon b Richards	55
C.W.J. Athey	c Marshall b Harper	64
D.I. Gower	c Haynes b Gray	29
I.T. Botham	c Logie b Walsh	7
A.J. Lamb	not out	33
M.W. Gatting*	c Dujon b Walsh	3
C.J. Richards+	b Marshall	18
J.E. Emburey	not out	16
P.A.J. DeFreitas		
G.C. Small		
G.R. Dilley		
Extras	(B 4, LB 13, W 5, NB 5)	27
TOTAL	(50 overs) (for 6 wkts)	252

						Fall	
Marshall	9	1	39	1	1st	121
Gray	10	0	43	1	2nd	148
Garner	9	1	31	0	3rd	161
Walsh	10	0	55	2	4th	177
Harper	9	0	46	1	5th	182
Richards	3	0	21	1	6th	220

WEST INDIES

C.G. Greenidge	lbw b DeFreitas	3
D.L. Haynes	b Small	22
R.B. Richardson	c Lamb b DeFreitas	3
I.V.A. Richards*	c Broad b Botham	43
A.L. Logie	c Gower b Dilley	43
P.J.L. Dujon+	c Dilley b Emburey	25
R.A. Harper	c Dilley b Emburey	4
M.D. Marshall	c Athey b Emburey	3
J. Garner	c DeFreitas b Emburey	0
A.H. Gray	not out	7
C.A. Walsh	b DeFreitas	3
Extras	(W 2, NB 5)	7
TOTAL	(45.5 overs)	163

						Fall	
Dilley	8	1	19	1	1st	3
DeFreitas	7.5	1	15	3	2nd	15
Botham	10	0	46	1	3rd	60
Small	10	1	46	1	4th	92
Emburey	10	0	37	4	5th	136
						6th	141
						7th	150
						8th	150
						9th	157
						10th	163

Match No: 126/37

AUSTRALIA v ENGLAND

Benson & Hedges World Series Cup
Played at Adelaide Oval on 26/01/1987
Toss: Australia
Umpires: A.R. Crafter and S.G. Randell
Man of the match: S.R. Waugh
Debuts: None

Result: Australia won by 33 runs

AUSTRALIA
G.R. Marsh	c Emburey b DeFreitas	8
D.M. Wellham	c Richards b DeFreitas	9
D.M. Jones	c Richards b DeFreitas	8
A.R. Border*	c Broad b DeFreitas	91
S.R. Waugh	not out	83
S.P. O'Donnell	run out	6
G.R.J. Matthews	c Lamb b Dilley	0
T.J. Zoehrer+	not out	5
K.H. MacLeay		
P.L. Taylor		
S.P. Davis		
Extras	(B 1, LB 8, W 4, NB 2)	15
TOTAL	(50 overs) (for 6 wkts)	**225**

	O	M	R	W		Fall
Dilley	10	1	41	1	1st	21
DeFreitas	10	1	35	4	2nd	24
Botham	10	0	42	0	3rd	37
Small	10	0	42	0	4th	201
Emburey	10	0	56	0	5th	211
					6th	219

ENGLAND
B.C. Broad	c Border b Waugh	46
C.W.J. Athey	lbw b Davis	12
D.I. Gower	c Waugh b O'Donnell	21
M.W. Gatting*	b Taylor	46
A.J. Lamb	run out	8
I.T. Botham	st Zoehrer b Taylor	18
C.J. Richards+	b Waugh	2
J.E. Emburey	run out	17
P.A.J. DeFreitas	c Jones b Taylor	8
G.C. Small	b MacLeay	2
G.R. Dilley	not out	3
Extras	(LB 8, W 1)	9
TOTAL	(48.1 overs)	**192**

	O	M	R	W		Fall
Davis	8	0	18	1	1st	23
MacLeay	10	1	43	1	2nd	55
Matthews	4	0	21	0	3rd	125
O'Donnell	9	0	43	1	4th	138
Waugh	10	1	30	2	5th	144
Taylor	7.1	0	29	3	6th	152
					7th	168
					8th	184
					9th	188
					10th	192

Match No: 127/26

ENGLAND v WEST INDIES

Benson & Hedges World Series Cup
Played at Melbourne Cricket Ground on 30/01/1987
Toss: England   **Result:** West Indies won by 6 wickets
Umpires: R.C. Bailhache and S.G. Randell
Man of the match: I.V.A. Richards
Debuts: None

ENGLAND

B.C. Broad	c Garner b Holding	33
C.W.J. Athey	lbw b Garner	2
D.I. Gower	b Marshall	8
A.J. Lamb	run out	0
M.W. Gatting*	b Harper	13
I.T. Botham	c & b Holding	15
J.E. Emburey	c Harper b Garner	34
C.J. Richards+	b Marshall	8
P.A.J. DeFreitas	c Haynes b Garner	13
N.A. Foster	b Marshall	5
G.C. Small	not out	1
Extras	(LB 3, W 4, NB 8)	15
TOTAL	**(48.2 overs)**	**147**

					Fall	
Marshall	9.2	2	30	3	1st	11
Garner	9	1	37	3	2nd	27
Holding	8.3	2	19	2	3rd	37
Walsh	5	1	16	0	4th	61
Harper	10	0	26	1	5th	77
Richards	6.3	1	16	0	6th	84
					7th	111
					8th	136
					9th	144
					10th	147

WEST INDIES

D.L. Haynes	lbw b Foster	13
R.B. Richardson	c Richards b DeFreitas	0
H.A. Gomes	run out	36
I.V.A. Richards*	b Foster	58
A.L. Logie	not out	19
P.J.L. Dujon+	not out	1
R.A. Harper		
M.D. Marshall		
M.A. Holding		
J. Garner		
C.A. Walsh		
Extras	(LB 10, W 8, NB 3)	21
TOTAL	**(48.3 overs) (for 4 wkts)**	**148**

					Fall	
DeFreitas	10	2	15	1	1st	7
Small	10	3	16	0	2nd	49
Botham	10	3	28	0	3rd	98
Foster	9	1	25	2	4th	146
Emburey	9.3	1	54	0		

Match No: 128/38

AUSTRALIA v ENGLAND

Benson & Hedges World Series Cup
Played at Melbourne Cricket Ground on 01/02/1987
Toss: England **Result:** Australia won by 109 runs
Umpires: R.A. French and B.E. Martin
Man of the match: S.R. Waugh
Debuts: None

AUSTRALIA
G.R. Marsh	c Emburey b Foster	28
A.R. Border*	c Athey b Small	45
D.M. Jones	c Athey b Gatting	93
G.M. Ritchie	st French b Gatting	9
D.M. Wellham	c Lamb b Gatting	3
S.R. Waugh	not out	49
S.P. O'Donnell	not out	4
T.J. Zoehrer+		
G.R.J. Matthews		
P.L. Taylor		
S.P. Davis		
Extras	(LB 7, W 9, NB 1)	17
TOTAL	(50 overs) (for 5 wkts)	248

						Fall	
DeFreitas	8	2	37	0	1st	61
Small	10	0	49	1	2nd	127
Botham	10	0	35	0	3rd	144
Foster	7	1	20	1	4th	154
Emburey	6	0	41	0	5th	223
Gatting	9	0	59	3		

ENGLAND
B.C. Broad	b O'Donnell	2
I.T. Botham	c & b Matthews	45
D.I. Gower	c Taylor b Davis	11
A.J. Lamb	run out	11
M.W. Gatting*	c Davis b Waugh	6
C.W.J. Athey	lbw b O'Donnell	29
J.E. Emburey	b Matthews	1
P.A.J. DeFreitas	b Waugh	11
N.A. Foster	b Waugh	4
B.N. French+	not out	5
G.C. Small	c Matthews b Jones	4
Extras	(B 2, LB 7, W 1)	10
TOTAL	(47.3 overs)	139

						Fall	
Davis	8	1	20	1	1st	4
O'Donnell	9	2	33	2	2nd	25
Matthews	10	1	24	2	3rd	52
Waugh	10	0	26	3	4th	65
Taylor	9	1	23	0	5th	87
Jones	1.3	0	4	1	6th	90
						7th	117
						8th	129
						9th	130
						10th	139

Match No: 129/27

ENGLAND v WEST INDIES

Benson & Hedges World Series Cup
Played at Devonport Oval on 03/02/1987
Toss: West Indies   **Result:** England won by 29 runs
Umpires: A.R. Crafter and S.G. Randell
Man of the match: B.C. Broad
Debuts: None

ENGLAND

B.C. Broad	c Dujon b Walsh	76
I.T. Botham	c Richardson b Gray	8
D.I. Gower	c Payne b Marshall	3
A.J. Lamb	c Logie b Harper	36
M.W. Gatting*	c Richardson b Gray	6
C.W.J. Athey	lbw b Marshall	3
J.E. Emburey	c Garner b Walsh	2
P.A.J. DeFreitas	not out	15
N.A. Foster	run out	0
B.N. French+	b Marshall	0
G.C. Small	not out	6
Extras	(LB 14, W 3, NB 5)	22
TOTAL	(50 overs) (for 9 wkts)	**177**

						Fall	
Marshall	10	0	31	3	1st	23
Gray	10	2	29	2	2nd	29
Garner	10	0	30	0	3rd	103
Walsh	10	1	31	2	4th	129
Harper	10	0	42	1	5th	133
					6th	143
					7th	158
					8th	159
					9th	160

WEST INDIES

R.B. Richardson	c French b DeFreitas	2
T.R.O. Payne	c French b Botham	18
A.L. Logie	b Foster	31
H.A. Gomes	c Emburey b Botham	19
I.V.A. Richards*	b Botham	1
P.J.L. Dujon+	c Gatting b Emburey	34
R.A. Harper	c French b Small	4
M.D. Marshall	c Athey b DeFreitas	27
J. Garner	b Emburey	4
A.H. Gray	c & b Emburey	0
C.A. Walsh	not out	1
Extras	(LB 5, W 2)	7
TOTAL	(48 overs)	**148**

						Fall	
DeFreitas	9	1	20	2	1st	10
Small	10	0	35	1	2nd	25
Foster	10	0	29	1	3rd	71
Botham	10	1	33	3	4th	73
Emburey	9	0	26	3	5th	90
					6th	95
					7th	132
					8th	147
					9th	147
					10th	148

Match No: 130/39

AUSTRALIA v ENGLAND

Benson & Hedges World Series Cup 1st Final
Played at Melbourne Cricket Ground on 08/02/1987
Toss: England   **Result:** England won by 6 wickets
Umpires: P.J. McConnell and S.G. Randell
Man of the match: None
Debuts: None

AUSTRALIA
G.R. Marsh	c Gatting b DeFreitas	2
T.J. Zoehrer+	c Gatting b Dilley	0
D.M. Jones	b DeFreitas	67
A.R. Border*	c French b Foster	42
G.M. Ritchie	run out	13
S.R. Waugh	c DeFreitas b Emburey	1
S.P. O'Donnell	b Dilley	10
G.R.J. Matthews	b Dilley	8
P.L. Taylor	not out	3
B.A. Reid	not out	5
S.P. Davis		
Extras	(LB 10, W 3, NB 7)	20
TOTAL	(44 overs) (for 8 wkts)	**171**

						Fall	
Dilley	9	2	32	3	1st	3
DeFreitas	9	0	32	2	2nd	3
Botham	9	0	26	0	3rd	106
Foster	9	0	42	1	4th	134
Emburey	8	0	29	1	5th	137
					6th	146
					7th	161
					8th	164

ENGLAND
B.C. Broad	c Jones b Matthews	12
I.T. Botham	c Marsh b Matthews	71
C.W.J. Athey	c & b Matthews	12
D.I. Gower	c Taylor b Reid	45
A.J. Lamb	not out	15
M.W. Gatting*	not out	3
J.E. Emburey		
P.A.J. DeFreitas		
N.A. Foster		
B.N. French+		
G.R. Dilley		
Extras	(B 5, LB 3, W 4, NB 2)	14
TOTAL	(36 overs) (for 4 wkts)	**172**

						Fall	
Davis	4	0	17	0	1st	91
O'Donnell	4	0	25	0	2nd	93
Reid	5	0	31	1	3rd	147
Waugh	8	1	36	0	4th	159
Matthews	9	1	27	3		
Taylor	5	0	24	0		
Jones	1	0	4	0		

Match No: 131/40

AUSTRALIA v ENGLAND

Benson & Hedges World Series Cup 2nd Final
Played at Sydney Cricket Ground on 11/02/1987
Toss: England   **Result:** England won by 8 runs
Umpires: A.R. Crafter and R.A. French
Man of the finals: I.T. Botham
Debuts: None

ENGLAND
B.C. Broad	c O'Donnell b Matthews	53
I.T. Botham	c Ritchie b O'Donnell	25
C.W.J. Athey	b Matthews	16
D.I. Gower	c Wellham b Taylor	17
M.W. Gatting*	run out	7
A.J. Lamb	c Zoehrer b O'Donnell	35
J.E. Emburey	c Zoehrer b Waugh	6
P.A.J. DeFreitas	c Jones b Taylor	1
N.A. Foster	c Taylor b Davis	7
B.N. French+	not out	9
G.R. Dilley	not out	6
Extras	(LB 4, W 1)	5
TOTAL	(50 overs) (for 9 wkts)	**187**

						Fall	
Davis	10	0	44	1		1st	36
O'Donnell	10	1	37	2		2nd	73
Waugh	10	0	42	1		3rd	102
Matthews	10	1	31	2		4th	120
Taylor	10	2	29	2		5th	121
						6th	143
						7th	146
						8th	170
						9th	170

AUSTRALIA
G.R. Marsh	lbw b Botham	28
A.R. Border*	c French b Botham	27
D.M. Jones	c & b Emburey	13
G.M. Ritchie	c DeFreitas b Botham	4
D.M. Wellham	c Gower b DeFreitas	30
S.R. Waugh	run out	22
S.P. O'Donnell	not out	40
T.J. Zoehrer+	lbw b DeFreitas	0
G.R.J. Matthews	run out	3
P.L. Taylor	not out	3
S.P. Davis		
Extras	(B 1, LB 6, W 2)	9
TOTAL	(50 overs) (for 8 wkts)	**179**

						Fall	
Dilley	10	1	34	0		1st	55
DeFreitas	10	1	34	2		2nd	70
Botham	10	1	26	3		3rd	72
Foster	10	0	51	0		4th	80
Emburey	10	2	27	1		5th	124
						6th	135
						7th	135
						8th	151

Match No: 132/18

ENGLAND v INDIA

Four Nations Tournament
Played at Sharjah CA Stadium, UAE on 02/04/1987
Toss: India   **Result:** India won by 3 wickets
Umpires: D.P. Buultjens and P.W. Vidanagamage
Man of the match: Kapil Dev
Debuts: Eng - D.J. Capel, N.H. Fairbrother, J.J. Whitaker

ENGLAND
G.A. Gooch	b Maninder Singh	31
B.C. Broad	st Viswanath b Shastri	57
R.T. Robinson	c Srikkanth b Shastri	34
N.H. Fairbrother	c Azharuddin b Shastri	14
J.J. Whitaker	b Gopal Sharma	4
D.J. Capel	run out	8
J.E. Emburey*	b Kapil Dev	25
P.A.J. DeFreitas	not out	18
C.J. Richards+	not out	14
P.H. Edmonds		
N.A. Foster		
Extras	(LB 4, W 2)	6
TOTAL	(50 overs) (for 7 wkts)	**211**

Fall
Kapil Dev	8 1 30 1	1st 60
Prabhakar	8 2 17 0	2nd 106
Arun	4 0 32 0	3rd 134
Gopal Sharma	10 0 38 1	4th 143
Shastri	10 1 47 3	5th 145
Maninder Singh	10 0 43 1	6th 167
		7th 184

INDIA
M. Prabhakar	c Edmonds b Foster	4
K. Srikkanth	c Fairbrother b Capel	56
R. Lamba	c Whitaker b Edmonds	4
D.B. Vengsarkar	c Robinson b Edmonds	40
R.J. Shastri	c Edmonds b Emburey	7
Kapil Dev*	c Capel b Emburey	64
M. Azharuddin	not out	24
S. Viswanath+	b Emburey	3
B. Arun	not out	7
Gopal Sharma		
Maninder Singh		
Extras	(B 2, LB 2, W 1)	5
TOTAL	(48.5 overs) (for 7 wkts)	**214**

Fall
DeFreitas	10 3 33 0	1st 22
Foster	9 1 46 1	2nd 33
Capel	10 0 45 1	3rd 86
Edmonds	10 0 48 2	4th 97
Emburey	9.5 0 38 3	5th 146
		6th 194
		7th 200

Match No: 133/19

ENGLAND v PAKISTAN

Four Nations Tournament
Played at Sharjah CA Stadium, UAE on 07/04/1987
Toss: England **Result:** England won by 5 wickets
Umpires: D.P. Buultjens and P.W. Vidanagamage
Man of the match: R.T. Robinson
Debuts: None

PAKISTAN

Mudassar Nazar	c Richards b DeFreitas	3
Ramiz Raja	run out	44
Ijaz Ahmed	run out	1
Javed Miandad	run out	60
Salim Malik	c Richards b Capel	1
Imran Khan*	c Richards b Foster	46
Manzoor Elahi	c & b Capel	3
Wasim Akram	c Fairbrother b Capel	10
Salim Yousuf+	b Emburey	8
Abdul Qadir	not out	13
Tausif Ahmed	not out	3
Extras	(B 8, LB 8, W 4, NB 5)	25
TOTAL	(50 overs) (for 9 wkts)	217

						Fall	
DeFreitas	10	0	47	1	1st	10
Small	10	2	25	0	2nd	11
Foster	10	0	47	1	3rd	77
Emburey	10	1	44	1	4th	83
Capel	10	0	38	3	5th	175
					6th	175
					7th	188
					8th	190
					9th	211

ENGLAND

G.A. Gooch	c Salim Malik b Imran Khan	1
B.C. Broad	c Ijaz Ahmed b Mudassar Nazar	65
R.T. Robinson	c Manzoor Elahi b Abdul Qadir	83
J.J. Whitaker	not out	44
N.H. Fairbrother	c Ramiz Raja b Abdul Qadir	6
D.J. Capel	st Salim Yousuf b Abdul Qadir	2
J.E. Emburey*	not out	5
C.J. Richards+		
P.A.J. DeFreitas		
N.A. Foster		
G.C. Small		
Extras	(B 2, LB 9, W 3)	14
TOTAL	(47.2 overs) (for 5 wkts)	220

						Fall	
Imran Khan	9	2	24	1	1st	3
Wasim Akram	9.2	0	38	0	2nd	143
Abdul Qadir	10	0	47	3	3rd	166
Mudassar Nazar	10	0	41	1	4th	182
Manzoor Elahi	6	0	39	0	5th	188
Tausif Ahmed	3	0	20	0		

Match No: 134/41

ENGLAND v AUSTRALIA

Four Nations Tournament
Played at Sharjah CA Stadium, UAE on 09/04/1987
Toss: Australia **Result:** England won by 11 runs
Umpires: D.P. Buultjens and P.W. Vidanagamage
Man of the match: G.A. Gooch
Debuts: None

ENGLAND
G.A. Gooch	lbw b Waugh	86
B.C. Broad	b Taylor	44
R.T. Robinson	lbw b O'Donnell	5
N.H. Fairbrother	run out	32
R.J. Bailey	c O'Donnell b Reid	11
D.J. Capel	run out	17
J.E. Emburey*	not out	18
P.A.J. DeFreitas	not out	1
C.J. Richards+		
N.A. Foster		
G.C. Small		
Extras	(B 1, LB 7, W 6, NB 2)	16
TOTAL	(50 overs) (for 6 wkts)	**230**

	O	M	R	W		Fall
Reid	10	0	50	1	1st	118
Davis	8	3	24	0	2nd	125
Matthews	7	0	31	0	3rd	167
Waugh	10	1	49	1	4th	188
Taylor	7	0	41	1	5th	193
O'Donnell	8	0	27	1	6th	229

AUSTRALIA
G.R. Marsh	lbw b DeFreitas	0
D.C. Boon	c Broad b Emburey	73
D.M. Wellham	c Robinson b Small	2
A.R. Border*	c Bailey b Emburey	84
S.P. O'Donnell	run out	6
S.R. Waugh	b Foster	14
G.R.J. Matthews	c Gooch b DeFreitas	13
T.J. Zoehrer+	run out	1
P.L. Taylor	not out	14
B.A. Reid	run out	2
S.P. Davis	not out	3
Extras	(LB 6, NB 1)	7
TOTAL	(50 overs) (for 9 wkts)	**219**

	O	M	R	W		Fall
DeFreitas	10	1	40	2	1st	0
Small	9	1	23	1	2nd	7
Capel	5	0	28	0	3rd	166
Gooch	6	0	34	0	4th	166
Emburey	10	1	38	2	5th	177
Foster	10	0	50	1	6th	195
					7th	200
					8th	200
					9th	204

Match No: 135/20

ENGLAND v PAKISTAN

Texaco Trophy
Played at The Oval, London on 21/05/1987
Toss: England   **Result:** England won by 7 wickets
Umpires: D.R. Shepherd and A.G.T. Whitehead
Man of the match: B.C. Broad
Debuts: None

PAKISTAN

Mudassar Nazar	c DeFreitas b Foster	45
Ramiz Raja	run out	0
Mansoor Akhtar	c Gatting b Dilley	12
Javed Miandad	c Lamb b Dilley	113
Imran Khan*	c Broad b Foster	7
Wasim Akram	b Emburey	12
Manzoor Elahi	not out	18
Salim Malik	not out	8
Ijaz Ahmed		
Salim Yousuf+		
Tausif Ahmed		
Extras	(B 1, LB 8, W 4, NB 4)	17
TOTAL	(55 overs) (for 6 wkts)	232

						Fall	
Dilley	11	1	63	2		1st	0
DeFreitas	11	3	50	0		2nd	18
Botham	11	2	38	0		3rd	128
Foster	11	0	36	2		4th	169
Emburey	11	1	36	1		5th	206
						6th	208

ENGLAND

B.C. Broad	c sub (Asif Mujtaba) b Wasim Akram	99
C.W.J. Athey	c Salim Malik b Mudassar Nazar	33
M.W. Gatting*	retired hurt	2
A.J. Lamb	c sub (Asif Mujtaba) Tausif Ahmed	61
D.I. Gower	not out	15
I.T. Botham	not out	6
C.J. Richards+		
J.E. Emburey		
P.A.J. DeFreitas		
N.A. Foster		
G.R. Dilley		
Extras	(LB 9, W 2, NB 6)	17
TOTAL	(53.1 overs) (for 3 wkts)	233

						Fall	
Imran Khan	8	0	30	0		1st	76
Manzoor Elahi	11	1	31	0		2nd	199
Wasim Akram	11	0	60	1		3rd	218
Mudassar Nazar	11	1	41	1			
Tausif Ahmed	10.1	0	47	1			
Mansoor Akhtar	2	0	15	0			

Match No: 136/21

ENGLAND v PAKISTAN

Texaco Trophy
Played at Trent Bridge, Nottingham on 23/05/1987
Toss: Pakistan **Result:** Pakistan won by 6 wickets
Umpires: D.J. Constant and B.J. Meyer
Man of the match: Javed Miandad
Debuts: None

ENGLAND		
B.C. Broad	c Salim Yousuf b Wasim Akram	52
C.W.J. Athey	lbw b Imran Khan	1
G.A. Gooch	lbw b Mohsin Kamal	9
A.J. Lamb	c Salim Yousuf b Tausif Ahmed	26
D.I. Gower	b Mudassar Nazar	24
I.T. Botham	c Mohsin Kamal b Tausif Ahmed	0
C.J. Richards+	c Manzoor Elahi b Mohsin Kamal	0
J.E. Emburey*	b Wasim Akram	25
P.A.J. DeFreitas	c Manzoor Elahi b Imran Khan	3
N.A. Foster	run out	5
G.R. Dilley	not out	0
Extras	(LB 8, W 4)	12
TOTAL	(51.1 overs)	**157**

	O	M	R	W	Fall	
Imran Khan	9	1	31	2	1st	15
Mohsin Kamal	11	1	31	2	2nd	45
Wasim Akram	9.1	1	18	2	3rd	75
Mudassar Nazar	11	1	36	1	4th	117
Tausif Ahmed	11	1	33	2	5th	117
					6th	117
					7th	121
					8th	144
					9th	157
					10th	157

PAKISTAN		
Mudassar Nazar	lbw b Foster	12
Ramiz Raja	c Gooch b DeFreitas	13
Mansoor Akhtar	b Foster	21
Javed Miandad	not out	71
Salim Malik	run out	9
Imran Khan*	not out	21
Manzoor Elahi		
Wasim Akram		
Salim Yousuf+		
Tausif Ahmed		
Mohsin Kamal		
Extras	(LB 8, W 2, NB 1)	11
TOTAL	(52 overs) (for 4 wkts)	**158**

	O	M	R	W	Fall	
Dilley	9	4	16	0	1st	23
DeFreitas	11	2	30	1	2nd	29
Foster	11	1	25	2	3rd	64
Botham	7	0	34	0	4th	81
Emburey	11	2	33	0		
Gooch	3	0	12	0		

Match No: 137/22

ENGLAND v PAKISTAN

Texaco Trophy
Played at Edgbaston, Birmingham on 25/05/1987
Toss: England **Result:** England won by 1 wicket
Umpires: H.D. Bird and K.E. Palmer
Man of the match: P.A.J. DeFreitas
Debuts: None

PAKISTAN

Batsman	Dismissal	Runs
Mudassar Nazar	lbw b Thomas	0
Ramiz Raja	run out	46
Mansoor Akhtar	c Richards b Thomas	0
Javed Miandad	c Gower b Foster	68
Salim Malik	b Emburey	45
Imran Khan*	not out	24
Manzoor Elahi	b Emburey	0
Salim Yousuf+	run out	0
Wasim Akram	c Richards b Foster	0
Tausif Ahmed	b Foster	0
Mohsin Kamal	not out	11
Extras	(B 2, LB 13, W 1, NB 3)	19
TOTAL	(55 overs) (for 9 wkts)	**213**

Bowler	O	M	R	W		Fall	
Thomas	11	0	59	2	1st	0
DeFreitas	11	1	30	0	2nd	0
Botham	11	1	31	0	3rd	73
Foster	11	1	29	3	4th	168
Emburey	11	1	49	2	5th	170
					6th	170
					7th	170
					8th	170
					9th	178

ENGLAND

Batsman	Dismissal	Runs
B.C. Broad	c Javed Miandad b Mohsin Kamal	15
C.W.J. Athey	c Salim Yousuf b Imran Khan	5
D.I. Gower	b Mudassar Nazar	11
A.J. Lamb	c Mansoor Akhtar b Mudassar Nazar	14
M.W. Gatting*	c Javed Miandad b Mohsin Kamal	41
I.T. Botham	c sub (Asif Mujtaba) b Tausif Ahmed	24
C.J. Richards+	run out	16
J.E. Emburey	run out	16
N.A. Foster	not out	14
P.A.J. DeFreitas	b Imran Khan	33
J.G. Thomas	not out	1
Extras	(LB 14, W 12, NB 1)	27
TOTAL	(54.3 overs) (for 9 wkts)	**217**

Bowler	O	M	R	W		Fall	
Imran Khan	11	0	43	2	1st	18
Mohsin Kamal	11	0	47	2	2nd	31
Wasim Akram	10.3	2	34	0	3rd	34
Mudassar Nazar	11	2	17	2	4th	75
Tausif Ahmed	11	0	62	1	5th	105
					6th	140
					7th	155
					8th	167
					9th	209

Match No: 138/28

ENGLAND v WEST INDIES

Reliance World Cup
Played at Municipal Stadium, Gujranwala on 09/10/1987
Toss: England   **Result:** England won by 2 wickets
Umpires: A.R. Crafter and R.B. Gupta
Man of the match: A.J. Lamb
Debuts: None

WEST INDIES
D.L. Haynes	run out	19
C.A. Best	b DeFreitas	5
R.B. Richardson	b Foster	53
I.V.A. Richards*	b Foster	27
P.J.L. Dujon+	run out	46
A.L. Logie	b Foster	49
R.A. Harper	b Small	24
C.L. Hooper	not out	1
W.K.M. Benjamin	not out	7
C.A. Walsh		
B.P. Patterson		
Extras	(LB 9, NB 3)	12
TOTAL	(50 overs) (for 7 wkts)	243

						Fall	
DeFreitas	10	2	31	1	1st	8
Foster	10	0	53	3	2nd	53
Emburey	10	1	22	0	3rd	105
Small	10	0	45	1	4th	122
Pringle	10	0	83	0	5th	205
					6th	235
					7th	235

ENGLAND
G.A. Gooch	c Dujon b Hooper	47
B.C. Broad	c Dujon b Walsh	3
R.T. Robinson	run out	12
M.W. Gatting*	b Hooper	25
A.J. Lamb	not out	67
D.R. Pringle	c Best b Hooper	12
P.R. Downton+	run out	3
J.E. Emburey	b Patterson	22
P.A.J. DeFreitas	b Patterson	23
N.A. Foster	not out	9
G.C. Small		
Extras	(LB 14, W 6, NB 3)	23
TOTAL	(49.3 overs) (for 8 wkts)	246

						Fall	
Patterson	10	0	49	2	1st	14
Walsh	9.3	0	65	1	2nd	40
Harper	10	0	44	0	3rd	98
Benjamin	10	2	32	0	4th	99
Hooper	10	0	42	3	5th	123
					6th	131
					7th	162
					8th	209

Match No: 139/23

PAKISTAN v ENGLAND

Reliance World Cup
Played at Pindi Club Ground, Rawalpindi on 12 & 13/10/1987
Toss: England   **Result:** Pakistan won by 18 runs
Umpires: A.R.Crafter and R.B.Gupta
Man of the match: Abdul Qadir
Debuts: None

PAKISTAN

Batsman	Dismissal	Runs
Mansoor Akhtar	c Downton b Foster	6
Ramiz Raja	run out	15
Salim Malik	c Downton b DeFreitas	65
Javed Miandad	lbw b DeFreitas	23
Ijaz Ahmed	c Robinson b Small	59
Imran Khan*	b Small	22
Wasim Akram	b DeFreitas	5
Salim Yousuf+	not out	16
Abdul Qadir	not out	12
Tausif Ahmed		
Salim Jaffer		
Extras	(LB 10, W 3, NB 3)	16
TOTAL	(50 overs) (for 7 wkts)	239

Bowler	O	M	R	W		Fall	
DeFreitas	10	1	42	3		1st	13
Foster	10	1	35	1		2nd	51
Small	10	1	47	2		3rd	112
Pringle	10	0	54	0		4th	123
Emburey	10	0	51	0		5th	202
						6th	210
						7th	210

ENGLAND

Batsman	Dismissal	Runs
G.A. Gooch	b Abdul Qadir	21
B.C. Broad	b Tausif Ahmed	36
R.T. Robinson	b Abdul Qadir	33
M.W. Gatting*	b Salim Jaffer	43
A.J. Lamb	lbw b Abdul Qadir	30
D.R. Pringle	run out	8
J.E. Emburey	run out	1
P.R. Downton+	c Salim Yousuf b Abdul Qadir	0
P.A.J. DeFreitas	not out	3
N.A. Foster	run out	6
G.C. Small	lbw b Salim Jaffer	0
Extras	(B 6, LB 26, W 8)	40
TOTAL	(48.4 overs)	221

Bowler	O	M	R	W		Fall	
Wasim Akram	9	0	32	0		1st	52
Salim Jaffer	9.4	0	42	2		2nd	92
Tausif Ahmed	10	0	39	1		3rd	141
Abdul Qadir	10	0	31	4		4th	186
Salim Malik	7	0	29	0		5th	206
Mansoor Akhtar	3	0	16	0		6th	207
						7th	207
						8th	213
						9th	221
						10th	221

Match No: 140/5

ENGLAND v SRI LANKA

Reliance World Cup
Played at Shahi Bagh Stadium, Peshawar on 17/10/1987
Toss: England   **Result:** England won on faster scoring rate
Umpires: R.B. Gupta and V.K. Ramaswamy
Man of the match: A.J. Lamb
Debuts: None

ENGLAND		
G.A. Gooch	c & b Anurasiri	84
B.C. Broad	c de Silva b Ratnayeke	28
M.W. Gatting*	b Ratnayake	58
A.J. Lamb	c de Silva b Ratnayeke	76
J.E. Emburey	not out	30
C.W.J. Athey	not out	2
P.R. Downton+		
P.A.J. DeFreitas		
D.R. Pringle		
E.E. Hemmings		
G.C. Small		
Extras	(LB 13, W 5)	18
TOTAL	(50 overs) (for 4 wkts)	**296**

	O	M	R	W		Fall
Ratnayeke	9	0	62	2	1st	89
John	10	0	44	0	2nd	142
de Silva	7	0	33	0	3rd	218
Ratnayake	10	0	60	1	4th	287
Anurasiri	8	0	44	1		
Ranatunga	6	0	40	0		

SRI LANKA		
R.S. Mahanama	c Gooch b Pringle	11
D.S.B.P. Kuruppu+	c Hemmings b Emburey	13
A.P. Gurusinha	run out	1
R.S. Madugalle	b Hemmings	30
A. Ranatunga	lbw b DeFreitas	40
L.R.D. Mendis*	run out	14
P.A. de Silva	c Emburey b Hemmings	6
J.R. Ratnayeke	c Broad b Emburey	1
R.J. Ratnayake	not out	14
V.B. John	not out	8
S.D. Anurasiri		
Extras	(B 2, LB 9, W 6, NB 3)	20
TOTAL	(45 overs) (for 8 wkts)	**158**

	O	M	R	W		Fall
DeFreitas	9	2	24	1	1st	31
Small	7	0	27	0	2nd	32
Pringle	4	0	11	1	3rd	37
Emburey	10	1	26	2	4th	99
Hemmings	10	1	31	2	5th	105
Gooch	2	0	9	0	6th	113
Athey	1	0	10	0	7th	119
Broad	1	0	6	0	8th	137
Lamb	1	0	3	0		

Match No: 141/24

PAKISTAN v ENGLAND

Reliance World Cup
Played at National Stadium, Karachi on 20/10/1987
Toss: Pakistan **Result:** Pakistan won by 7 wickets
Umpires: A.R. Crafter and V.K. Ramaswamy
Man of the match: Imran Khan
Debuts: None

ENGLAND

G.A. Gooch	c Wasim Akram b Imran Khan	16
R.T. Robinson	b Abdul Qadir	16
C.W.J. Athey	b Tausif Ahmed	86
M.W. Gatting*	c Salim Yousuf b Abdul Qadir	60
A.J. Lamb	b Imran Khan	9
J.E. Emburey	lbw b Abdul Qadir	3
P.R. Downton+	c Salim Yousuf b Imran Khan	6
P.A.J. DeFreitas	c Salim Yousuf b Imran Khan	13
N.A. Foster	not out	20
G.C. Small	run out	0
E.E. Hemmings	not out	4
Extras	(LB 7, W 4)	11
TOTAL	(50 overs) (for 9 wkts)	**244**

						Fall	
Imran Khan	9	0	37	4		1st	26
Wasim Akram	8	0	44	0		2nd	52
Tausif Ahmed	10	0	46	1		3rd	187
Abdul Qadir	10	0	31	3		4th	187
Salim Jaffer	8	0	44	0		5th	192
Salim Malik	5	0	35	0		6th	203
						7th	206
						8th	230
						9th	230

PAKISTAN

Ramiz Raja	c Gooch b DeFreitas	113
Mansoor Akhtar	run out	29
Salim Malik	c Athey b Emburey	88
Javed Miandad	not out	6
Ijaz Ahmed	not out	4
Imran Khan*		
Salim Yousuf+		
Wasim Akram		
Abdul Qadir		
Tausif Ahmed		
Salim Jaffer		
Extras	(LB 6, W 1)	7
TOTAL	(49 overs) (for 3 wkts)	**247**

						Fall	
DeFreitas	8	2	41	1		1st	61
Foster	10	0	51	0		2nd	228
Hemmings	10	1	40	0		3rd	243
Emburey	10	0	34	1			
Small	9	0	63	0			
Gooch	2	0	12	0			

Match No: 142/29

ENGLAND v WEST INDIES

Reliance World Cup
Played at Sawai Mansingh Stadium, Jaipur on 26/10/1987
Toss: West Indies   **Result:** England won by 34 runs
Umpires: Mahboob Shah and P.W. Vidanagamage
Man of the match: G.A. Gooch
Debuts: None

ENGLAND
G.A. Gooch	c Harper b Patterson	92
R.T. Robinson	b Patterson	13
C.W.J. Athey	c Patterson b Harper	21
M.W. Gatting*	lbw b Richards	25
A.J. Lamb	c Richardson b Patterson	40
J.E. Emburey	not out	24
P.A.J. DeFreitas	not out	16
P.R. Downton+		
N.A. Foster		
G.C. Small		
E.E. Hemmings		
Extras	(B 5, LB 10, W 22, NB 1)	38
TOTAL	(50 overs) (for 5 wkts)	**269**

						Fall	
Patterson	9	0	56	3	1st	35
Walsh	10	0	24	0	2nd	90
Benjamin	10	0	63	0	3rd	154
Harper	10	1	52	1	4th	209
Hooper	3	0	27	0	5th	250
Richards	8	0	32	1		

WEST INDIES
D.L. Haynes	c Athey b DeFreitas	9
P.V. Simmons	b Emburey	25
R.B. Richardson	c Downton b Small	93
I.V.A. Richards*	b Hemmings	51
A.L. Logie	c Hemmings b Emburey	22
C.L. Hooper	c Downton b DeFreitas	8
P.J.L. Dujon+	c Downton b Foster	1
R.A. Harper	run out	3
W.K.M. Benjamin	c Foster b DeFreitas	8
C.A. Walsh	b Hemmings	2
B.P. Patterson	not out	4
Extras	(LB 7, W 1, NB 1)	9
TOTAL	(48.1 overs)	**235**

						Fall	
DeFreitas	9.1	2	28	3	1st	18
Foster	10	0	52	1	2nd	65
Emburey	9	0	41	2	3rd	147
Small	10	0	61	1	4th	182
Hemmings	10	0	46	2	5th	208
					6th	211
					7th	219
					8th	221
					9th	224
					10th	235

Match No: 143/6

ENGLAND v SRI LANKA

Reliance World Cup
Played at Nehru Stadium, Poona on 30/10/1987
Toss: Sri Lanka   Result: England won by 8 wickets
Umpires: D.M. Archer and Khizar Hayat
Man of the match: G.A. Gooch
Debuts: None

SRI LANKA

R.S. Mahanama	c Emburey b DeFreitas	14
J.R. Ratnayeke	lbw b Small	7
A.P. Gurusinha+	run out	34
R.L. Dias	st Downton b Hemmings	80
L.R.D. Mendis*	b DeFreitas	7
R.S. Madugalle	c sub (P.W. Jarvis) b Hemmings	22
P.A. de Silva	not out	23
A.L.F. de Mel	c Lamb b Hemmings	0
S. Jeganathan	not out	20
V.B. John		
S.D. Anurasiri		
Extras	(LB 3, W 3, NB 5)	11
TOTAL	(50 overs) (for 7 wkts)	218

						Fall	
DeFreitas	10	2	46	2	1st	23
Small	10	1	33	1	2nd	25
Foster	10	0	37	0	3rd	113
Emburey	10	1	42	0	4th	125
Hemmings	10	0	57	3	5th	170
					6th	177
					7th	180

ENGLAND

G.A. Gooch	c & b Jeganathan	61
R.T. Robinson	b Jeganathan	55
C.W.J. Athey	not out	40
M.W. Gatting*	not out	46
A.J. Lamb		
P.R. Downton+		
J.E. Emburey		
P.A.J. DeFreitas		
N.A. Foster		
G.C. Small		
E.E. Hemmings		
Extras	(B 1, LB 13, W 3)	17
TOTAL	(41.2 overs) (for 2 wkts)	219

						Fall	
Ratnayeke	8	1	37	0	1st	123
John	6	2	19	0	2nd	132
de Mel	4.2	0	34	0		
Jeganathan	10	0	45	2		
Anurasiri	10	0	45	0		
de Silva	3	0	25	0		

Match No: 144/19

INDIA v ENGLAND

Reliance World Cup Semi-Final
Played at Wankhede Stadium, Bombay on 05/11/1987
Toss: India **Result:** England won by 35 runs
Umpires: A.R. Crafter and S.J. Woodward
Man of the match: G.A. Gooch
Debuts: None

ENGLAND

G.A. Gooch	c Srikkanth b Maninder Singh	115
R.T. Robinson	st More b Maninder Singh	13
C.W.J. Athey	c More b Chetan Sharma	4
M.W. Gatting*	b Maninder Singh	56
A.J. Lamb	not out	32
J.E. Emburey	lbw b Kapil Dev	6
P.A.J. DeFreitas	b Kapil Dev	7
P.R. Downton+	not out	1
N.A. Foster		
G.C. Small		
E.E. Hemmings		
Extras	(B 1, LB 18, W 1)	20
TOTAL	(50 overs) (for 6 wkts)	**254**

						Fall	
Kapil Dev	10	1	38	2	1st	40
Prabhakar	9	1	40	0	2nd	79
Maninder Singh	10	0	54	3	3rd	196
Chetan Sharma	9	0	41	1	4th	203
Shastri	10	0	49	0	5th	219
Azharuddin	2	0	13	0	6th	231

INDIA

K. Srikkanth	b Foster	31
S.M. Gavaskar	b DeFreitas	4
N.S. Sidhu	c Athey b Foster	22
M. Azharuddin	lbw b Hemmings	64
C.S. Pandit	lbw b Foster	24
Kapil Dev*	c Gatting b Hemmings	30
R.J. Shastri	c Downton b Hemmings	21
K.S. More+	c & b Emburey	0
M. Prabhakar	c Downton b Small	4
Chetan Sharma	c Lamb b Hemmings	0
Maninder Singh	not out	0
Extras	(B 1, LB 9, W 6, NB 3)	19
TOTAL	(45.3 overs)	**219**

						Fall	
DeFreitas	7	0	37	1	1st	7
Small	6	0	22	1	2nd	58
Emburey	10	1	35	1	3rd	73
Foster	10	0	47	3	4th	121
Hemmings	9.3	1	52	4	5th	168
Gooch	3	0	16	0	6th	204
					7th	205
					8th	218
					9th	219
					10th	219

Match No: 145/42

AUSTRALIA v ENGLAND

Reliance World Cup Final
Played at Eden Gardens, Calcutta on 08/11/1987
Toss: Australia   **Result:** Australia won by 7 runs
Umpires: R.B. Gupta and Mahboob Shah
Man of the match: D.C. Boon
Debuts: None

AUSTRALIA
D.C. Boon	c Downton b Hemmings	75
G.R. Marsh	b Foster	24
D.M. Jones	c Athey b Hemmings	33
C.J. McDermott	b Gooch	14
A.R. Border*	run out	31
M.R.J. Veletta	not out	45
S.R. Waugh	not out	5
S.P. O'Donnell		
G.C. Dyer+		
T.B.A. May		
B.A. Reid		
Extras	(B 1, LB 13, W 5, NB 7)	26
TOTAL	(50 overs) (for 5 wkts)	**253**

						Fall	
DeFreitas	6	1	34	0	1st	75
Small	6	0	33	0	2nd	151
Foster	10	0	38	1	3rd	166
Hemmings	10	1	48	2	4th	168
Emburey	10	0	44	0	5th	241
Gooch	8	1	42	1		

ENGLAND
G.A. Gooch	lbw b O'Donnell	35
R.T. Robinson	lbw b McDermott	0
C.W.J. Athey	run out	58
M.W. Gatting*	c Dyer b Border	41
A.J. Lamb	b Waugh	45
P.R. Downton+	c O'Donnell b Border	9
J.E. Emburey	run out	10
P.A.J. DeFreitas	c Reid b Waugh	17
N.A. Foster	not out	7
G.C. Small	not out	3
E.E. Hemmings		
Extras	(B 1, LB 14, W 2, NB 4)	21
TOTAL	(50 overs) (for 8 wkts)	**246**

						Fall	
McDermott	10	1	51	1	1st	1
Reid	10	0	43	0	2nd	66
Waugh	9	0	37	2	3rd	135
O'Donnell	10	1	35	1	4th	170
May	4	0	27	0	5th	188
Border	7	0	38	2	6th	218
					7th	220
					8th	235

Match No: 146/25

PAKISTAN v ENGLAND

Played at Gaddafi Stadium, Lahore on 18/11/1987
Toss: Pakistan   Result: England won by 2 wickets
Umpires: Shakeel Khan and Shakoor Rana
Man of the match: J.E. Emburey
Debuts: Pak - Zhahid Ahmed

PAKISTAN
Ramiz Raja	c Gatting b Capel	38
Shoaib Mohammad	c French b Foster	11
Salim Malik	run out	30
Ijaz Ahmed	c Gooch b Hemmings	17
Mudassar Nazar	c Fairbrother b Foster	10
Salim Yousuf+	c French b Hemmings	22
Manzoor Elahi	b Emburey	14
Wasim Akram	b Emburey	5
Abdul Qadir*	run out	7
Zahid Ahmed	c & b Emburey	0
Salim Jaffer	not out	2
Extras	(B 1, LB 5, W 2, NB 2)	10
TOTAL	(41.3 overs)	**166**

						Fall	
DeFreitas	7	1	19	0	1st	25
Foster	8	1	37	2	2nd	62
Capel	9	0	43	1	3rd	96
Emburey	8.3	2	17	3	4th	102
Hemmings	9	1	44	2	5th	132
					6th	138
					7th	154
					8th	163
					9th	163
					10th	166

ENGLAND
G.A. Gooch	b Abdul Qadir	43
B.C. Broad	c Manzoor Elahi b Wasim Akram	1
M.W. Gatting*	lbw b Abdul Qadir	16
C.W.J. Athey	lbw b Wasim Akram	20
D.J. Capel	run out	8
N.H. Fairbrother	b Zahid Ahmed	25
J.E. Emburey	c Ijaz Ahmed b Zahid Ahmed	4
P.A.J. DeFreitas	not out	14
N.A. Foster	lbw b Wasim Akram	0
B.N. French+	not out	7
E.E. Hemmings		
Extras	(B 13, LB 10, W 4, NB 2)	29
TOTAL	(44.3 overs) (for 8 wkts)	**167**

						Fall	
Wasim Akram	9	0	25	3	1st	5
Salim Jaffer	3	0	18	0	2nd	61
Mudassar Nazar	9	1	19	0	3rd	74
Manzoor Elahi	2	0	12	0	4th	89
Abdul Qadir	8.3	2	32	2	5th	120
Zahid Ahmed	9	1	24	2	6th	127
Shoaib Mohammad	4	0	14	0	7th	137
						8th	140

Match No: 147/26

PAKISTAN v ENGLAND

Played at National Stadium, Karachi on 20/11/1987
Toss: England Result: England won by 23 runs
Umpires: Khizar Hayat and Mahboob Shah
Man of the match: G.A. Gooch
Debuts: None

ENGLAND
G.A. Gooch	st Zulqarnain b Abdul Qadir	142
B.C. Broad	c Manzoor Elahi b Abdul Qadir	22
M.W. Gatting*	run out	21
N.H. Fairbrother	b Zahid Ahmed	2
D.J. Capel	not out	50
J.E. Emburey	c Manzoor Elahi b Abdul Qadir	1
P.A.J. DeFreitas	b Mohsin Kamal	0
N.A. Foster	not out	5
C.W.J. Athey		
B.N. French+		
E.E. Hemmings		
Extras	(B 3, LB 9, W 6, NB 2)	20
TOTAL	(44 overs) (for 6 wkts)	263

					Fall	
Wasim Akram	4	1	9	0	1st	70
Mohsin Kamal	9	0	57	1	2nd	135
Manzoor Elahi	3	0	19	0	3rd	140
Zahid Ahmed	7	0	37	1	4th	249
Asif Mujtaba	3	0	25	0	5th	251
Abdul Qadir	8	0	30	3	6th	251
Salim Malik	5	0	32	0		
Shoaib Mohammad	5	0	42	0		

PAKISTAN
Ramiz Raja	obstructed the field	99
Shoaib Mohammad	run out	37
Salim Malik	c Fairbrother b Foster	35
Manzoor Elahi	run out	17
Abdul Qadir*	c Broad b Foster	0
Ijaz Ahmed	c Athey b Emburey	26
Wasim Akram	c Foster b Emburey	9
Asif Mujtaba	b Capel	0
Zahid Ahmed	not out	3
Zulqarnain+		
Mohsin Kamal		
Extras	(LB 7, W 7)	14
TOTAL	(44 overs) (for 8 wkts)	240

					Fall	
DeFreitas	9	1	35	0	1st	77
Foster	9	0	47	2	2nd	138
Capel	8	1	41	1	3rd	172
Hemmings	9	0	45	0	4th	172
Emburey	9	0	65	2	5th	214
					6th	228
					7th	230
					8th	240

Match No: 148/27

PAKISTAN v ENGLAND

Played at Shahi Bagh Stadium, Peshawar on 22/11/1987
Toss: England **Result:** England won by 98 runs
Umpires: Amanullah Khan and Javed Akhtar
Man of the match: N.A. Foster
Debuts: Eng - R.C. Russell   Pak - Shakil Khan

ENGLAND
G.A. Gooch	c Zulqarnain b Mudassar Nazar	57
B.C. Broad	b Shakil Khan	66
M.W. Gatting*	c Manzoor Elahi b Abdul Qadir	53
D.J. Capel	st Zulqarnain b Tausif Ahmed	25
J.E. Emburey	run out	3
P.A.J. DeFreitas	c Shoaib Mohammad b Abdul Qadir	3
C.W.J. Athey	st Zulqarnain b Abdul Qadir	6
N.H. Fairbrother	run out	1
N.A. Foster	not out	2
R.C. Russell+	not out	2
N.G.B. Cook		
Extras	(B 1, LB 7, W 5, NB 5)	18
TOTAL	(45 overs) (for 8 wkts)	**236**

	O	M	R	W		Fall	
Mohsin Kamal	9	0	37	0	1st	101
Shakil Khan	9	0	50	1	2nd	168
Mudassar Nazar	9	0	33	1	3rd	214
Tausif Ahmed	9	0	59	1	4th	221
Abdul Qadir	9	0	49	3	5th	221
					6th	231
					7th	232
					8th	234

PAKISTAN
Ramiz Raja	lbw b Foster	5
Shoaib Mohammad	retired hurt	6
Salim Malik	b Cook	52
Ijaz Ahmed	c Russell b Cook	15
Mudassar Nazar	b Capel	1
Manzoor Elahi	c Gooch b Emburey	21
Abdul Qadir*	c Russell b DeFreitas	21
Zulqarnain+	c Russell b DeFreitas	0
Mohsin Kamal	b Foster	5
Tausif Ahmed	not out	0
Shakil Khan	b Foster	0
Extras	(LB 3, W 3, NB 6)	12
TOTAL	(31.5 overs)	**138**

	O	M	R	W		Fall	
DeFreitas	7	0	31	2	1st	11
Foster	6.5	0	20	3	2nd	34
Cook	6	1	18	2	3rd	43
Capel	9	0	44	1	4th	78
Emburey	3	0	22	1	5th	122
					6th	126
					7th	138
					8th	138
					9th	138

Match No: 149/43

AUSTRALIA v ENGLAND

Australia Bicentennial Match
Played at Melbourne Cricket Ground on 04/02/1988
Toss: Australia   **Result:** Australia won by 22 runs
Umpires: R.C. Bailhache and A.R. Crafter
Man of the match: G.R. Marsh
Debuts: Eng - P.W. Jarvis, N.V. Radford

AUSTRALIA

D.C. Boon	c & b Capel	33
G.R. Marsh	run out	87
D.M. Jones	c sub (M.D. Moxon) b Emburey	30
M.R.J. Veletta	c Capel b Emburey	13
S.R. Waugh	run out	27
A.R. Border*	c Gatting b DeFreitas	19
A.I.C. Dodemaide	not out	7
P.L. Taylor	not out	1
G.C. Dyer+		
S.P. Davis		
M.R. Whitney		
Extras	(LB 6, W 5, NB 7)	18
TOTAL	(48 overs) (for 6 wkts)	**235**

	O	M	R	W		Fall
DeFreitas	10	1	43	1	1st	70
Radford	10	0	61	0	2nd	133
Capel	8	1	30	1	3rd	169
Jarvis	10	0	42	0	4th	184
Emburey	10	0	53	2	5th	222
					6th	233

ENGLAND

B.C. Broad	c Dyer b Waugh	25
R.T. Robinson	c Dodemaide b Whitney	35
P.A.J. DeFreitas	run out	21
C.W.J. Athey	c Border b Davis	4
N.H. Fairbrother	st Dyer b Taylor	22
M.W. Gatting*	c Border b Whitney	37
D.J. Capel	c Taylor b Davis	18
J.E. Emburey	b Dodemaide	26
C.J. Richards+	not out	14
N.V. Radford	not out	0
P.W. Jarvis		
Extras	(LB 9, W 1, NB 1)	11
TOTAL	(48 overs) (for 8 wkts)	**213**

	O	M	R	W		Fall
Whitney	10	1	37	2	1st	58
Dodemaide	10	1	35	1	2nd	65
Davis	10	0	55	2	3rd	82
Waugh	10	0	42	1	4th	96
Taylor	8	0	35	1	5th	123
					6th	172
					7th	175
					8th	213

Match No: 150/24
NEW ZEALAND v ENGLAND

Rothmans Cup
Played at Carisbrook, Dunedin on 09/03/1988
Toss: New Zealand   **Result:** England won by 5 wickets
Umpires: R.L. McHarg and G.C. Morris
Man of the match: J.G. Wright
Debuts: NZ - M.J. Greatbatch, C.M. Kuggeleign, R.B. Reid

NEW ZEALAND

R.B. Reid	c Broad b DeFreitas	8
J.G. Wright*	c Moxon b Radford	70
M.D. Crowe	b Jarvis	18
M.J. Greatbatch	c Capel b Emburey	28
K.R. Rutherford	c French b Capel	13
C.M. Kuggeleijn	c Gatting b DeFreitas	34
J.G. Bracewell	run out	7
I.D.S. Smith+	b Emburey	0
M.C. Snedden	b Emburey	7
W. Watson	not out	0
E.J. Chatfield	st French b Emburey	0
Extras	(LB 13, W 5, NB 1)	19
TOTAL	(49.4 overs)	**204**

						Fall	
DeFreitas	10	1	26	2		1st	24
Radford	10	0	47	1		2nd	50
Capel	10	1	45	1		3rd	127
Jarvis	10	2	34	1		4th	140
Emburey	9.4	0	39	4		5th	157
						6th	188
						7th	190
						8th	204
						9th	204
						10th	204

ENGLAND

B.C. Broad	run out	33
M.D. Moxon	c Smith b Chatfield	6
R.T. Robinson	lbw b Snedden	17
M.W. Gatting*	c Kuggeleijn b Rutherford	42
N.H. Fairbrother	not out	50
D.J. Capel	c Smith b Chatfield	48
J.E. Emburey	not out	2
P.A.J. DeFreitas		
B.N. French+		
P.W. Jarvis		
N.V. Radford		
Extras	(LB 6, W 2, NB 1)	9
TOTAL	(49.2 overs) (for 5 wkts)	**207**

						Fall	
Watson	10	2	46	0		1st	28
Chatfield	10	2	15	2		2nd	53
Kuggeleijn	7	0	31	0		3rd	69
Snedden	10	1	46	1		4th	114
Bracewell	7.2	0	42	0		5th	192
Rutherford	5	0	21	1			

Match No: 151/25

NEW ZEALAND v ENGLAND

Rothmans Cup
Played at Lancaster Park, Christchurch on 12/03/1988
Toss: England   Result: England won by 6 wickets
Umpires: B.L. Aldridge and G.C. Morris
Man of the match: B.C. Broad
Debuts: None

NEW ZEALAND
R.B. Reid	c Broad b Capel	8
J.G. Wright*	c DeFreitas b Emburey	43
M.D. Crowe	c French b DeFreitas	2
M.J. Greatbatch	run out	15
K.R. Rutherford	run out	5
C.M. Kuggeleijn	b Emburey	40
J.G. Bracewell	run out	43
I.D.S. Smith+	c Fairbrother b Emburey	19
M.C. Snedden	not out	1
W. Watson	not out	2
E.J. Chatfield		
Extras	(LB 5, W 3)	8
TOTAL	(45 overs) (for 8 wkts)	186

						Fall	
DeFreitas	9	0	53	1	1st	24
Capel	9	3	27	1	2nd	26
Jarvis	9	0	33	0	3rd	53
Radford	9	0	30	0	4th	68
Emburey	9	1	38	3	5th	86
					6th	149
					7th	183
					8th	183

ENGLAND
B.C. Broad	c Rutherford b Snedden	56
M.D. Moxon	c Kuggeleijn b Watson	17
R.T. Robinson	c Chatfield b Rutherford	44
M.W. Gatting*	b Watson	33
N.H. Fairbrother	not out	25
D.J. Capel	not out	6
J.E. Emburey		
P.A.J. DeFreitas		
B.N. French+		
P.W. Jarvis		
N.V. Radford		
Extras	(LB 4, W 3)	7
TOTAL	(42.5 overs) (for 4 wkts)	188

						Fall	
Watson	9	1	31	2	1st	37
Chatfield	7	0	32	0	2nd	112
Bracewell	5	0	28	0	3rd	151
Snedden	9	0	33	1	4th	167
Kuggeleijn	6	0	31	0		
Rutherford	6.5	0	29	1		

Match No: 152/26

NEW ZEALAND v ENGLAND

Rothmans Cup
Played at McLean Park, Napier on 16/03/1988
Toss: New Zealand   **Result:** New Zealand won by 7 wickets
Umpires: F.R. Goodall and S.J. Woodward
Man of the match: J.G. Wright
Debuts: NZ - R.H. Vance

ENGLAND
B.C. Broad	b Snedden	106
C.W.J. Athey	run out	0
R.T. Robinson	c Smith b Snedden	36
P.A.J. DeFreitas	c Kuggeleijn b Rutherford	23
M.W. Gatting*	b Rutherford	6
N.H. Fairbrother	c & b Kuggeleijn	1
D.J. Capel	c Morrison b Kuggeleijn	14
J.E. Emburey	c & b Snedden	15
P.W. Jarvis	not out	5
B.N. French+	b Chatfield	0
N.V. Radford	c Rutherford b Snedden	0
Extras	(LB 10, W 2, NB 1)	13
TOTAL	(47.3 overs)	**219**

						Fall	
Morrison	7	0	32	0	1st	1
Watson	5	0	24	0	2nd	80
Chatfield	9	0	40	1	3rd	114
Snedden	8.3	0	34	4	4th	137
Rutherford	10	0	39	2	5th	142
Kuggeleijn	8	0	40	2	6th	186
					7th	205
					8th	216
					9th	218
					10th	219

NEW ZEALAND
J.G. Wright*	c Robinson b Emburey	101
R.H. Vance	b DeFreitas	5
A.H. Jones	b Jarvis	16
M.J. Greatbatch	not out	64
K.R. Rutherford	not out	27
C.M. Kuggeleijn		
I.D.S. Smith+		
M.C. Snedden		
D.K. Morrison		
W. Watson		
E.J. Chatfield		
Extras	(LB 6, W 4)	10
TOTAL	(46.3 overs) (for 3 wkts)	**223**

						Fall	
DeFreitas	10	2	30	1	1st	24
Capel	9	0	50	0	2nd	62
Radford	8	0	31	0	3rd	172
Jarvis	9.3	1	45	1		
Emburey	7	0	47	1		
Gatting	3	0	14	0		

Match No: 153/27

NEW ZEALAND v ENGLAND

Rothmans Cup
Played at Eden Park, Auckland on 19/03/1988
Toss: New Zealand   **Result:** New Zealand won by 4 wickets
Umpires: R.L. McHarg and S.J. Woodward
Man of the match: A.H. Jones
Debuts: None

ENGLAND

B.C. Broad	b Snedden	12
M.D. Moxon	b Watson	19
P.A.J. DeFreitas	c Crowe b Watson	6
R.T. Robinson	c Kuggeleijn b Rutherford	13
M.W. Gatting*	c Wright b Watson	48
N.H. Fairbrother	b Kuggeleijn	54
D.J. Capel	b Chatfield	25
J.E. Emburey	b Chatfield	11
P.W. Jarvis	run out	0
B.N. French+	c Greatbatch b Chatfield	2
N.V. Radford	not out	0
Extras	(LB 12, W 5, NB 1)	18
TOTAL	(50 overs)	**208**

						Fall	
Hadlee	10	0	43	0	1st	33
Watson	10	0	36	3	2nd	33
Snedden	10	2	30	1	3rd	41
Chatfield	10	2	31	3	4th	71
Kuggeleijn	5	0	28	1	5th	146
Rutherford	5	0	28	1	6th	179
					7th	197
					8th	197
					9th	208
					10th	208

NEW ZEALAND

J.G. Wright*	b Radford	47
A.H. Jones	c Radford b Jarvis	90
M.D. Crowe	c French b Jarvis	13
M.J. Greatbatch	c Radford b Jarvis	5
K.R. Rutherford	lbw b Jarvis	0
C.M. Kuggeleijn	b Capel	2
R.J. Hadlee	not out	33
I.D.S. Smith+	not out	1
M.C. Snedden		
W. Watson		
E.J. Chatfield		
Extras	(B 3, LB 12, W 5)	20
TOTAL	(49.2 overs) (for 6 wkts)	**211**

						Fall	
DeFreitas	10	0	45	0	1st	86
Capel	10	0	42	1	2nd	115
Radford	10	2	32	1	3rd	129
Jarvis	9.2	1	33	4	4th	129
Emburey	10	0	44	0	5th	138
					6th	199

Match No: 154/30

ENGLAND v WEST INDIES

Texaco Trophy
Played at Edgbaston, Birmingham on 19/05/1988
Toss: England   **Result:** England won by 6 wickets
Umpires: J. Birkenshaw and B.J. Meyer
Man of the match: G.C. Small
Debuts: Eng - M.A. Lynch

WEST INDIES
C.G. Greenidge	b Small	18
P.V. Simmons	c Lamb b Dilley	22
R.B. Richardson	lbw b Pringle	11
I.V.A. Richards*	c Emburey b Small	13
A.L. Logie	c Downton b Small	51
C.L. Hooper	c Emburey b Small	51
P.J.L. Dujon+	run out	27
R.A. Harper	b Emburey	4
M.D. Marshall	c Lamb b DeFreitas	6
C.E.L. Ambrose	b Emburey	1
C.A. Walsh	not out	2
Extras	(LB 2, W 3, NB 6)	11
TOTAL	(55 overs)	**217**

						Fall	
DeFreitas	11	2	45	1	1st	34
Dilley	11	0	64	1	2nd	50
Small	11	0	31	4	3rd	66
Pringle	11	5	26	1	4th	72
Emburey	11	1	49	2	5th	169
					6th	180
					7th	195
					8th	209
					9th	212
					10th	217

ENGLAND
G.A. Gooch	c Harper b Ambrose	43
B.C. Broad	c Greenidge b Marshall	35
M.W. Gatting*	not out	82
M.A. Lynch	run out	0
A.J. Lamb	b Hooper	11
D.R. Pringle	not out	23
P.R. Downton+		
J.E. Emburey		
P.A.J. DeFreitas		
G.C. Small		
G.R. Dilley		
Extras	(B 2, LB 10, W 7, NB 6)	25
TOTAL	(53 overs) (for 4 wkts)	**219**

						Fall	
Ambrose	11	1	39	1	1st	70
Walsh	11	1	50	0	2nd	119
Richards	7	1	29	0	3rd	121
Marshall	11	1	32	1	4th	153
Harper	7	0	33	0		
Hooper	6	0	24	1		

Match No: 155/31

ENGLAND v WEST INDIES

Texaco Trophy
Played at Headingley, Leeds on 21/05/1988
Toss: West Indies   **Result:** England won by 47 runs
Umpires: D.J. Constant and D.R. Shepherd
Man of the match: D.R. Pringle
Debuts: WI - I.R. Bishop

ENGLAND
G.A. Gooch	c Greenidge b Simmons	32
B.C. Broad	c Dujon b Ambrose	13
M.W. Gatting*	c Richards b Marshall	18
M.A. Lynch	lbw b Marshall	2
A.J. Lamb	c Dujon b Simmons	2
D.R. Pringle	c Dujon b Walsh	39
P.R. Downton+	c Dujon b Bishop	30
J.E. Emburey	c Ambrose b Bishop	8
P.A.J. DeFreitas	not out	15
G.C. Small	not out	7
G.R. Dilley		
Extras	(B 3, LB 1, W 3, NB 13)	20
TOTAL	(55 overs) (for 8 wkts)	186

						Fall	
Walsh	11	0	39	1	1st	29
Ambrose	7	2	19	1	2nd	64
Marshall	9	1	29	2	3rd	72
Bishop	11	1	32	2	4th	80
Simmons	9	2	30	2	5th	83
Richards	8	0	33	0	6th	149
					7th	154
					8th	169

WEST INDIES
C.G. Greenidge	c Downton b Small	21
P.V. Simmons	b DeFreitas	1
R.B. Richardson	c Downton b Dilley	1
I.V.A. Richards*	b Small	31
A.L. Logie	c Lynch b Dilley	8
C.L. Hooper	lbw b Pringle	12
P.J.L. Dujon+	b Pringle	12
M.D. Marshall	c Downton b Gooch	1
C.E.L. Ambrose	c Downton b Pringle	23
C.A. Walsh	b Emburey	18
I.R. Bishop	not out	2
Extras	(LB 3, W 3, NB 3)	9
TOTAL	(46.3 overs)	139

						Fall	
Dilley	11	0	45	2	1st	2
DeFreitas	9	2	29	1	2nd	11
Small	9	2	11	2	3rd	38
Pringle	11	0	30	3	4th	67
Gooch	3	0	12	1	5th	67
Emburey	3.3	0	9	1	6th	83
					7th	84
					8th	104
					9th	132
					10th	139

Match No: 156/32

ENGLAND v WEST INDIES

Texaco Trophy
Played at Lord's, London on 23 & 24/05/1988
Toss: England   **Result:** England won by 7 wickets
Umpires: H.D. Bird and N.T. Plews
Man of the match: P.A.J. DeFreitas
Debuts: None

WEST INDIES
C.G. Greenidge	c DeFreitas b Emburey	39
D.L. Haynes	run out	10
R.B. Richardson	c Downton b Pringle	13
I.V.A. Richards*	c Emburey b DeFreitas	9
A.L. Logie	run out	0
C.L. Hooper	run out	12
P.J.L. Dujon+	not out	30
M.D. Marshall	b Emburey	41
W.K.M. Benjamin		
C.A. Walsh		
I.R. Bishop		
Extras	(B 2, LB 10, W 12)	24
TOTAL	(55 overs) (for 7 wkts)	**178**

						Fall	
DeFreitas	11	5	20	1	1st	40
Radford	11	2	29	0	2nd	75
Small	10	1	34	0	3rd	79
Pringle	11	4	27	1	4th	79
Emburey	10	1	53	2	5th	95
Gooch	2	1	3	0	6th	111
					7th	178

ENGLAND
G.A. Gooch	st Dujon b Hooper	28
B.C. Broad	b Bishop	34
M.W. Gatting*	not out	40
M.A. Lynch	b Bishop	6
A.J. Lamb	not out	30
D.R. Pringle		
P.R. Downton+		
J.E. Emburey		
P.A.J. DeFreitas		
G.C. Small		
N.V. Radford		
Extras	(B 6, LB 17, W 5, NB 14)	42
TOTAL	(50 overs) (for 3 wkts)	**180**

						Fall	
Marshall	9	2	21	0	1st	71
Walsh	11	5	11	0	2nd	108
Bishop	11	1	33	2	3rd	124
Benjamin	9	0	38	0		
Hooper	10	0	54	1		

Match No: 157/7

ENGLAND v SRI LANKA

Texaco Trophy
Played at The Oval, London on 04/09/1988
Toss: England   Result: England won by 5 wickets
Umpires: J.W. Holder and K.E. Palmer
Man of the match: K.J. Barnett
Debuts: Eng - K.J. Barnett, R.A. Smith   SL - M.A.W.R. Madurasinghe

SRI LANKA
D.S.B.P. Kuruppu+	lbw b Gooch	38
M.A.R. Samarasekera	b Small	10
P.A. de Silva	b Gooch	16
A. Ranatunga	run out	37
L.R.D. Mendis	b Small	60
R.S. Madugalle*	c Foster b Pringle	17
J.R. Ratnayeke	c Pringle b Small	19
H.P. Tillekeratne	not out	15
G.F. Labrooy	not out	10
M.A.W.R. Madurasinghe		
S.D. Anurasiri		
Extras	(B 1, LB 10, W 8, NB 1)	20
TOTAL	(55 overs) (for 7 wkts)	242

						Fall	
Foster	11	0	47	0	1st	21
Small	11	1	44	3	2nd	54
Gooch	11	1	35	2	3rd	75
Pringle	11	0	46	1	4th	144
Marks	11	0	59	0	5th	190
					6th	193
					7th	224

ENGLAND
G.A. Gooch*	c de Silva b Labrooy	7
R.T. Robinson	lbw b Ratnayeke	13
K.J. Barnett	run out	84
A.J. Lamb	c sub (B.E.A.Rajadurai) b Labrooy	66
R.A. Smith	c Kuruppu b Labrooy	9
R.J. Bailey	not out	43
D.R. Pringle	not out	19
R.C. Russell+		
V.J. Marks		
N.A. Foster		
G.C. Small		
Extras	(W 3, NB 1)	4
TOTAL	(52.4 overs) (for 5 wkts)	245

						Fall	
Ratnayeke	9.4	3	37	1	1st	9
Labrooy	10	0	40	3	2nd	22
Samarasekera	11	0	52	0	3rd	140
Ranatunga	11	0	42	0	4th	154
Anurasiri	6	0	31	0	5th	213
de Silva	2	0	19	0		
Madurasinghe	3	0	24	0		

Match No: 158/44

ENGLAND v AUSTRALIA

Texaco Trophy
Played at Old Trafford, Manchester on 25/05/1989
Toss: England   **Result:** England won by 95 runs
Umpires: J.W. Holder and N.T. Plews
Man of the match: P.A.J. DeFreitas
Debuts: Eng - S.J. Rhodes

ENGLAND
G.A. Gooch	c Jones b Border	52
D.I. Gower*	c Healy b Rackemann	36
M.W. Gatting	c Boon b Waugh	3
A.J. Lamb	b Lawson	35
R.A. Smith	c & b Alderman	35
I.T. Botham	c Boon b Lawson	4
D.R. Pringle	lbw b Waugh	9
S.J. Rhodes+	b Lawson	8
P.A.J. DeFreitas	not out	17
J.E. Emburey	b Rackemann	10
N.A. Foster	not out	5
Extras	(LB 12, W 3, NB 2)	17
TOTAL	(55 overs) (for 9 wkts)	**231**

						Fall	
Alderman	11	2	38	1	1st	55
Lawson	11	1	48	3	2nd	70
Rackemann	10	1	33	2	3rd	125
Waugh	11	1	45	2	4th	161
Moody	8	0	37	0	5th	167
Border	4	0	18	1	6th	179
					7th	190
					8th	203
					9th	220

AUSTRALIA
G.R. Marsh	c Rhodes b Emburey	17
D.C. Boon	b DeFreitas	5
D.M. Jones	c Rhodes b Foster	4
A.R. Border*	b Foster	4
S.R. Waugh	c Smith b DeFreitas	35
T.M. Moody	b Emburey	24
M.R.J. Veletta	lbw b Pringle	17
I.A. Healy+	c Emburey b Foster	10
G.F. Lawson	c DeFreitas b Emburey	0
C.G. Rackemann	b Botham	6
T.M. Alderman	not out	0
Extras	(B 1, LB 9, W 4)	14
TOTAL	(47.1 overs)	**136**

						Fall	
Foster	10	3	29	3	1st	8
DeFreitas	8	1	19	2	2nd	13
Pringle	8	2	19	1	3rd	17
Botham	10.1	1	28	1	4th	64
Emburey	11	0	31	3	5th	85
					6th	115
					7th	119
					8th	120
					9th	136
					10th	136

170   England - The Complete One-Day International Record

Match No: 159/45

ENGLAND v AUSTRALIA

Texaco Trophy
Played at Trent Bridge, Nottingham on 27/05/1989
Toss: England   **Result:** Match tied
Umpires: H.D. Bird and J.H. Hampshire
Man of the match: A.J. Lamb
Debuts: None

ENGLAND
G.A. Gooch	c Jones b Alderman	10
D.I. Gower*	b Waugh	28
M.W. Gatting	b May	37
A.J. Lamb	not out	100
R.A. Smith	st Healy b May	3
I.T. Botham	run out	8
D.R. Pringle	not out	25
S.J. Rhodes+		
P.A.J. DeFreitas		
J.E. Emburey		
N.A. Foster		
Extras	(LB 14, W 1)	15
TOTAL	(55 overs) (for 5 wkts)	**226**

					Fall	
Alderman	9	2	38	1	1st	30
Lawson	11	0	47	0	2nd	57
Rackemann	11	1	37	0	3rd	119
Waugh	11	1	47	1	4th	123
May	11	1	35	2	5th	138
Moody	2	0	8	0		

AUSTRALIA
D.C. Boon	b Botham	28
G.R. Marsh	lbw b Emburey	34
D.M. Jones	b Emburey	29
A.R. Border*	c Rhodes b Pringle	39
S.R. Waugh	run out	43
T.M. Moody	run out	10
I.A. Healy+	not out	26
G.F. Lawson	c Gooch b Foster	1
T.B.A. May	b DeFreitas	2
C.G. Rackemann	not out	0
T.M. Alderman		
Extras	(B 1, LB 6, W 7)	14
TOTAL	(55 overs) (for 8 wkts)	**226**

					Fall	
Foster	11	2	44	1	1st	59
DeFreitas	11	0	48	1	2nd	81
Pringle	11	1	38	1	3rd	116
Botham	11	0	42	1	4th	153
Emburey	11	0	47	2	5th	174
					6th	205
					7th	218
					8th	225

Match No: 160/46

ENGLAND v AUSTRALIA

Texaco Trophy
Played at Lord's, London on 29/05/1989
Toss: England
Umpires: B.J. Meyer and D.R. Shepherd
Man of the match: G.R. Marsh
Debuts: None

Result: Australia won by 6 wickets

ENGLAND

G.A. Gooch	b Alderman	136
D.I. Gower*	c Veletta b Moody	61
M.W. Gatting	run out	18
A.J. Lamb	lbw b Alderman	0
R.A. Smith	b Rackemann	21
I.T. Botham	not out	25
P.A.J. DeFreitas	c Rackemann b Alderman	0
D.R. Pringle	run out	0
S.J. Rhodes+	not out	1
J.E. Emburey		
N.A. Foster		
Extras	(LB 14, W 2)	16
TOTAL	(54.3 overs) (for 7 wkts)	**278**

						Fall	
Alderman	11	2	36	3	1st	123
Rackemann	11	0	56	1	2nd	180
Lawson	11	0	48	0	3rd	182
Waugh	11	0	70	0	4th	239
May	6	0	33	0	5th	266
Moody	5	0	21	1	6th	266
					7th	268

AUSTRALIA

G.R. Marsh	not out	111
D.C. Boon	lbw b Foster	19
D.M. Jones	c Gower b Emburey	27
A.R. Border*	b Pringle	53
S.R. Waugh	c Gooch b Foster	35
T.M. Moody	not out	6
M.R.J. Veletta+		
G.F. Lawson		
T.B.A. May		
C.G. Rackemann		
T.M. Alderman		
Extras	(LB 18, W 8, NB 2)	28
TOTAL	(54.3 overs) (for 4 wkts)	**279**

						Fall	
DeFreitas	11	1	50	0	1st	24
Foster	11	0	57	2	2nd	84
Pringle	10.3	0	50	1	3rd	197
Botham	11	0	43	0	4th	268
Emburey	11	0	61	1		

Match No: 161/8
ENGLAND v SRI LANKA

Nehru Cup
Played at Feroz Shah Kotla, Delhi on 15/10/1989
Toss: England   Result: England won by 5 wickets
Umpires: R.B. Gupta and P.J. McConnell
Man of the match: R.A. Smith
Debuts: Eng - A.J. Stewart, A.R.C. Fraser

SRI LANKA
R.S. Mahanama	run out	1
D.S.B.P. Kuruppu+	c Russell b Fraser	5
A.P. Gurusinha	c Lamb b Capel	19
P.A. de Silva	lbw b Hemmings	80
A. Ranatunga*	b Gooch	7
M.A.R. Samarasekera	c Stewart b Gooch	24
J.R. Ratnayeke	c Gooch b DeFreitas	6
G.F. Labrooy	lbw b DeFreitas	0
E.A.R. de Silva	b DeFreitas	2
S.D. Anurasiri	not out	5
K.I. Wijegunawardene	b Fraser	3
Extras	(B 6, LB 22, W 10, NB 3)	41
TOTAL	(48.3 overs)	193

					Fall	
DeFreitas	10	3	38	3	1st	1
Fraser	8.3	1	25	2	2nd	17
Small	6	0	26	0	3rd	42
Capel	4	0	16	1	4th	82
Gooch	10	2	26	2	5th	154
Hemmings	10	1	34	1	6th	174
					7th	180
					8th	180
					9th	186
					10th	193

ENGLAND
G.A. Gooch*	c P.A. de Silva b Labrooy	5
W. Larkins	c P.A. de Silva b Ranatunga	19
R.A. Smith	not out	81
A.J. Lamb	c P.A. de Silva b Wijegunawardene	52
A.J. Stewart	c Kuruppu b Ranatunga	4
D.J. Capel	lbw b Wijegunawardene	4
R.C. Russell+	not out	10
P.A.J. DeFreitas		
G.C. Small		
E.E. Hemmings		
A.R.C. Fraser		
Extras	(B 1, LB 8, W 10, NB 2)	21
TOTAL	(48.4 overs) (for 5 wkts)	196

					Fall	
Ratnayeke	7	1	10	0	1st	18
Labrooy	7	1	34	1	2nd	34
Ranatunga	10	0	39	2	3rd	137
E.A.R. de Silva	10	0	29	0	4th	157
Anurasiri	3	0	22	0	5th	170
P.A. de Silva	3	0	16	0		
Wijegunawardene	8.4	1	37	2		

Match No: 162/47

AUSTRALIA v ENGLAND

Nehru Cup
Played at Lal Bahadur Stadium, Hyderabad on 19/10/1989
Toss: Australia   **Result:** England won by 7 wickets
Umpires: L.H. Barker and Khizar Hayat
Man of the match: W. Larkins
Debuts: None

AUSTRALIA

D.C. Boon	c Gooch b Fraser				0		
G.R. Marsh	c Lamb b Small				54		
D.M. Jones	run out				50		
P.L. Taylor	not out				36		
A.R. Border*	not out				84		
S.R. Waugh							
S.P. O'Donnell							
I.A. Healy+							
T.B.A. May							
G.F. Lawson							
T.M. Alderman							
Extras	(LB 6, W 4, NB 8)				18		
TOTAL	(50 overs) (for 3 wkts)				242		
						Fall	
Fraser	10	2	48	1		1st	0
Pringle	10	3	42	0		2nd	108
Small	10	0	55	1		3rd	122
Capel	8	0	39	0			
Gooch	10	3	35	0			
Hemmings	2	0	17	0			

ENGLAND

G.A. Gooch*	lbw b Border				56		
W. Larkins	c Border b May				124		
R.A. Smith	not out				24		
A.J. Lamb	b Lawson				23		
A.J. Stewart	not out				4		
D.J. Capel							
R.C. Russell+							
D.R. Pringle							
G.C. Small							
E.E. Hemmings							
A.R.C. Fraser							
Extras	(B 1, LB 9, NB 2)				12		
TOTAL	(47.3 overs) (for 3 wkts)				243		
						Fall	
Alderman	7	1	28	0		1st	185
Lawson	10	1	51	1		2nd	191
May	10	0	55	1		3rd	234
O'Donnell	7.3	0	27	0			
Border	10	0	43	1			
Taylor	3	0	29	0			

Match No: 163/28
ENGLAND v PAKISTAN

Nehru Cup
Played at Barabati Stadium, Cuttack on 22/10/1989
Toss: Pakistan   **Result:** England won by 4 wickets
Umpires: R.B. Gupta and V.K. Ramaswamy
Man of the match: G.A. Gooch
Debuts: None

PAKISTAN
Shahid Saeed	b Capel	5
Shoaib Mohammad	c Cook b Capel	3
Ijaz Ahmed	b Cook	15
Javed Miandad	b Gooch	14
Salim Malik	b Small	42
Imran Khan*	st Russell b Hemmings	19
Salim Yousuf+	c Lamb b Gooch	6
Abdul Qadir	c Russell b Cook	13
Wasim Akram	lbw b Gooch	0
Mushtaq Ahmed	not out	9
Waqar Younis	not out	4
Extras	(B 5, LB 8, W 2, NB 3)	18
TOTAL	(50 overs) (for 9 wkts)	**148**

						Fall	
Fraser	10	3	15	0	1st	8
Capel	8	2	16	2	2nd	16
Small	8	2	29	1	3rd	37
Gooch	10	4	19	3	4th	53
Cook	10	0	43	2	5th	107
Hemmings	4	0	13	1	6th	111
					7th	128
					8th	128
					9th	132

ENGLAND
G.A. Gooch*	b Wasim Akram	7
W. Larkins	c Javed Miandad b Wasim Akram	0
R.A. Smith	c Javed Miandad b Mushtaq Ahmed	19
A.J. Lamb	b Salim Malik	42
A.J. Stewart	c Javed Miandad b Abdul Qadir	31
D.J. Capel	run out	23
R.C. Russell+	not out	7
G.C. Small	not out	0
E.E. Hemmings		
A.R.C. Fraser		
N.G.B. Cook		
Extras	(B 8, LB 4, W 8)	20
TOTAL	(43.2 overs) (for 6 wkts)	**149**

						Fall	
Wasim Akram	10	1	32	2	1st	1
Waqar Younis	10	1	30	0	2nd	21
Abdul Qadir	9.2	2	29	1	3rd	68
Mushtaq Ahmed	6	2	25	1	4th	92
Salim Malik	2	0	9	1	5th	139
Imran Khan	6	1	12	0	6th	148

Match No: 164/20
INDIA v ENGLAND

Nehru Cup
Played at Green Park, Modi Stadium, Kanpur on 25/10/1989
Toss: India					**Result:** India won by 6 wickets
Umpires: K.T. Francis and Khizar Hayat
Man of the match: C. Sharma
Debuts: None

ENGLAND
G.A. Gooch*	c Azharuddin b Chetan Sharma	21
W. Larkins	lbw b A.K. Sharma	42
R.A. Smith	c Azharuddin b Prabhakar	0
A.J. Lamb	c Srikkanth b Chetan Sharma	91
A.J. Stewart	run out	61
D.J. Capel	b Kapil Dev	2
P.A.J. DeFreitas	c Azharuddin b Kapil Dev	11
R.C. Russell+	not out	10
G.C. Small	not out	0
E.E. Hemmings		
A.R.C. Fraser		
Extras	(LB 7, W 7, NB 3)	17
TOTAL	(50 overs) (for 7 wkts)	**255**

						Fall	
Kapil Dev	10	0	56	2	1st	43
Prabhakar	10	0	50	1	2nd	48
Chetan Sharma	10	0	78	2	3rd	80
Arshad Ayub	10	0	27	0	4th	210
A.K. Sharma	10	1	37	1	5th	219
					6th	239
					7th	251

INDIA
K. Srikkanth*	st Russell b Hemmings	32
R. Lamba	c Russell b Small	16
N.S. Sidhu	run out	61
Chetan Sharma	not out	101
D.B. Vengsarkar	c Larkins b DeFreitas	31
Kapil Dev	not out	4
M. Azharuddin		
A.K. Sharma		
K.S. More+		
M. Prabhakar		
Arshad Ayub		
Extras	(LB 6, W 6, NB 2)	14
TOTAL	(48.1 overs) (for 4 wkts)	**259**

						Fall	
Fraser	10	2	31	0	1st	41
DeFreitas	10	0	66	1	2nd	65
Hemmings	10	0	51	1	3rd	170
Small	10	0	44	1	4th	251
Capel	3	0	24	0		
Gooch	5.1	0	37	0		

Match No: 165/33

ENGLAND v WEST INDIES

Nehru Cup
Played at Roop Singh Stadium, Gwalior on 27/10/1989
Toss: West Indies **Result:** West Indies won by 26 runs
Umpires: S.K. Ghosh and V.K. Ramaswamy
Man of the match: D.L. Haynes
Debuts: None

WEST INDIES
D.L. Haynes	not out	138
P.V. Simmons	run out	13
R.B. Richardson	run out	44
I.V.A. Richards*	c Hemmings b Small	16
A.L. Logie	c Stewart b Small	17
M.D. Marshall	c Smith b Small	16
R.C. Haynes	not out	0
P.J.L. Dujon+		
W.K.M. Benjamin		
C.E.L. Ambrose		
C.A. Walsh		
Extras	(LB 10, W 9, NB 2)	21
TOTAL	(50 overs) (for 5 wkts)	265

						Fall	
Fraser	10	1	47	0		1st	31
DeFreitas	10	1	42	0		2nd	155
Capel	8	0	49	0		3rd	188
Small	10	0	39	3		4th	236
Hemmings	7	0	44	0		5th	264
Gooch	5	0	34	0			

ENGLAND
G.A. Gooch*	c Dujon b Marshall	59
W. Larkins	c sub (K.L.T. Arthurton) b Marshall	29
R.A. Smith	c Dujon b Marshall	65
A.J. Lamb	b Marshall	0
A.J. Stewart	c Logie b Simmons	20
D.J. Capel	b Benjamin	21
P.A.J. DeFreitas	c sub (K.L.T. Arthurton) b Walsh	7
R.C. Russell+	not out	8
G.C. Small	b Benjamin	4
E.E. Hemmings	not out	1
A.R.C. Fraser		
Extras	(B 1, LB 13, W 11)	25
TOTAL	(50 overs) (for 8 wkts)	239

						Fall	
Ambrose	10	0	33	0		1st	58
Benjamin	10	1	46	2		2nd	150
Walsh	10	0	41	1		3rd	150
Marshall	10	0	33	4		4th	189
R.C. Haynes	4	0	25	0		5th	191
Richards	5	0	44	0		6th	209
Simmons	1	0	3	1		7th	229
						8th	238

Match No: 166/29

ENGLAND v PAKISTAN

Nehru Cup
Played at Vidarbha C.A. Ground, Nagpur on 30/10/1989
Toss: Pakistan   **Result:** Pakistan won by 6 wickets
Umpires: R.B. Gupta and V.K. Ramaswamy
Man of the match: Ramiz Raja
Debuts: Eng - N. Hussain

ENGLAND
G.A. Gooch*	c sub (Shoaib Mohammad) b Waqar Younis	35
W. Larkins	c & b Akram Raza	25
R.A. Smith	b Abdul Qadir	55
A.J. Stewart+	b Waqar Younis	0
N. Hussain	lbw b Abdul Qadir	2
A.J. Lamb	c Aamer Malik b Abdul Qadir	6
D.J. Capel	run out	20
D.R. Pringle	not out	21
P.A.J. DeFreitas	not out	4
G.C. Small		
A.R.C. Fraser		
Extras	(B 3, LB 20, W 3)	26
TOTAL	(30 overs) (for 7 wkts)	**194**

					Fall	
Imran Khan	4	0	26	0	1st	44
Wasim Akram	6	0	28	0	2nd	102
Akram Raza	5	0	28	1	3rd	103
Waqar Younis	6	1	40	2	4th	136
Mushtaq Ahmed	3	0	19	0	5th	144
Abdul Qadir	6	0	30	3	6th	145
					7th	184

PAKISTAN
Ramiz Raja	not out	85
Javed Miandad	b DeFreitas	17
Ijaz Ahmed	c Smith b DeFreitas	2
Imran Khan*	lbw b Small	15
Salim Malik	c Lamb b Fraser	66
Wasim Akram	not out	0
Aamer Malik+		
Abdul Qadir		
Akram Raza		
Mushtaq Ahmed		
Waqar Younis		
Extras	(LB 10)	10
TOTAL	(28.3 overs) (for 4 wkts)	**195**

					Fall	
Fraser	6	0	58	1	1st	26
DeFreitas	6	0	40	2	2nd	32
Capel	6	0	24	0	3rd	69
Pringle	5	0	33	0	4th	191
Small	5.3	0	30	1		

Match No: 167/34

WEST INDIES v ENGLAND

Cable & Wireless Series
Played at Queen's Park Oval, Port of Spain, Trinidad on 14/02/1990
Toss: England   **Result:** Match abandoned
Umpires: D.M. Archer and C.E. Cumberbatch
Man of the match: None
Debuts: Eng - C.C. Lewis   WI - E.A. Moseley

WEST INDIES

C.G. Greenidge	c Stewart b Capel	21
D.L. Haynes	c Russell b Lewis	25
R.B. Richardson	c Stewart b Fraser	51
C.L. Hooper	c Smith b Hemmings	17
C.A. Best	c & b Gooch	6
I.V.A. Richards*	b Small	32
E.A. Moseley	c Lewis b Fraser	2
M.D. Marshall	b Small	9
P.J.L. Dujon+	not out	15
I.R. Bishop	not out	18
C.A. Walsh		
Extras	(B 4, LB 4, W 3, NB 1)	12
TOTAL	(50 overs) (for 8 wkts)	**208**

						Fall	
Small	10	1	41	2	1st	49
Fraser	10	1	37	2	2nd	49
Capel	6	0	25	1	3rd	89
Lewis	7	1	30	1	4th	100
Hemmings	9	0	41	1	5th	155
Gooch	8	0	26	1	6th	162
					7th	172
					8th	180

ENGLAND

G.A. Gooch*	not out	13
W. Larkins	c Best b Marshall	2
R.A. Smith	not out	6
A.J. Lamb		
A.J. Stewart		
D.J. Capel		
R.C. Russell+		
C.C. Lewis		
G.C. Small		
E.E. Hemmings		
A.R.C. Fraser		
Extras	(LB 1, NB 4)	5
TOTAL	(13 overs) (for 1 wkt)	**26**

						Fall	
Marshall	6	1	12	1	1st	9
Bishop	5	2	6	0		
Walsh	1	0	1	0		
Moseley	1	0	6	0		

Match No: 168/35
WEST INDIES v ENGLAND

Cable & Wireless Series
Played at Queens Park Oval, Port of Spain, Trinidad on 17/02/1990
Toss: England   **Result:** Match abandoned
Umpires: D.M. Archer and C.E. Cumberbatch
Man of the match: None
Debuts: None

WEST INDIES
C.G. Greenidge	not out	8
D.L. Haynes	not out	4
R.B. Richardson		
C.L. Hooper		
C.A. Best		
I.V.A. Richards*		
P.J.L. Dujon+		
M.D. Marshall		
E.A. Moseley		
I.R. Bishop		
C.A. Walsh		
Extras	(LB 1)	1
TOTAL	(5.5 overs) (for 0 wkts)	13

Small	3	1	7	0
Fraser	2.5	0	5	0

ENGLAND
G.A. Gooch*
W. Larkins
R.A. Smith
A.J. Lamb
A.J. Stewart
D.J. Capel
R.C. Russell+
C.C. Lewis
G.C. Small
E.E. Hemmings
A.R.C. Fraser

Match No: 169/36

WEST INDIES v ENGLAND

Cable & Wireless Series
Played at Sabina Park, Kingston, Jamaica on 03/03/1990
Toss: England   **Result:** West Indies won by 3 wickets
Umpires: L.H. Barker and S. Bucknor
Man of the match: R.B. Richardson
Debuts: None

ENGLAND

Batsman	Dismissal	Runs
G.A. Gooch*	b Bishop	2
W. Larkins	b Walsh	33
R.A. Smith	c Marshall b Hooper	43
A.J. Lamb	b Bishop	66
A.J. Stewart	c Dujon b Hooper	0
D.J. Capel	c Dujon b Bishop	28
R.C. Russell+	b Marshall	2
P.A.J. DeFreitas	not out	3
G.C. Small	b Bishop	0
E.E. Hemmings		
A.R.C. Fraser		
Extras	(B 3, LB 25, W 6, NB 3)	37
TOTAL	(50 overs) (for 8 wkts)	214

Bowler	O	M	R	W	Fall	
Marshall	10	1	39	1	1st	20
Bishop	10	1	28	4	2nd	71
Walsh	6	0	38	1	3rd	117
Moseley	6	1	15	0	4th	117
Richards	9	0	32	0	5th	185
Hooper	9	0	34	2	6th	206
					7th	212
					8th	214

WEST INDIES

Batsman	Dismissal	Runs
D.L. Haynes	c Smith b DeFreitas	8
C.A. Best	b Small	4
R.B. Richardson	not out	108
C.L. Hooper	b Hemmings	20
I.V.A. Richards*	c Small b Hemmings	25
K.L.T. Arthurton	c Russell b Hemmings	0
P.J.L. Dujon+	c Smith b Small	27
E.A. Moseley	c Gooch b Fraser	0
I.R. Bishop	not out	6
M.D. Marshall		
C.A. Walsh		
Extras	(B 12, LB 4, W 1, NB 1)	18
TOTAL	(50 overs) (for 7 wkts)	216

Bowler	O	M	R	W	Fall	
Small	9	0	37	2	1st	11
DeFreitas	10	2	29	1	2nd	23
Capel	9	1	47	0	3rd	74
Fraser	10	0	41	1	4th	158
Hemmings	10	0	31	3	5th	158
Gooch	2	0	15	0	6th	204
					7th	210

Match No: 170/37

WEST INDIES v ENGLAND

Cable & Wireless Series
Played at Bourda, Georgetown, Guyana on 07/03/1990
Toss: West Indies **Result:** West Indies won by 6 wickets
Umpires: D.M. Archer and C. Duncan
Man of the match: C.A. Best
Debuts: None

ENGLAND

G.A. Gooch*	b Moseley	33
W. Larkins	c Richards b Moseley	34
R.A. Smith	c Hooper b Walsh	18
A.J. Lamb	c Dujon b Bishop	22
A.J. Stewart	c Dujon b Walsh	0
D.J. Capel	b Hooper	1
R.C. Russell+	b Bishop	28
P.A.J. DeFreitas	run out	11
G.C. Small	not out	18
E.E. Hemmings	not out	0
A.R.C. Fraser		
Extras	(B 1, LB 8, W 6, NB 8)	23
TOTAL	(48 overs) (for 8 wkts)	**188**

	O	M	R	W	Fall	
Bishop	10	1	41	2	1st	71
Walsh	10	1	33	2	2nd	88
Baptiste	8	3	21	0	3rd	109
Moseley	10	0	52	2	4th	109
Hooper	10	0	32	1	5th	112
					6th	132
					7th	156
					8th	181

WEST INDIES

D.L. Haynes	c DeFreitas b Hemmings	50
C.A. Best	run out	100
R.B. Richardson	c Russell b Capel	19
C.L. Hooper	not out	16
I.V.A. Richards*	c DeFreitas b Fraser	2
K.L.T. Arthurton	not out	0
P.J.L. Dujon+		
E.A.E. Baptiste		
E.A. Moseley		
I.R. Bishop		
C.A. Walsh		
Extras	(LB 2, W 1, NB 1)	4
TOTAL	(45.2 overs) (for 4 wkts)	**191**

	O	M	R	W	Fall	
DeFreitas	7	1	32	0	1st	113
Small	9.2	1	43	0	2nd	155
Capel	9	2	39	1	3rd	179
Fraser	10	1	42	1	4th	182
Hemmings	10	1	33	1		

182 England - The Complete One-Day International Record

Match No: 171/38

WEST INDIES v ENGLAND

Cable & Wireless Series
Played at Bourda, Georgetown, Guyana on 15/03/1990
Toss: West Indies   **Result:** West Indies won by 7 wickets
Umpires: D.M. Archer and C. Duncan
Man of the match: None
Debuts: WI - C.B. Lambert

ENGLAND

G.A. Gooch*	b Hooper	42
W. Larkins	c & b Bishop	1
R.A. Smith	c Dujon b Bishop	1
A.J. Lamb	c Richardson b Moseley	9
A.J. Stewart	b Hooper	13
R.J. Bailey	c & b Ambrose	42
D.J. Capel	c Dujon b Ambrose	7
R.C. Russell+	c Best b Ambrose	19
G.C. Small	c Dujon b Ambrose	0
E.E. Hemmings	not out	3
A.R.C. Fraser	not out	3
Extras	(B 2, LB 9, W 13, NB 2)	26
TOTAL	**(49 overs) (for 9 wkts)**	**166**

					Fall	
Bishop	7	2	22	2	1st	13
Ambrose	9	1	18	4	2nd	18
Moseley	10	1	48	1	3rd	46
Baptiste	10	1	31	0	4th	86
Hooper	10	0	28	2	5th	88
Best	3	0	8	0	6th	102
					7th	149
					8th	150
					9th	160

WEST INDIES

C.G. Greenidge	lbw b Fraser	77
C.B. Lambert	b Hemmings	48
R.B. Richardson	c Capel b Small	7
C.L. Hooper	not out	19
C.A. Best	not out	7
K.L.T. Arthurton		
P.J.L. Dujon*+		
E.A.E. Baptiste		
E.A. Moseley		
I.R. Bishop		
C.E.L. Ambrose		
Extras	(LB 2, W 4, NB 3)	9
TOTAL	**(40.2 overs) (for 3 wkts)**	**167**

					Fall	
Capel	9	1	41	0	1st	88
Small	7	0	32	1	2nd	105
Fraser	9.2	1	33	1	3rd	152
Gooch	5	1	22	0		
Hemmings	10	1	37	1		

Match No: 172/39

WEST INDIES v ENGLAND

Cable & Wireless Series
Played at Kensington Oval, Bridgetown, Barbados on 03/04/1990
Toss: West Indies **Result:** West Indies won by 4 wickets
Umpires: D.M. Archer and L.H. Barker
Man of the match: R.B. Richardson
Debuts: None

ENGLAND

D.M. Smith	b Moseley	5
W. Larkins	hit wicket b Walsh	34
R.A. Smith	run out	69
A.J. Lamb*	not out	55
N. Hussain	not out	15
D.J. Capel		
R.C. Russell+		
P.A.J. DeFreitas		
C.C. Lewis		
G.C. Small		
E.E. Hemmings		
Extras	(B 2, LB 8, W 14, NB 12)	36
TOTAL	(38 overs) (for 3 wkts)	**214**

					Fall	
Ambrose	9	2	31	0	1st	47
Walsh	8	0	49	1	2nd	98
Moseley	7	0	43	1	3rd	161
Marshall	8	0	50	0		
Hooper	6	0	31	0		

WEST INDIES

C.G. Greenidge	c Russell b Small	6
D.L. Haynes*	c Hussain b Hemmings	45
R.B. Richardson	b Small	80
C.A. Best	c sub (A.J. Stewart) b Capel	51
A.L. Logie	c R.A. Smith b DeFreitas	2
C.L. Hooper	c Larkins b Small	12
P.J.L. Dujon+	not out	11
E.A. Moseley	not out	1
M.D. Marshall		
C.E.L. Ambrose		
C.A. Walsh		
Extras	(LB 6, W 1, NB 2)	9
TOTAL	(37.3 overs) (for 6 wkts)	**217**

					Fall	
Small	9	1	29	3	1st	39
DeFreitas	8.3	0	63	1	2nd	78
Lewis	5	0	35	0	3rd	190
Capel	6	0	52	1	4th	193
Hemmings	9	0	32	1	5th	199
					6th	212

Match No: 173/28

ENGLAND v NEW ZEALAND

Texaco Trophy
Played at Headingley, Leeds on 23/05/1990
Toss: New Zealand   **Result:** New Zealand won by 4 wickets
Umpires: B.J. Meyer and N.T. Plews
Man of the match: M.J. Greatbatch
Debuts: NZ - C. Pringle

ENGLAND
G.A. Gooch*	c Millmow b Pringle	55
D.I. Gower	c Priest b Hadlee	1
R.A. Smith	c Crowe b Hadlee	128
A.J. Lamb	run out	18
A.J. Stewart	lbw b Morrison	33
D.R. Pringle	not out	30
R.C. Russell+	c Crowe b Pringle	13
P.A.J. DeFreitas	not out	1
C.C. Lewis		
G.C. Small		
E.E. Hemmings		
Extras	(LB 10, W 1, NB 5)	16
TOTAL	(55 overs) (for 6 wkts)	295

						Fall	
Hadlee	11	4	46	2	1st	5
Pringle	11	2	45	2	2nd	118
Morrison	11	0	70	1	3rd	168
Millmow	11	0	65	0	4th	225
Priest	11	0	59	0	5th	261
					6th	274

NEW ZEALAND
J.G. Wright*	c Stewart b Gooch	52
A.H. Jones	st Russell b Gooch	51
M.D. Crowe	c Russell b Lewis	46
M.J. Greatbatch	not out	102
K.R. Rutherford	lbw b Lewis	0
R.J. Hadlee	c Lamb b Lewis	12
M.W. Priest	c Gower b Small	2
I.D.S. Smith+	not out	17
C. Pringle		
J.P. Millmow		
D.K. Morrison		
Extras	(B 5, LB 7, W 3, NB 1)	16
TOTAL	(54.5 overs) (for 6 wkts)	298

						Fall	
Small	11	1	43	1	1st	97
DeFreitas	10.5	0	70	0	2nd	106
Pringle	7	0	45	0	3rd	224
Lewis	11	0	54	3	4th	224
Hemmings	11	0	51	0	5th	254
Gooch	4	0	23	2	6th	259

Match No: 174/29

ENGLAND v NEW ZEALAND

Texaco Trophy
Played at The Oval, London on 25/05/1990
Toss: England
Result: England won by 6 wickets
Umpires: D.J. Constant and J.H. Hampshire
Man of the match: D.E. Malcolm
Debuts: Eng - D.E. Malcolm

NEW ZEALAND
J.G. Wright*	c Small b Malcolm	15
A.H. Jones	run out	15
M.D. Crowe	c Russell b Lewis	7
M.J. Greatbatch	c Smith b Malcolm	111
K.R. Rutherford	retired hurt	0
R.J. Hadlee	retired hurt	9
M.W. Priest	c Smith b DeFreitas	24
I.D.S. Smith+	not out	25
C. Pringle	b Small	1
J.P. Millmow		
D.K. Morrison		
Extras	(LB 2, W 3)	5
TOTAL	(55 overs) (for 6 wkts)	212

Fall

DeFreitas	11	1	47	1	1st	25
Malcolm	11	5	19	2	2nd	34
Lewis	11	1	51	1	3rd	53
Small	11	0	59	1	4th	174
Hemmings	11	2	34	0	5th	202
					6th	212

ENGLAND
G.A. Gooch*	not out	112
D.I. Gower	b Hadlee	4
R.A. Smith	c Smith b Hadlee	5
A.J. Lamb	lbw b Pringle	4
A.J. Stewart	c Morrison b Priest	28
R.C. Russell+	not out	47
C.C. Lewis		
P.A.J. DeFreitas		
G.C. Small		
E.E. Hemmings		
D.E. Malcolm		
Extras	(LB 7, W 5, NB 1)	13
TOTAL	(49.3 overs) (for 4 wkts)	213

Fall

Hadlee	11	2	34	2	1st	5
Pringle	9.3	0	53	1	2nd	15
Millmow	9	1	47	0	3rd	29
Morrison	9	0	38	0	4th	104
Priest	11	2	34	1		

Match No: 175/21

ENGLAND v INDIA

Texaco Trophy
Played at Headingley, Leeds on 18/07/1990
Toss: India **Result:** India won by 6 wickets
Umpires: J.H. Hampshire and J.W. Holder
Man of the match: A.R. Kumble
Debuts: Eng - M.A. Atherton   Ind - A.R. Kumble

ENGLAND
G.A. Gooch*	c & b Shastri	45
M.A. Atherton	lbw b Prabhakar	7
D.I. Gower	b Kumble	50
A.J. Lamb	c Prabhakar b Kapil Dev	56
R.A. Smith	c More b Kumble	6
R.C. Russell+	c Manjrekar b Kapil Dev	14
P.A.J. DeFreitas	b Sharma	11
C.C. Lewis	lbw b Prabhakar	6
E.E. Hemmings	b Sharma	3
A.R.C. Fraser	not out	4
D.E. Malcolm	c Kapil Dev b Prabhakar	4
Extras	(B 6, LB 8, W 9)	23
TOTAL	(54.3 overs)	**229**

						Fall	
Kapil Dev	11	1	49	2		1st	22
Prabhakar	10.3	1	40	3		2nd	86
Sharma	11	1	57	2		3rd	134
Shastri	11	0	40	1		4th	142
Kumble	11	2	29	2		5th	186
						6th	196
						7th	211
						8th	221
						9th	224
						10th	229

INDIA
W.V. Raman	c Atherton b DeFreitas	0
N.S. Sidhu	lbw b Lewis	39
S.V. Manjrekar	c Gower b Lewis	82
S.R. Tendulkar	b Malcolm	19
M. Azharuddin*	not out	55
R.J. Shastri	not out	23
Kapil Dev		
M. Prabhakar		
K.S. More+		
S.K. Sharma		
A.R. Kumble		
Extras	(LB 5, W 9, NB 1)	15
TOTAL	(53 overs) (for 4 wkts)	**233**

						Fall	
DeFreitas	10	1	40	1		1st	1
Malcolm	11	0	57	1		2nd	76
Fraser	11	3	37	0		3rd	115
Lewis	10	0	58	2		4th	183
Hemmings	11	0	36	0			

Match No: 176/22

ENGLAND v INDIA

Texaco Trophy
Played at Trent Bridge, Nottingham on 20/07/1990
Toss: India   **Result:** India won by 5 wickets
Umpires: M.J. Kitchen and D.R. Shepherd
Man of the match: R.A. Smith
Debuts: None

ENGLAND

Batsman	Dismissal	Runs
G.A. Gooch*	b Prabhakar	7
M.A. Atherton	c More b Prabhakar	59
D.I. Gower	run out	25
A.J. Lamb	run out	3
R.A. Smith	b Shastri	103
R.C. Russell+	c Azharuddin b Kapil Dev	50
P.A.J. DeFreitas	c Vengsarkar b Sharma	1
C.C. Lewis	lbw b Prabhakar	7
G.C. Small	c Azharuddin b Kapil Dev	4
E.E. Hemmings	run out	0
A.R.C. Fraser	not out	0
Extras	(B 1, LB 12, W 8, NB 1)	22
TOTAL	(55 overs)	**281**

Bowler	O	M	R	W		Fall	
Kapil Dev	11	2	40	2	1st	12
Prabhakar	11	0	58	3	2nd	47
Sharma	10	0	50	1	3rd	62
Shastri	11	0	52	1	4th	173
Kumble	11	1	58	0	5th	246
Tendulkar	1	0	10	0	6th	254
					7th	275
					8th	280
					9th	281
					10th	281

INDIA

Batsman	Dismissal	Runs
R.J. Shastri	c Atherton b Hemmings	33
N.S. Sidhu	b Small	23
S.V. Manjrekar	st Russell b Hemmings	59
D.B. Vengsarkar	b Lewis	54
M. Azharuddin*	not out	63
S.R. Tendulkar	b Fraser	31
Kapil Dev	not out	5
M. Prabhakar		
K.S. More+		
S.K. Sharma		
A.R. Kumble		
Extras	(LB 5, W 9)	14
TOTAL	(53 overs) (for 5 wkts)	**282**

Bowler	O	M	R	W		Fall	
Small	10	0	73	1	1st	42
DeFreitas	11	0	59	0	2nd	69
Fraser	11	1	38	1	3rd	166
Hemmings	11	1	53	2	4th	186
Lewis	10	0	54	1	5th	249

Match No: 177/30

ENGLAND v NEW ZEALAND

Benson & Hedges World Series Cup
Played at Adelaide Oval on 01/12/1990
Toss: England   Result: New Zealand won by 7 runs
Umpires: A.R. Crafter and I.S. Thomas
Man of the match: J.G. Wright
Debuts: Eng - J.E. Morris   NZ - R.T. Latham

NEW ZEALAND
J.G. Wright	c Russell b Malcolm	67
A.H. Jones	c Russell b Malcolm	6
M.D. Crowe*	c Gower b Hemmings	16
K.R. Rutherford	b Small	50
R.T. Latham	b Small	27
I.D.S. Smith+	not out	10
C.Z. Harris	b Fraser	4
R.G. Petrie		
C. Pringle		
D.K. Morrison		
W. Watson		
Extras	(LB 12, W 5, NB 2)	19
TOTAL	(40 overs) (for 6 wkts)	199

						Fall	
Fraser	8	1	33	1	1st	16
Malcolm	9	0	39	2	2nd	62
Small	7	1	25	2	3rd	114
Lewis	8	0	39	0	4th	185
Hemmings	8	0	51	1	5th	188
					6th	199

ENGLAND
D.I. Gower	c Crowe b Pringle	6
M.A. Atherton	c Smith b Morrison	33
R.A. Smith	c Crowe b Pringle	8
A.J. Lamb*	b Watson	49
J.E. Morris	not out	63
R.C. Russell+	b Petrie	7
C.C. Lewis	c Morrison b Petrie	6
G.C. Small	c Wright b Morrison	5
E.E. Hemmings	b Pringle	3
A.R.C. Fraser	run out	0
D.E. Malcolm	not out	3
Extras	(LB 5, W 4)	9
TOTAL	(40 overs) (for 9 wkts)	192

						Fall	
Pringle	8	1	36	3	1st	6
Petrie	8	0	26	2	2nd	20
Morrison	8	0	38	2	3rd	91
Watson	8	1	29	1	4th	106
Harris	8	0	58	0	5th	126
					6th	158
					7th	173
					8th	182
					9th	188

Match No: 178/31

ENGLAND v NEW ZEALAND

Benson & Hedges World Series Cup
Played at WACA Ground, Perth on 07/12/1990
Toss: New Zealand   **Result:** England won by 4 wickets
Umpires: R.J. Evans and T.A. Prue
Man of the match: A.J. Stewart
Debuts: Eng - M.P. Bicknell, P.C.R. Tufnell

NEW ZEALAND
J.G. Wright	c Lewis b Bicknell	6
A.H. Jones	run out	26
M.D. Crowe*	c Russell b Lewis	37
M.J. Greatbatch+	c Larkins b Small	19
K.R. Rutherford	b Fraser	11
I.D.S. Smith	c Lamb b Bicknell	15
C.Z. Harris	c Russell b Tufnell	0
R.G. Petrie	not out	14
C. Pringle	c & b Small	2
D.K. Morrison	c Russell b Lewis	7
W. Watson	b Lewis	1
Extras	(B 4, LB 8, W 4, NB 4)	20
TOTAL	(49.2 overs)	**158**

						Fall	
Fraser	10	3	23	1	1st	16
Bicknell	10	1	36	2	2nd	52
Lewis	9.2	1	26	3	3rd	94
Small	10	1	30	2	4th	99
Tufnell	10	1	31	1	5th	126
					6th	126
					7th	126
					8th	128
					9th	154
					10th	158

ENGLAND
J.E. Morris	c Rutherford b Morrison	31
W. Larkins	c Crowe b Morrison	44
R.A. Smith	c sub (R.T. Latham) b Watson	0
A.J. Lamb*	lbw b Watson	20
A.J. Stewart	not out	29
R.C. Russell+	c Crowe b Pringle	5
C.C. Lewis	c Greatbatch b Pringle	0
G.C. Small	not out	9
M.P. Bicknell		
A.R.C. Fraser		
P.C.R. Tufnell		
Extras	(B 4, LB 8, W 10, NB 1)	23
TOTAL	(43.5 overs) (for 6 wkts)	**161**

						Fall	
Pringle	10	1	45	2	1st	72
Petrie	10	0	39	0	2nd	73
Morrison	10	1	27	2	3rd	100
Watson	10	1	26	2	4th	101
Harris	3.5	0	12	0	5th	115
					6th	129

Match No: 179/48

AUSTRALIA v ENGLAND

Benson & Hedges World Series Cup
Played at WACA Ground, Perth on 09/12/1990
Toss: England   **Result:** Australia won by 6 wickets
Umpires: R.J. Evans and P.J. McConnell
Man of the match: D.M. Jones
Debuts: None

ENGLAND
J.E. Morris	b S.R. Waugh	7
W. Larkins	b O'Donnell	38
R.A. Smith	c Healy b Rackemann	37
A.J. Lamb*	c Alderman b O'Donnell	3
A.J. Stewart	c Alderman b Matthews	41
C.C. Lewis	lbw b Matthews	2
R.C. Russell+	c O'Donnell b Alderman	13
G.C. Small	c Border b O'Donnell	5
M.P. Bicknell	not out	31
A.R.C. Fraser	c M.E. Waugh b O'Donnell	4
P.C.R. Tufnell		
Extras	(B 3, LB 3, W 2, NB 3)	11
TOTAL	(50 overs) (for 9 wkts)	**192**

						Fall	
Alderman	10	0	34	1	1st	31
Rackemann	10	2	19	1	2nd	58
S.R. Waugh	10	1	52	1	3rd	62
O'Donnell	10	0	45	4	4th	128
Matthews	10	0	36	2	5th	136
					6th	139
					7th	154
					8th	156
					9th	192

AUSTRALIA
D.C. Boon	b Small	38
G.R. Marsh	c Lewis b Tufnell	37
D.M. Jones	not out	63
A.R. Border*	c Russell b Bicknell	24
M.E. Waugh	c Lewis b Bicknell	0
S.R. Waugh	not out	12
G.R.J. Matthews		
S.P. O'Donnell		
I.A. Healy+		
C.G. Rackemann		
T.M. Alderman		
Extras	(LB 8, W 10, NB 1)	19
TOTAL	(41 overs) (for 4 wkts)	**193**

						Fall	
Fraser	9	2	30	0	1st	56
Bicknell	9	0	55	2	2nd	110
Small	4.3	1	14	1	3rd	155
Lewis	8	1	36	0	4th	155
Larkins	0.3	0	1	0		
Tufnell	10	1	49	1		

Match No: 180/32

ENGLAND v NEW ZEALAND

Benson & Hedges World Series Cup
Played at Sydney Cricket Ground on 13/12/1990
Toss: New Zealand   **Result:** England won by 33 runs
Umpires: A.R. Crafter and I.S. Thomas
Man of the match: A.J. Lamb
Debuts: None

ENGLAND
G.A. Gooch*	c Young b Petrie	3
W. Larkins	c Watson b Pringle	8
R.A. Smith	c Latham b Petrie	4
A.J. Lamb	b Morrison	72
J.E. Morris	run out	19
A.J. Stewart+	run out	42
C.C. Lewis	c & b Bradburn	4
M.P. Bicknell	b Pringle	8
E.E. Hemmings	not out	8
A.R.C. Fraser	lbw b Pringle	5
P.C.R. Tufnell	b Pringle	2
Extras	(LB 7, W 10, NB 2)	19
TOTAL	(46.4 overs)	**194**

						Fall	
Pringle	8.4	0	35	4		1st	7
Petrie	8	2	25	2		2nd	16
Watson	10	0	38	0		3rd	23
Morrison	10	0	45	1		4th	66
Bradburn	10	0	44	1		5th	143
						6th	156
						7th	179
						8th	179
						9th	188
						10th	194

NEW ZEALAND
M.D. Crowe*	lbw b Fraser	76
J.G. Wright	c Lamb b Lewis	23
G.E. Bradburn	b Lewis	2
K.R. Rutherford	b Hemmings	1
R.T. Latham	c Smith b Hemmings	10
B.A. Young+	c Morris b Bicknell	25
C.Z. Harris	c Stewart b Lewis	12
R.G. Petrie	c Stewart b Lewis	2
C. Pringle	c Hemmings b Fraser	1
D.K. Morrison	not out	2
W. Watson	run out	0
Extras	(LB 5, W 2)	7
TOTAL	(48.1 overs)	**161**

						Fall	
Bicknell	10	0	39	1		1st	56
Fraser	9	1	21	2		2nd	64
Lewis	9.1	0	35	4		3rd	66
Tufnell	10	1	27	0		4th	84
Hemmings	10	1	34	2		5th	138
						6th	151
						7th	158
						8th	159
						9th	160
						10th	161

Match No: 181/33

ENGLAND v NEW ZEALAND

Benson & Hedges World Series Cup
Played at Woolloongabba, Brisbane on 15/12/1990
Toss: New Zealand **Result:** New Zealand won by 8 wickets
Umpires: S.G. Randell and C.D. Timmins
Man of the match: M.D. Crowe
Debuts: None

ENGLAND
G.A. Gooch*	b Harris	48
W. Larkins	c Young b Petrie	15
R.A. Smith	b Morrison	41
A.J. Lamb	run out	10
J.E. Morris	c Young b Petrie	16
A.J. Stewart+	not out	30
C.C. Lewis	run out	3
P.A.J. DeFreitas	not out	27
A.R.C. Fraser		
D.E. Malcolm		
P.C.R. Tufnell		
Extras	(LB 8, W 5)	13
TOTAL	(50 overs) (for 6 wkts)	203

						Fall	
Pringle	10	1	36	0		1st	27
Petrie	10	1	32	2		2nd	99
Morrison	10	2	41	1		3rd	115
Watson	10	0	40	0		4th	122
Harris	8	0	36	1		5th	143
Latham	2	0	10	0		6th	149

NEW ZEALAND
M.D. Crowe*	c Gooch b Malcolm	78
J.G. Wright	c Stewart b Tufnell	54
A.H. Jones	not out	41
R.T. Latham	not out	17
K.R. Rutherford		
B.A. Young+		
C.Z. Harris		
R.G. Petrie		
C. Pringle		
D.K. Morrison		
W. Watson		
Extras	(B 1, LB 4, W 4, NB 5)	14
TOTAL	(44.3 overs) (for 2 wkts)	204

						Fall	
Fraser	9	2	38	0		1st	109
Malcolm	8	0	56	1		2nd	178
DeFreitas	8	0	31	0			
Lewis	9.3	1	31	0			
Tufnell	10	0	43	1			

Match No: 182/49

AUSTRALIA v ENGLAND

Benson & Hedges World Series Cup
Played at Woolloongabba, Brisbane on 16/12/1990
Toss: Australia   **Result:** Australia won by 37 runs
Umpires: A.R. Crafter and L.J. King
Man of the match: D.M. Jones
Debuts: None

AUSTRALIA
D.C. Boon	lbw b Fraser	10
G.R. Marsh	c Larkins b Bicknell	82
D.M. Jones	c Tufnell b DeFreitas	145
S.R. Waugh	not out	14
M.E. Waugh	c Tufnell b DeFreitas	5
S.P. O'Donnell	c Morris b DeFreitas	0
A.R. Border*	not out	4
G.R.J. Matthews		
I.A. Healy+		
C.G. Rackemann		
B.A. Reid		
Extras	(B 3, LB 12, W 7, NB 1)	23
TOTAL	(50 overs) (for 5 wkts)	**283**

						Fall	
Fraser	10	1	47	1		1st	24
Bicknell	10	0	64	1		2nd	209
DeFreitas	10	0	57	3		3rd	261
Hemmings	10	0	57	0		4th	272
Tufnell	10	0	43	0		5th	272

ENGLAND
G.A. Gooch*	b Matthews	41
W. Larkins	b O'Donnell	19
A.J. Lamb	c Border b Matthews	35
A.J. Stewart+	run out	40
R.A. Smith	run out	6
J.E. Morris	c S.R. Waugh b Matthews	13
P.A.J. DeFreitas	not out	49
M.P. Bicknell	b Rackemann	25
E.E. Hemmings	not out	3
A.R.C. Fraser		
P.C.R. Tufnell		
Extras	(B 1, LB 8, W 5, NB 1)	15
TOTAL	(50 overs) (for 7 wkts)	**246**

						Fall	
Reid	10	1	41	0		1st	26
O'Donnell	10	2	43	1		2nd	104
Rackemann	10	0	41	1		3rd	121
S.R. Waugh	4	0	20	0		4th	141
Matthews	10	0	54	3		5th	151
M.E. Waugh	4	0	23	0		6th	174
Border	1	0	9	0		7th	213
Jones	1	0	6	0			

Match No: 183/50

AUSTRALIA v ENGLAND

Benson & Hedges World Series Cup
Played at Sydney Cricket Ground on 01/01/1991
Toss: England   **Result:** Australia won by 68 runs
Umpires: L.J. King and S.G. Randell
Man of the match: P.L. Taylor
Debuts: None

AUSTRALIA

G.R. Marsh	lbw b Tufnell	29
D.C. Boon	lbw b Fraser	4
D.M. Jones	c Small b Tufnell	25
A.R. Border*	c Small b Hemmings	4
M.E. Waugh	c Larkins b Fraser	62
S.R. Waugh	c Stewart b Tufnell	3
S.P. O'Donnell	not out	71
I.A. Healy+	c Atherton b Fraser	4
P.L. Taylor	not out	2
C.G. Rackemann		
T.M. Alderman		
Extras	(LB 5, W 11, NB 1)	17
TOTAL	(50 overs) (for 7 wkts)	**221**

					Fall	
Fraser	10	2	28	3	1st	15
Small	10	1	43	0	2nd	55
DeFreitas	10	0	48	0	3rd	72
Tufnell	10	2	40	3	4th	82
Hemmings	10	0	57	1	5th	93
					6th	205
					7th	218

ENGLAND

G.A. Gooch*	b O'Donnell	37
W. Larkins	b Taylor	40
M.A. Atherton	c Healy b S.R. Waugh	8
A.J. Stewart+	c S.R. Waugh b Border	18
R.A. Smith	b Taylor	1
J.E. Morris	c M.E. Waugh b Taylor	8
P.A.J. DeFreitas	st Healy b Border	9
G.C. Small	st Healy b Border	15
E.E. Hemmings	run out	1
A.R.C. Fraser	c Boon b Rackemann	4
P.C.R. Tufnell	not out	0
Extras	(B 2, LB 7, W 1, NB 2)	12
TOTAL	(45.5 overs)	**153**

					Fall	
Alderman	8	0	28	0	1st	65
Rackemann	7.5	1	25	1	2nd	81
O'Donnell	5	0	15	1	3rd	103
S.R. Waugh	6	0	25	1	4th	109
Taylor	10	2	27	3	5th	117
Border	9	1	24	3	6th	125
					7th	135
					8th	136
					9th	153
					10th	153

Match No: 184/51

AUSTRALIA v ENGLAND

Benson & Hedges World Series Cup
Played at Melbourne Cricket Ground on 10/01/1991
Toss: Australia   **Result:** Australia won by 3 runs
Umpires: R.J. Evans and L.J. King
Man of the match: I.A. Healy
Debuts: None

AUSTRALIA
D.C. Boon	c Small b DeFreitas	42
G.R. Marsh	c Stewart b Bicknell	7
D.M. Jones	c Stewart b Bicknell	2
A.R. Border*	c Larkins b Small	10
M.E. Waugh	run out	36
S.R. Waugh	not out	65
S.P. O'Donnell	c Bicknell b Gooch	7
I.A. Healy+	not out	50
P.L. Taylor		
C.G. Rackemann		
T.M. Alderman		
Extras	(LB 1, W 1, NB 1)	3
TOTAL	(50 overs) (for 6 wkts)	222

						Fall	
Fraser	10	2	39	0		1st	14
Bicknell	9.5	0	33	2		2nd	16
Small	10	2	50	1		3rd	30
Tufnell	3	0	23	0		4th	81
DeFreitas	7.1	0	37	1		5th	112
Gooch	10	0	39	1		6th	127

ENGLAND
G.A. Gooch*	c Healy b M.E. Waugh	37
D.I. Gower	lbw b Alderman	26
W. Larkins	b Alderman	0
A.J. Stewart+	b Taylor	55
R.A. Smith	b M.E. Waugh	7
J.E. Morris	c Healy b M.E. Waugh	10
P.A.J. DeFreitas	c Border b M.E. Waugh	6
G.C. Small	b Taylor	0
M.P. Bicknell	c Alderman b S.R. Waugh	23
A.R.C. Fraser	not out	38
P.C.R. Tufnell	not out	5
Extras	(LB 6, W 5, NB 1)	12
TOTAL	(50 overs) (for 9 wkts)	219

						Fall	
Alderman	9	2	31	2		1st	39
Rackemann	7	0	52	0		2nd	39
O'Donnell	7	0	28	0		3rd	93
S.R. Waugh	7	1	25	1		4th	119
M.E. Waugh	10	0	37	4		5th	139
Taylor	10	1	40	2		6th	142
						7th	142
						8th	146
						9th	176

Match No: 185/34

NEW ZEALAND v ENGLAND

Bank of New Zealand Series
Played at Lancaster Park, Christchurch on 09/02/1991
Toss: England   Result: England won by 14 runs
Umpires: B.L. Aldridge and R.S. Dunne
Man of the match: K.R. Rutherford
Debuts: None

ENGLAND

G.A. Gooch*	b Pringle	17
D.I. Gower	b Petrie	4
M.A. Atherton	b Watson	0
A.J. Lamb	run out	61
R.A. Smith	c Jones b Pringle	65
A.J. Stewart	c Wright b Pringle	40
R.C. Russell+	c sub (R.T. Latham) b Petrie	10
P.A.J. DeFreitas	not out	10
M.P. Bicknell	not out	0
E.E. Hemmings		
A.R.C. Fraser		
Extras	(LB 8, W 12, NB 3)	23
TOTAL	(50 overs) (for 7 wkts)	230

						Fall	
Petrie	10	0	51	2	1st	6
Watson	10	2	15	1	2nd	9
Pringle	10	0	54	3	3rd	46
Larsen	10	0	47	0	4th	129
Harris	8	0	46	0	5th	192
Rutherford	2	0	9	0	6th	217
					7th	220

NEW ZEALAND

M.D. Crowe*	c & b Bicknell	13
J.G. Wright	c Smith b DeFreitas	27
A.H. Jones	run out	17
K.R. Rutherford	c Gooch b Bicknell	77
M.J. Greatbatch	c Russell b Hemmings	0
I.D.S. Smith+	run out	4
C.Z. Harris	c Russell b Bicknell	56
G.R. Larsen	not out	1
R.G. Petrie	c Gower b Fraser	0
C. Pringle	not out	0
W. Watson		
Extras	(B 2, LB 14, W 5)	21
TOTAL	(50 overs) (for 8 wkts)	216

						Fall	
Fraser	10	0	28	1	1st	38
Bicknell	10	2	55	3	2nd	50
DeFreitas	10	3	36	1	3rd	82
Gooch	10	0	31	0	4th	86
Hemmings	10	0	50	1	5th	90
						6th	212
						7th	213
						8th	215

Match No: 186/35

NEW ZEALAND v ENGLAND

Bank of New Zealand Series
Played at Basin Reserve, Wellington on 13/02/1991
Toss: England   **Result:** New Zealand won by 9 runs
Umpires: G.I.J. Cowan and S.J. Woodward
Man of the match: A.H. Jones
Debuts: NZ - C.L. Cairns

NEW ZEALAND

R.B. Reid	c Russell b Fraser	9
J.G. Wright	b Fraser	9
M.D. Crowe*	c Russell b Bicknell	5
A.H. Jones	b Fraser	64
K.R. Rutherford	c & b Tufnell	19
C.Z. Harris	st Russell b Tufnell	9
I.D.S. Smith+	b Bicknell	28
C.L. Cairns	c Smith b DeFreitas	5
G.R. Larsen	not out	10
C. Pringle	not out	18
W. Watson		
Extras	(LB 9, W 11)	20
TOTAL	(49 overs) (for 8 wkts)	**196**

						Fall	
Fraser	9	1	22	3	1st	20
Bicknell	10	0	65	2	2nd	25
DeFreitas	10	2	22	1	3rd	43
Gooch	10	2	33	0	4th	91
Tufnell	10	0	45	2	5th	109
					6th	150
					7th	158
					8th	171

ENGLAND

G.A. Gooch*	c Wright b Cairns	41
M.A. Atherton	c Cairns b Harris	26
D.I. Gower	run out	11
A.J. Lamb	b Cairns	33
R.A. Smith	b Pringle	38
A.J. Stewart	c Watson b Harris	5
R.C. Russell+	c Cairns b Harris	2
P.A.J. DeFreitas	run out	2
M.P. Bicknell	c Jones b Pringle	9
A.R.C. Fraser	c Crowe b Pringle	5
P.C.R. Tufnell	not out	0
Extras	(LB 8, W 7)	15
TOTAL	(48 overs)	**187**

						Fall	
Pringle	10	1	43	3	1st	73
Watson	10	1	34	0	2nd	81
Cairns	9	1	41	2	3rd	93
Larsen	9	1	28	0	4th	147
Harris	10	0	33	3	5th	160
					6th	170
					7th	173
					8th	174
					9th	179
					10th	187

Match No: 187/36

NEW ZEALAND v ENGLAND

Bank of New Zealand Series
Played at Eden Park, Auckland on 16/02/1991
Toss: England   Result: New Zealand won by 7 runs
Umpires: R.L. McHarg and S.J. Woodward
Man of the match: C.Z.Harris
Debuts: None

NEW ZEALAND
M.D. Crowe*	b DeFreitas	6
R.B. Reid	c Lamb b Tufnell	26
A.H. Jones	run out	64
K.R. Rutherford	lbw b Gooch	12
M.J. Greatbatch	c Lamb b DeFreitas	12
C.Z. Harris	b Fraser	39
I.D.S. Smith+	not out	51
C.L. Cairns	run out	6
C. Pringle	not out	0
G.R. Larsen		
W. Watson		
Extras	(LB 5, W 3)	8
TOTAL	(50 overs) (for 7 wkts)	224

						Fall	
Fraser	10	3	31	1		1st	7
DeFreitas	10	0	51	2		2nd	66
Small	10	2	51	0		3rd	98
Gooch	10	0	40	1		4th	120
Tufnell	10	1	46	1		5th	135
						6th	209
						7th	215

ENGLAND
G.A. Gooch*	b Larsen	47
M.A. Atherton	c Crowe b Harris	34
D.I. Gower	c Jones b Harris	13
A.J. Lamb	c Smith b Cairns	42
R.A. Smith	b Cairns	35
A.J. Stewart	c Smith b Cairns	3
P.A.J. DeFreitas	c Crowe b Pringle	7
R.C. Russell+	b Cairns	13
G.C. Small	b Pringle	0
A.R.C. Fraser	b Pringle	6
P.C.R. Tufnell	not out	3
Extras	(LB 10, W 4)	14
TOTAL	(49.5 overs)	217

						Fall	
Pringle	9.5	0	43	3		1st	83
Watson	10	1	38	0		2nd	91
Cairns	10	0	55	4		3rd	118
Larsen	10	0	35	1		4th	171
Harris	10	1	36	2		5th	185
						6th	194
						7th	200
						8th	203
						9th	209
						10th	217

Match No: 188/40

ENGLAND v WEST INDIES

Texaco Trophy
Played at Edgbaston, Birmingham on 23 & 24/05/1991
Toss: England   **Result:** England won by 1 wicket
Umpires: J.H. Hampshire and M.J. Kitchen
Man of the match: M.A. Atherton
Debuts: Eng - G.A. Hick, R.K. Illingworth

WEST INDIES
C.G. Greenidge	c Russell b Botham	23
P.V. Simmons	c Gooch b Lewis	4
R.B. Richardson	c Illingworth b Botham	3
I.V.A. Richards*	c Fairbrother b Gooch	30
C.L. Hooper	c Russell b Botham	10
A.L. Logie	c DeFreitas b Botham	18
P.J. Dujon+	c Lewis b Illingworth	5
M.D. Marshall	c Lewis b DeFreitas	17
C.E.L. Ambrose	not out	21
C.A. Walsh	not out	29
B.P. Patterson		
Extras	(B 1, LB 5, W 6, NB 1)	13
TOTAL	(55 overs) (for 8 wkts)	**173**

						Fall	
DeFreitas	11	3	22	1	1st	8
Lewis	11	3	41	1	2nd	16
Pringle	7	0	22	0	3rd	48
Botham	11	2	45	4	4th	78
Gooch	5	0	17	1	5th	84
Illingworth	10	1	20	1	6th	98
					7th	103
					8th	121

ENGLAND
G.A. Gooch*	lbw b Ambrose	0
M.A. Atherton	not out	69
G.A. Hick	c Richardson b Marshall	14
A.J. Lamb	b Hooper	18
N.H. Fairbrother	c Dujon b Hooper	4
I.T. Botham	lbw b Walsh	8
D.R. Pringle	c Richardson b Walsh	1
R.C. Russell+	c Dujon b Patterson	1
P.A.J. DeFreitas	c Richardson b Marshall	8
C.C. Lewis	c Richardson b Patterson	0
R.K. Illingworth	not out	9
Extras	(LB 9, W 18, NB 16)	43
TOTAL	(49.4 overs) (for 9 wkts)	**175**

						Fall	
Ambrose	11	2	34	1	1st	1
Patterson	11	2	38	2	2nd	41
Marshall	11	1	32	2	3rd	80
Walsh	11	0	34	2	4th	87
Simmons	3	0	10	0	5th	123
Hooper	2.4	0	18	2	6th	126
					7th	134
					8th	147
					9th	152

Match No: 189/41

ENGLAND v WEST INDIES

Texaco Trophy
Played at Old Trafford, Manchester on 25/05/1991
Toss: West Indies   Result: England won by 9 runs
Umpires: H.D. Bird and D.R. Shepherd
Man of the match: A.J. Lamb
Debuts: Eng - M.R. Ramprakash

ENGLAND
G.A. Gooch*	b Hooper	54
M.A. Atherton	c sub (B.C. Lara) b Ambrose	74
G.A. Hick	b Ambrose	29
A.J. Lamb	c Dujon b Patterson	62
N.H. Fairbrother	not out	5
M.R. Ramprakash	not out	6
D.R. Pringle		
R.C. Russell+		
C.C. Lewis		
P.A.J. DeFreitas		
R.K. Illingworth		
Extras	(B 4, LB 16, W 14, NB 6)	40
TOTAL	(55 overs) (for 4 wkts)	**270**

						Fall	
Ambrose	11	3	36	2	1st	156
Patterson	10	1	39	1	2nd	156
Walsh	11	0	56	0	3rd	258
Marshall	10	0	45	0	4th	260
Simmons	4	0	30	0		
Hooper	9	0	44	1		

WEST INDIES
P.V. Simmons	run out	28
P.J.L. Dujon+	c DeFreitas b Lewis	21
R.B. Richardson	c Russell b Gooch	13
C.L. Hooper	c sub (D.A. Reeve) b Lewis	48
I.V.A. Richards*	lbw b Lewis	78
A.L. Logie	c Illingworth b Pringle	24
M.D. Marshall	c & b Pringle	22
C.G. Greenidge	run out	4
C.E.L. Ambrose	not out	5
C.A. Walsh	not out	1
B.P. Patterson		
Extras	(LB 4, W 10, NB 3)	17
TOTAL	(55 overs) (for 8 wkts)	**261**

						Fall	
DeFreitas	11	3	50	0	1st	34
Lewis	11	0	62	3	2nd	61
Pringle	11	2	52	2	3rd	69
Illingworth	11	1	42	0	4th	190
Gooch	11	1	51	1	5th	208
					6th	250
					7th	250
					8th	256

Match No: 190/42

ENGLAND v WEST INDIES

Texaco Trophy
Played at Lord's, London on 27/05/1991
Toss: England   **Result:** England won by 7 wickets
Umpires: M.J. Kitchen and D.R. Shepherd
Man of the match: N.H. Fairbrother
Debuts: Eng - D.V. Lawrence, D.A. Reeve

WEST INDIES
P.V. Simmons	c Russell b DeFreitas	5
P.J.L. Dujon+	b Lawrence	0
R.B. Richardson	c DeFreitas b Illingworth	41
B.C. Lara	c & b Illingworth	23
I.V.A. Richards*	c Illingworth b DeFreitas	37
A.L. Logie	c & b Gooch	82
C.L. Hooper	c Fairbrother b Lawrence	26
M.D. Marshall	c DeFreitas b Lawrence	13
C.E.L. Ambrose	not out	6
C.A. Walsh	lbw b Lawrence	0
B.P. Patterson	not out	2
Extras	(B 1, LB 9, W 14, NB 5)	29
TOTAL	(55 overs) (for 9 wkts)	**264**

					Fall	
Lawrence	11	1	67	4	1st	8
DeFreitas	11	1	26	2	2nd	8
Reeve	11	1	43	0	3rd	71
Illingworth	11	1	53	2	4th	91
Pringle	9	0	56	0	5th	164
Gooch	2	0	9	1	6th	227
					7th	241
					8th	258
					9th	258

ENGLAND
G.A. Gooch*	run out	11
M.A. Atherton	c Dujon b Marshall	25
G.A. Hick	not out	86
N.H. Fairbrother	c Richards b Patterson	113
M.R. Ramprakash	not out	0
D.A. Reeve		
D.R. Pringle		
R.C. Russell+		
P.A.J. DeFreitas		
R.K. Illingworth		
D.V. Lawrence		
Extras	(B 4, LB 12, W 10, NB 4)	30
TOTAL	(46.1 overs) (for 3 wkts)	**265**

					Fall	
Ambrose	8	0	31	0	1st	28
Patterson	10	0	62	1	2nd	48
Marshall	11	1	49	1	3rd	261
Walsh	11	1	50	0		
Hooper	4.1	0	36	0		
Simmons	2	0	21	0		

Matches   201

Match No: 191/37
NEW ZEALAND v ENGLAND

Bank of New Zealand Series
Played at Eden Park, Auckland on 11/01/1992
Toss: New Zealand   Result: England won by 7 wickets
Umpires: D.B. Cowie and S.J. Woodward
Man of the match: D.A. Reeve
Debuts: None

NEW ZEALAND
J.G. Wright	c Stewart b Lewis	6
R.T. Latham	lbw b Pringle	25
M.D. Crowe*	b Reeve	31
A.H. Jones	c Stewart b Reeve	1
M.J. Greatbatch	c Hick b Reeve	4
C.Z. Harris	not out	38
C.L. Cairns	c Hick b Pringle	42
I.D.S. Smith+	c Gooch b Lewis	2
C. Pringle	not out	9
G.R. Larsen		
D.K. Morrison		
Extras	(LB 13, W 4, NB 3)	20
TOTAL	(50 overs) (for 7 wkts)	178

						Fall	
DeFreitas	10	1	34	0	1st	21
Lewis	8	0	33	2	2nd	45
Pringle	6	1	32	2	3rd	51
Reeve	10	3	20	3	4th	61
Tufnell	10	3	17	0	5th	81
Hick	6	0	29	0	6th	165
					7th	167

ENGLAND
G.A. Gooch*	c Greatbatch b Harris	47
G.A. Hick	b Cairns	23
R.A. Smith	not out	61
A.J. Lamb	c Crowe b Harris	12
N.H. Fairbrother	not out	23
A.J. Stewart+		
D.A. Reeve		
C.C. Lewis		
D.R. Pringle		
P.A.J. DeFreitas		
P.C.R. Tufnell		
Extras	(LB 6, W 3, NB 4)	13
TOTAL	(33.5 overs) (for 3 wkts)	179

						Fall	
Morrison	5.5	0	35	0	1st	64
Pringle	5	0	26	0	2nd	109
Cairns	5	0	32	1	3rd	123
Larsen	9	3	36	0		
Harris	9	0	44	2		

Match No: 192/38

NEW ZEALAND v ENGLAND

Bank of New Zealand Series
Played at Carisbrook, Dunedin on 12/02/1992
Toss: New Zealand   **Result:** England won by 3 wickets
Umpires: B.L. Aldridge and R.S. Dunne
Man of the match: K.R. Rutherford
Debuts: NZ - M.L. Su'a

NEW ZEALAND
R.T. Latham	run out	12
A.H. Jones	b Botham	20
M.J. Greatbatch	c Stewart b Reeve	10
M.D. Crowe*	c sub (M.R. Ramprakash) b Illingworth	29
K.R. Rutherford	run out	52
C.Z. Harris	b Pringle	32
C.L. Cairns	b Lewis	3
I.D.S. Smith+	not out	5
M.L. Su'a	not out	4
D.K. Morrison		
G.R. Larsen		
Extras	(B 1, LB 12, W 3, NB 3)	19
TOTAL	(50 overs) (for 7 wkts)	**186**

						Fall	
Pringle	10	2	31	1	1st	14
Lewis	9	0	32	1	2nd	35
Reeve	8	1	19	1	3rd	54
Botham	6	1	27	1	4th	89
Illingworth	9	1	33	1	5th	163
Tufnell	8	0	31	0	6th	170
					7th	180

ENGLAND
G.A. Gooch*	c Smith b Larsen	24
G.A. Hick	lbw b Morrison	7
R.A. Smith	b Larsen	17
A.J. Lamb	lbw b Latham	40
I.T. Botham	c Rutherford b Latham	28
A.J. Stewart+	b Latham	0
D.A. Reeve	not out	31
C.C. Lewis	c Greatbatch b Morrison	18
D.R. Pringle	not out	14
R.K. Illingworth		
P.C.R. Tufnell		
Extras	(LB 2, W 7)	9
TOTAL	(49.1 overs) (for 7 wkts)	**188**

						Fall	
Morrison	7	0	27	2	1st	21
Su'a	8	1	35	0	2nd	54
Larsen	10	1	24	2	3rd	63
Cairns	6.1	0	36	0	4th	108
Harris	10	1	39	0	5th	108
Latham	8	1	25	3	6th	131
					7th	165

Match No: 193/39
NEW ZEALAND v ENGLAND

Bank of New Zealand Series
Played at Lancaster Park, Christchurch on 15/02/1992
Toss: New Zealand **Result:** England won by 71 runs
Umpires: R.L. McHarg and S.J. Woodward
Man of the match: I.T. Botham
Debuts: None

ENGLAND
I.T. Botham	c Greatbatch b Latham	79
G.A. Hick	c Greatbatch b Larsen	18
R.A. Smith	c Smith b Cairns	85
A.J. Stewart*+	c Crowe b Su'a	13
A.J. Lamb	c Harris b Watson	25
G.A. Gooch	not out	22
C.C. Lewis	c Latham b Watson	0
D.R. Pringle	c Watson b Cairns	5
D.A. Reeve	not out	2
R.K. Illingworth		
G.C. Small		
Extras	(LB 2, W 4)	6
TOTAL	(40 overs) (for 7 wkts)	255

						Fall	
Cairns	6	0	37	2	1st	60
Watson	8	1	64	2	2nd	125
Larsen	6	2	34	1	3rd	166
Su'a	5	0	35	1	4th	220
Harris	8	0	35	0	5th	228
Latham	7	0	48	1	6th	231
					7th	248

NEW ZEALAND
R.T. Latham	c Reeve b Lewis	0
J.G. Wright	c Hick b Reeve	36
M.J. Greatbatch	b Pringle	5
M.D. Crowe*	c Stewart b Pringle	6
K.R. Rutherford	c sub (M.R. Ramprakash) b Botham	37
C.Z. Harris	run out	37
C.L. Cairns	c Smith b Illingworth	6
I.D.S. Smith+	c sub (P.A.J. DeFreitas) b Small	27
M.L. Su'a	not out	12
G.R. Larsen	not out	3
W. Watson		
Extras	(LB 6, W 6, NB 3)	15
TOTAL	(40 overs) (for 8 wkts)	184

						Fall	
Lewis	6	1	21	1	1st	4
Pringle	6	2	11	2	2nd	20
Small	8	0	46	1	3rd	23
Reeve	5	0	26	1	4th	92
Botham	7	1	36	1	5th	100
Illingworth	8	0	38	1	6th	112
						7th	148
						8th	171

Match No: 194/23

ENGLAND v INDIA

Benson & Hedges World Cup
Played at WACA Ground, Perth on 22/02/1992
Toss: England   Result: England won by 9 runs
Umpires: J.D. Buultjens and P.J. McConnell
Man of the match: I.T. Botham
Debuts: None

ENGLAND

G.A. Gooch*	c Tendulkar b Shastri	51
I.T. Botham	c More b Kapil Dev	9
R.A. Smith	c Azharuddin b Prabhakar	91
G.A. Hick	c More b Banerjee	5
N.H. Fairbrother	c Srikkanth b Srinath	24
A.J. Stewart+	b Prabhakar	13
C.C. Lewis	c Banerjee b Kapil Dev	10
D.R. Pringle	c Srikkanth b Srinath	1
D.A. Reeve	not out	8
P.A.J. DeFreitas	run out	1
P.C.R. Tufnell	not out	3
Extras	(B 1, LB 6, W 13)	20
TOTAL	(50 overs) (for 9 wkts)	236

						Fall	
Kapil Dev	10	0	38	2	1st	21
Prabhakar	10	3	34	2	2nd	131
Srinath	9	1	47	2	3rd	137
Banerjee	7	0	45	1	4th	197
Tendulkar	10	0	37	0	5th	198
Shastri	4	0	28	1	6th	214
					7th	222
					8th	223
					9th	224

INDIA

R.J. Shastri	run out	57
K. Srikkanth	c Botham b DeFreitas	39
M. Azharuddin*	c Stewart b Reeve	0
S.R. Tendulkar	c Stewart b Botham	35
V.G. Kambli	c Hick b Botham	3
P.K. Amre	run out	22
Kapil Dev	c DeFreitas b Reeve	17
S. Banerjee	not out	25
K.S. More+	run out	1
M. Prabhakar	b Reeve	0
J. Srinath	run out	11
Extras	(LB 9, W 7, NB 1)	17
TOTAL	(49.2 overs)	227

						Fall	
Pringle	10	0	53	0	1st	63
Lewis	9.2	0	36	0	2nd	63
DeFreitas	10	0	39	1	3rd	126
Reeve	6	0	38	3	4th	140
Botham	10	0	27	2	5th	149
Tufnell	4	0	25	0	6th	187
					7th	194
					8th	200
					9th	201
					10th	227

Match No: 195/43

ENGLAND v WEST INDIES

Benson & Hedges World Cup
Played at Melbourne Cricket Ground on 27/02/1992
Toss: England   **Result:** England won by 6 wickets
Umpires: K.E. Liebenberg and S.J. Woodward
Man of the match: C.C. Lewis
Debuts: None

WEST INDIES
D.L. Haynes	c Fairbrother b DeFreitas	38
B.C. Lara	c Stewart b Lewis	0
R.B. Richardson*	c Botham b Lewis	5
C.L. Hooper	c Reeve b Botham	5
K.L.T. Arthurton	c Fairbrother b DeFreitas	54
A.L. Logie	run out	20
R.A. Harper	c Hick b Reeve	3
M.D. Marshall	run out	3
D. Williams+	c Pringle b DeFreitas	6
C.E.L. Ambrose	c DeFreitas b Lewis	4
W.K.M. Benjamin	not out	11
Extras	(LB 4, W 3, NB 1)	8
TOTAL	(49.2 overs)	**157**

						Fall	
Pringle	7	3	16	0		1st	0
Lewis	8.2	1	30	3		2nd	22
DeFreitas	9	2	34	3		3rd	36
Botham	10	0	30	1		4th	55
Reeve	10	1	23	1		5th	91
Tufnell	5	0	20	0		6th	102
						7th	116
						8th	131
						9th	145
						10th	157

ENGLAND
G.A. Gooch*	st Williams b Hooper	65
I.T. Botham	c Williams b Benjamin	8
R.A. Smith	c Logie b Benjamin	8
G.A. Hick	c & b Harper	54
N.H. Fairbrother	not out	13
A.J. Stewart+	not out	0
D.A. Reeve		
C.C. Lewis		
D.R. Pringle		
P.A.J. DeFreitas		
P.C.R. Tufnell		
Extras	(LB 7, W 4, NB 1)	12
TOTAL	(39.5 overs) (for 4 wkts)	**160**

						Fall	
Ambrose	8	1	26	0		1st	50
Marshall	8	0	37	0		2nd	71
Benjamin	9.5	2	22	2		3rd	126
Hooper	10	1	38	1		4th	156
Harper	4	0	30	1			

Match No: 196/30

ENGLAND v PAKISTAN

Benson & Hedges World Cup
Played at Adelaide Oval on 01/03/1992
Toss: England   Result: Match abandoned
Umpires: S.A. Bucknor and P.J. McConnell
Man of the match: None
Debuts: None

PAKISTAN
Ramiz Raja	c Reeve b DeFreitas	1
Aamir Sohail	c & b Pringle	9
Inzamam-ul-Haq	c Stewart b DeFreitas	0
Javed Miandad*	b Pringle	3
Salim Malik	c Reeve b Botham	17
Ijaz Ahmed	c Stewart b Small	0
Wasim Akram	b Botham	1
Moin Khan+	c Hick b Small	2
Wasim Haider	c Stewart b Reeve	13
Mushtaq Ahmed	c Reeve b Pringle	17
Aqib Javed	not out	1
Extras	(LB 1, W 8, NB 1)	10
TOTAL	**(40.2 overs)**	**74**

						Fall	
Pringle	8.2	5	8	3	1st	5
DeFreitas	7	1	22	2	2nd	5
Small	10	1	29	2	3rd	14
Botham	10	4	12	2	4th	20
Reeve	5	3	2	1	5th	32
					6th	35
					7th	42
					8th	47
					9th	62
					10th	74

ENGLAND
G.A. Gooch*	c Moin Khan b Wasim Akram	3
I.T. Botham	not out	6
R.A. Smith	not out	5
G.A. Hick		
N.H. Fairbrother		
A.J. Stewart+		
C.C. Lewis		
D.A. Reeve		
D.R. Pringle		
P.A.J. DeFreitas		
G.C. Small		
Extras	(B 1, LB 3, W 5, NB 1)	10
TOTAL	**(8 overs) (for 1 wkt)**	**24**

						Fall	
Wasim Akram	3	0	7	1	1st	14
Aqib Javed	3	1	7	0		
Wasim Haider	1	0	1	0		
Ijaz Ahmed	1	0	5	0		

Match No: 197/52

AUSTRALIA v ENGLAND

Benson & Hedges World Cup
Played at Sydney Cricket Ground on 05/03/1992
Toss: Australia   Result: England won by 8 wickets
Umpires: S.A. Bucknor and Khizar Hayat
Man of the match: I.T. Botham
Debuts: None

AUSTRALIA

T.M. Moody	b Tufnell	51
M.A. Taylor	lbw b Pringle	0
D.C. Boon	run out	18
D.M. Jones	c Lewis b DeFreitas	22
S.R. Waugh	run out	27
A.R. Border*	b Botham	16
I.A. Healy+	c Fairbrother b Botham	9
P.L. Taylor	lbw b Botham	0
C.J. McDermott	c DeFreitas b Botham	0
M.R. Whitney	not out	8
B.A. Reid	b Reeve	1
Extras	(B 2, LB 8, W 5, NB 4)	19
TOTAL	(49 overs)	171

					Fall	
Pringle	9	1	24	1	1st	5
Lewis	10	2	28	0	2nd	35
DeFreitas	10	3	23	1	3rd	106
Botham	10	1	31	4	4th	114
Tufnell	9	0	52	1	5th	145
Reeve	1	0	3	1	6th	155
					7th	155
					8th	155
					9th	164
					10th	171

ENGLAND

G.A. Gooch*	b Waugh	58
I.T. Botham	c Healy b Whitney	53
R.A. Smith	not out	30
G.A. Hick	not out	7
N.H. Fairbrother		
A.J. Stewart+		
C.C. Lewis		
D.A. Reeve		
D.R. Pringle		
P.A.J. DeFreitas		
P.C.R. Tufnell		
Extras	(LB 13, W 8, NB 4)	25
TOTAL	(40.5 overs) (for 2 wkts)	173

					Fall	
McDermott	10	1	29	0	1st	107
Reid	7.5	0	49	0	2nd	153
Whitney	10	2	28	1		
Waugh	6	0	29	1		
P.L. Taylor	3	0	7	0		
Moody	4	0	18	0		

Match No: 198/9

ENGLAND v SRI LANKA

Benson & Hedges World Cup
Played at Eastern Oval, Ballarat on 09/03/1992
Toss: England   **Result:** England won by 106 runs
Umpires: Khizar Hayat and P.D. Reporter
Man of the match: C.C. Lewis
Debuts: None

ENGLAND

G.A. Gooch*	b Labrooy	8
I.T. Botham	b Anurasiri	47
R.A. Smith	run out	19
G.A. Hick	b Ramanayake	41
N.H. Fairbrother	c Ramanayake b Gurusinha	63
A.J. Stewart+	c Jayasuriya b Gurusinha	59
C.C. Lewis	not out	20
D.R. Pringle	not out	0
D.A. Reeve		
P.A.J. DeFreitas		
R.K. Illingworth		
Extras	(B 1, LB 9, W 9, NB 4)	23
TOTAL	(50 overs) (for 6 wkts)	**280**

						Fall	
Wickremasinghe	9	0	54	0	1st	44
Ramanayake	10	1	42	1	2nd	80
Labrooy	10	1	68	1	3rd	105
Anurasiri	10	1	27	1	4th	164
Gurusinha	10	0	67	2	5th	244
Jayasuriya	1	0	12	0	6th	268

SRI LANKA

R.S. Mahanama	c Botham b Lewis	9
M.A.R. Samarasekera	c Illingworth b Lewis	23
A.P. Gurusinha	c & b Lewis	7
P.A. de Silva*	c Fairbrother b Lewis	7
A. Ranatunga	c Stewart b Botham	36
H.P. Tillekeratne+	run out	4
S.T. Jayasuriya	c DeFreitas b Illingworth	19
G.F. Labrooy	c Smith b Illingworth	19
C.P.H. Ramanayake	c & b Reeve	12
S.D. Anurasiri	lbw b Reeve	11
G.P. Wickremasinghe	not out	6
Extras	(LB 7, W 8, NB 6)	21
TOTAL	(49 overs)	**174**

						Fall	
Pringle	7	1	27	0	1st	33
Lewis	8	0	30	4	2nd	46
DeFreitas	5	1	31	0	3rd	56
Botham	10	0	33	1	4th	60
Illingworth	10	0	32	2	5th	91
Reeve	4	0	14	2	6th	119
						7th	123
						8th	156
						9th	158
						10th	174

Match No: 199/1

ENGLAND v SOUTH AFRICA

Benson & Hedges World Cup
Played at Melbourne Cricket Ground on 12/03/1992
Toss: England   Result: England won by 3 wickets
                                          (revised target)
Umpires: B.L. Aldridge and J.D. Buultjens
Man of the match: A.J. Stewart
Debuts: None

SOUTH AFRICA
K.C. Wessels*	c Smith b Hick	85
A.C. Hudson	c & b Hick	79
P.N. Kirsten	c Smith b DeFreitas	11
J.N. Rhodes	run out	18
A.P. Kuiper	not out	15
W.J. Cronje	not out	13
B.M. McMillan		
D.J. Richardson+		
R.P. Snell		
M.W. Pringle		
A.A. Donald		
Extras	(B 4, LB 4, W 4, NB 3)	15
TOTAL	(50 overs) (for 4 wkts)	236

						Fall	
Pringle	9	2	34	0	1st	151
DeFreitas	10	1	41	1	2nd	170
Botham	8	0	37	0	3rd	201
Small	2	0	14	0	4th	205
Illingworth	10	0	43	0		
Reeve	2.4	0	15	0		
Hick	8.2	0	44	2		

ENGLAND
A.J. Stewart*+	run out	77
I.T. Botham	b McMillan	22
R.A. Smith	c Richardson b McMillan	0
G.A. Hick	c Richardson b Snell	1
N.H. Fairbrother	not out	75
C.C. Lewis	run out	33
D.A. Reeve	c McMillan b Snell	10
D.R. Pringle	c Kuiper b Snell	1
P.A.J. DeFreitas	not out	1
R.K. Illingworth		
G.C. Small		
Extras	(LB 3, W 1, NB 2)	6
TOTAL	(40.5 overs) (for 7 wkts)	226

						Fall	
Donald	9	1	43	0	1st	63
Pringle	8	0	44	0	2nd	63
Snell	7.5	0	42	3	3rd	64
McMillan	8	1	39	2	4th	132
Kuiper	4	0	32	0	5th	166
Cronje	3	0	14	0	6th	216
Kirsten	1	0	9	0	7th	225

Match No: 200/40

NEW ZEALAND v ENGLAND

Benson & Hedges World Cup
Played at Basin Reserve, Wellington on 15/03/1992
Toss: New Zealand   **Result:** New Zealand won by 7 wickets
Umpires: S.G. Randell and I.D. Robinson
Man of the match: A.H. Jones
Debuts: None

ENGLAND
A.J. Stewart*+	c Harris b Patel	41
I.T. Botham	b Patel	8
G.A. Hick	c Greatbatch b Harris	56
R.A. Smith	c Patel b Jones	38
A.J. Lamb	c Cairns b Watson	12
C.C. Lewis	c & b Watson	0
D.A. Reeve	not out	21
D.R. Pringle	c sub (R.T. Latham) b Jones	10
P.A.J. DeFreitas	c Cairns b Harris	0
R.K. Illingworth	not out	2
G.C. Small		
Extras	(B 1, LB 7, W 4)	12
TOTAL	(50 overs) (for 8 wkts)	**200**

						Fall	
Patel	10	1	26	2	1st	25
Harris	8	0	39	2	2nd	95
Watson	10	0	40	2	3rd	135
Cairns	3	0	21	0	4th	162
Larsen	10	3	24	0	5th	162
Jones	9	0	42	2	6th	169
					7th	189
					8th	195

NEW ZEALAND
M.J. Greatbatch	c DeFreitas b Botham	35
J.G. Wright	b DeFreitas	1
A.H. Jones	run out	78
M.D. Crowe*	not out	73
K.R. Rutherford	not out	3
C.Z. Harris		
C.L. Cairns		
I.D.S. Smith+		
D.N. Patel		
G.R. Larsen		
W. Watson		
Extras	(B 1, LB 8, W 1, NB 1)	11
TOTAL	(40.5 overs) (for 3 wkts)	**201**

						Fall	
Pringle	6.2	1	34	0	1st	5
DeFreitas	8.3	1	45	1	2nd	64
Botham	4	0	19	1	3rd	172
Illingworth	9	1	46	0		
Hick	6	0	26	0		
Reeve	3	0	9	0		
Small	4	0	13	0		

Match No: 201/1

ENGLAND v ZIMBABWE

Benson & Hedges World Cup
Played at Lavington Oval, Albury on 18/03/1992
Toss: England   **Result:** Zimbabwe won by 9 runs
Umpires: B.L. Aldridge and Khizar Hayat
Man of the match: E.A. Brandes
Debuts: None

ZIMBABWE

W.R. James	c & b Illingworth	13
A. Flower+	b DeFreitas	7
A.J. Pycroft	c Gooch b Botham	3
K.J. Arnott	lbw b Botham	11
D.L. Houghton*	c Fairbrother b Small	29
A.C. Waller	b Tufnell	8
A.H. Shah	c Lamb b Tufnell	3
I.P. Butchart	c Fairbrother b Botham	24
E.A. Brandes	st Stewart b Illingworth	14
A.J. Traicos	not out	0
M.P. Jarvis	lbw b Illingworth	6
Extras	(LB 8, W 8)	16
TOTAL	(46.1 overs)	134

Fall

DeFreitas	8	1	14	1	1st	12
Small	9	1	20	1	2nd	19
Botham	10	2	23	3	3rd	30
Illingworth	9.1	0	33	3	4th	52
Tufnell	10	2	36	2	5th	65
					6th	77
					7th	96
					8th	127
					9th	127
					10th	134

ENGLAND

G.A. Gooch*	lbw b Brandes	0
I.T. Botham	c Flower b Shah	18
A.J. Lamb	c James b Brandes	17
R.A. Smith	b Brandes	2
G.A. Hick	b Brandes	0
N.H. Fairbrother	c Flower b Butchart	20
A.J. Stewart+	c Waller b Shah	29
P.A.J. DeFreitas	c Flower b Butchart	4
R.K. Illingworth	run out	11
G.C. Small	c Pycroft b Jarvis	5
P.C.R. Tufnell	not out	0
Extras	(B 4, LB 3, W 11, NB 1)	19
TOTAL	(49.1 overs)	125

Fall

Brandes	10	4	21	4	1st	0
Jarvis	9.1	0	32	1	2nd	32
Shah	10	3	17	2	3rd	42
Traicos	10	4	16	0	4th	42
Butchart	10	2	32	2	5th	43
					6th	95
					7th	101
					8th	108
					9th	124
					10th	125

Match No: 202/2

ENGLAND v SOUTH AFRICA

Benson & Hedges World Cup Semi-Final
Played at Sydney Cricket Ground on 22/03/1992
Toss: South Africa   **Result:** England won by 19 runs (revised target)
Umpires: B.L. Aldridge and S.G. Randell
Man of the match: G.A. Hick
Debuts: None

ENGLAND
G.A. Gooch*	c Richardson b Donald	2
I.T. Botham	b Pringle	21
A.J. Stewart+	c Richardson b McMillan	33
G.A. Hick	c Rhodes b Snell	83
N.H. Fairbrother	b Pringle	28
A.J. Lamb	c Richardson b Donald	19
C.C. Lewis	not out	18
D.A. Reeve	not out	25
P.A.J. DeFreitas		
G.C. Small		
R.K. Illingworth		
Extras	(B 1, LB 7, W 9, NB 6)	23
TOTAL	(45 overs) (for 6 wkts)	**252**

	O	M	R	W		Fall	
Donald	10	0	69	2		1st	20
Pringle	9	2	36	2		2nd	39
Snell	8	0	52	1		3rd	110
McMillan	9	0	47	1		4th	183
Kuiper	5	0	26	0		5th	187
Cronje	4	0	14	0		6th	221

SOUTH AFRICA
K.C. Wessels*	c Lewis b Botham	17
A.C. Hudson	lbw b Illingworth	46
P.N. Kirsten	b DeFreitas	11
A.P. Kuiper	b Illingworth	36
W.J. Cronje	c Hick b Small	24
J.N. Rhodes	c Lewis b Small	43
B.M. McMillan	not out	21
D.J. Richardson+	not out	13
R.P. Snell		
M.W. Pringle		
A.A. Donald		
Extras	(LB 17, W 4)	21
TOTAL	(43 overs) (for 6 wkts)	**232**

	O	M	R	W		Fall	
Botham	10	0	52	1		1st	26
Lewis	5	0	38	0		2nd	61
DeFreitas	8	1	28	1		3rd	90
Illingworth	10	1	46	2		4th	131
Small	10	1	51	2		5th	176
						6th	206

Match No: 203/31

ENGLAND v PAKISTAN

Benson & Hedges World Cup Final
Played at Melbourne Cricket Ground on 25/03/1992
Toss: Pakistan   **Result:** Pakistan won by 22 runs
Umpires: B.L. Aldridge and S.A. Bucknor
Man of the match: Wasim Akram
Debuts: None

PAKISTAN
Aamir Sohail	c Stewart b Pringle	4
Ramiz Raja	lbw b Pringle	8
Imran Khan*	c Illingworth b Botham	72
Javed Miandad	c Botham b Illingworth	58
Inzamam-ul-Haq	b Pringle	42
Wasim Akram	run out	33
Salim Malik	not out	0
Ijaz Ahmed		
Moin Khan+		
Mushtaq Ahmed		
Aqib Javed		
Extras	(LB 19, W 6, NB 7)	32
TOTAL	(50 overs) (for 6 wkts)	**249**

						Fall	
Pringle	10	2	22	3	1st	20
Lewis	10	2	52	0	2nd	24
Botham	7	0	42	1	3rd	163
DeFreitas	10	1	42	0	4th	197
Illingworth	10	0	50	1	5th	249
Reeve	3	0	22	0	6th	249

ENGLAND
G.A. Gooch*	c Aqib Javed b Mushtaq Ahmed	29
I.T. Botham	c Moin Khan b Wasim Akram	0
A.J. Stewart+	c Moin Khan b Aqib Javed	7
G.A. Hick	lbw b Mushtaq Ahmed	17
N.H. Fairbrother	c Moin Khan b Aqib Javed	62
A.J. Lamb	b Wasim Akram	31
C.C. Lewis	b Wasim Akram	0
D.A. Reeve	c Ramiz Raja b Mushtaq Ahmed	15
D.R. Pringle	not out	18
P.A.J. DeFreitas	run out	10
R.K. Illingworth	c Ramiz Raja b Imran Khan	14
Extras	(LB 5, W 13, NB 6)	24
TOTAL	(49.2 overs)	**227**

						Fall	
Wasim Akram	10	0	49	3	1st	6
Aqib Javed	10	2	27	2	2nd	21
Mushtaq Ahmed	10	1	41	3	3rd	59
Ijaz Ahmed	3	0	13	0	4th	69
Imran Khan	6.2	0	43	1	5th	141
Aamir Sohail	10	0	49	0	6th	141
					7th	180
					8th	183
					9th	208
					10th	227

Match No: 204/32

ENGLAND v PAKISTAN

Texaco Trophy
Played at Lord's, London on 20/05/1992
Toss: Pakistan **Result:** England won by 79 runs
Umpires: B.J. Meyer and D.R. Shepherd
Man of the match: R.A. Smith
Debuts: None

ENGLAND
G.A. Gooch*	c Moin Khan b Aqib Javed	9
A.J. Stewart+	c Asif Mujtaba b Naved Anjum	50
R.A. Smith	c Moin Khan b Aqib Javed	85
A.J. Lamb	c Javed Miandad b Naved Anjum	60
N.H. Fairbrother	c Asif Mujtaba b Aqib Javed	25
G.A. Hick	b Wasim Akram	3
I.T. Botham	not out	10
C.C. Lewis	not out	6
D.R. Pringle		
P.A.J. DeFreitas		
R.K. Illingworth		
Extras	(LB 14, W 9, NB 7)	30
TOTAL	(55 overs) (for 6 wkts)	278

	O	M	R	W		Fall
Wasim Akram	11	0	39	1	1st	20
Aqib Javed	11	0	54	3	2nd	115
Naved Anjum	11	0	48	2	3rd	213
Mushtaq Ahmed	11	0	56	0	4th	238
Asif Mujtaba	11	0	67	0	5th	250
					6th	268

PAKISTAN
Aamir Sohail	run out	36
Ramiz Raja	c & b Pringle	0
Salim Malik	c Stewart b Botham	24
Javed Miandad*	c Hick b Pringle	7
Inzamam-ul-Haq	c & b Botham	2
Asif Mujtaba	c Smith b Hick	52
Wasim Akram	st Stewart b Illingworth	34
Naved Anjum	c Hick b Pringle	3
Moin Khan+	c Stewart b Pringle	11
Mushtaq Ahmed	not out	7
Aqib Javed	b Hick	8
Extras	(LB 8, W 5, NB 2)	15
TOTAL	(54.2 overs)	199

	O	M	R	W		Fall
DeFreitas	9	2	17	0	1st	0
Pringle	11	1	42	4	2nd	49
Lewis	8	1	35	0	3rd	74
Botham	11	0	45	2	4th	78
Illingworth	11	0	36	1	5th	78
Hick	3.2	0	7	2	6th	161
Fairbrother	1	0	9	0	7th	164
					8th	181
					9th	184
					10th	199

Match No: 205/33

ENGLAND v PAKISTAN

Texaco Trophy
Played at The Oval, London on 22/05/1992
Toss: England   **Result:** England won by 39 runs
Umpires: M.J. Kitchen and R. Palmer
Man of the match: A.J. Stewart
Debuts: Pak - Tanvir Mehdi

ENGLAND
G.A. Gooch*	run out	25
A.J. Stewart+	b Aqib Javed	103
R.A. Smith	b Mushtaq Ahmed	7
A.J. Lamb	st Moin Khan b Aamir Sohail	11
N.H. Fairbrother	b Tanvir Mehdi	63
G.A. Hick	not out	71
I.T. Botham	not out	2
C.C. Lewis		
D.R. Pringle		
P.A.J. DeFreitas		
R.K. Illingworth		
Extras	(LB 8, W 9, NB 3)	20
TOTAL	(55 overs) (for 5 wkts)	302

						Fall	
Aqib Javed	10	0	70	1		1st	71
Naved Anjum	9	0	37	0		2nd	81
Tanvir Mehdi	11	0	72	1		3rd	108
Mushtaq Ahmed	11	0	47	1		4th	202
Aamir Sohail	11	0	52	1		5th	295
Asif Mujtaba	3	0	16	0			

PAKISTAN
Aamir Sohail	b Illingworth	32
Ramiz Raja	c sub (M.R. Ramprakash) b DeFreitas	86
Salim Malik	b Pringle	26
Inzamam-ul-Haq	lbw b Pringle	15
Javed Miandad*	lbw b Botham	38
Asif Mujtaba	lbw b Illingworth	29
Naved Anjum	run out	6
Moin Khan+	c & b Lewis	15
Mushtaq Ahmed	c Illingworth b Lewis	8
Tanvir Mehdi	b DeFreitas	0
Aqib Javed	not out	0
Extras	(LB 4, W 3, NB 1)	8
TOTAL	(50.5 overs)	263

						Fall	
DeFreitas	10.5	0	59	2		1st	81
Lewis	8	0	47	2		2nd	144
Botham	11	0	52	1		3rd	148
Illingworth	11	0	58	2		4th	174
Pringle	9	1	35	2		5th	220
Hick	1	0	8	0		6th	232
						7th	249
						8th	263
						9th	263
						10th	263

Match No: 206/34

ENGLAND v PAKISTAN

Texaco Trophy
Played at Trent Bridge, Nottingham on 20/08/1992
Toss: Pakistan **Result:** England won by 198 runs
Umpires: B. Dudleston and D.R. Shepherd
Man of the match: R.A. Smith
Debuts: Pak - Rashid Latif

ENGLAND

G.A. Gooch*	b Waqar Younis	42
A.J. Stewart+	c Wasim Akram b Waqar Younis	34
R.A. Smith	c Ramiz Raja b Aqib Javed	77
N.H. Fairbrother	b Aqib Javed	62
A.J. Lamb	lbw b Waqar Younis	16
G.A. Hick	b Wasim Akram	63
I.T. Botham	c Ramiz Raja b Waqar Younis	24
C.C. Lewis	not out	1
P.A.J. DeFreitas	not out	5
R.K. Illingworth		
G.C. Small		
Extras	(B 4, LB 12, W 18, NB 5)	39
TOTAL	(55 overs) (for 7 wkts)	**363**

Bowler	O	M	R	W	Fall	
Wasim Akram	11	0	55	1	1st	84
Aqib Javed	11	0	55	2	2nd	95
Waqar Younis	11	0	73	4	3rd	224
Mushtaq Ahmed	11	1	58	0	4th	250
Ijaz Ahmed	4	0	29	0	5th	269
Aamir Sohail	3	0	34	0	6th	353
Asif Mujtaba	4	0	43	0	7th	357

PAKISTAN

Aamir Sohail	c Botham b Lewis	17
Ramiz Raja	c Gooch b DeFreitas	0
Salim Malik*	c Small b Illingworth	45
Asif Mujtaba	c Lewis b DeFreitas	1
Inzamam-ul-Haq	run out	10
Ijaz Ahmed	c Gooch b Botham	23
Wasim Akram	lbw b Illingworth	1
Rashid Latif+	st Stewart b Illingworth	29
Waqar Younis	c Hick b DeFreitas	13
Mushtaq Ahmed	not out	14
Aqib Javed	c Stewart b Small	2
Extras	(LB 5, W 5,)	10
TOTAL	(46.1 overs)	**165**

Bowler	O	M	R	W	Fall	
DeFreitas	11	1	33	3	1st	2
Lewis	8	2	24	1	2nd	22
Botham	11	1	41	1	3rd	27
Small	5.1	0	28	1	4th	60
Illingworth	11	1	34	3	5th	87
					6th	98
					7th	103
					8th	129
					9th	153
					10th	165

Match No: 207/35

ENGLAND v PAKISTAN

Texaco Trophy
Played at Lord's, London on 22 & 23/08/1992
Toss: Pakistan **Result:** Pakistan won by 3 runs
Umpires: J.H. Hampshire and K.E. Palmer
Man of the match: Javed Miandad
Debuts: Eng - R.J. Blakey

PAKISTAN
Aamir Sohail	c Stewart b DeFreitas	20
Ramiz Raja	c Stewart b Botham	23
Salim Malik	st Blakey b Illingworth	48
Javed Miandad*	not out	50
Inzamam-ul-Haq	c Blakey b Reeve	16
Wasim Akram	b DeFreitas	23
Naved Anjum	not out	4
Moin Khan+		
Waqar Younis		
Mushtaq Ahmed		
Aqib Javed		
Extras	(B 2, LB 7, W 11)	20
TOTAL	(50 overs) (for 5 wkts)	**204**

						Fall	
DeFreitas	10	2	39	2	1st	32
Lewis	10	0	49	0	2nd	91
Botham	10	1	33	1	3rd	102
Reeve	10	1	31	1	4th	137
Illingworth	10	0	43	1	5th	189

ENGLAND
I.T. Botham	st Moin Khan b Aamir Sohail	40
A.J. Stewart*	lbw b Waqar Younis	0
R.A. Smith	c Moin Khan b Aqib Javed	4
N.H. Fairbrother	b Aqib Javed	33
A.J. Lamb	c Moin Khan b Mushtaq Ahmed	55
G.A. Hick	b Aamir Sohail	8
R.J. Blakey+	b Waqar Younis	25
D.A. Reeve	not out	6
C.C. Lewis	c sub (Asif Mujtaba) b Wasim Akram	1
P.A.J. DeFreitas	c Mushtaq Ahmed b Wasim Akram	0
R.K. Illingworth	b Waqar Younis	4
Extras	(LB 8, W 11, NB 6)	25
TOTAL	(49.2 overs)	**201**

						Fall	
Wasim Akram	10	2	41	2	1st	15
Waqar Younis	9.2	0	36	3	2nd	30
Mushtaq Ahmed	10	1	34	1	3rd	72
Aqib Javed	9	0	39	2	4th	111
Aamir Sohail	5	0	22	2	5th	139
Naved Anjum	6	0	21	0	6th	172
						7th	191
						8th	193
						9th	193
						10th	201

Match No: 208/36

ENGLAND v PAKISTAN

Texaco Trophy
Played at Old Trafford, Manchester on 24/08/1992
Toss: Pakistan   **Result:** England won by 6 wickets
Umpires: H.D. Bird and M.J. Kitchen
Man of the match : R.A. Smith
Debuts: Eng - D.G. Cork

PAKISTAN
Aamir Sohail	run out	87
Ramiz Raja*	run out	37
Shoaib Mohammad	b Reeve	9
Inzamam-ul-Haq	lbw b Cork	75
Asif Mujtaba	c Smith b DeFreitas	10
Wasim Akram	not out	15
Naved Anjum	not out	12
Moin Khan+		
Waqar Younis		
Mushtaq Ahmed		
Aqib Javed		
Extras	(LB 6, W 2, NB 1)	9
TOTAL	(55 overs) (for 5 wkts)	**254**

						Fall	
DeFreitas	11	1	52	1	1st	69
Cork	11	1	37	1	2nd	90
Botham	11	0	43	0	3rd	189
Reeve	11	1	57	1	4th	210
Illingworth	11	0	59	0	5th	240

ENGLAND
G.A. Gooch*	b Aamir Sohail	45
A.J. Stewart+	st Moin Khan b Aamir Sohail	51
R.A. Smith	not out	85
N.H. Fairbrother	b Waqar Younis	15
A.J. Lamb	c Moin Khan b Waqar Younis	2
G.A. Hick	not out	42
I.T. Botham		
D.A. Reeve		
D.G. Cork		
P.A.J. DeFreitas		
R.K. Illingworth		
Extras	(LB 7, W 3, NB 5)	15
TOTAL	(43.4 overs) (for 4 wkts)	**255**

						Fall	
Wasim Akram	9.4	1	45	0	1st	98
Waqar Younis	8	0	58	2	2nd	101
Aqib Javed	6	0	42	0	3rd	149
Mushtaq Ahmed	9	0	48	0	4th	159
Aamir Sohail	7	0	29	2		
Naved Anjum	4	0	26	0		

Match No: 209/24

INDIA v ENGLAND

Charminar Challenge Series
Played at Sawai Mansingh Stadium, Jaipur on 18/01/1993
Toss: England   **Result:** England won by 4 wickets
Umpires: S.K. Bansal and S. Venkataraghavan
Man of the match: V.G. Kambli
Debuts: None

INDIA
M. Prabhakar	b Jarvis	25
N.S. Sidhu	b Jarvis	0
V.G. Kambli	not out	100
M. Azharuddin*	lbw b Lewis	6
S.R. Tendulkar	not out	82
P.K. Amre		
Kapil Dev		
V. Yadav+		
A.R. Kumble		
Venkatapathy Raju		
J. Srinath		
Extras	(B 2, LB 7, W 1)	10
TOTAL	(48 overs) (for 3 wkts)	223

						Fall	
DeFreitas	9	3	40	0		1st	0
Jarvis	10	0	49	2		2nd	31
Reeve	10	0	37	0		3rd	59
Lewis	9	0	26	1			
Emburey	8	0	49	0			
Gooch	2	0	13	0			

ENGLAND
G.A. Gooch*	lbw b Kapil Dev	4
A.J. Stewart+	c Yadav b Kapil Dev	91
R.A. Smith	c & b Prabhakar	16
M.W. Gatting	b Kumble	30
N.H. Fairbrother	not out	46
G.A. Hick	run out	13
D.A. Reeve	lbw b Prabhakar	2
C.C. Lewis	not out	8
J.E. Emburey		
P.A.J. DeFreitas		
P.W. Jarvis		
Extras	(B 1, LB 8, W 3, NB 2)	14
TOTAL	(48 overs) (for 6 wkts)	224

						Fall	
Kapil Dev	10	1	36	2		1st	29
Prabhakar	10	0	43	2		2nd	85
Srinath	10	0	47	0		3rd	145
Venkatapathy Raju	8	1	35	0		4th	161
Kumble	10	0	54	1		5th	200
						6th	203

Match No: 210/25

INDIA v ENGLAND

Charminar Challenge Series
Played at Sector 16 Stadium, Chandigarh on 21/01/1993
Toss: India **Result:** India won by 5 wickets
Umpires: R.V. Ramani and V.K. Ramaswamy
Man of the match: N.S. Sidhu
Debuts: Eng - I.D.K. Salisbury

ENGLAND
G.A. Gooch*	c Tendulkar b Srinath	7
A.J. Stewart+	c Azharuddin b Kapil Dev	7
R.A. Smith	lbw b Kumble	42
M.W. Gatting	c & b Srinath	0
N.H. Fairbrother	lbw b Venkatapathy Raju	7
G.A. Hick	b Kapil Dev	56
D.A. Reeve	not out	33
C.C. Lewis	not out	16
P.A.J. DeFreitas		
P.W. Jarvis		
I.D.K. Salisbury		
Extras	(LB 13, W 13, NB 4)	30
TOTAL	(50 overs) (for 6 wkts)	198

Fall

Kapil Dev	10	2	40	2	1st	19
Prabhakar	8	0	30	0	2nd	20
Srinath	10	2	34	2	3rd	22
Tendulkar	3	0	16	0	4th	49
Venkatapathy Raju	9	0	28	1	5th	132
Kumble	10	0	37	1	6th	153

INDIA
N.S. Sidhu	c Reeve b DeFreitas	76
M. Prabhakar	c Reeve b Lewis	36
V.G. Kambli	c & b Jarvis	9
M. Azharuddin*	lbw b Reeve	36
S.R. Tendulkar	lbw b DeFreitas	1
P.K. Amre	not out	24
Kapil Dev	not out	5
V. Yadav+		
A.R. Kumble		
Venkatapathy Raju		
J. Srinath		
Extras	(LB 3, W 5, NB 6)	14
TOTAL	(45.1 overs) (for 5 wkts)	201

Fall

DeFreitas	10	1	31	2	1st	79
Jarvis	10	1	43	1	2nd	99
Reeve	6.1	0	33	1	3rd	148
Lewis	10	0	47	1	4th	161
Salisbury	8	1	42	0	5th	195
Gatting	1	0	2	0		

Match No: 211/26

INDIA v ENGLAND

Charminar Challenge Series
Played at Chinnaswamy Stadium, Bangalore on 26/02/1993
Toss: India   **Result:** England won by 48 runs
Umpires: V.K. Ramaswamy and M.R. Singh
Man of the match: P.W. Jarvis and J. Srinath
Debuts: None

ENGLAND

R.A. Smith	c More b Srinath	29
A.J. Stewart+	lbw b Srinath	14
G.A. Hick	c Amre b Prabhakar	56
M.W. Gatting	b Srinath	7
N.H. Fairbrother	run out	5
G.A. Gooch*	b Prabhakar	45
C.C. Lewis	c Tendulkar b Srinath	19
D.A. Reeve	not out	13
P.A.J. DeFreitas	c Prabhakar b Srinath	2
P.W. Jarvis	c Azharuddin b Kapil Dev	1
D.E. Malcolm	not out	0
Extras	(LB 15, W 4, NB 8)	27
TOTAL	(47 overs) (for 9 wkts)	**218**

					Fall	
Kapil Dev	8	1	27	1	1st	42
Prabhakar	10	0	50	2	2nd	65
Srinath	9	1	41	5	3rd	79
Venkatapathy Raju	10	0	46	0	4th	102
Kumble	10	1	39	0	5th	157
					6th	185
					7th	210
					8th	213
					9th	218

INDIA

M. Prabhakar	run out	0
N.S. Sidhu	c Gooch b DeFreitas	40
V.G. Kambli	c Stewart b Jarvis	33
S.R. Tendulkar	c Hick b Lewis	3
M. Azharuddin*	lbw b Jarvis	1
P.K. Amre	c Hick b Jarvis	16
Kapil Dev	c Gooch b Malcolm	32
K.S. More+	lbw b Jarvis	0
A.R. Kumble	b Jarvis	24
J. Srinath	c Hick b Malcolm	2
Venkatapathy Raju	not out	1
Extras	(LB 4, W 11, NB 3)	18
TOTAL	(41.4 overs)	**170**

					Fall	
Malcolm	9	1	47	2	1st	3
DeFreitas	8	0	27	1	2nd	61
Lewis	10	0	32	1	3rd	66
Jarvis	8.4	1	35	5	4th	67
Reeve	6	0	25	0	5th	100
					6th	114
					7th	115
					8th	160
					9th	166
					10th	170

Match No: 212/27

INDIA v ENGLAND

Charminar Challenge Series
Played at Keenan Stadium, Jamshedpur on 01/03/1993
Toss: England **Result:** England won by 6 wickets
Umpires: L. Narasimhan and C.S. Sathe
Man of the match: N.H. Fairbrother
Debuts: None

INDIA
N.S. Sidhu	c DeFreitas b Malcolm	18
M. Prabhakar	c Blakey b DeFreitas	2
V.G. Kambli	run out	23
S.R. Tendulkar	b Jarvis	24
M. Azharuddin*	c Fairbrother b Lewis	23
Kapil Dev	not out	15
P.K. Amre	c Gooch b Jarvis	19
S.A. Ankola	run out	2
K.S. More+	not out	1
A.R. Kumble		
J. Srinath		
Extras	(LB 6, W 3, NB 1)	10
TOTAL	(26 overs) (for 7 wkts)	**137**

					Fall	
DeFreitas	4	0	17	1	1st	11
Malcolm	6	0	17	1	2nd	46
Lewis	5	0	25	1	3rd	51
Reeve	6	0	32	0	4th	96
Jarvis	5	0	40	2	5th	99
					6th	122
					7th	127

ENGLAND
G.A. Gooch*	c More b Kapil Dev	15
R.A. Smith	run out	17
G.A. Hick	c Azharuddin b Ankola	1
N.H. Fairbrother	not out	53
C.C. Lewis	lbw b Prabhakar	25
D.A. Reeve	not out	17
M.W. Gatting		
R.J. Blakey+		
P.A.J. DeFreitas		
P.W. Jarvis		
D.E. Malcolm		
Extras	(LB 8, W 5)	13
TOTAL	(25.4 overs) (for 4 wkts)	**141**

					Fall	
Kapil Dev	4	1	10	1	1st	27
Prabhakar	5.4	0	34	1	2nd	33
Srinath	6	0	38	0	3rd	43
Ankola	6	0	28	1	4th	93
Kumble	4	0	23	0		

Match No: 213/28

INDIA v ENGLAND

Charminar Challenge Series
Played at Roop Singh Stadium, Gwalior on 04/03/1993
Toss: India **Result:** India won by 3 wickets
Umpires: A.V. Jayaprakash and P.D. Reporter
Man of the match: N.S. Sidhu
Debuts: None

ENGLAND

R.A. Smith	lbw b Srinath	129
A.J. Stewart	b Kumble	33
G.A. Hick	c More b Prabhakar	18
N.H. Fairbrother	c Maninder singh b Srinath	37
C.C. Lewis	lbw b Prabhakar	4
G.A. Gooch*	run out	1
D.A. Reeve	run out	3
R.J. Blakey+	lbw b Srinath	0
P.A.J. DeFreitas	not out	2
P.W. Jarvis	b Prabhakar	0
D.E. Malcolm	b Prabhakar	0
Extras	(B 1, LB 16, W 8, NB 4)	29
TOTAL	(50 overs)	256

	O	M	R	W		Fall
Kapil Dev	9	0	39	0	1st	101
Prabhakar	10	0	54	4	2nd	154
Srinath	10	0	41	3	3rd	227
Kumble	10	0	41	1	4th	246
Maninder Singh	8	0	46	0	5th	246
Sharma	3	0	18	0	6th	251
					7th	251
					8th	256
					9th	256
					10th	256

INDIA

N.S. Sidhu	not out	134
M. Prabhakar	lbw b DeFreitas	0
V.G. Kambli	c Gooch b Malcolm	2
M. Azharuddin	c Stewart b Malcolm	74
S.R. Tendulkar	b Jarvis	5
A.K. Sharma	run out	0
Kapil Dev*	c Hick b Jarvis	2
K.S. More+	c Hick b Malcolm	1
A.R. Kumble	not out	19
Maninder Singh		
J. Srinath		
Extras	(B 2, LB 9, W 8, NB 1)	20
TOTAL	(48 overs) (for 7 wkts)	257

	O	M	R	W		Fall
DeFreitas	10	0	52	1	1st	1
Malcolm	10	0	40	3	2nd	4
Lewis	10	0	56	0	3rd	179
Jarvis	10	0	43	2	4th	189
Reeve	6	0	37	0	5th	190
Hick	2	0	18	0	6th	202
					7th	205

Match No: 214/29

INDIA v ENGLAND

Charminar Challenge Series
Played at Roop Singh Stadium, Gwalior on 05/03/1993
Toss: India   Result: India won by 4 wickets
Umpires: S.K. Bansal and S. Venkataraghavan
Man of the match: M. Azharuddin
Debuts: None

ENGLAND
R.A. Smith	c Sharma b Maninder Singh	72
A.J. Stewart+	c More b Srinath	11
G.A. Hick	not out	105
N.H. Fairbrother	c Kapil Dev b Srinath	41
M.W. Gatting	c Sidhu b Srinath	6
C.C. Lewis	not out	3
G.A. Gooch*		
D.A. Reeve		
P.A.J. DeFreitas		
P.W. Jarvis		
D.E. Malcolm		
Extras	(LB 8, W 17, NB 2)	27
TOTAL	(48 overs) (for 4 wkts)	265

						Fall	
Kapil Dev	10	2	48	0		1st	42
Prabhakar	9	0	52	0		2nd	158
Srinath	9	0	37	3		3rd	246
Maninder Singh	10	0	62	1		4th	258
Kumble	10	0	58	0			

INDIA
M. Prabhakar	b Jarvis	73
N.S. Sidhu	c Hick b Lewis	19
V.G. Kambli	c Reeve b DeFreitas	22
M. Azharuddin*	not out	95
S.R. Tendulkar	c sub (J.P. Taylor) b Lewis	34
Kapil Dev	c Reeve b Jarvis	2
A.K. Sharma	c Gooch b Jarvis	2
K.S. More+	not out	10
A.R. Kumble		
Maninder Singh		
J. Srinath		
Extras	(LB 1, W 7, NB 2)	10
TOTAL	(46.4 overs) (for 6 wkts)	267

						Fall	
Malcolm	8	0	56	0		1st	41
Lewis	10	1	51	2		2nd	99
Jarvis	10	0	39	3		3rd	166
Reeve	8.4	0	64	0		4th	245
DeFreitas	10	0	56	1		5th	251
						6th	253

226 *England - The Complete One-Day International Record*

Match No: 215/10

SRI LANKA v ENGLAND

Played at Khettarama Stadium, Colombo on 10/03/1993
Toss: Sri Lanka   **Result:** Sri Lanka won by 80 runs
Umpires: K.T. Francis and S. Ponnadhurai
Man of the match: H.P. Tillekeratne
Debuts: None

SRI LANKA

U.C. Hathurusinghe	lbw b Emburey	43
R.S. Mahanama	c Hick b Malcolm	7
A.P. Gurusinha	c DeFreitas b Jarvis	5
P.A. de Silva	c & b Reeve	34
A. Ranatunga*	c Stewart b Lewis	36
H.P. Tillekeratne	not out	66
S.T. Jayasuriya	not out	34
A.M. de Silva		
R.S. Kalpage		
C.P.H. Ramanayake		
G.P. Wickremasinghe		
Extras	(B 3, LB 4, W 10, NB 8)	25
TOTAL	(47 overs) (for 5 wkts)	250

						Fall	
Malcolm	7	1	32	1	1st	16
Lewis	9	0	40	1	2nd	33
Jarvis	9	0	57	1	3rd	101
DeFreitas	3	0	25	0	4th	109
Emburey	10	1	42	1	5th	180
Reeve	9	1	47	1		

ENGLAND

R.A. Smith	c & b Wickremasinghe	3
A.J. Stewart*+	lbw b Ramanayake	5
G.A. Hick	c Mahanama b Hathurusinghe	31
N.H. Fairbrother	lbw b Jayasuriya	34
M.W. Gatting	b Kalpage	1
C.C. Lewis	b Kalpage	16
D.A. Reeve	c Ranatunga b Kalpage	16
P.A.J. DeFreitas	c Ranatunga b Wickremasinghe	21
J.E. Emburey	st A.M. de Silva b Jayasuriya	10
P.W. Jarvis	not out	16
D.E. Malcolm	run out	2
Extras	(LB 10, W 4, NB 1)	15
TOTAL	(36.1 overs)	170

						Fall	
Ramanayake	7	0	25	1	1st	7
Wickremasinghe	6.1	1	21	2	2nd	9
Hathurusinghe	6	0	28	1	3rd	67
Gurusinha	2	0	7	0	4th	71
Kalpage	8	0	34	3	5th	99
Jayasuriya	7	0	45	2	6th	103
					7th	120
					8th	137
					9th	152
					10th	170

Match No: 216/11

SRI LANKA v ENGLAND

Played at Tyronne Fernando Stadium, Moratuwa on 20/03/1993
Toss: Sri Lanka **Result:** Sri Lanka won by 8 wickets
Umpires: B.C. Cooray and T.M. Samarasinghe
Man of the match: S.T. Jayasuriya
Debuts: Eng - J.P. Taylor

ENGLAND
C.C. Lewis	c Ramanayake b Wickremasinghe	8
R.A. Smith	st A.M. de Silva b Jayasuriya	31
G.A. Hick	lbw b Kalpage	36
N.H. Fairbrother	c A.M. de Silva b Jayasuriya	21
A.J. Stewart*+	lbw b Tillekeratne	14
M.W. Gatting	lbw b P.A. de Silva	2
D.A. Reeve	b Jayasuriya	21
J.E. Emburey	c Ramanayake b Jayasuriya	20
I.D.K. Salisbury	not out	2
P.W. Jarvis	c A.M. de Silva b Jayasuriya	4
J.P. Taylor	b Jayasuriya	1
Extras	(B 2, LB 9, W 3, NB 6)	20
TOTAL	**(48.5 overs)**	**180**

						Fall	
Ramanayake	4	0	20	0	1st	23
Wickremasinghe	8	0	23	1	2nd	77
Gurusinha	4	0	21	0	3rd	85
Hathurusinghe	2	0	13	0	4th	111
Kalpage	10	0	27	1	5th	114
Jayasuriya	9.5	0	29	6	6th	125
P.A. de Silva	7	1	22	1	7th	168
Tillekeratne	4	0	14	1	8th	172
					9th	177
					10th	180

SRI LANKA
R.S. Mahanama	c Stewart b Salisbury	29
U.C. Hathurusinghe	c & b Salisbury	33
A.P. Gurusinha	not out	35
P.A. de Silva	not out	75
A. Ranatunga*		
H.P. Tillekeratne		
S.T. Jayasuriya		
A.M. de Silva+		
R.S. Kalpage		
C.P.H. Ramanayake		
G.P. Wickremasinghe		
Extras	(B 1, LB 2, W 2, NB 6)	11
TOTAL	**(35.2 overs) (for 2 wkts)**	**183**

						Fall	
Lewis	7	1	13	0	1st	66
Jarvis	4	0	22	0	2nd	68
Taylor	3	0	20	0		
Emburey	6	0	29	0		
Salisbury	4	0	36	2		
Hick	6.2	1	36	0		
Reeve	5	0	24	0		

Match No: 217/53

ENGLAND v AUSTRALIA

Texaco Trophy
Played at Old Trafford, Manchester on 19/05/1993
Toss: England   **Result:** Australia won by 4 runs
Umpires: B.J. Meyer and D.R. Shepherd
Man of the match: C.J. McDermott
Debuts: Eng - A.R. Caddick, G.P. Thorpe   Aus - M.L. Hayden

AUSTRALIA

M.L. Hayden	c Stewart b Lewis	29
M.A. Taylor	c Fairbrother b Illingworth	79
M.E. Waugh	c Fairbrother b Jarvis	56
D.C. Boon	c Fairbrother b Illingworth	2
A.R. Border*	c Lewis b Illingworth	4
S.R. Waugh	c & b Lewis	27
I.A. Healy+	c Thorpe b Caddick	20
M.G. Hughes	b Lewis	20
P.R. Reiffel	run out	2
C.J. McDermott	not out	3
T.B.A. May	not out	1
Extras	(B 1, LB 8, W 2, NB 4)	15
TOTAL	(55 overs) (for 9 wkts)	**258**

	O	M	R	W		Fall
Caddick	11	1	50	1	1st	60
Pringle	10	3	36	0	2nd	168
Lewis	11	1	54	3	3rd	171
Jarvis	11	0	55	1	4th	178
Illingworth	11	0	48	3	5th	186
Hick	1	0	6	0	6th	219
					7th	237
					8th	254
					9th	255

ENGLAND

G.A. Gooch*	c M.E. Waugh b McDermott	4
A.J. Stewart+	b Hughes	22
R.A. Smith	c & b McDermott	9
G.A. Hick	b Reiffel	85
N.H. Fairbrother	c Reiffel b S.R. Waugh	59
G.P. Thorpe	c Taylor b McDermott	31
C.C. Lewis	run out	4
D.R. Pringle	c Taylor b S.R. Waugh	6
R.K. Illingworth	run out	12
P.W. Jarvis	c Reiffel b S.R. Waugh	2
A.R. Caddick	not out	1
Extras	(LB 8, W 9, NB 2)	19
TOTAL	(54.5 overs)	**254**

	O	M	R	W		Fall
McDermott	11	2	38	3	1st	11
Hughes	9.5	1	40	1	2nd	38
May	11	2	40	0	3rd	44
Reiffel	11	0	63	1	4th	171
M.E. Waugh	2	0	12	0	5th	194
S.R. Waugh	10	0	53	3	6th	211
					7th	227
					8th	240
					9th	247
					10th	254

Match No: 218/54

ENGLAND v AUSTRALIA

Texaco Trophy
Played at Edgbaston, Birmingham on 21/05/1993
Toss: Australia   **Result:** Australia won by 6 wickets
Umpires: M.J. Kitchen and K.E. Palmer
Man of the match: R.A. Smith
Debuts: None

ENGLAND
G.A. Gooch*	c Healy b McDermott	17
A.J. Stewart+	b McDermott	0
R.A. Smith	not out	167
G.A. Hick	c Healy b Reiffel	2
N.H. Fairbrother	c Taylor b S.R. Waugh	23
G.P. Thorpe	c Border b McDermott	36
C.C. Lewis	not out	13
D.R. Pringle		
D.G. Cork		
P.W. Jarvis		
A.R. Caddick		
Extras	(B 2, LB 4, W 2, NB 11)	19
TOTAL	(55 overs) (for 5 wkts)	**277**

						Fall	
McDermott	11	1	29	3	1st	3
Hughes	11	2	51	0	2nd	40
Reiffel	11	1	70	1	3rd	55
May	11	0	45	0	4th	105
S.R. Waugh	8	0	55	1	5th	247
M.E. Waugh	3	0	21	0		

AUSTRALIA
M.A. Taylor	b Lewis	26
M.L. Hayden	b Jarvis	14
M.E. Waugh	c Fairbrother b Lewis	113
D.C. Boon	c Stewart b Pringle	21
A.R. Border*	not out	86
S.R. Waugh	not out	6
I.A. Healy+		
M.G. Hughes		
P.R. Reiffel		
C.J. McDermott		
T.B.A. May		
Extras	(LB 5, W 3, NB 6)	14
TOTAL	(53.3 overs) (for 4 wkts)	**280**

						Fall	
Caddick	11	1	43	0	1st	28
Jarvis	10	1	51	1	2nd	55
Lewis	10.3	0	61	2	3rd	95
Pringle	11	0	63	1	4th	263
Cork	11	1	57	0		

Match No: 219/55

ENGLAND v AUSTRALIA

Texaco Trophy
Played at Lord's, London on 23/05/1993
Toss: England   **Result:** Australia won by 19 runs
Umpires: H.D. Bird and R. Palmer
Man of the match: B.P. Julian
Debuts: Aus - B.P. Julian

AUSTRALIA

M.L. Hayden	c Stewart b Caddick	4
M.A. Taylor*	c Stewart b Reeve	57
M.E. Waugh	c Stewart b Caddick	14
D.C. Boon	b Illingworth	73
D.R. Martyn	not out	51
S.R. Waugh	c Gooch b Caddick	8
I.A. Healy+	not out	12
M.G. Hughes		
B.P. Julian		
C.J. McDermott		
T.B.A. May		
Extras	(LB 3, W 6, NB 2)	11
TOTAL	(55 overs) (for 5 wkts)	**230**

						Fall	
Jarvis	11	1	51	0	1st	12
Caddick	11	3	39	3	2nd	31
Cork	9	2	24	0	3rd	139
Illingworth	10	0	46	1	4th	193
Reeve	11	1	50	1	5th	208
Hick	3	0	17	0		

ENGLAND

G.A. Gooch*	c Hughes b May	42
A.J. Stewart+	c M.E. Waugh b Julian	74
R.A. Smith	st Healy b May	6
G.A. Hick	b Julian	7
N.H. Fairbrother	c Boon b Julian	18
G.P. Thorpe	c Healy b S.R. Waugh	22
D.A. Reeve	run out	2
D.G. Cork	b Hughes	11
R.K. Illingworth	c Healy b Hughes	9
P.W. Jarvis	c Hayden b McDermott	3
A.R. Caddick	not out	2
Extras	(LB 6, W 8, NB 1)	15
TOTAL	(53.1 overs)	**211**

						Fall	
McDermott	10	1	35	1	1st	96
Hughes	10.1	0	41	2	2nd	115
Julian	11	1	50	3	3rd	129
May	11	1	36	2	4th	159
S.R. Waugh	11	0	43	1	5th	160
					6th	169
					7th	195
					8th	201
					9th	208
					10th	211

Match No: 220/44

WEST INDIES v ENGLAND

Cable & Wireless Series
Played at Kensington Oval, Bridgetown, Barbados on 16/02/1994
Toss: England   **Result:** England won by 61 runs
Umpires: L.H. Barker and C.R. Duncan
Man of the match: M.A. Atherton
Debuts: Eng - A.P. Igglesden, M.P. Maynard, S.L. Watkin

ENGLAND

M.A. Atherton*	c Richardson b Cummins	86
A.J. Stewart+	c Lara b Benjamin	11
G.P. Thorpe	c Adams b Benjamin	4
R.A. Smith	c & b Harper	12
G.A. Hick	c Simmons b Cummins	47
M.P. Maynard	not out	22
C.C. Lewis	not out	6
S.L. Watkin		
A.P. Igglesden		
P.C.R. Tufnell		
D.E. Malcolm		
Extras	(B 4, LB 7, NB 3)	14
TOTAL	(50 overs) (for 5 wkts)	202

	O	M	R	W	Fall	
Ambrose	10	2	35	0	1st	35
Walsh	10	0	42	0	2nd	45
Benjamin	10	2	38	2	3rd	73
Cummins	10	1	28	2	4th	166
Harper	10	0	48	1	5th	176

WEST INDIES

D.L. Haynes	c Malcolm b Igglesden	17
B.C. Lara	c Igglesden b Malcolm	9
R.B. Richardson*	c Maynard b Lewis	12
K.L.T. Arthurton	b Lewis	6
P.V. Simmons	b Lewis	0
J.C. Adams+	c Thorpe b Igglesden	29
R.A. Harper	lbw b Watkin	11
A.C. Cummins	c Thorpe b Malcolm	24
W.K.M. Benjamin	c Thorpe b Tufnell	0
C.E.L. Ambrose	c Smith b Malcolm	10
C.A. Walsh	not out	1
Extras	(B 1, LB 10, W 11)	22
TOTAL	(40.4 overs)	141

	O	M	R	W	Fall	
Malcolm	8.4	1	41	3	1st	17
Watkin	8	1	27	1	2nd	43
Lewis	8	2	18	3	3rd	48
Igglesden	8	2	12	2	4th	48
Tufnell	8	0	32	1	5th	55
					6th	82
					7th	121
					8th	122
					9th	136
					10th	141

Match No: 221/45

WEST INDIES v ENGLAND

Cable & Wireless Series
Played at Sabina Park, Kingston, Jamaica on 26/02/1994
Toss: West Indies   **Result:** West Indies won by 3 wickets
                               (revised target)

Umpires: L.H. Barker and S.A. Bucknor
Man of the match: J.C. Adams
Debuts: None

ENGLAND

Batsman	Dismissal	Runs
M.A. Atherton*	c Arthurton b Harper	46
A.J. Stewart+	run out	66
R.A. Smith	c Harper b K.C.G. Benjamin	56
G.A. Hick	c Cummins b Arthurton	31
M.P. Maynard	b Cummins	22
N. Hussain	c Richardson b Cummins	10
C.C. Lewis	b K.C.G. Benjamin	0
S.L. Watkin	b K.C.G. Benjamin	0
A.P. Igglesden	not out	2
P.C.R. Tufnell	not out	2
A.R.C. Fraser		
Extras	(LB 9, W 7, NB 2)	18
TOTAL	(50 overs) (for 8 wkts)	**253**

Bowler	O	M	R	W		Fall	
Walsh	5	1	26	0		1st	112
K.C.G. Benjamin	10	1	44	3		2nd	128
Cummins	8	1	42	2		3rd	209
W.K.M. Benjamin	8	0	33	0		4th	214
Harper	8	0	45	1		5th	247
Simmons	7	0	32	0		6th	248
Arthurton	4	0	22	1		7th	248
						8th	249

WEST INDIES

Batsman	Dismissal	Runs
D.L. Haynes	c & b Hick	53
B.C. Lara	lbw b Watkin	8
P.V. Simmons	b Fraser	39
K.L.T. Arthurton	st Stewart b Hick	12
R.B. Richardson*	c Fraser b Watkin	32
J.C. Adams+	not out	52
R.A. Harper	lbw b Watkin	0
A.C. Cummins	c Smith b Watkin	16
W.K.M. Benjamin	not out	9
K.C.G. Benjamin		
C.A. Walsh		
Extras	(B 3, LB 7, W 6, NB 3)	19
TOTAL	(45.5 overs) (for 7 wkts)	**240**

Bowler	O	M	R	W		Fall	
Igglesden	7	1	29	0		1st	13
Watkin	9.5	1	49	4		2nd	111
Fraser	9	0	50	1		3rd	128
Lewis	9	0	48	0		4th	130
Tufnell	4	0	22	0		5th	186
Hick	7	0	32	2		6th	186
						7th	223

Match No: 222/46

WEST INDIES v ENGLAND

Cable & Wireless Series
Played at Arnos Vale, St Vincent on 02/03/1994
Toss: England   Result: West Indies won by 165 runs
Umpires: L.H. Barker and G.A. Johnson
Man of the match: D.L. Haynes
Debuts: None

WEST INDIES
D.L. Haynes	c Lewis b Tufnell	83
P.V. Simmons	c Hussain b Tufnell	63
B.C. Lara	c Stewart b Fraser	60
K.L.T. Arthurton	c Smith b Watkin	28
R.B. Richardson*	not out	52
J.C. Adams+	c Smith b Watkin	6
R.A. Harper	run out	15
A.C. Cummins	not out	0
W.K.M. Benjamin		
C.E.L. Ambrose		
K.C.G. Benjamin		
Extras	(LB 4, W 2)	6
TOTAL	(50 overs) (for 6 wkts)	313

	O	M	R	W		Fall
Igglesden	10	1	65	0	1st	145
Watkin	9	0	61	2	2nd	156
Lewis	9	0	67	0	3rd	230
Fraser	10	1	46	1	4th	242
Hick	3	0	18	0	5th	256
Tufnell	9	0	52	2	6th	300

ENGLAND
C.C. Lewis	lbw b Cummins	2
A.J. Stewart+	c Adams b K.C.J. Benjamin	13
R.A. Smith	b Ambrose	18
G.A. Hick	c Cummins b Harper	32
M.P. Maynard	c Simmons b Cummins	6
N. Hussain	c & b Harper	16
M.A. Atherton*	not out	19
S.L. Watkin	c Lara b Arthurton	4
A.P. Igglesden	c Ambrose b Lara	18
A.R.C. Fraser	st Adams b Lara	1
P.C.R. Tufnell	not out	0
Extras	(B 1, LB 12, W 6)	19
TOTAL	(50 overs) (for 9 wkts)	148

	O	M	R	W		Fall
K.C.G. Benjamin	6	0	21	1	1st	7
Cummins	8	1	22	2	2nd	24
W.K.M. Benjamin	5	1	15	0	3rd	41
Ambrose	6	2	13	1	4th	64
Simmons	7	1	18	0	5th	98
Harper	10	0	29	2	6th	105
Arthurton	6	1	12	1	7th	119
Lara	2	0	5	2	8th	144
					9th	148

Match No: 223/47

WEST INDIES v ENGLAND

Cable & Wireless Series
Played at Queens Park Oval, Port of Spain, Trinidad on 05/03/1994
Toss: England   Result: West Indies won by 72 runs
                                                (revised target)
Umpires: S.A. Bucknor and C.E. Cumberbatch
Man of the match: D.L. Haynes
Debuts: None

WEST INDIES

D.L. Haynes	b Lewis	115
P.V. Simmons	c Hick b Lewis	16
B.C. Lara	lbw b Fraser	19
K.L.T. Arthurton	c Stewart b Fraser	0
R.B. Richardson*	c Ramprakash b Caddick	13
J.C. Adams+	c Caddick b Fraser	40
R.A. Harper	b Lewis	23
A.C. Cummins	not out	13
W.K.M. Benjamin	not out	0
C.E.L. Ambrose		
K.C.G. Benjamin		
Extras	(B 4, LB 4, W 13, NB 5)	26
TOTAL	(45.4 overs) (for 7 wkts)	265

						Fall	
Igglesden	3	0	16	0	1st	45
Caddick	10	0	60	1	2nd	75
Fraser	10	0	31	3	3rd	75
Lewis	9.4	1	59	3	4th	98
Salisbury	9	0	58	0	5th	222
Hick	4	0	33	0	6th	238
					7th	265

ENGLAND

M.A. Atherton*	b K.C.G. Benjamin	41
A.J. Stewart+	b K.C.G. Benjamin	2
R.A. Smith	b Harper	45
G.A. Hick	c & b Harper	10
M.P. Maynard	b Harper	8
M.R. Ramprakash	b Ambrose	31
C.C. Lewis	c Lara b Harper	4
A.R. Caddick	not out	20
I.D.K. Salisbury	b Cummins	5
A.P. Igglesden	run out	0
A.R.C. Fraser	not out	4
Extras	(B 1, LB 9, W 11, NB 2)	23
TOTAL	(36 overs) (for 9 wkts)	193

						Fall	
K.C.G. Benjamin	8	0	37	2	1st	23
Cummins	6	0	34	1	2nd	86
Ambrose	8	0	34	1	3rd	110
W.K.M. Benjamin	7	0	38	0	4th	121
Harper	7	0	40	4	5th	130
						6th	145
						7th	177
						8th	184
						9th	184

Match No: 224/48

WEST INDIES v ENGLAND

Cable & Wireless Series
Played at Queens Park Oval, Port of Trinidad on 06/03/1994
Toss: West Indies **Result:** England won by 5 wickets
(revised target)
Umpires: S.A. Bucknor and C.E. Cumberbatch
Man of the match: A.J. Stewart
Debuts: None

WEST INDIES

P.V. Simmons	b Salisbury	84
J.C. Adams+	c Atherton b Salisbury	23
B.C. Lara	c Stewart b Caddick	16
K.L.T. Arthurton	c Ramprakash b Lewis	17
R.B. Richardson*	c Stewart b Salisbury	15
R.I.C. Holder	run out	26
R.A. Harper	c & b Lewis	37
A.C. Cummins	c Smith b Lewis	11
W.K.M. Benjamin	c Ramprakash b Lewis	8
K.C.G. Benjamin	not out	0
C.A. Walsh		
Extras	(B 1, LB 10, W 1, NB 1)	13
TOTAL	(50 overs) (for 9 wkts)	**250**

						Fall	
Fraser	10	2	41	0	1st	89
Watkin	10	0	56	0	2nd	126
Lewis	10	0	35	4	3rd	135
Caddick	10	2	66	1	4th	164
Salisbury	10	0	41	3	5th	164
					6th	230
					7th	232
					8th	248
					9th	250

ENGLAND

M.A. Atherton*	b K.C.G Benjamin	51
A.J. Stewart+	b Cummins	53
R.A. Smith	lbw b Cummins	4
G.A. Hick	not out	47
M.P. Maynard	c Adams b K.C.G. Benjamin	1
M.R. Ramprakash	c Adams b Walsh	10
C.C. Lewis	not out	16
A.R. Caddick		
I.D.K. Salisbury		
S.L. Watkin		
A.R.C. Fraser		
Extras	(B 2, LB 9, W 4, NB 4)	19
TOTAL	(36.4 overs) (for 5 wkts)	**201**

						Fall	
W.K.M. Benjamin	8	1	33	0	1st	62
Walsh	10	0	58	1	2nd	83
Cummins	7.4	0	36	2	3rd	151
K.C.G. Benjamin	9	0	55	2	4th	156
Harper	2	0	8	0	5th	174

Match No: 225/41

ENGLAND v NEW ZEALAND

Texaco Trophy
Played at Edgbaston, Birmingham on 19/05/1994
Toss: New Zealand   **Result:** England won by 42 runs
Umpires: R. Palmer and N.T. Plews
Man of the match: M.A. Atherton
Debuts: Eng - D. Gough, S.D. Udal

ENGLAND
M.A. Atherton*	run out	81
A.J. Stewart	c Nash b Pringle	24
R.A. Smith	c Parore b Thomson	15
G.A. Gooch	b Thomson	23
G.A. Hick	b Pringle	18
D.A. Reeve	c Fleming b Pringle	16
S.J. Rhodes+	c Thomson b Pringle	12
C.C. Lewis	b Pringle	19
S.D. Udal	not out	3
D. Gough		
A.R.C. Fraser		
Extras	(B 1, LB 5, W 7)	13
TOTAL	(55 overs) (for 8 wkts)	224

						Fall	
Morrison	6	0	31	0	1st	33
Pringle	11	1	45	5	2nd	84
Nash	6	1	20	0	3rd	140
Larsen	10	1	43	0	4th	161
Hart	11	0	45	0	5th	180
Thomson	11	0	34	2	6th	199
					7th	199
					8th	224

NEW ZEALAND
B.A. Young	b Gough	65
M.D. Crowe	c Stewart b Gough	0
A.C. Parore+	b Udal	42
K.R. Rutherford*	lbw b Udal	0
S.P. Fleming	c & b Hick	17
S.A. Thomson	c Lewis b Hick	7
G.R. Larsen	c & b Lewis	13
D.J. Nash	b Lewis	0
M.N. Hart	c Stewart b Lewis	13
C. Pringle	c Hick b Fraser	3
D.K. Morrison	not out	17
Extras	(LB 4, W 1)	5
TOTAL	(52.5 overs)	182

						Fall	
Fraser	10	0	37	1	1st	2
Gough	11	1	36	2	2nd	78
Udal	11	0	39	2	3rd	81
Reeve	4	0	15	0	4th	110
Lewis	9.5	2	20	3	5th	134
Hick	7	0	31	2	6th	136
					7th	136
					8th	149
					9th	152
					10th	182

Match No: 226/3

ENGLAND v SOUTH AFRICA

Texaco Trophy
Played at Edgbaston, Birmingham on 25/08/1994
Toss: South Africa   **Result:** England won by 6 wickets
Umpires: J.C. Balderstone and H.D. Bird
Man of the match: G.A. Hick
Debuts: None

SOUTH AFRICA

Batsman	Dismissal	Runs
K.C. Wessels*	b DeFreitas	4
G. Kirsten	c DeFreitas b Lewis	30
P.N. Kirsten	c Rhodes b DeFreitas	8
J.N. Rhodes	c Thorpe b Cork	35
D.J. Cullinan	b DeFreitas	45
W.J. Cronje	b Lewis	36
D.J. Richardson+	not out	20
R.P. Snell	c Gough b Lewis	2
T.G. Shaw	not out	17
C.R. Matthews		
P.S. de Villiers		
Extras	(LB 6, W 10, NB 2)	18
TOTAL	(55 overs) (for 7 wkts)	215

Bowler	O	M	R	W	Fall	
DeFreitas	9	1	38	3	1st	5
Gough	11	2	40	0	2nd	30
Lewis	8	0	32	3	3rd	58
Udal	11	0	34	0	4th	103
Cork	11	0	46	1	5th	174
Hick	5	1	19	0	6th	176
					7th	182

ENGLAND

Batsman	Dismissal	Runs
M.A. Atherton*	run out	49
A.J. Stewart	c de Villiers b Shaw	32
G.A. Hick	c Shaw b Snell	81
G.P. Thorpe	run out	26
N.H. Fairbrother	not out	19
S.J. Rhodes+	not out	0
C.C. Lewis		
D.G. Cork		
P.A.J. DeFreitas		
D. Gough		
S.D. Udal		
Extras	(LB 9, W 2, NB 1)	12
TOTAL	(54 overs) (for 4 wkts)	219

Bowler	O	M	R	W	Fall	
de Villiers	11	2	27	0	1st	57
Matthews	11	1	42	0	2nd	126
Shaw	11	0	34	1	3rd	181
Cronje	9	0	50	0	4th	215
Snell	11	0	49	1		
G. Kirsten	1	0	8	0		

Match No: 227/4

ENGLAND v SOUTH AFRICA

Texaco Trophy
Played at Old Trafford, Manchester on 27 & 28/08/1994
Toss: England   Result: England won by 4 wickets
Umpires: M.J. Kitchen and K.E. Palmer
Man of the match: S.J. Rhodes
Debuts: None

SOUTH AFRICA
G. Kirsten	c Lewis b Cork	30
K.C. Wessels*	lbw b DeFreitas	21
W.J. Cronje	run out	0
J.N. Rhodes	lbw b Cork	0
D.J. Cullinan	run out	54
B.M. McMillan	st Rhodes b Udal	0
D.J. Richardson+	c Lewis b Gough	14
T.G. Shaw	b Gough	6
C.R. Matthews	b Cork	26
P.S. de Villiers	not out	14
A.A. Donald	not out	2
Extras	(LB 6, W 4, NB 4)	14
TOTAL	(55 overs) (for 9 wkts)	**181**

						Fall	
DeFreitas	11	4	12	1	1st	43
Gough	10	1	39	2	2nd	47
Lewis	9	0	44	0	3rd	47
Udal	11	2	17	1	4th	64
Cork	11	1	49	3	5th	68
Hick	3	0	14	0	6th	113
					7th	121
					8th	163
					9th	163

ENGLAND
M.A. Atherton*	c Wessels b Matthews	19
A.J. Stewart	c Cullinan b Donald	11
G.A. Hick	lbw b Donald	0
G.P. Thorpe	c Cullinan b Shaw	55
N.H. Fairbrother	run out	3
S.J. Rhodes+	run out	56
C.C. Lewis	not out	17
P.A.J. DeFreitas	not out	7
D.G. Cork		
D. Gough		
S.D. Udal		
Extras	(W 4, NB 10)	14
TOTAL	(48.2 overs) (for 6 wkts)	**182**

						Fall	
Donald	10.2	1	47	2	1st	27
de Villiers	8	1	29	0	2nd	28
McMillan	10	1	53	0	3rd	42
Matthews	9	2	20	1	4th	60
Shaw	11	0	33	1	5th	130
					6th	171

Match No: 228/56

AUSTRALIA v ENGLAND

Benson & Hedges World Series Cup
Played at Sydney Cricket Ground on 06/12/1994
Toss: Australia   **Result:** Australia won by 28 runs
Umpires: D.B. Hair and P.D. Parker
Man of the match: D.C. Boon
Debuts: Eng - J.E. Benjamin, C. White

AUSTRALIA

M.A. Taylor*	c & b Hick	57
M.J. Slater	c Hick b Udal	50
M.E. Waugh	b Udal	4
D.C. Boon	not out	64
M.G. Bevan	c Gooch b Gough	46
S.G. Law	not out	0
I.A. Healy+		
S.K. Warne		
C.J. McDermott		
T.B.A. May		
G.D. McGrath		
Extras	(LB 2, W 1)	3
TOTAL	(50 overs) (for 4 wkts)	**224**

						Fall	
Benjamin	6	0	25	0	1st	96
DeFreitas	9	1	43	0	2nd	106
Gough	10	0	51	1	3rd	126
White	5	0	22	0	4th	218
Udal	10	1	37	2		
Hick	10	0	44	1		

ENGLAND

M.A. Atherton*	lbw b Law	60
A.J. Stewart	c Law b May	48
G.A. Hick	c Boon b May	6
G.P. Thorpe	c Bevan b McDermott	21
G.A. Gooch	c McDermott b Warne	21
C. White	b McDermott	0
S.J. Rhodes+	c Warne b Law	8
P.A.J. DeFreitas	run out	6
D. Gough	not out	8
S.D. Udal	b McGrath	4
J.E. Benjamin	b McDermott	0
Extras	(LB 7, W 6, NB 1)	14
TOTAL	(48.3 overs)	**196**

						Fall	
McDermott	9.3	0	34	3	1st	100
McGrath	9	4	22	1	2nd	112
Warne	10	0	46	1	3rd	133
Law	10	0	52	2	4th	147
May	10	1	35	2	5th	149
					6th	164
					7th	180
					8th	187
					9th	195
					10th	196

Match No: 229/2

ENGLAND v ZIMBABWE

Benson and Hedges World Series Cup
Played at Sydney Cricket Ground on 15/12/1994
Toss: Zimbabwe　　　　　　　　　　　　**Result:** Zimbabwe won by 13 runs
Umpires: D.B. Hair and C.D. Timmins
Man of the match: G.W. Flower
Debuts: None

ZIMBABWE

A. Flower*+	c Stewart b Fraser	12
G.W. Flower	not out	84
A.D.R. Campbell	b Gough	23
G.J. Whittall	c Stewart b Gough	0
D.L. Houghton	c Stewart b Gough	57
M.H. Dekker	c DeFreitas b Fraser	5
G.C. Martin	b DeFreitas	7
P.A. Strang	run out	0
H.H. Streak	run out	1
S.G. Peall	c Stewart b Gough	0
D.H. Brain	b Gough	7
Extras	(LB 7, W 1, NB 1)	9
TOTAL	(49.3 overs)	205

Fall

DeFreitas	10	2	27	1	1st	24
Fraser	10	0	45	2	2nd	61
Gough	9.3	0	44	5	3rd	61
Tufnell	10	0	43	0	4th	171
Udal	8	0	31	0	5th	179
Hick	2	0	8	0	6th	192
					7th	192
					8th	198
					9th	198
					10th	205

ENGLAND

G.A. Gooch	c & b Strang	38
M.A. Atherton*	c A. Flower b Whittall	14
G.A. Hick	run out	64
G.P. Thorpe	lbw b Strang	0
J.P. Crawley	lbw b Dekker	18
A.J. Stewart+	b Streak	29
P.A.J. DeFreitas	run out	5
D. Gough	b Streak	2
S.D. Udal	run out	10
A.R.C. Fraser	b Dekker	2
P.C.R. Tufnell	not out	0
Extras	(LB 5, W5)	10
TOTAL	(49.1 overs)	192

Fall

Brain	8	1	27	0	1st	49
Streak	8.1	1	36	2	2nd	60
Whittall	4	1	21	1	3rd	60
Strang	10	2	30	2	4th	105
Peall	10	2	29	0	5th	169
Dekker	9	0	44	2	6th	178
					7th	179
					8th	181
					9th	192
					10th	192

Match No: 230/3

ENGLAND v ZIMBABWE

Benson and Hedges World Series Cup
Played at Woolloongabba, Brisbane on 07/01/1995
Toss: England   **Result:** England won by 26 runs
Umpires: A.J. McQuillan and C.D. Timmins
Man of the match: G.P. Thorpe
Debuts: None

ENGLAND

G.A. Gooch	b Brain	0
M.A. Atherton*	lbw b Martin	26
G.A. Hick	c A. Flower b Streak	8
G.P. Thorpe	c Brain b Strang	89
N.H. Fairbrother	run out	7
J.P. Crawley	lbw b G.W. Flower	14
S.J. Rhodes+	st A. Flower b Dekker	20
D. Gough	c Campbell b Dekker	4
P.A.J. DeFreitas	not out	12
S.D. Udal	not out	11
J.E. Benjamin		
Extras	(B 4, LB 2, W3)	9
TOTAL	(50 overs) (for 8 wkts)	**200**

						Fall	
Brain	8	0	27	1	1st	0
Streak	7	1	26	1	2nd	20
Whittall	5	0	19	0	3rd	72
Martin	5	1	15	1	4th	82
Peall	5	0	19	0	5th	107
Strang	10	0	42	1	6th	164
G.W. Flower	3	0	16	1	7th	170
Dekker	7	0	30	2	8th	182

ZIMBABWE

G.W. Flower	c Rhodes b Udal	19
A.D.R. Campbell	c Fairbrother b DeFreitas	3
M.H. Dekker	c Benjamin	5
A. Flower*+	c Rhodes b Gough	52
G.J. Whittall	c Rhodes b DeFreitas	53
I.P. Butchart	run out	2
G.C. Martin	st Rhodes b Hick	1
P.A. Strang	b Gough	16
D.H. Brain	c Hick b Udal	2
H.H. Streak	not out	9
S.G. Peall	run out	3
Extras	(LB 7, W 2)	9
TOTAL	(48.1 overs)	**174**

						Fall	
Gough	9.1	3	17	2	1st	8
DeFreitas	10	0	28	2	2nd	16
Benjamin	6	0	22	1	3rd	56
Udal	8	0	41	2	4th	103
Hick	7	1	29	1	5th	123
Gooch	8	0	30	0	6th	124
					7th	149
					8th	156
					9th	169
					10th	174

Match No: 231/57

AUSTRALIA v ENGLAND

Benson & Hedges World Series Cup
Played at Melbourne Cricket Ground on 10/01/1995
Toss: England **Result:** England won by 37 runs
Umpires: S.G. Randell and P.D. Parker
Man of the match: G.A. Hick
Debuts: Aus - G.R. Robertson

ENGLAND

G.A. Gooch	c Taylor b McGrath	2
M.A. Atherton*	c S.R. Waugh b M.E. Waugh	14
G.A. Hick	c Fleming b Warne	91
G.P. Thorpe	c Healy b M.E. Waugh	8
N.H. Fairbrother	c Healy b Warne	35
J.P. Crawley	c Healy b McGrath	2
S.J. Rhodes+	lbw b McGrath	2
D. Gough	b McGrath	45
P.A.J. DeFreitas	not out	2
S.D. Udal	not out	2
A.R.C. Fraser		
Extras	(B 4, LB 10, W 6, NB 2)	22
TOTAL	(50 overs) (for 8 wkts)	**225**

	O	M	R	W		Fall
Fleming	10	1	36	0	1st	11
McGrath	10	1	25	4	2nd	31
M.E. Waugh	10	1	43	2	3rd	44
Warne	10	0	37	2	4th	133
Robertson	5	0	38	0	5th	136
Law	5	0	32	0	6th	142
					7th	216
					8th	223

AUSTRALIA

M.A. Taylor*	c Rhodes b Fraser	6
M.J. Slater	b Fraser	2
M.E. Waugh	b Hick	41
S.R. Waugh	c Rhodes b Fraser	0
S.G. Law	c & b Udal	17
D.C. Boon	b Hick	26
I.A. Healy+	c Atherton b Hick	56
G.R. Robertson	run out	1
S.K. Warne	b Fraser	21
D.W. Fleming	not out	5
G.D. McGrath	b DeFreitas	10
Extras	(W 3)	3
TOTAL	(48 overs)	**188**

	O	M	R	W		Fall
Fraser	10	2	22	4	1st	3
DeFreitas	9	0	32	1	2nd	16
Gooch	10	0	50	0	3rd	19
Udal	9	1	43	1	4th	62
Hick	10	1	41	3	5th	76
					6th	125
					7th	131
					8th	173
					9th	173
					10th	188

ONE-DAY INTERNATIONAL PLAYERS

1971-1995

JONATHAN AGNEW

Full Name: Jonathan Philip Agnew
Born: 04/04/60 - Macclesfield, Cheshire
Right-arm fast bowler - Right-hand lower order batsman

No	Date	Opposition	Venue	Bat	C	Bowling		
1	23/01/85	India	Nagpur			10	0	38	3
2	27/01/85	India	Chandigarh		1	3	0	23	0
3	17/02/85	Australia	Melbourne	2*		8	0	59	0

Batting & Fielding

Mat	Inns	N/O	Runs	H/S	Avg	100s	50s	Cat
3	1	1	2	2*	-	0	0	1

Bowling

Overs	Mds	Runs	Wkts	Avg	Best	5WI	E/R
21	0	120	3	40.00	3-38	0	5.71

PAUL ALLOTT

Full Name: Paul John Walter Allott
Born: 14/09/56 - Altrincham, Cheshire
Right-arm fast medium bowler - Right-hand lower order batsman

No	Date	Opposition	Venue	Bat	C	Bowling			
1	13/02/82	Sri Lanka	Colombo	0		9	0	40	2
2	02/06/82	India	Headingley			11	4	21	2
3	04/06/82	India	The Oval	5		8	3	24	1
4	09/06/83	New Zealand	The Oval			12	1	47	0
5	11/06/83	Sri Lanka	Taunton	0*		12	1	82	1
6	13/06/83	Pakistan	Lord's			12	2	48	1
7	15/06/83	New Zealand	Edgbaston	0		11.5	2	44	1
8	18/06/83	Pakistan	Old Trafford			12	1	33	1
9	20/06/83	Sri Lanka	Headingley			10.4	0	41	3
10	22/06/83	India	Old Trafford	8	1	10	3	40	1
11	30/05/85	Australia	Old Trafford	2	1	11	0	47	1
12	01/06/85	Australia	Edgbaston			10	1	40	1
13	03/06/85	Australia	Lord's			7	1	45	0

Batting & Fielding

Mat	Inns	N/O	Runs	H/S	Avg	100s	50s	Cat
13	6	1	15	8	3.00	0	0	2

Bowling

Overs	Mds	Runs	Wkts	Avg	Best	5WI	E/R
136.3	19	552	15	36.80	3-41	0	4.04

DENNIS AMISS

Full Name: Dennis Leslie Amiss MBE
Born: 07/04/43 - Harborne, Birmingham
Right-hand opening batsman - Left-arm slow bowler

No	Date	Opposition	Venue	Bat	C
1	24/08/72	Australia	Old Trafford	103	
2	26/08/72	Australia	Lord's	25	
3	28/08/72	Australia	Edgbaston	40	
4	18/07/73	New Zealand	Swansea	100	
5	20/07/73	New Zealand	Old Trafford	34	
6	13/07/74	India	Headingley	20	
7	01/01/75	Australia	Melbourne	47	
8	08/03/75	New Zealand	Dunedin	3	
9	07/06/75	India	Lord's	137	
10	11/06/75	New Zealand	Trent Bridge	16	
11	14/06/75	East Africa	Edgbaston	88	1
12	18/06/75	Australia	Headingley	2	
13	26/08/76	West Indies	Scarborough	34	
14	28/08/76	West Indies	Lord's	12	
15	30/08/76	West Indies	Edgbaston	47	
16	02/06/77	Australia	Old Trafford	8	1
17	04/06/77	Australia	Edgbaston	35	
18	06/06/77	Australia	The Oval	108	

Batting & Fielding

Mat	Inns	N/O	Runs	H/S	Avg	100s	50s	Cat
18	18	0	859	137	47.72	4	1	2

GEOFF ARNOLD

Full Name: Geoffrey Graham Arnold
Born: 03/09/44 - Earlsfield, Surrey
Right-arm fast medium bowler - Right-hand lower order batsman

No	Date	Opposition	Venue	Bat	C	Bowling			
1	24/08/72	Australia	Old Trafford			11	0	38	2
2	26/08/72	Australia	Lord's	11*		11	0	47	0
3	28/08/72	Australia	Edgbaston			11	3	27	4
4	18/07/73	New Zealand	Swansea			11	2	28	3
5	20/07/73	New Zealand	Old Trafford	0*					
6	07/09/73	West Indies	The Oval	17		9	1	24	2
7	13/07/74	India	Headingley			10	1	42	2
8	15/07/74	India	The Oval		1	7	0	20	0
9	03/09/74	Pakistan	Edgbaston	2		6	3	7	1
10	01/01/75	Australia	Melbourne			*8	2	30	2
11	08/03/75	New Zealand	Dunedin	0		*2	0	6	0
12	07/06/75	India	Lord's			10	2	20	1
13	11/06/75	New Zealand	Trent Bridge		1	12	3	35	1
14	18/06/75	Australia	Headingley	18*		7.4	2	15	1

Batting & Fielding

Mat	Inns	N/O	Runs	H/S	Avg	100s	50s	Cat
14	6	3	48	18*	16.00	0	0	2

Bowling

Overs	Mds	Runs	Wkts	Avg	Best	5WI	E/R
119	19	339	19	17.84	4-27	0	2.84

246   *England - The Complete One-Day International Record*

MICHAEL ATHERTON

Full Name: Michael Andrew Atherton
Born: 23/03/68 - Manchester, Lancashire
Right-hand opening batsman - Leg break bowler

No	Date	Opposition	Venue	Bat	C
1	18/07/90	India	Headingley	7	1
2	20/07/90	India	Trent Bridge	59	1
3	01/12/90	New Zealand	Adelaide	33	
4	01/01/91	Australia	Sydney	8	1
5	09/02/91	New Zealand	Christchurch	0	
6	13/02/91	New Zealand	Wellington	26	
7	16/02/91	New Zealand	Auckland	34	
8	23/05/91	West Indies	Edgbaston	69*	
9	25/05/91	West Indies	Old Trafford	74	
10	27/05/91	West Indies	Lord's	25	
11	16/02/94	West Indies	Bridgetown	86	
12	26/02/94	West Indies	Kingston	46	
13	02/03/94	West Indies	Arnos Vale	19*	
14	05/03/94	West Indies	Port of Spain	41	
15	06/03/94	West Indies	Port of Spain	51	1
16	19/05/94	New Zealand	Edgbaston	81	
17	25/08/94	South Africa	Edgbaston	49	
18	27/08/94	South Africa	Old Trafford	19	
19	06/12/94	Australia	Sydney	60	
20	15/12/94	Zimbabwe	Sydney	14	
21	07/01/95	Zimbabwe	Brisbane	26	
22	10/01/95	Australia	Melbourne	14	1

Batting & Fielding

Mat	Inns	N/O	Runs	H/S	Avg	100s	50s	Cat
22	22	2	841	86	42.05	0	7	5

BILL ATHEY

Full Name: Charles William Jeffrey Athey
Born: 27/09/57 - Middlesbrough, Yorkshire
Right-hand middle order batsman - Off break bowler

No	Date	Opposition	Venue	Bat	C	Bowling
1	20/08/80	Australia	The Oval	32	1	
2	22/08/80	Australia	Edgbaston	51		
3	18/07/86	New Zealand	Old Trafford	142*		
4	01/01/87	Australia	Perth	34		
5	03/01/87	West Indies	Perth	1		
6	05/01/87	Pakistan	Perth	42	1	
7	07/01/87	Pakistan	Perth	1	2	
8	17/01/87	West Indies	Brisbane	14		
9	18/01/87	Australia	Brisbane	111		
10	22/01/87	Australia	Sydney	2	3	
11	24/01/87	West Indies	Adelaide	64	1	
12	26/01/87	Australia	Adelaide	12		

No	Date	Opposition	Venue	Bat					
13	30/01/87	West Indies	Melbourne	2					
14	01/02/87	Australia	Melbourne	29	2				
15	03/02/87	West Indies	Devonport	3	1				
16	08/02/87	Australia	Melbourne	12					
17	11/02/87	Australia	Sydney	16					
18	21/05/87	Pakistan	The Oval	33					
19	23/05/87	Pakistan	Trent Bridge	1					
20	25/05/87	Pakistan	Edgbaston	5					
21	17/10/87	Sri Lanka	Peshawar	2*		1	0	10	0
22	20/10/87	Pakistan	Karachi	86	1				
23	26/10/87	West Indies	Jaipur	21	1				
24	30/10/87	Sri Lanka	Poona	40*					
25	05/11/87	India	Bombay	4	1				
26	08/11/87	Australia	Calcutta	58	1				
27	18/11/87	Pakistan	Lahore	20					
28	20/11/87	Pakistan	Karachi		1				
29	22/11/87	Pakistan	Peshawar	6					
30	04/02/88	Australia	Melbourne	4					
31	16/03/88	New Zealand	Napier	0					

Batting & Fielding

Mat	Inns	N/O	Runs	H/S	Avg	100s	50s	Cat
31	30	3	848	142*	31.40	2	4	16

Bowling

Overs	Mds	Runs	Wkts	Avg	Best	5WI	E/R
1	0	10	0	-	-	0	10.00

ROB BAILEY

Full Name: Robert John Bailey
Born: 28/10/63 - Biddulph, Staffordshire
Right-hand middle order batsman - Off break bowler

No	Date	Opposition	Venue	Bat	C		Bowling		
1	26/03/85	Pakistan	Sharjah	41*		6	0	25	0
2	09/04/87	Australia	Sharjah	11	1				
3	04/09/88	Sri Lanka	The Oval	43*					
4	15/03/90	West Indies	Georgetown	42					

Batting & Fielding

Mat	Inns	N/O	Runs	H/S	Avg	100s	50s	Cat
4	4	2	137	43*	68.50	0	0	1

Bowling

Overs	Mds	Runs	Wkts	Avg	Best	5WI	E/R
6	0	25	0	-	-	0	4.16

DAVID BAIRSTOW

Full Name: David Leslie Bairstow
Born: 01/09/51 - Horton, Bradford, Yorkshire
Right-hand middle/lower order batsman - Wicket-keeper

No	Date	Opposition	Venue	Bat	C/S
1	24/01/79	Australia	Melbourne		1
2	04/02/79	Australia	Melbourne	1	

248   England - The Complete One-Day International Record

3	07/02/79	Australia	Melbourne	3	1
4	28/11/79	West Indies	Sydney	0	
5	08/12/79	Australia	Melbourne	15*	1+1
6	11/12/79	Australia	Sydney	18	2+1
7	23/12/79	West Indies	Brisbane	12	
8	26/12/79	Australia	Sydney	7*	2
9	14/01/80	Australia	Sydney	21*	2+1
10	16/01/80	West Indies	Adelaide	23*	
11	20/01/80	West Indies	Melbourne	4	3
12	22/01/80	West Indies	Sydney	18*	
13	28/05/80	West Indies	Headingley	16	
14	30/05/80	West Indies	Lord's	2	
15	20/08/80	Australia	The Oval	9*	2
16	22/08/80	Australia	Edgbaston	6	
17	04/02/81	West Indies	Arnos Vale	5	+1
18	26/02/81	West Indies	Berbice	16	
19	31/05/84	West Indies	Old Trafford	13	2
20	02/06/84	West Indies	Trent Bridge	9	
21	04/06/84	West Indies	Lord's	8	1

Batting & Fielding

Mat	Inns	N/O	Runs	H/S	Avg	100s	50s	Cat	St
21	20	6	206	23*	14.71	0	0	17	4

GRAHAM BARLOW

Full Name: Graham Derek Barlow
Born: 26/03/50 - Folkstone, Kent
Left-hand opening/middle order batsman - Right-arm medium bowler

No	Date	Opposition	Venue	Bat	C
1	26/08/76	West Indies	Scarborough	80*	
2	28/08/76	West Indies	Lord's	0	2
3	30/08/76	West Indies	Edgbaston	0	1
4	02/06/77	Australia	Old Trafford	42	1
5	04/06/77	Australia	Edgbaston	25	
6	06/06/77	Australia	The Oval	2	

Batting & Fielding

Mat	Inns	N/O	Runs	H/S	Avg	100s	50s	Cat
6	6	1	149	80*	29.80	0	1	4

KIM BARNETT

Full Name: Kim John Barnett
Born: 17/07/60 - Stoke-on-Trent, Staffordshire
Right-hand opening batsman - Leg break bowler

No	Date	Opposition	Venue	Bat	C
1	04/09/88	Sri Lanka	The Oval	84	

Batting & Fielding

Mat	Inns	N/O	Runs	H/S	Avg	100s	50s	Cat
1	1	0	84	84	84.00	0	1	0

JOEY BENJAMIN

Full Name: Joseph Emmanuel Benjamin
Born: 02/02/61 - Christchurch, St Kitts
Right-arm fast medium bowler - Right-hand lower order batsman

No	Date	Opposition	Venue	Bat	C	Bowling			
1	06/12/94	Australia	Sydney	0		6	0	25	0
2	07/01/95	Zimbabwe	Brisbane			6	0	22	1

Batting & Fielding

Mat	Inns	N/O	Runs	H/S	Avg	100s	50s	Cat
2	1	0	0	0	0.00	0	0	0

Bowling

Overs	Mds	Runs	Wkts	Avg	Best	5WI	E/R
12	0	47	1	47.00	1-22	0	3.91

MARK BENSON

Full Name: Mark Richard Benson
Born: 06/07/58 - Shoreham-by-Sea, Sussex
Left-hand opening batsman - Off-break bowler

No	Date	Opposition	Venue	Bat	C
1	16/07/86	New Zealand	Headingley	24	

Batting & Fielding

Mat	Inns	N/O	Runs	H/S	Avg	100s	50s	Cat
1	1	0	24	24	24.00	0	0	0

MARTIN BICKNELL

Full Name: Martin Paul Bicknell
Born: 14/01/69 - Guildford, Surrey
Right-arm fast medium bowler - Right-hand lower order batsman

No	Date	Opposition	Venue	Bat	C	Bowling			
1	07/12/90	New Zealand	Perth			10	1	36	2
2	09/12/90	Australia	Perth	31*		9	0	55	2
3	13/12/90	New Zealand	Sydney	8		10	0	39	1
4	16/12/90	Australia	Brisbane	25		10	0	64	1
5	10/01/91	Australia	Melbourne	23	1	9.5	0	33	2
6	09/02/91	New Zealand	Christchurch	0*	1	10	2	55	3
7	13/02/91	New Zealand	Wellington	9		10	0	65	2

Batting & Fielding

Mat	Inns	N/O	Runs	H/S	Avg	100s	50s	Cat
7	6	2	96	31*	24.00	0	0	2

Bowling

Overs	Mds	Runs	Wkts	Avg	Best	5WI	E/R
68.5	3	347	13	26.69	3-55	0	5.04

RICHARD BLAKEY

Full Name: Richard John Blakey
Born: 15/01/67 - Huddersfield, Yorkshire
Right-hand middle order batsman - Wicket-keeper

No	Date	Opposition	Venue	Bat	C/S
1	22/08/92	Pakistan	Lord's	25	1+1
2	01/03/93	India	Jamshedpur		1
3	04/03/93	India	Gwalior	0	

Batting & Fielding

Mat	Inns	N/O	Runs	H/S	Avg	100s	50s	Cat	St
3	2	0	25	25	12.50	0	0	2	1

IAN BOTHAM

Full Name: Ian Terence Botham OBE
Born: 24/11/55 - Oldfield, Heswall, Cheshire
Right-arm fast medium bowler - Right-hand middle order batsman

No	Date	Opposition	Venue	Bat	C	Bowling			
1	26/08/76	West Indies	Scarborough	1		3	0	26	1
2	30/08/76	West Indies	Edgbaston	20		3	0	31	1
3	23/12/77	Pakistan	Sahiwal	15*		*7	0	39	3
4	30/12/77	Pakistan	Sialkot	17*		*6.7	0	21	1
5	13/01/78	Pakistan	Lahore	11		*7	0	41	0
6	24/05/78	Pakistan	Old Trafford	31		8	1	17	2
7	26/05/78	Pakistan	The Oval	1		11	2	36	1
8	15/07/78	New Zealand	Scarborough	3		11	1	43	1
9	17/07/78	New Zealand	Old Trafford	34	1	7	0	24	1
10	13/01/79	Australia	Sydney						
11	24/01/79	Australia	Melbourne		2	*4.5	2	16	3
12	04/02/79	Australia	Melbourne	31		*7.6	0	58	0
13	07/02/79	Australia	Melbourne	13		*5.5	0	30	1
14	09/06/79	Australia	Lord's	18*		8	0	32	0
15	13/06/79	Canada	Old Trafford		1	9	5	12	1
16	16/06/79	Pakistan	Headingley	22	1	12	3	38	2
17	20/06/79	New Zealand	Old Trafford	21		12	3	42	1
18	23/06/79	West Indies	Lord's	4		12	2	44	2
19	28/11/79	West Indies	Sydney	11		7	1	26	1
20	08/12/79	Australia	Melbourne	10		9	2	27	1
21	11/12/79	Australia	Sydney	5		10	1	36	2
22	23/12/79	West Indies	Brisbane	4		10	1	39	0
23	26/12/79	Australia	Sydney	6		9	1	33	2
24	14/01/80	Australia	Sydney	0		7	0	33	0
25	16/01/80	West Indies	Adelaide	22	1	10	0	35	2
26	20/01/80	West Indies	Melbourne	19		10	2	33	3
27	22/01/80	West Indies	Sydney	37	1	10	1	28	1
28	28/05/80	West Indies	Headingley	30	2	11	1	45	2
29	30/05/80	West Indies	Lord's	42*		11	2	71	1
30	20/08/80	Australia	The Oval	4		9	1	28	0
31	22/08/80	Australia	Edgbaston	2		11	1	41	0
32	04/02/81	West Indies	Arnos Vale	60		8	1	32	1
33	26/02/81	West Indies	Berbice	27		7	1	24	0
34	04/06/81	Australia	Lord's	13*		11	1	39	2

Players 251

35	06/06/81	Australia	Edgbaston	24		11	1	44	2
36	08/06/81	Australia	Headingley	5		11	2	42	1
37	25/11/81	India	Ahmedabad	25 *		10	4	20	2
38	20/12/81	India	Jullundur	5		7	0	33	1
39	27/01/82	India	Cuttack	52		8	0	48	1
40	13/02/82	Sri Lanka	Colombo	60		9	0	45	2
41	14/02/82	Sri Lanka	Colombo	13	1	9	4	29	2
42	02/06/82	India	Headingley		1	11	0	56	4
43	04/06/82	India	The Oval	4	2	9	2	22	1
44	17/07/82	Pakistan	Trent Bridge	10 *		11	0	57	3
45	19/07/82	Pakistan	Old Trafford	49	1	8.4	0	40	1
46	11/01/83	Australia	Sydney	18		7	1	41	1
47	13/01/83	New Zealand	Melbourne	41	1	10	0	40	3
48	15/01/83	New Zealand	Brisbane	0	1	9	2	47	3
49	16/01/83	Australia	Brisbane	29		8	1	29	3
50	20/01/83	New Zealand	Sydney			8.2	0	30	2
51	23/01/83	Australia	Melbourne	19		7	1	45	0
52	26/01/83	Australia	Sydney	0		2	0	13	1
53	29/01/83	New Zealand	Adelaide	65		8	0	61	2
54	30/01/83	Australia	Adelaide	14		7	0	49	2
55	05/02/83	New Zealand	Perth	19	1	2	0	9	0
56	19/02/83	New Zealand	Auckland	12		8	0	40	2
57	23/02/83	New Zealand	Wellington	15	1	7	0	46	1
58	26/02/83	New Zealand	Christchurch	3	1	5	1	17	1
59	09/06/83	New Zealand	The Oval	22	1	12	0	42	2
60	11/06/83	Sri Lanka	Taunton	0	1	12	0	60	0
61	13/06/83	Pakistan	Lord's		2	12	3	36	2
62	15/06/83	New Zealand	Edgbaston	12		12	1	47	1
63	18/06/83	Pakistan	Old Trafford			12	1	51	0
64	20/06/83	Sri Lanka	Headingley			9	4	12	2
65	22/06/83	India	Old Trafford	6		11	4	40	1
66	18/02/84	New Zealand	Christchurch	1	1	6	3	7	2
67	22/02/84	New Zealand	Wellington	15		8.1	1	25	2
68	25/02/84	New Zealand	Auckland	18		7	1	22	1
69	09/03/84	Pakistan	Lahore	18 *		7	0	43	0
70	31/05/84	West Indies	Old Trafford	2		11	0	67	2
71	02/06/84	West Indies	Trent Bridge	15	1	9	1	33	1
72	04/06/84	West Indies	Lord's	22		8	0	25	0
73	30/05/85	Australia	Old Trafford	72	2	11	2	41	1
74	01/06/85	Australia	Edgbaston	29		10	2	38	2
75	03/06/85	Australia	Lord's			8	1	27	1
76	04/03/86	West Indies	Port of Spain	8		8	1	59	1
77	19/03/86	West Indies	Bridgetown	14	1	9	2	39	2
78	31/03/86	West Indies	Port of Spain	29		5	0	24	0
79	01/01/87	Australia	Perth	68	1	10	0	52	1
80	03/01/87	West Indies	Perth	11		10	1	29	1
81	05/01/87	Pakistan	Perth	10		10	1	37	1
82	07/01/87	Pakistan	Perth	23 *		10	2	29	3
83	17/01/87	West Indies	Brisbane	14 *	1	10	1	46	0
84	18/01/87	Australia	Brisbane	22		10	0	54	0
85	22/01/87	Australia	Sydney	27		10	0	51	0
86	24/01/87	West Indies	Adelaide	7		10	0	46	1
87	26/01/87	Australia	Adelaide	18		10	0	42	0
88	30/01/87	West Indies	Melbourne	15		10	3	28	0
89	01/02/87	Australia	Melbourne	45		10	0	35	0
90	03/02/87	West Indies	Devonport	8		10	1	33	3
91	08/02/87	Australia	Melbourne	71		9	0	26	0
92	11/02/87	Australia	Sydney	25		10	1	26	3
93	21/05/87	Pakistan	The Oval	6 *		11	2	38	0
94	23/05/87	Pakistan	Trent Bridge	0		7	0	34	1
95	25/05/87	Pakistan	Edgbaston	24		11	1	31	0
96	25/05/89	Australia	Old Trafford	4		10.1	1	28	1

97	27/05/89	Australia	Trent Bridge	8		11	0	42	1
98	29/05/89	Australia	Lord's	25*		11	0	43	0
99	23/05/91	West Indies	Edgbaston	8		11	2	45	4
100	12/02/92	New Zealand	Dunedin	28		6	1	27	1
101	15/02/92	New Zealand	Christchurch	79		7	1	36	1
102	22/02/92	India	Perth	9	1	10	0	27	2
103	27/02/92	West Indies	Melbourne	8	1	10	0	30	1
104	01/03/92	Pakistan	Adelaide	6*		10	4	12	2
105	05/03/92	Australia	Sydney	53		10	1	31	4
106	09/03/92	Sri Lanka	Ballarat	47	1	10	0	33	1
107	12/03/92	South Africa	Melbourne	22		8	0	37	0
108	15/03/92	New Zealand	Wellington	8		4	0	19	1
109	18/03/92	Zimbabwe	Albury	18		10	2	23	3
110	22/03/92	South Africa	Sydney	21		10	0	52	1
111	25/03/92	Pakistan	Melbourne	0	1	7	0	42	1
112	20/05/92	Pakistan	Lord's	10*	1	11	0	45	2
113	22/05/92	Pakistan	The Oval	2*		11	0	52	1
114	20/08/92	Pakistan	Trent Bridge	24	1	11	1	41	1
115	22/08/92	Pakistan	Lord's	40		10	1	33	1
116	24/08/92	Pakistan	Old Trafford			11	0	43	0

Batting & Fielding
Mat	Inns	N/O	Runs	H/S	Avg	100s	50s	Cat
116	106	15	2113	79	23.21	0	9	36

Bowling
Overs	Mds	Runs	Wkts	Avg	Best	5WI	E/R
1045.1	109	4139	145	28.54	4-31	0	3.96

GEOFF BOYCOTT

Full Name: Geoffrey Boycott OBE
Born: 21/10/40 - Fitzwilliam, Yorkshire
Right-hand opening batsman - Right-arm medium bowler

No	Date	Opposition	Venue	Bat	C	Bowling			
1	05/01/71	Australia	Melbourne	8					
2	24/08/72	Australia	Old Trafford	25					
3	26/08/72	Australia	Lord's	8					
4	28/08/72	Australia	Edgbaston	41					
5	18/07/73	New Zealand	Swansea	20					
6	20/07/73	New Zealand	Old Trafford	15					
7	05/09/73	West Indies	Headingley	0					
8	30/12/77	Pakistan	Sialkot						
9	13/01/78	Pakistan	Lahore	6	3				
10	24/05/78	Pakistan	Old Trafford	3					
11	13/01/79	Australia	Sydney						
12	24/01/79	Australia	Melbourne	39*					
13	04/02/79	Australia	Melbourne	33	2				
14	07/02/79	Australia	Melbourne	2					
15	09/06/79	Australia	Lord's	1		6	0	15	2
16	13/06/79	Canada	Old Trafford	14*	1	1	0	3	0
17	16/06/79	Pakistan	Headingley	18		5	0	14	2
18	20/06/79	New Zealand	Old Trafford	2		9	1	24	1
19	23/06/79	West Indies	Lord's	57		6	0	38	0
20	08/12/79	Australia	Melbourne	68					
21	11/12/79	Australia	Sydney	105					
22	23/12/79	West Indies	Brisbane	68					

23	26/12/79	Australia	Sydney	86*				
24	20/01/80	West Indies	Melbourne	35				
25	22/01/80	West Indies	Sydney	63				
26	28/05/80	West Indies	Headingley	5				
27	30/05/80	West Indies	Lord's	70				
28	20/08/80	Australia	The Oval	99				
29	22/08/80	Australia	Edgbaston	78	1	0	11	0
30	04/02/81	West Indies	Arnos Vale	2				
31	26/02/81	West Indies	Berbice	7				
32	04/06/81	Australia	Lord's	75*				
33	06/06/81	Australia	Edgbaston	14				
34	08/06/81	Australia	Headingley	4				
35	25/11/81	India	Ahmedabad	5				
36	20/12/81	India	Jullundur	6				

Batting & Fielding

Mat	Inns	N/O	Runs	H/S	Avg	100s	50s	Cat
36	34	4	1082	105	36.06	1	9	5

Bowling

Overs	Mds	Runs	Wkts	Avg	Best	5WI	E/R
28	1	105	5	21.00	2-14	0	3.75

MIKE BREARLEY

Full Name: John Michael Brearley OBE
Born: 28/04/42 - Harrow, Middlesex
Right-hand opening/middle order batsman - Right-arm medium bowler

No	Date	Opposition	Venue	Bat	C
1	02/06/77	Australia	Old Trafford	29	1
2	04/06/77	Australia	Edgbaston	10	
3	06/06/77	Australia	The Oval	78	2
4	23/12/77	Pakistan	Sahiwal	30	
5	13/01/78	Pakistan	Lahore	1	
6	15/07/78	New Zealand	Scarborough	31	
7	17/07/78	New Zealand	Old Trafford	27	
8	13/01/79	Australia	Sydney		
9	24/01/79	Australia	Melbourne	0	
10	04/02/79	Australia	Melbourne	0	
11	07/02/79	Australia	Melbourne	46	2
12	09/06/79	Australia	Lord's	44	
13	13/06/79	Canada	Old Trafford	0	
14	16/06/79	Pakistan	Headingley	0	2
15	20/06/79	New Zealand	Old Trafford	53	1
16	23/06/79	West Indies	Lord's	64	1
17	28/11/79	West Indies	Sydney	25	1
18	08/12/79	Australia	Melbourne	27	1
19	11/12/79	Australia	Sydney	2*	
20	23/12/79	West Indies	Brisbane	9*	
21	26/12/79	Australia	Sydney	0	
22	14/01/80	Australia	Sydney	5	1
23	16/01/80	West Indies	Adelaide	0	
24	20/01/80	West Indies	Melbourne	25*	
25	22/01/80	West Indies	Sydney	4	

Batting & Fielding

Mat	Inns	N/O	Runs	H/S	Avg	100s	50s	Cat
25	24	3	510	78	24.28	0	3	12

CHRIS BROAD

Full Name: Brian Christopher Broad
Born: 29/09/57 - Knowle, Bristol
Left-hand opening batsman - Right-arm medium bowler

No	Date	Opposition	Venue	Bat	C	Bowling
1	01/01/87	Australia	Perth	76		
2	03/01/87	West Indies	Perth	0	1	
3	05/01/87	Pakistan	Perth	97		
4	07/01/87	Pakistan	Perth	0	1	
5	17/01/87	West Indies	Brisbane	49		
6	18/01/87	Australia	Brisbane	15		
7	22/01/87	Australia	Sydney	45		
8	24/01/87	West Indies	Adelaide	55	1	
9	26/01/87	Australia	Adelaide	46	1	
10	30/01/87	West Indies	Melbourne	33		
11	01/02/87	Australia	Melbourne	2		
12	03/02/87	West Indies	Devonport	76		
13	08/02/87	Australia	Melbourne	12		
14	11/02/87	Australia	Sydney	53		
15	02/04/87	India	Sharjah	57		
16	07/04/87	Pakistan	Sharjah	65		
17	09/04/87	Australia	Sharjah	44	1	
18	21/05/87	Pakistan	The Oval	99	1	
19	23/05/87	Pakistan	Trent Bridge	52		
20	25/05/87	Pakistan	Edgbaston	15		
21	09/10/87	West Indies	Gujranwala	3		
22	12/10/87	Pakistan	Rawalpindi	36		
23	17/10/87	Sri Lanka	Peshawar	28	1	1 0 6 0
24	18/11/87	Pakistan	Lahore	1		
25	20/11/87	Pakistan	Karachi	22	1	
26	22/11/87	Pakistan	Peshawar	66		
27	04/02/88	Australia	Melbourne	25		
28	09/03/88	New Zealand	Dunedin	33	1	
29	12/03/88	New Zealand	Christchurch	56	1	
30	16/03/88	New Zealand	Napier	106		
31	19/03/88	New Zealand	Auckland	12		
32	19/05/88	West Indies	Edgbaston	35		
33	21/05/88	West Indies	Headingley	13		
34	23/05/88	West Indies	Lord's	34		

Batting & Fielding

Mat	Inns	N/O	Runs	H/S	Avg	100s	50s	Cat
34	34	0	1361	106	40.02	1	11	10

Bowling

Overs	Mds	Runs	Wkts	Avg	Best	5WI	E/R
1	0	6	0	-	-	0	6.00

ALAN BUTCHER

Full Name: Alan Raymond Butcher
Born: 07/01/54 - Croydon, Surrey
Left-hand opening batsman - Left-arm slow/medium bowler

No	Date	Opposition	Venue	Bat	C
1	20/08/80	Australia	The Oval	14	

Batting & Fielding

Mat	Inns	N/O	Runs	H/S	Avg	100s	50s	Cat
1	1	0	14	14	14.00	0	0	0

ROLAND BUTCHER

Full Name: Roland Orlando Butcher
Born: 14/10/53 - East Point, St Philip, Barbados
Right-hand middle order batsman - Right-arm medium bowler

No	Date	Opposition	Venue	Bat	C
1	22/08/80	Australia	Edgbaston	52	
2	04/02/81	West Indies	Arnos Vale	1	
3	26/02/81	West Indies	Berbice	5	

Batting & Fielding

Mat	Inns	N/O	Runs	H/S	Avg	100s	50s	Cat
3	3	0	58	52	19.33	0	1	0

ANDREW CADDICK

Full Name: Andrew Richard Caddick
Born: 21/11/68 - Christchurch, New Zealand
Right-arm fast medium bowler - Right-hand lower order batsman

No	Date	Opposition	Venue	Bat	C	Bowling			
1	19/05/93	Australia	Old Trafford	1*		11	1	50	1
2	21/05/93	Australia	Edgbaston			11	1	43	0
3	23/05/93	Australia	Lord's	2*		11	3	39	3
4	05/03/94	West Indies	Port of Spain	20*	1	10	0	60	1
5	06/03/94	West Indies	Port of Spain			10	2	66	1

Batting & Fielding

Mat	Inns	N/O	Runs	H/S	Avg	100s	50s	Cat
5	3	3	23	20*	-	0	0	1

Bowling

Overs	Mds	Runs	Wkts	Avg	Best	5WI	E/R
53	7	258	6	43.00	3-39	0	4.86

DAVID CAPEL

Full Name: David John Capel
Born: 06/02/63 - Northampton
Right-arm medium bowler - Right-hand middle order batsman

No	Date	Opposition	Venue	Bat	C	Bowling			
1	02/04/87	India	Sharjah	8	1	10	0	45	1
2	07/04/87	Pakistan	Sharjah	2	1	10	0	38	3
3	09/04/87	Australia	Sharjah	17		5	0	28	0
4	18/11/87	Pakistan	Lahore	8		9	0	43	1
5	20/11/87	Pakistan	Karachi	50*		8	1	41	1
6	22/11/87	Pakistan	Peshawar	25		9	0	44	1
7	04/02/88	Australia	Melbourne	18	2	8	1	30	1
8	09/03/88	New Zealand	Dunedin	48	1	10	1	45	1
9	12/03/88	New Zealand	Christchurch	6*		9	3	27	1
10	16/03/88	New Zealand	Napier	14		9	0	50	0

11	19/03/88	New Zealand	Auckland	25		10	0	42	1
12	15/10/89	Sri Lanka	Delhi	4		4	0	16	1
13	19/10/89	Australia	Hyderabad			8	0	39	0
14	22/10/89	Pakistan	Cuttack	23		8	2	16	2
15	25/10/89	India	Kanpur	2		3	0	24	0
16	27/10/89	West Indies	Gwalior	21		8	0	49	0
17	30/10/89	Pakistan	Nagpur	20		6	0	24	0
18	14/02/90	West Indies	Port of Spain			6	0	25	1
19	17/02/90	West Indies	Port of Spain						
20	03/03/90	West Indies	Kingston	28		9	1	47	0
21	07/03/90	West Indies	Georgetown	1		9	2	39	1
22	15/03/90	West Indies	Georgetown	7	1	9	1	41	0
23	03/04/90	West Indies	Bridgetown			6	0	52	1

Batting & Fielding
Mat	Inns	N/O	Runs	H/S	Avg	100s	50s	Cat
23	19	2	327	50*	19.23	0	1	6

Bowling
Overs	Mds	Runs	Wkts	Avg	Best	5WI	E/R
173	12	805	17	47.35	3-38	0	4.65

BRIAN CLOSE

Full Name: Dennis Brian Close CBE
Born: 24/02/31 - Rawdon, Leeds, Yorkshire
Left-hand middle order batsman - Right-arm medium or off break bowler

No	Date	Opposition	Venue	Bat	C	Bowling		
1	24/08/72	Australia	Old Trafford	1	1	3	0	21	0
2	26/08/72	Australia	Lord's	43				
3	28/08/72	Australia	Edgbaston	5				

Batting & Fielding
Mat	Inns	N/O	Runs	H/S	Avg	100s	50s	Cat
3	3	0	49	43	16.33	0	0	1

Bowling
Overs	Mds	Runs	Wkts	Avg	Best	5WI	E/R
3	0	21	0	-	-	0	7.00

GEOFF COOK

Full Name: Geoffrey Cook
Born: 09/10/51 - Middlesbrough, Yorkshire
Right-hand opening batsman - Left-arm slow bowler

No	Date	Opposition	Venue	Bat	C
1	25/11/81	India	Ahmedabad	13	1
2	20/12/81	India	Jullundur	1	
3	27/01/82	India	Cuttack	30	
4	13/02/82	Sri Lanka	Colombo	28	1
5	14/02/82	Sri Lanka	Colombo	32	
6	16/01/83	Australia	Brisbane	2	

Batting & Fielding

Mat	Inns	N/O	Runs	H/S	Avg	100s	50s	Cat
6	6	0	106	32	17.66	0	0	2

NICK COOK

Full Name: Nicholas Grant Billson Cook
Born: 17/06/56 - Leicester
Left-arm slow bowler - Right-hand lower order batsman

No	Date	Opposition	Venue	Bat	C	Bowling			
1	26/03/84	Pakistan	Karachi		1	8	0	34	1
2	22/11/87	Pakistan	Peshawar			6	1	18	2
3	22/10/89	Pakistan	Cuttack		1	10	0	43	2

Batting & Fielding

Mat	Inns	N/O	Runs	H/S	Avg	100s	50s	Cat
3	0	0	0	-	-	0	0	2

Bowling

Overs	Mds	Runs	Wkts	Avg	Best	5WI	E/R
24	1	95	5	19.00	2-18	0	3.95

GEOFF COPE

Full Name: Geoffrey Alan Cope
Born: 23/02/47 - Burmantofts, Leeds, Yorkshire
Off break bowler - Right-hand lower order batsman

No	Date	Opposition	Venue	Bat	C	Bowling			
1	30/12/77	Pakistan	Sialkot			*7	0	19	1
2	13/01/78	Pakistan	Lahore	1*		*7	0	16	1

Batting & Fielding

Mat	Inns	N/O	Runs	H/S	Avg	100s	50s	Cat
2	1	1	1	1*	-	0	0	0

Bowling

Overs	Mds	Runs	Wkts	Avg	Best	5WI	E/R
18.4	0	35	2	17.50	1-16	0	1.87

DOMINIC CORK

Full Name: Dominic Gerald Cork
Born: 07/08/71 - Newcastle-under-Lyme, Staffordshire
Right-arm fast medium bowler - Right-hand lower order batsman

No	Date	Opposition	Venue	Bat	C	Bowling			
1	24/08/92	Pakistan	Old Trafford			11	1	37	1
2	21/05/93	Australia	Edgbaston			11	1	57	0

3	23/05/93	Australia	Lord's		11		9	2	24	0
4	25/08/94	South Africa	Edgbaston				11	1	46	1
5	27/08/94	South Africa	Old Trafford				11	1	49	3

Batting & Fielding

Mat	Inns	N/O	Runs	H/S	Avg	100s	50s	Cat
5	1	0	11	11	11.00	0	0	0

Bowling

Overs	Mds	Runs	Wkts	Avg	Best	5WI	E/R
53	6	213	5	42.60	3-49	0	4.01

NORMAN COWANS

Full Name: Norman George Cowans
Born: 17/04/61 - Enfield, St Mary, Jamaica
Right-arm fast bowler - Right-hand lower order batsman

No	Date	Opposition	Venue	Bat	C	Bowling			
1	11/01/83	Australia	Sydney	4	1	7	0	20	2
2	13/01/83	New Zealand	Melbourne			10	0	50	0
3	15/01/83	New Zealand	Brisbane		1	10	0	52	1
4	16/01/83	Australia	Brisbane	0		9	1	35	0
5	20/01/83	New Zealand	Sydney			10	1	26	1
6	23/01/83	Australia	Melbourne			6	0	46	2
7	05/02/83	New Zealand	Perth			8	0	32	1
8	26/02/83	New Zealand	Christchurch	1*		10	3	55	1
9	20/06/83	Sri Lanka	Headingley		1	12	3	31	2
10	18/02/84	New Zealand	Christchurch	4*		10	2	37	0
11	22/02/84	New Zealand	Wellington			10	1	33	0
12	25/02/84	New Zealand	Auckland	0		9.3	0	59	0
13	26/03/84	Pakistan	Karachi			5	0	20	1
14	05/12/84	India	Poona			8	0	32	0
15	27/12/84	India	Cuttack			10	0	39	0
16	20/01/85	India	Bangalore			10	1	31	1
17	23/01/85	India	Nagpur			10	0	44	3
18	17/02/85	Australia	Melbourne		1	10	0	52	0
19	26/02/85	India	Sydney	3*	1	10	0	59	3
20	02/03/85	Pakistan	Melbourne	0		10	0	52	1
21	30/05/85	Australia	Old Trafford	1		10.1	1	44	2
22	01/06/85	Australia	Edgbaston			11	2	42	2
23	03/06/85	Australia	Lord's			8	2	22	0

Batting & Fielding

Mat	Inns	N/O	Runs	H/S	Avg	100s	50s	Cat
23	8	3	13	4*	2.60	0	0	5

Bowling

Overs	Mds	Runs	Wkts	Avg	Best	5WI	E/R
213.4	17	913	23	39.69	3-44	0	4.27

CHRIS COWDREY

Full Name: Christopher Stuart Cowdrey
Born: 20/10/57 - Farnborough, Kent
Right-arm medium bowler - Right-hand middle order batsman

No	Date	Opposition	Venue	Bat	C	Bowling		
1	23/01/85	India	Nagpur	46*		7.4	0	52	1
2	27/01/85	India	Chandigarh	5		1	0	3	1
3	17/02/85	Australia	Melbourne	0				

Batting & Fielding

Mat	Inns	N/O	Runs	H/S	Avg	100s	50s	Cat
3	3	1	51	46*	25.50	0	0	0

Bowling

Overs	Mds	Runs	Wkts	Avg	Best	5WI	E/R
8.4	0	55	2	27.50	1-3	0	6.34

COLIN COWDREY

Full Name: Sir Michael Colin Cowdrey
Born: 24/12/32 - Bangalore, India
Right-hand middle order batsman - Leg break bowler

No	Date	Opposition	Venue	Bat	C
1	05/01/71	Australia	Melbourne	1	

Batting & Fielding

Mat	Inns	N/O	Runs	H/S	Avg	100s	50s	Cat
1	1	0	1	1	1.00	0	0	0

JOHN CRAWLEY

Full Name: John Paul Crawley
Born: 21/09/71 - Malden, Essex
Right-hand middle order batsman - Right-arm medium bowler

No	Date	Opposition	Venue	Bat	C
1	15/12/94	Zimbabwe	Sydney	18	
2	07/01/95	Zimbabwe	Brisbane	14	
3	10/01/95	Australia	Melbourne	2	

Batting & Fielding

Mat	Inns	N/O	Runs	H/S	Avg	100s	50s	Cat
3	3	0	34	18	11.33	0	0	0

PHILLIP DEFREITAS

Full Name: Phillip Anthony Jason DeFreitas
Born: 18/12/66 - Scotts Head, Dominica
Right-arm fast medium bowler - Right-hand middle order batsman

No	Date	Opposition	Venue	Bat	C	Bowling		
1	01/01/87	Australia	Perth	0*		9.2	0	42	3
2	05/01/87	Pakistan	Perth	13*	1	9	1	24	1
3	07/01/87	Pakistan	Perth			10	1	33	0

260 England - The Complete One-Day International Record

4	17/01/87	West Indies	Brisbane		1	9	2	17	2
5	18/01/87	Australia	Brisbane	6		10	2	41	0
6	22/01/87	Australia	Sydney	6 *	1	10	0	46	1
7	24/01/87	West Indies	Adelaide		1	7.5	1	15	3
8	26/01/87	Australia	Adelaide	8		10	1	35	4
9	30/01/87	West Indies	Melbourne	13		10	2	15	1
10	01/02/87	Australia	Melbourne	11		8	2	37	0
11	03/02/87	West Indies	Devonport	15 *		9	1	20	2
12	08/02/87	Australia	Melbourne		1	9	0	32	2
13	11/02/87	Australia	Sydney	1	1	10	1	34	2
14	02/04/87	India	Sharjah	18 *		10	3	33	0
15	07/04/87	Pakistan	Sharjah			10	0	47	1
16	09/04/87	Australia	Sharjah	1 *		10	1	40	2
17	21/05/87	Pakistan	The Oval		1	11	3	50	0
18	23/05/87	Pakistan	Trent Bridge	3		11	2	30	1
19	25/05/87	Pakistan	Edgbaston	33		11	1	30	0
20	09/10/87	West Indies	Gujranwala	23		10	2	31	1
21	12/10/87	Pakistan	Rawalpindi	3 *		10	1	42	3
22	17/10/87	Sri Lanka	Peshawar			9	2	24	1
23	20/10/87	Pakistan	Karachi	13		8	2	41	1
24	26/10/87	West Indies	Jaipur	16 *		9.1	2	28	3
25	30/10/87	Sri Lanka	Poona			10	2	46	2
26	05/11/87	India	Bombay	7		7	0	37	1
27	08/11/87	Australia	Calcutta	17		6	1	34	0
28	18/11/87	Pakistan	Lahore	14 *		7	1	19	0
29	20/11/87	Pakistan	Karachi	0		9	1	35	0
30	22/11/87	Pakistan	Peshawar	3		7	0	31	2
31	04/02/88	Australia	Melbourne	21		10	1	43	1
32	09/03/88	New Zealand	Dunedin			10	1	26	2
33	12/03/88	New Zealand	Christchurch		1	9	0	53	1
34	16/03/88	New Zealand	Napier	23		10	2	30	1
35	19/03/88	New Zealand	Auckland	6		10	0	45	0
36	19/05/88	West Indies	Edgbaston			11	2	45	1
37	21/05/88	West Indies	Headingley	15 *		9	2	29	1
38	23/05/88	West Indies	Lord's		1	11	5	20	1
39	25/05/89	Australia	Old Trafford	17 *	1	8	1	19	2
40	27/05/89	Australia	Trent Bridge			11	0	48	1
41	29/05/89	Australia	Lord's	0		11	1	50	0
42	15/10/89	Sri Lanka	Delhi			10	3	38	3
43	25/10/89	India	Kanpur	11		10	0	66	1
44	27/10/89	West Indies	Gwalior	7		10	1	42	0
45	30/10/89	Pakistan	Nagpur	4 *		6	0	40	2
46	03/03/90	West Indies	Kingston	3 *		10	2	29	1
47	07/03/90	West Indies	Georgetown	11	2	7	1	32	0
48	03/04/90	West Indies	Bridgetown			8.3	0	63	1
49	23/05/90	New Zealand	Headingley	1 *		10.5	0	70	0
50	25/05/90	New Zealand	The Oval			11	1	47	0
51	18/07/90	India	Headingley	11		10	1	40	1
52	20/07/90	India	Trent Bridge	1		11	0	59	0
53	15/12/90	New Zealand	Brisbane	27 *		8	0	31	0
54	16/12/90	Australia	Brisbane	49 *		10	0	57	3
55	01/01/91	Australia	Sydney	9		10	0	48	0
56	10/01/91	Australia	Melbourne	6		7.1	0	37	1
57	09/02/91	New Zealand	Christchurch	10 *		10	3	36	1
58	13/02/91	New Zealand	Wellington	2		10	2	22	1
59	16/02/91	New Zealand	Auckland	7		10	0	51	2
60	23/05/91	West Indies	Edgbaston	8	1	11	3	22	1
61	25/05/91	West Indies	Old Trafford		1	11	3	50	0
62	27/05/91	West Indies	Lord's		2	11	1	26	2
63	11/01/92	New Zealand	Auckland			10	1	34	0
64	22/02/92	India	Perth	1	1	10	0	39	1

65	27/02/92	West Indies	Melbourne		1	9	2	34	3
66	01/03/92	Pakistan	Adelaide			7	1	22	2
67	05/03/92	Australia	Sydney		1	10	3	23	1
68	09/03/92	Sri Lanka	Ballarat		1	5	1	31	0
69	12/03/92	South Africa	Melbourne	1*		10	1	41	1
70	15/03/92	New Zealand	Wellington	0	1	8.3	1	45	1
71	18/03/92	Zimbabwe	Albury	4		8	1	14	1
72	22/03/92	South Africa	Sydney			8	1	28	1
73	25/03/92	Pakistan	Melbourne	10		10	1	42	0
74	20/05/92	Pakistan	Lord's			9	2	17	0
75	22/05/92	Pakistan	The Oval			10.5	0	59	2
76	20/08/92	Pakistan	Trent Bridge	5*		11	1	33	3
77	22/08/92	Pakistan	Lord's	0		10	2	39	2
78	24/08/92	Pakistan	Old Trafford			11	1	52	1
79	18/01/93	India	Jaipur			9	3	40	0
80	21/01/93	India	Chandigarh			10	1	31	2
81	26/02/93	India	Bangalore	2		8	0	27	1
82	01/03/93	India	Jamshedpur		1	4	0	17	1
83	04/03/93	India	Gwalior	2*		10	0	52	1
84	05/03/93	India	Gwalior			10	0	56	1
85	10/03/93	Sri Lanka	Colombo (2)	21	1	3	0	25	0
86	25/08/94	South Africa	Edgbaston		1	9	1	38	3
87	27/08/94	South Africa	Old Trafford	7*		11	4	12	1
88	06/12/94	Australia	Sydney	6		9	1	43	0
89	15/12/94	Zimbabwe	Sydney	5	1	10	2	27	1
90	07/01/95	Zimbabwe	Brisbane	12*		10	0	28	2
91	10/01/95	Australia	Melbourne	2*		9	0	32	1

Batting & Fielding

Mat	Inns	N/O	Runs	H/S	Avg	100s	50s	Cat
91	59	23	551	49*	15.30	0	0	25

Bowling

Overs	Mds	Runs	Wkts	Avg	Best	5WI	E/R
848.1	105	3284	104	31.57	4-35	0	3.87

MIKE DENNESS

Full Name: Michael Henry Denness
Born: 01/12/40 - Bellshill, Lanarkshire, Scotland
Right-hand opening/middle order batsman - Right-arm medium bowler

No	Date	Opposition	Venue	Bat	C
1	05/09/73	West Indies	Headingley	66	
2	07/09/73	West Indies	The Oval	0	
3	13/07/74	India	Headingley	8	
4	15/07/74	India	The Oval	24	1
5	31/08/74	Pakistan	Trent Bridge	32	
6	03/09/74	Pakistan	Edgbaston	9	
7	01/01/75	Australia	Melbourne	12	
8	09/03/75	New Zealand	Wellington		
9	07/06/75	India	Lord's	37*	
10	11/06/75	New Zealand	Trent Bridge	37	
11	14/06/75	East Africa	Edgbaston	12*	
12	18/06/75	Australia	Headingley	27	

Batting & Fielding

Mat	Inns	N/O	Runs	H/S	Avg	100s	50s	Cat
12	11	2	264	66	29.33	0	1	1

GRAHAM DILLEY

Full Name: Graham Roy Dilley
Born: 18/05/59 - Dartford, Kent
Right-arm fast bowler - Left-hand lower order batsman

No	Date	Opposition	Venue	Bat	C	Bowling			
1	28/11/79	West Indies	Sydney	1		6	2	21	1
2	08/12/79	Australia	Melbourne	0*		10	1	30	2
3	11/12/79	Australia	Sydney			9	0	29	1
4	23/12/79	West Indies	Brisbane	0		8	1	25	0
5	26/12/79	Australia	Sydney			10	1	32	1
6	20/01/80	West Indies	Melbourne			10	0	39	2
7	22/01/80	West Indies	Sydney			7	0	37	0
8	28/05/80	West Indies	Headingley	0		11	3	41	1
9	26/02/81	West Indies	Berbice	3		5	0	21	1
10	02/06/82	India	Headingley			5	1	20	0
11	04/06/82	India	The Oval	1		7	1	19	1
12	09/06/83	New Zealand	The Oval	31*		8	0	33	1
13	11/06/83	Sri Lanka	Taunton	29	1	11	0	45	4
14	13/06/83	Pakistan	Lord's			12	1	33	0
15	15/06/83	New Zealand	Edgbaston	10		12	1	43	0
16	18/06/83	Pakistan	Old Trafford			12	2	46	2
17	22/06/83	India	Old Trafford	20*		11	0	43	0
18	09/03/84	Pakistan	Lahore	1		8	0	38	1
19	24/05/86	India	The Oval	6		11	0	53	1
20	26/05/86	India	Old Trafford			11	2	46	2
21	16/07/86	New Zealand	Headingley	2*		11	1	37	1
22	18/07/86	New Zealand	Old Trafford			9	0	55	1
23	01/01/87	Australia	Perth			10	1	31	2
24	03/01/87	West Indies	Perth	1		10	0	46	4
25	07/01/87	Pakistan	Perth			10	0	23	1
26	17/01/87	West Indies	Brisbane			8.3	1	23	4
27	18/01/87	Australia	Brisbane	0*		10	2	40	2
28	22/01/87	Australia	Sydney		1	9	2	28	2
29	24/01/87	West Indies	Adelaide		2	8	1	19	1
30	26/01/87	Australia	Adelaide	3*		10	1	41	1
31	08/02/87	Australia	Melbourne			9	2	32	3
32	11/02/87	Australia	Sydney	6*		10	1	34	0
33	21/05/87	Pakistan	The Oval			11	1	63	2
34	23/05/87	Pakistan	Trent Bridge	0*		9	4	16	0
35	19/05/88	West Indies	Edgbaston			11	0	64	1
36	21/05/88	West Indies	Headingley			11	0	45	2

Batting & Fielding

Mat	Inns	N/O	Runs	H/S	Avg	100s	50s	Cat
36	18	8	114	31*	11.40	0	0	4

Bowling

Overs	Mds	Runs	Wkts	Avg	Best	5WI	E/R
340.3	33	1291	48	26.89	4-23	0	3.79

BASIL D'OLIVEIRA

Full Name: Basil Lewis D'Oliveira OBE
Born: 04/10/31 - Signal Hill, Cape Town, South Africa
Right-hand middle order batsman - Right arm medium or off break bowler

No	Date	Opposition	Venue	Bat	C	Bowling			
1	05/01/71	Australia	Melbourne	17	*6	1	38	1
2	24/08/72	Australia	Old Trafford	5*	1	9	1	37	0
3	26/08/72	Australia	Lord's	6		11	0	46	1
4	28/08/72	Australia	Edgbaston	2		6	1	19	1

Batting & Fielding

Mat	Inns	N/O	Runs	H/S	Avg	100s	50s	Cat
4	4	1	30	17	10.00	0	0	1

Bowling

Overs	Mds	Runs	Wkts	Avg	Best	5WI	E/R
34	3	140	3	46.66	1-19	0	4.11

PAUL DOWNTON

Full Name: Paul Rupert Downton
Born: 04/04/57 - Farnborough, Kent
Right-hand middle order batsman - Wicket-keeper

No	Date	Opposition	Venue	Bat	C/S
1	23/12/77	Pakistan	Sahiwal		1
2	05/12/84	India	Poona	27*	
3	27/12/84	India	Cuttack	44*	
4	20/01/85	India	Bangalore	12	+1
5	23/01/85	India	Nagpur	13	2
6	17/02/85	Australia	Melbourne	27	
7	26/02/85	India	Sydney	9	2
8	02/03/85	Pakistan	Melbourne	6	1
9	30/05/85	Australia	Old Trafford	11	1
10	01/06/85	Australia	Edgbaston	16*	
11	03/06/85	Australia	Lord's		
12	18/02/86	West Indies	Kingston	8	2+1
13	04/03/86	West Indies	Port of Spain		
14	19/03/86	West Indies	Bridgetown	0	1
15	31/03/86	West Indies	Port of Spain	12	
16	24/05/86	India	The Oval	4	1
17	26/05/86	India	Old Trafford	4*	1
18	09/10/87	West Indies	Gujranwala	3	
19	12/10/87	Pakistan	Rawalpindi	0	2
20	17/10/87	Sri Lanka	Peshawar		
21	20/10/87	Pakistan	Karachi	6	
22	26/10/87	West Indies	Jaipur		3
23	30/10/87	Sri Lanka	Poona		+1
24	05/11/87	India	Bombay	1*	2
25	08/11/87	Australia	Calcutta	9	1
26	19/05/88	West Indies	Edgbaston		1
27	21/05/88	West Indies	Headingley	30	4
28	23/05/88	West Indies	Lord's		1

Batting & Fielding

Mat	Inns	N/O	Runs	H/S	Avg	100s	50s	Cat	St
28	20	5	242	44*	16.13	0	0	26	3

PHIL EDMONDS

Full Name: Philippe-Henri Edmonds
Born: 08/03/51 - Lusaka, Northern Rhodesia
Left-arm slow bowler - Right-hand middle order batsman

No	Date	Opposition	Venue	Bat	C	Bowling			
1	23/12/77	Pakistan	Sahiwal	5		*7	0	19	0
2	30/12/77	Pakistan	Sialkot		1	*7	0	28	2
3	13/01/78	Pakistan	Lahore	0		*7	1	28	2
4	24/05/78	Pakistan	Old Trafford	4 *		10	4	17	0
5	17/07/78	New Zealand	Old Trafford			7.2	1	39	3
6	13/01/79	Australia	Sydney						
7	24/01/79	Australia	Melbourne		1	*7	0	26	1
8	07/02/79	Australia	Melbourne	15					
9	09/06/79	Australia	Lord's			11	1	25	1
10	16/06/79	Pakistan	Headingley	2		3	0	8	0
11	23/06/79	West Indies	Lord's	5 *		12	2	40	2
12	05/12/84	India	Poona			10	0	43	1
13	27/12/84	India	Cuttack			10	0	47	0
14	20/01/85	India	Bangalore	7		10	0	44	1
15	23/01/85	India	Nagpur	8 *		10	0	44	0
16	27/01/85	India	Chandigarh	5		3	0	20	2
17	17/02/85	Australia	Melbourne	20		10	0	33	0
18	26/02/85	India	Sydney	5		10	1	38	0
19	02/03/85	Pakistan	Melbourne	0 *		10	1	29	1
20	24/03/85	Australia	Sharjah	15 *		10	2	31	2
21	26/03/85	Pakistan	Sharjah	3		10	0	47	1
22	30/05/85	Australia	Old Trafford	0	1	11	2	33	1
23	01/06/85	Australia	Edgbaston	6 *		10	0	48	0
24	31/03/86	West Indies	Port of Spain	0		10	1	38	0
25	26/05/86	India	Old Trafford			11	1	49	1
26	18/07/86	New Zealand	Old Trafford			11	1	42	1
27	03/01/87	West Indies	Perth	16 *	1	9	1	53	0
28	22/01/87	Australia	Sydney			10	0	48	2
29	02/04/87	India	Sharjah		2	10	0	48	2

Batting & Fielding

Mat	Inns	N/O	Runs	H/S	Avg	100s	50s	Cat
29	18	7	116	20	10.54	0	0	6

Bowling

Overs	Mds	Runs	Wkts	Avg	Best	5WI	E/R
255.4	19	965	26	37.11	3-39	0	3.77

JOHN EDRICH

Full Name: John Hugh Edrich MBE
Born: 21/06/37 - Blofield, Norfolk
Left-hand opening batsman

No	Date	Opposition	Venue	Bat	C
1	05/01/71	Australia	Melbourne	82	
2	13/07/74	India	Headingley	90	
3	15/07/74	India	The Oval	19	
4	31/08/74	Pakistan	Trent Bridge	18	

5	03/09/74	Pakistan	Edgbaston	6
6	08/03/75	New Zealand	Dunedin	8
7	09/03/75	New Zealand	Wellington	

Batting & Fielding

Mat	Inns	N/O	Runs	H/S	Avg	100s	50s	Cat
7	6	0	223	90	37.16	0	2	0

RICHARD ELLISON

Full Name: Richard Mark Ellison
Born: 21/09/59 - Willesborough, Ashford, Kent
Right-arm fast medium bowler - Left-hand middle order batsman

No	Date	Opposition	Venue	Bat	C	Bowling			
1	05/12/84	India	Poona	4	2	7	0	45	1
2	27/12/84	India	Cuttack	14*		6	0	31	0
3	20/01/85	India	Bangalore	1*		6	0	25	0
4	27/01/85	India	Chandigarh	4*		3	0	20	0
5	17/02/85	Australia	Melbourne	2*		10	4	34	1
6	26/02/85	India	Sydney	1		10	1	46	1
7	02/03/85	Pakistan	Melbourne	6		10	0	42	3
8	24/03/85	Australia	Sharjah	24		10	1	28	2
9	26/03/85	Pakistan	Sharjah	3		7	1	18	0
10	04/03/86	West Indies	Port of Spain			8	0	57	0
11	31/03/86	West Indies	Port of Spain	5		7	0	30	0
12	24/05/86	India	The Oval	10		10	1	36	0
13	26/05/86	India	Old Trafford			11	0	55	1
14	16/07/86	New Zealand	Headingley	12		11	1	43	3

Batting & Fielding

Mat	Inns	N/O	Runs	H/S	Avg	100s	50s	Cat
14	12	4	86	24	10.75	0	0	2

Bowling

Overs	Mds	Runs	Wkts	Avg	Best	5WI	E/R
116	9	510	12	42.50	3-42	0	4.39

JOHN EMBUREY

Full Name: John Ernest Emburey
Born: 20/08/52 - Peckham, London
Off break bowler - Right-hand middle order batsman

No	Date	Opposition	Venue	Bat	C	Bowling			
1	14/01/80	Australia	Sydney	18		10	1	33	2
2	16/01/80	West Indies	Adelaide	1	1	10	0	39	0
3	20/01/80	West Indies	Melbourne			10	0	31	0
4	22/01/80	West Indies	Sydney	6		9.3	0	48	0
5	22/08/80	Australia	Edgbaston	1*	1	8	0	51	0
6	04/02/81	West Indies	Arnos Vale	5	1	10	4	20	1
7	26/02/81	West Indies	Berbice	0		10	4	22	2
8	13/02/82	Sri Lanka	Colombo	0		5	0	18	0
9	18/02/86	West Indies	Kingston	5		10	3	19	0

#	Date	Opponent	Venue	Runs	H/S	Overs	Mds	Runs	Wkts
10	04/03/86	West Indies	Port of Spain			8	2	48	0
11	19/03/86	West Indies	Bridgetown	15		9	0	55	2
12	31/03/86	West Indies	Port of Spain	2*		10	2	31	1
13	24/05/86	India	The Oval	20		11	2	15	0
14	26/05/86	India	Old Trafford			11	1	46	2
15	16/07/86	New Zealand	Headingley	0		11	0	30	0
16	18/07/86	New Zealand	Old Trafford			11	1	34	1
17	01/01/87	Australia	Perth		2	10	0	41	1
18	03/01/87	West Indies	Perth	18		9.2	0	31	2
19	05/01/87	Pakistan	Perth	11*		10	0	65	2
20	07/01/87	Pakistan	Perth			8	0	34	1
21	17/01/87	West Indies	Brisbane			9	0	35	3
22	18/01/87	Australia	Brisbane	24*	1	10	0	60	1
23	22/01/87	Australia	Sydney	4		9	0	42	3
24	24/01/87	West Indies	Adelaide	16*		10	0	37	4
25	26/01/87	Australia	Adelaide	17	1	10	0	56	0
26	30/01/87	West Indies	Melbourne	34		9.3	1	54	0
27	01/02/87	Australia	Melbourne	1	1	6	0	41	0
28	03/02/87	West Indies	Devonport	2	2	9	0	26	3
29	08/02/87	Australia	Melbourne			8	0	29	1
30	11/02/87	Australia	Sydney	6	1	10	2	27	1
31	02/04/87	India	Sharjah	25		9.5	0	38	3
32	07/04/87	Pakistan	Sharjah	5*		10	1	44	1
33	09/04/87	Australia	Sharjah	18*		10	1	38	2
34	21/05/87	Pakistan	The Oval			11	1	36	1
35	23/05/87	Pakistan	Trent Bridge	25		11	2	33	0
36	25/05/87	Pakistan	Edgbaston	16		11	1	49	2
37	09/10/87	West Indies	Gujranwala	22		10	1	22	0
38	12/10/87	Pakistan	Rawalpindi	1		10	0	51	0
39	17/10/87	Sri Lanka	Peshawar	30*	1	10	1	26	2
40	20/10/87	Pakistan	Karachi	3		10	0	34	1
41	26/10/87	West Indies	Jaipur	24*		9	0	41	2
42	30/10/87	Sri Lanka	Poona		1	10	1	42	0
43	05/11/87	India	Bombay	6	1	10	1	35	1
44	08/11/87	Australia	Calcutta	10		10	0	44	0
45	18/11/87	Pakistan	Lahore	4	1	8.3	2	17	3
46	20/11/87	Pakistan	Karachi	1		9	0	65	2
47	22/11/87	Pakistan	Peshawar	3		3	0	22	1
48	04/02/88	Australia	Melbourne	26		10	0	53	2
49	09/03/88	New Zealand	Dunedin	2*		9.4	0	39	4
50	12/03/88	New Zealand	Christchurch			9	1	38	3
51	16/03/88	New Zealand	Napier	15		7	0	47	1
52	19/03/88	New Zealand	Auckland	11		10	0	44	0
53	19/05/88	West Indies	Edgbaston		2	11	1	49	2
54	21/05/88	West Indies	Headingley	8		3.3	0	9	1
55	23/05/88	West Indies	Lord's		1	10	1	53	2
56	25/05/89	Australia	Old Trafford	10	1	11	0	31	3
57	27/05/89	Australia	Trent Bridge			11	0	47	2
58	29/05/89	Australia	Lord's			11	0	61	1
59	18/01/93	India	Jaipur			8	0	49	0
60	10/03/93	Sri Lanka	Colombo (2)	10		10	1	42	1
61	20/03/93	Sri Lanka	Moratuwa	20		6	0	29	0

Batting & Fielding

Mat	Inns	N/O	Runs	H/S	Avg	100s	50s	Cat
61	45	10	501	34	14.31	0	0	19

Bowling

Overs	Mds	Runs	Wkts	Avg	Best	5WI	E/R
570.5	39	2346	76	30.86	4-37	0	4.10

NEIL FAIRBROTHER

Full Name: Neil Harvey Fairbrother
Born: 09/09/63 - Warrington, Lancashire
Left-hand middle order batsman - Left-arm medium bowler

No	Date	Opposition	Venue	Bat	C	Bowling
1	02/04/87	India	Sharjah	14	1	
2	07/04/87	Pakistan	Sharjah	6	1	
3	09/04/87	Australia	Sharjah	32		
4	18/11/87	Pakistan	Lahore	25	1	
5	20/11/87	Pakistan	Karachi	2	1	
6	22/11/87	Pakistan	Peshawar	1		
7	04/02/88	Australia	Melbourne	22		
8	09/03/88	New Zealand	Dunedin	50*		
9	12/03/88	New Zealand	Christchurch	25*	1	
10	16/03/88	New Zealand	Napier	1		
11	19/03/88	New Zealand	Auckland	54		
12	23/05/91	West Indies	Edgbaston	4	1	
13	25/05/91	West Indies	Old Trafford	5*		
14	27/05/91	West Indies	Lord's	113	1	
15	11/01/92	New Zealand	Auckland	23*		
16	22/02/92	India	Perth	24		
17	27/02/92	West Indies	Melbourne	13*	2	
18	01/03/92	Pakistan	Adelaide			
19	05/03/92	Australia	Sydney		1	
20	09/03/92	Sri Lanka	Ballarat	63	1	
21	12/03/92	South Africa	Melbourne	75*		
22	18/03/92	Zimbabwe	Albury	20	2	
23	22/03/92	South Africa	Sydney	28		
24	25/03/92	Pakistan	Melbourne	62		
25	20/05/92	Pakistan	Lord's	25		1 0 9 0
26	22/05/92	Pakistan	The Oval	63		
27	20/08/92	Pakistan	Trent Bridge	62		
28	22/08/92	Pakistan	Lord's	33		
29	24/08/92	Pakistan	Old Trafford	15		
30	18/01/93	India	Jaipur	46*		
31	21/01/93	India	Chandigarh	7		
32	26/02/93	India	Bangalore	5		
33	01/03/93	India	Jamshedpur	53*	1	
34	04/03/93	India	Gwalior	37		
35	05/03/93	India	Gwalior	41		
36	10/03/93	Sri Lanka	Colombo (2)	34		
37	20/03/93	Sri Lanka	Moratuwa	21		
38	19/05/93	Australia	Old Trafford	59	3	
39	21/05/93	Australia	Edgbaston	23	1	
40	23/05/93	Australia	Lord's	18		
41	25/08/94	South Africa	Edgbaston	19*		
42	25/08/94	South Africa	Old Trafford	3		
43	07/01/95	Zimbabwe	Brisbane	7	1	
44	10/01/95	Australia	Melbourne	35		

Batting & Fielding

Mat	Inns	N/O	Runs	H/S	Avg	100s	50s	Cat
44	42	9	1268	113	38.42	1	9	19

Bowling

Overs	Mds	Runs	Wkts	Avg	Best	5WI	E/R
1	0	9	0	-	-	0	9.00

268   England - The Complete One-Day International Record

KEITH FLETCHER

Full Name: Keith William Robert Fletcher OBE
Born: 20/05/44 - Worcester
Right-hand middle order batsman - Leg break bowler

No	Date	Opposition	Venue	Bat	C
1	05/01/71	Australia	Melbourne	24	
2	24/08/72	Australia	Old Trafford	60	
3	26/08/72	Australia	Lord's	20	
4	28/08/72	Australia	Edgbaston	34	
5	18/07/73	New Zealand	Swansea	16*	1
6	20/07/73	New Zealand	Old Trafford	25	
7	05/09/73	West Indies	Headingley	2	
8	07/09/73	West Indies	The Oval	63	
9	13/07/74	India	Headingley	39	1
10	15/07/74	India	The Oval	55*	
11	31/08/74	Pakistan	Trent Bridge		
12	03/09/74	Pakistan	Edgbaston	2	
13	01/01/75	Australia	Melbourne	31	1
14	08/03/75	New Zealand	Dunedin	11	
15	09/03/75	New Zealand	Wellington	18*	
16	07/06/75	India	Lord's	68	1
17	11/06/75	New Zealand	Trent Bridge	131	
18	14/06/75	East Africa	Edgbaston		
19	18/06/75	Australia	Headingley	8	
20	25/11/81	India	Ahmedabad	26	
21	20/12/81	India	Jullundur	5	
22	27/01/82	India	Cuttack	69	
23	13/02/82	Sri Lanka	Colombo	12	
24	14/02/82	Sri Lanka	Colombo	38	

Batting & Fielding

Mat	Inns	N/O	Runs	H/S	Avg	100s	50s	Cat
24	22	3	757	131	39.84	1	5	4

NEIL FOSTER

Full Name: Neil Alan Foster
Born: 06/05/62 - Colchester, Essex
Right-arm fast bowler - Right-hand lower order batsman

No	Date	Opposition	Venue	Bat	C		Bowling		
1	18/02/84	New Zealand	Christchurch	0		10	4	19	2
2	22/02/84	New Zealand	Wellington		2	10	3	29	2
3	25/02/84	New Zealand	Auckland	1		6	0	37	0
4	09/03/84	Pakistan	Lahore	6*		8	0	34	0
5	26/03/84	Pakistan	Karachi		1	8	0	36	0
6	31/05/84	West Indies	Old Trafford	24	1	11	0	61	1
7	02/06/84	West Indies	Trent Bridge			10	0	46	0
8	04/06/84	West Indies	Lord's	4*		11	1	40	0
9	05/12/84	India	Poona			10	0	44	3
10	27/12/84	India	Cuttack			5	0	26	0
11	20/01/85	India	Bangalore			6	0	33	0
12	27/01/85	India	Chandigarh			3	0	17	0
13	26/02/85	India	Sydney	1		10	0	33	2

14	02/03/85	Pakistan	Melbourne	1	1	10	0	56	2
15	24/03/85	Australia	Sharjah	5*	1	10	1	34	1
16	03/06/85	Australia	Lord's			11	0	55	1
17	18/02/86	West Indies	Kingston	5*		10	1	44	1
18	04/03/86	West Indies	Port of Spain		1	10	1	42	1
19	19/03/86	West Indies	Bridgetown	9*	1	9	0	39	3
20	31/03/86	West Indies	Port of Spain			6	1	27	1
21	16/07/86	New Zealand	Headingley	5	1	9	1	27	2
22	18/07/86	New Zealand	Old Trafford			7	0	40	0
23	05/01/87	Pakistan	Perth			4	0	23	0
24	30/01/87	West Indies	Melbourne	5		9	1	25	2
25	01/02/87	Australia	Melbourne	4		7	1	20	1
26	03/02/87	West Indies	Devonport	0		10	0	29	1
27	08/02/87	Australia	Melbourne			9	0	42	1
28	11/02/87	Australia	Sydney	7		10	0	51	0
29	02/04/87	India	Sharjah			9	1	46	1
30	07/04/87	Pakistan	Sharjah			10	0	47	1
31	09/04/87	Australia	Sharjah			10	0	50	1
32	21/05/87	Pakistan	The Oval			11	0	36	2
33	23/05/87	Pakistan	Trent Bridge	5		11	1	25	2
34	25/05/87	Pakistan	Edgbaston	14*		11	1	29	3
35	09/10/87	West Indies	Gujranwala	9*		10	0	53	3
36	12/10/87	Pakistan	Rawalpindi	6		10	1	35	1
37	20/10/87	Pakistan	Karachi	20*		10	0	51	0
38	26/10/87	West Indies	Jaipur		1	10	0	52	1
39	30/10/87	Sri Lanka	Poona			10	0	37	0
40	05/11/87	India	Bombay			10	0	47	3
41	08/11/87	Australia	Calcutta	7*		10	0	38	1
42	18/11/87	Pakistan	Lahore	0		8	1	37	2
43	20/11/87	Pakistan	Karachi	5*	1	9	0	47	2
44	22/11/87	Pakistan	Peshawar	2*		6.5	0	20	3
45	04/09/88	Sri Lanka	The Oval		1	11	0	47	0
46	25/05/89	Australia	Old Trafford	5*		10	3	29	3
47	27/05/89	Australia	Trent Bridge			11	2	44	1
48	29/05/89	Australia	Lord's			11	0	57	2

Batting & Fielding
Mat	Inns	N/O	Runs	H/S	Avg	100s	50s	Cat
48	25	12	150	24	11.53	0	0	12

Bowling
Overs	Mds	Runs	Wkts	Avg	Best	5WI	E/R
437.5	25	1836	59	31.11	3-20	0	4.19

GRAEME FOWLER

Full Name: Graeme Fowler
Born: 20/04/57 - Accrington, Lancashire
Left-hand opening batsman - Right-arm medium bowler - Wicket-keeper

No	Date	Opposition	Venue	Bat	C/S
1	20/01/83	New Zealand	Sydney	0	
2	09/06/83	New Zealand	The Oval	8	
3	11/06/83	Sri Lanka	Taunton	22	
4	13/06/83	Pakistan	Lord's	78*	
5	15/06/83	New Zealand	Edgbaston	69	
6	18/06/83	Pakistan	Old Trafford	69	
7	20/06/83	Sri Lanka	Headingley	81*	

270 England - The Complete One-Day International Record

8	22/06/83	India	Old Trafford	33	
9	09/03/84	Pakistan	Lahore	43	1
10	26/03/84	Pakistan	Karachi	25	1+2
11	31/05/84	West Indies	Old Trafford	1	
12	02/06/84	West Indies	Trent Bridge	25	
13	04/06/84	West Indies	Lord's	34	
14	05/12/84	India	Poona	5	
15	27/12/84	India	Cuttack	15	
16	20/01/85	India	Bangalore	45	
17	23/01/85	India	Nagpur	37	
18	27/01/85	India	Chandigarh	17	
19	17/02/85	Australia	Melbourne	26	
20	26/02/85	India	Sydney	26	1
21	02/03/85	Pakistan	Melbourne	0	
22	24/03/85	Australia	Sharjah	26	
23	26/03/85	Pakistan	Sharjah	19	
24	30/05/85	Australia	Old Trafford	10	
25	24/05/86	India	The Oval	20	
26	26/05/86	India	Old Trafford	10	1

Batting & Fielding

Mat	Inns	N/O	Runs	H/S	Avg	100s	50s	Cat	St
26	26	2	744	81*	31.00	0	4	4	2

ANGUS FRASER

Full Name: Angus Robert Charles Fraser
Born: 08/08/65 - Billinge, Lancashire
Right-arm fast medium bowler - Right-hand lower order batsman

No	Date	Opposition	Venue	Bat	C	Bowling			
1	15/10/89	Sri Lanka	Delhi			8.3	1	25	2
2	19/10/89	Australia	Hyderabad			10	2	48	1
3	22/10/89	Pakistan	Cuttack			10	3	15	0
4	25/10/89	India	Kanpur			10	2	31	0
5	27/10/89	West Indies	Gwalior			10	1	47	0
6	30/10/89	Pakistan	Nagpur			6	0	58	1
7	14/02/90	West Indies	Port of Spain			10	1	37	2
8	17/02/90	West Indies	Port of Spain			2.5	0	5	0
9	03/03/90	West Indies	Kingston			10	0	41	1
10	07/03/90	West Indies	Georgetown			10	1	42	1
11	15/03/90	West Indies	Georgetown	3*		9.2	1	33	1
12	18/07/90	India	Headingley	4*		11	3	37	0
13	20/07/90	India	Trent Bridge	0*		11	1	38	1
14	01/12/90	New Zealand	Adelaide	0		8	1	33	1
15	07/12/90	New Zealand	Perth			10	3	23	1
16	09/12/90	Australia	Perth	4		9	2	30	0
17	13/12/90	New Zealand	Sydney	5		9	1	21	2
18	15/12/90	New Zealand	Brisbane			9	2	38	0
19	16/12/90	Australia	Brisbane			10	1	47	1
20	01/01/91	Australia	Sydney	4		10	2	28	3
21	10/01/91	Australia	Melbourne	38*		10	2	39	0
22	09/02/91	New Zealand	Christchurch			10	0	28	1
23	13/02/91	New Zealand	Wellington	5		9	1	22	3
24	16/02/91	New Zealand	Auckland	6		10	3	31	1
25	26/02/94	West Indies	Kingston		1	9	0	50	1
26	02/03/94	West Indies	Arnos Vale	1		10	1	46	1
27	05/03/94	West Indies	Port of Spain	4*		10	0	31	3

28	06/03/94	West Indies	Port of Spain		10	2	41	0
29	19/05/94	New Zealand	Edgbaston		10	0	37	1
30	15/12/94	Zimbabwe	Sydney	2	10	0	45	2
31	10/01/95	Australia	Melbourne		10	2	22	4

Batting & Fielding

Mat	Inns	N/O	Runs	H/S	Avg	100s	50s	Cat
31	13	5	76	38*	9.50	0	0	1

Bowling

Overs	Mds	Runs	Wkts	Avg	Best	5WI	E/R
291.4	39	1069	35	30.54	4-22	0	3.66

BRUCE FRENCH

Full Name: Bruce Nicholas French
Born: 13/08/59 - Warsop, Nottinghamshire
Right-hand middle/lower order batsman - Wicket-keeper

No	Date	Opposition	Venue	Bat	C/S
1	27/01/85	India	Chandigarh		
2	24/03/85	Australia	Sharjah	4	2
3	26/03/85	Pakistan	Sharjah	7	1+1
4	01/02/87	Australia	Melbourne	5*	+1
5	03/02/87	West Indies	Devonport	0	3
6	08/02/87	Australia	Melbourne		1
7	11/02/87	Australia	Sydney	9*	1
8	18/11/87	Pakistan	Lahore	7*	2
9	20/11/87	Pakistan	Karachi		
10	09/03/88	New Zealand	Dunedin		1+1
11	12/03/88	New Zealand	Christchurch		1
12	16/03/88	New Zealand	Napier	0	
13	19/03/88	New Zealand	Auckland	2	1

Batting & Fielding

Mat	Inns	N/O	Runs	H/S	Avg	100s	50s	Cat	St
13	8	3	34	9*	6.80	0	0	13	3

MIKE GATTING

Full Name: Michael William Gatting OBE
Born: 06/06/57 - Kingsbury, Middlesex
Right-hand middle order batsman - Right-arm medium bowler

No	Date	Opposition	Venue	Bat	C	Bowling		
1	23/12/77	Pakistan	Sahiwal	17				
2	30/12/77	Pakistan	Sialkot	5	*1	0	15	0
3	13/01/78	Pakistan	Lahore	3				
4	20/08/80	Australia	The Oval	17*				
5	22/08/80	Australia	Edgbaston	2				
6	04/02/81	West Indies	Arnos Vale	3				
7	26/02/81	West Indies	Berbice	29				
8	04/06/81	Australia	Lord's	0				
9	06/06/81	Australia	Edgbaston	96				

272 England - The Complete One-Day International Record

10	08/06/81	Australia	Headingley	32	1				
11	25/11/81	India	Ahmedabad	47*					
12	20/12/81	India	Jullundur	71*					
13	27/01/82	India	Cuttack	8*					
14	13/02/82	Sri Lanka	Colombo	3					
15	14/02/82	Sri Lanka	Colombo	18					
16	17/07/82	Pakistan	Trent Bridge	37*					
17	19/07/82	Pakistan	Old Trafford	76					
18	09/06/83	New Zealand	The Oval	43		8	1	35	1
19	11/06/83	Sri Lanka	Taunton	7	1				
20	13/06/83	Pakistan	Lord's						
21	15/06/83	New Zealand	Edgbaston	1					
22	18/06/83	Pakistan	Old Trafford	14*					
23	20/06/83	Sri Lanka	Headingley		1	4	2	13	0
24	22/06/83	India	Old Trafford	18					
25	18/02/84	New Zealand	Christchurch	0					
26	22/02/84	New Zealand	Wellington	0*					
27	25/02/84	New Zealand	Auckland	4					
28	09/03/84	Pakistan	Lahore	9					
29	26/03/84	Pakistan	Karachi	38*	1	8	1	32	3
30	31/05/84	West Indies	Old Trafford	0	1				
31	02/06/84	West Indies	Trent Bridge	6					
32	05/12/84	India	Poona	115*					
33	27/12/84	India	Cuttack	59		10	0	49	2
34	20/01/85	India	Bangalore	3	1	4	0	27	0
35	23/01/85	India	Nagpur	1	1	4	0	14	0
36	27/01/85	India	Chandigarh	31	1	2	0	27	0
37	17/02/85	Australia	Melbourne	34	1				
38	26/02/85	India	Sydney	7					
39	02/03/85	Pakistan	Melbourne	11	1				
40	30/05/85	Australia	Old Trafford	31*	1				
41	01/06/85	Australia	Edgbaston	6	1				
42	03/06/85	Australia	Lord's						
43	18/02/86	West Indies	Kingston	10					
44	24/05/86	India	The Oval	27					
45	26/05/86	India	Old Trafford	39					
46	16/07/86	New Zealand	Headingley	19					
47	18/07/86	New Zealand	Old Trafford	7					
48	01/01/87	Australia	Perth	5*					
49	03/01/87	West Indies	Perth	15	1				
50	05/01/87	Pakistan	Perth	7		7	0	24	0
51	07/01/87	Pakistan	Perth	49	1	2	0	14	1
52	17/01/87	West Indies	Brisbane	3*					
53	18/01/87	Australia	Brisbane	30					
54	22/01/87	Australia	Sydney	1		2	0	11	0
55	24/01/87	West Indies	Adelaide	3					
56	26/01/87	Australia	Adelaide	46					
57	30/01/87	West Indies	Melbourne	13					
58	01/02/87	Australia	Melbourne	6		9	0	59	3
59	03/02/87	West Indies	Devonport	6	1				
60	08/02/87	Australia	Melbourne	3*	2				
61	11/02/87	Australia	Sydney	7					
62	21/05/87	Pakistan	The Oval	2*	1				
63	25/05/87	Pakistan	Edgbaston	41					
64	09/10/87	West Indies	Gujranwala	25					
65	12/10/87	Pakistan	Rawalpindi	43					
66	17/10/87	Sri Lanka	Peshawar	58					
67	20/10/87	Pakistan	Karachi	60					
68	26/10/87	West Indies	Jaipur	25					
69	30/10/87	Sri Lanka	Poona	46*					
70	05/11/87	India	Bombay	56	1				
71	08/11/87	Australia	Calcutta	41					

No	Date	Opposition	Venue	Bat	C			
72	18/11/87	Pakistan	Lahore	16	1			
73	20/11/87	Pakistan	Karachi	21				
74	22/11/87	Pakistan	Peshawar	53				
75	04/02/88	Australia	Melbourne	37	1			
76	09/03/88	New Zealand	Dunedin	42	1			
77	12/03/88	New Zealand	Christchurch	33				
78	16/03/88	New Zealand	Napier	6		3	0	14	0
79	19/03/88	New Zealand	Auckland	48				
80	19/05/88	West Indies	Edgbaston	82 *				
81	21/05/88	West Indies	Headingley	18				
82	23/05/88	West Indies	Lord's	40 *				
83	25/05/89	Australia	Old Trafford	3				
84	27/05/89	Australia	Trent Bridge	37				
85	29/05/89	Australia	Lord's	18				
86	18/01/93	India	Jaipur	30				
87	21/01/93	India	Chandigarh	0		1	0	2	0
88	26/02/93	India	Bangalore	7				
89	01/03/93	India	Jamshedpur					
90	05/03/93	India	Gwalior	6				
91	10/03/93	Sri Lanka	Colombo (2)	1				
92	20/03/93	Sri Lanka	Moratuwa	2				

Batting & Fielding

Mat	Inns	N/O	Runs	H/S	Avg	100s	50s	Cat
92	88	17	2095	115*	29.50	1	9	22

Bowling

Overs	Mds	Runs	Wkts	Avg	Best	5WI	E/R
65.2	4	336	10	33.60	3-32	0	5.14

NORMAN GIFFORD

Full Name: Norman Gifford MBE
Born: 30/03/40 - Ulverston, Lancashire
Left-arm slow bowler - Left-hand lower order batsman

No	Date	Opposition	Venue	Bat	C	Bowling			
1	24/03/85	Australia	Sharjah			10	1	27	0
2	26/03/85	Pakistan	Sharjah	0	1	10	0	23	4

Batting & Fielding

Mat	Inns	N/O	Runs	H/S	Avg	100s	50s	Cat
2	1	0	0	0	0.00	0	0	1

Bowling

Overs	Mds	Runs	Wkts	Avg	Best	5WI	E/R
20	1	50	4	12.50	4-23	0	2.50

GRAHAM GOOCH

Full Name: Graham Alan Gooch OBE
Born: 23/07/53 - Whipps Cross, Leytonstone, Essex
Right-hand opening batsman - Right-arm medium bowler

No	Date	Opposition	Venue	Bat	C	Bowling			
1	26/08/76	West Indies	Scarborough	32					
2	28/08/76	West Indies	Lord's	5					
3	30/08/76	West Indies	Edgbaston	3					
4	15/07/78	New Zealand	Scarborough	94		10	1	29	2
5	17/07/78	New Zealand	Old Trafford	0	1				
6	13/01/79	Australia	Sydney						
7	24/01/79	Australia	Melbourne	23		*1	0	2	0
8	04/02/79	Australia	Melbourne	19					
9	07/02/79	Australia	Melbourne	4					
10	09/06/79	Australia	Lord's	53					
11	13/06/79	Canada	Old Trafford	21*					
12	16/06/79	Pakistan	Headingley	33		1	0	1	0
13	20/06/79	New Zealand	Old Trafford	71		3	1	8	0
14	23/06/79	West Indies	Lord's	32		4	0	27	0
15	28/11/79	West Indies	Sydney	2					
16	08/12/79	Australia	Melbourne	1	2	6	0	32	2
17	11/12/79	Australia	Sydney	11	1	7	0	33	0
18	23/12/79	West Indies	Brisbane	17		3.5	0	38	1
19	26/12/79	Australia	Sydney	29		8	0	38	1
20	14/01/80	Australia	Sydney	69		3	0	13	0
21	16/01/80	West Indies	Adelaide	20	1	2	0	22	0
22	20/01/80	West Indies	Melbourne	9					
23	22/01/80	West Indies	Sydney	23		1	0	5	0
24	28/05/80	West Indies	Headingley	2		7	2	30	2
25	30/05/80	West Indies	Lord's	12					
26	20/08/80	Australia	The Oval	54		7	0	29	1
27	22/08/80	Australia	Edgbaston	108	1	3	0	16	1
28	04/02/81	West Indies	Arnos Vale	11		6	1	12	2
29	26/02/81	West Indies	Berbice	11	1	2	0	8	0
30	04/06/81	Australia	Lord's	53	1	5	1	21	0
31	06/06/81	Australia	Edgbaston	11		5	0	38	0
32	08/06/81	Australia	Headingley	37	2	11	0	50	0
33	25/11/81	India	Ahmedabad	23	1	7	0	28	1
34	20/12/81	India	Jullundur	12		7	0	25	2
35	27/01/82	India	Cuttack	3	2	8	0	39	1
36	13/02/82	Sri Lanka	Colombo	64	1	6	1	18	0
37	14/02/82	Sri Lanka	Colombo	74	1	9	0	50	0
38	30/05/85	Australia	Old Trafford	57		2	0	10	1
39	01/06/85	Australia	Edgbaston	115		2	0	14	0
40	03/06/85	Australia	Lord's	117*	1	11	0	46	1
41	18/02/86	West Indies	Kingston	36		2	2	0	1
42	04/03/86	West Indies	Port of Spain	129*					
43	19/03/86	West Indies	Bridgetown	6		6	1	41	0
44	31/03/86	West Indies	Port of Spain	10	1				
45	24/05/86	India	The Oval	30					
46	26/05/86	India	Old Trafford	10	1				
47	16/07/86	New Zealand	Headingley	18		4	0	20	0
48	18/07/86	New Zealand	Old Trafford	91		7	0	48	0
49	02/04/87	India	Sharjah	31					
50	07/04/87	Pakistan	Sharjah	1					
51	09/04/87	Australia	Sharjah	86	1	6	0	34	0
52	23/05/87	Pakistan	Trent Bridge	9	1	3	0	12	0
53	09/10/87	West Indies	Gujranwala	47					

#	Date	Country	Venue	Score					
54	12/10/87	Pakistan	Rawalpindi	21					
55	17/10/87	Sri Lanka	Peshawar	84	1	2	0	9	0
56	20/10/87	Pakistan	Karachi	16	1	2	0	12	0
57	26/10/87	West Indies	Jaipur	92					
58	30/10/87	Sri Lanka	Poona	61					
59	05/11/87	India	Bombay	115		3	0	16	0
60	08/11/87	Australia	Calcutta	35		8	1	42	1
61	18/11/87	Pakistan	Lahore	43	1				
62	20/11/87	Pakistan	Karachi	142					
63	22/11/87	Pakistan	Peshawar	57	1				
64	19/05/88	West Indies	Edgbaston	43					
65	21/05/88	West Indies	Headingley	32		3	0	12	1
66	23/05/88	West Indies	Lord's	28		2	1	3	0
67	04/09/88	Sri Lanka	The Oval	7		11	1	35	2
68	25/05/89	Australia	Old Trafford	52					
69	27/05/89	Australia	Trent Bridge	10	1				
70	29/05/89	Australia	Lord's	136	1				
71	15/10/89	Sri Lanka	Delhi	5	1	10	2	26	2
72	19/10/89	Australia	Hyderabad	56	1	10	3	35	0
73	22/10/89	Pakistan	Cuttack	7		10	4	19	3
74	25/10/89	India	Kanpur	21		5.1	0	37	0
75	27/10/89	West Indies	Gwalior	59		5	0	34	0
76	30/10/89	Pakistan	Nagpur	35					
77	14/02/90	West Indies	Port of Spain	13 *	1	8	0	26	1
78	17/02/90	West Indies	Port of Spain						
79	03/03/90	West Indies	Kingston	2	1	2	0	15	0
80	07/03/90	West Indies	Georgetown	33					
81	15/03/90	West Indies	Georgetown	42		5	1	22	0
82	23/05/90	New Zealand	Headingley	55		4	0	23	2
83	25/05/90	New Zealand	The Oval	112 *					
84	18/07/90	India	Headingley	45					
85	20/07/90	India	Trent Bridge	7					
86	13/12/90	New Zealand	Sydney	3					
87	15/12/90	New Zealand	Brisbane	48	1				
88	16/12/90	Australia	Brisbane	41					
89	01/01/91	Australia	Sydney	37					
90	10/01/91	Australia	Melbourne	37		10	0	39	1
91	09/02/91	New Zealand	Christchurch	17	1	10	0	31	0
92	13/02/91	New Zealand	Wellington	41		10	2	33	0
93	16/02/91	New Zealand	Auckland	47		10	0	40	1
94	23/05/91	West Indies	Edgbaston	0	1	5	0	17	1
95	25/05/91	West Indies	Old Trafford	54		11	1	51	1
96	27/05/91	West Indies	Lord's	11	1	2	0	9	1
97	11/01/92	New Zealand	Auckland	47	1				
98	12/02/92	New Zealand	Dunedin	24					
99	15/02/92	New Zealand	Christchurch	22 *					
100	22/02/92	India	Perth	51					
101	27/02/92	West Indies	Melbourne	65					
102	01/03/92	Pakistan	Adelaide	3					
103	05/03/92	Australia	Sydney	58					
104	09/03/92	Sri Lanka	Ballarat	8					
105	18/03/92	Zimbabwe	Albury	0	1				
106	22/03/92	South Africa	Sydney	2					
107	25/03/92	Pakistan	Melbourne	29					
108	20/05/92	Pakistan	Lord's	9					
109	22/05/92	Pakistan	The Oval	25					
110	20/08/92	Pakistan	Trent Bridge	42	2				
111	24/08/92	Pakistan	Old Trafford	45					
112	18/01/93	India	Jaipur	4		2	0	13	0
113	21/01/93	India	Chandigarh	7					
114	26/02/93	India	Bangalore	45	2				
115	01/03/93	India	Jamshedpur	15	1				

276   *England - The Complete One-Day International Record*

116	04/03/93	India	Gwalior	1	1				
117	05/03/93	India	Gwalior		1				
118	19/05/93	Australia	Old Trafford	4					
119	21/05/93	Australia	Edgbaston	17					
120	23/05/93	Australia	Lord's	42	1				
121	19/05/94	New Zealand	Edgbaston	23					
122	06/12/94	Australia	Sydney	21	1				
123	15/12/94	Zimbabwe	Syndey	38					
124	07/01/95	Zimbabwe	Brisbane	0		8	0	30	0
125	10/01/95	Australia	Melbourne	2		10	0	50	0

Batting & Fielding
Mat	Inns	N/O	Runs	H/S	Avg	100s	50s	Cat
125	122	6	4290	142	36.98	8	23	45

Bowling
Overs	Mds	Runs	Wkts	Avg	Best	5WI	E/R
344.2	26	1516	36	42.11	3-19	0	4.40

DARREN GOUGH

Full Name: Darren Gough
Born: 18/09/70 - Barnsley, Yorkshire
Right-arm fast bowler - Right-hand middle/lower order batsman

No	Date	Opposition	Venue	Bat	C	Bowling			
1	19/05/94	New Zealand	Edgbaston			11	1	36	2
2	25/08/94	South Africa	Edgbaston			11	2	40	0
3	27/08/94	South Africa	Old Tafford			10	1	39	2
4	06/12/94	Australia	Sydney	8*		10	0	51	1
5	15/12/94	Zimbabwe	Sydney	2	1	9.3	0	44	5
6	07/01/95	Zimbabwe	Brisbane	4		9.1	3	17	2
7	10/01/95	Australia	Melbourne	45					

Batting & Fielding
Mat	Inns	N/O	Runs	H/S	Avg	100s	50s	Cat
7	4	1	59	45	19.66	0	0	1

Bowling
Overs	Mds	Runs	Wkts	Avg	Best	5WI	E/R
60.4	7	227	12	18.91	5-44	1	3.74

IAN GOULD

Full Name: Ian James Gould
Born: 19/08/57 - Taplow, Buckinghamshire
Left-hand middle/lower order batsman - Wicket-keeper

No	Date	Opposition	Venue	Bat	C/S
1	15/01/83	New Zealand	Brisbane	15	2+1
2	16/01/83	Australia	Brisbane	2	1
3	20/01/83	New Zealand	Sydney		
4	23/01/83	Australia	Melbourne	3	
5	26/01/83	Australia	Sydney	42	1
6	29/01/83	New Zealand	Adelaide	1*	

7	30/01/83	Australia	Adelaide	9		
8	05/02/83	New Zealand	Perth	0		
9	19/02/83	New Zealand	Auckland	3		
10	23/02/83	New Zealand	Wellington	14		
11	26/02/83	New Zealand	Christchurch	0	+1	
12	09/06/83	New Zealand	The Oval	14*	2	
13	11/06/83	Sri Lanka	Taunton	35	+1	
14	13/06/83	Pakistan	Lord's		3	
15	15/06/83	New Zealand	Edgbaston	4	1	
16	18/06/83	Pakistan	Old Trafford		2	
17	20/06/83	Sri Lanka	Headingley		2	
18	22/06/83	India	Old Trafford	13	1	

Batting & Fielding

Mat	Inns	N/O	Runs	H/S	Avg	100s	50s	Cat	St
18	14	2	155	42	12.91	0	0	15	3

DAVID GOWER

Full Name: David Ivon Gower OBE
Born: 01/04/57 - Tunbridge Wells, Kent
Left-hand middle order batsman

No	Date	Opposition	Venue	Bat	C	Bowling
1	24/05/78	Pakistan	Old Trafford	33		
2	26/05/78	Pakistan	The Oval	114*	1	
3	15/07/78	New Zealand	Scarborough	4	1	
4	17/07/78	New Zealand	Old Trafford	50	1	
5	13/01/79	Australia	Sydney			
6	24/01/79	Australia	Melbourne	19*	1	
7	04/02/79	Australia	Melbourne	101*	1	
8	07/02/79	Australia	Melbourne	3		
9	09/06/79	Australia	Lord's	22*		
10	13/06/79	Canada	Old Trafford			
11	16/06/79	Pakistan	Headingley	27		
12	20/06/79	New Zealand	Old Trafford	1		
13	23/06/79	West Indies	Lord's	0	1	
14	28/11/79	West Indies	Sydney	44	2	
15	08/12/79	Australia	Melbourne	17		
16	11/12/79	Australia	Sydney	7		
17	23/12/79	West Indies	Brisbane	59		
18	26/12/79	Australia	Sydney	2	1	
19	14/01/80	Australia	Sydney	3		
20	16/01/80	West Indies	Adelaide	12		
21	20/01/80	West Indies	Melbourne	10		
22	22/01/80	West Indies	Sydney	27		
23	28/05/80	West Indies	Headingley	12	1	
24	30/05/80	West Indies	Lord's	12		
25	04/02/81	West Indies	Arnos Vale	23		
26	26/02/81	West Indies	Berbice	3		.3 0 5 0
27	04/06/81	Australia	Lord's	47		
28	06/06/81	Australia	Edgbaston	2		
29	08/06/81	Australia	Headingley	5		
30	25/11/81	India	Ahmedabad	8		
31	20/12/81	India	Jullundur	53	1	
32	27/01/82	India	Cuttack	42		
33	13/02/82	Sri Lanka	Colombo	15	2	

278 *England - The Complete One-Day International Record*

34	14/02/82	Sri Lanka	Colombo	6	
35	02/06/82	India	Headingley		
36	04/06/82	India	The Oval	76	1
37	17/07/82	Pakistan	Trent Bridge	17	
38	19/07/82	Pakistan	Old Trafford	33	1
39	11/01/83	Australia	Sydney	9	
40	13/01/83	New Zealand	Melbourne	122	
41	15/01/83	New Zealand	Brisbane	158	
42	16/01/83	Australia	Brisbane	22	
43	20/01/83	New Zealand	Sydney	0	2
44	23/01/83	Australia	Melbourne	6	1
45	26/01/83	Australia	Sydney	25	
46	29/01/83	New Zealand	Adelaide	109	1
47	30/01/83	Australia	Adelaide	77	2
48	05/02/83	New Zealand	Perth	35*	
49	19/02/83	New Zealand	Auckland	84	
50	23/02/83	New Zealand	Wellington	2	
51	26/02/83	New Zealand	Christchurch	53	
52	09/06/83	New Zealand	The Oval	39	
53	11/06/83	Sri Lanka	Taunton	130	
54	13/06/83	Pakistan	Lord's	48	
55	15/06/83	New Zealand	Edgbaston	92*	
56	18/06/83	Pakistan	Old Trafford	31	
57	20/06/83	Sri Lanka	Headingley	27*	1
58	22/06/83	India	Old Trafford	17	
59	18/02/84	New Zealand	Christchurch	3	2
60	22/02/84	New Zealand	Wellington	21	1
61	25/02/84	New Zealand	Auckland	35	
62	09/03/84	Pakistan	Lahore	7	
63	26/03/84	Pakistan	Karachi	31	1
64	31/05/84	West Indies	Old Trafford	15	
65	02/06/84	West Indies	Trent Bridge	36	1
66	04/06/84	West Indies	Lord's	29	
67	05/12/84	India	Poona	3	
68	27/12/84	India	Cuttack	21	1
69	20/01/85	India	Bangalore	38	1
70	23/01/85	India	Nagpur	11	
71	27/01/85	India	Chandigarh	19	
72	17/02/85	Australia	Melbourne	6	
73	26/02/85	India	Sydney	25	
74	02/03/85	Pakistan	Melbourne	27	
75	30/05/85	Australia	Old Trafford	3	
76	01/06/85	Australia	Edgbaston	0	
77	03/06/85	Australia	Lord's	102	1
78	18/02/86	West Indies	Kingston	0	
79	04/03/86	West Indies	Port of Spain	9	
80	19/03/86	West Indies	Bridgetown	0	
81	31/03/86	West Indies	Port of Spain	20	.2 0 9 0
82	24/05/86	India	The Oval	0	
83	26/05/86	India	Old Trafford	81	1
84	16/07/86	New Zealand	Headingley	18	
85	18/07/86	New Zealand	Old Trafford	9	
86	01/01/87	Australia	Perth	6	1
87	03/01/87	West Indies	Perth	11	
88	05/01/87	Pakistan	Perth	2	1
89	07/01/87	Pakistan	Perth	31	3
90	17/01/87	West Indies	Brisbane	42	
91	18/01/87	Australia	Brisbane	15	
92	22/01/87	Australia	Sydney	50	
93	24/01/87	West Indies	Adelaide	29	1
94	26/01/87	Australia	Adelaide	21	
95	30/01/87	West Indies	Melbourne	8	

96	01/02/87	Australia	Melbourne	11				
97	03/02/87	West Indies	Devonport	3				
98	08/02/87	Australia	Melbourne	45				
99	11/02/87	Australia	Sydney	17	1			
100	21/05/87	Pakistan	The Oval	15 *				
101	23/05/87	Pakistan	Trent Bridge	24				
102	25/05/87	Pakistan	Edgbaston	11	1			
103	25/05/89	Australia	Old Trafford	36				
104	27/05/89	Australia	Trent Bridge	28				
105	29/05/89	Australia	Lord's	61	1			
106	23/05/90	New Zealand	Headingley	1	1			
107	25/05/90	New Zealand	The Oval	4				
108	18/07/90	India	Headingley	50	1			
109	20/07/90	India	Trent Bridge	25				
110	01/12/90	New Zealand	Adelaide	6	1			
111	10/01/91	Australia	Melbourne	26				
112	09/02/91	New Zealand	Christchurch	4	1			
113	13/02/91	New Zealand	Wellington	11				
114	16/02/91	New Zealand	Auckland	13				

Batting & Fielding

Mat	Inns	N/O	Runs	H/S	Avg	100s	50s	Cat
114	111	8	3170	158	30.77	7	12	44

Bowling

Overs	Mds	Runs	Wkts	Avg	Best	5WI	E/R
0.5	0	14	0	-	-	0	16.80

TONY GREIG

Full Name: Anthony William Greig
Born: 06/10/46 - Queenstown, South Africa
Right-hand middle order batsman - Right-arm medium or off break bowler

No	Date	Opposition	Venue	Bat	C	Bowling			
1	24/08/72	Australia	Old Trafford			11	0	50	1
2	26/08/72	Australia	Lord's	31		9	1	29	0
3	28/08/72	Australia	Edgbaston	24 *		10	3	24	0
4	18/07/73	New Zealand	Swansea			9.5	2	26	1
5	20/07/73	New Zealand	Old Trafford	14					
6	05/09/73	West Indies	Headingley	48	3	11	0	40	0
7	07/09/73	West Indies	The Oval	17		6	2	21	0
8	13/07/74	India	Headingley	40		11	0	63	1
9	15/07/74	India	The Oval	24 *	1	9	0	27	2
10	31/08/74	Pakistan	Trent Bridge	7 *		4.5	0	40	0
11	03/09/74	Pakistan	Edgbaston	1					
12	01/01/75	Australia	Melbourne	3	1	*7.5	0	48	2
13	09/03/75	New Zealand	Wellington		1	*5	0	34	0
14	07/06/75	India	Lord's	4		9	1	26	0
15	11/06/75	New Zealand	Trent Bridge	9		12	0	45	4
16	14/06/75	East Africa	Edgbaston	9		10	1	18	2
17	18/06/75	Australia	Headingley	7					
18	28/08/76	West Indies	Lord's	3		5.5	0	31	2
19	30/08/76	West Indies	Edgbaston	2		6	0	48	1
20	02/06/77	Australia	Old Trafford	22	1	4	0	11	2
21	04/06/77	Australia	Edgbaston	0		1.2	0	2	1
22	06/06/77	Australia	The Oval	4		6	0	36	0

280   England - The Complete One-Day International Record

Batting & Fielding

Mat	Inns	N/O	Runs	H/S	Avg	100s	50s	Cat
22	19	3	269	48	16.81	0	0	7

Bowling

Overs	Mds	Runs	Wkts	Avg	Best	5WI	E/R
152.4	10	619	19	32.57	4-45	0	4.05

JOHN HAMPSHIRE

Full Name: John Harry Hampshire
Born: 10/02/41 - Thurnscoe, Yorkshire
Right-hand middle order batsman - Leg break bowler

No	Date	Opposition	Venue	Bat	C
1	05/01/71	Australia	Melbourne	10	
2	24/08/72	Australia	Old Trafford	25*	
3	26/08/72	Australia	Lord's	13	

Batting & Fielding

Mat	Inns	N/O	Runs	H/S	Avg	100s	50s	Cat
3	3	1	48	25*	24.00	0	0	0

FRANK HAYES

Full Name: Frank Charles Hayes
Born: 06/12/46 - Preston, Lancashire
Right-hand middle order batsman

No	Date	Opposition	Venue	Bat	C
1	18/07/73	New Zealand	Swansea	20*	
2	20/07/73	New Zealand	Old Trafford	9	
3	05/09/73	West Indies	Headingley	9	
4	11/06/75	New Zealand	Trent Bridge	34	
5	14/06/75	East Africa	Edgbaston	52	
6	18/06/75	Australia	Headingley	4	

Batting & Fielding

Mat	Inns	N/O	Runs	H/S	Avg	100s	50s	Cat
6	6	1	128	52	25.60	0	1	0

EDDIE HEMMINGS

Full Name: Edward Ernest Hemmings
Born: 20/02/49 - Leamington Spa, Warwickshire
Right-arm medium or off break bowler - Right-hand lower order batsman

No	Date	Opposition	Venue	Bat	C		Bowling		
1	17/07/82	Pakistan	Trent Bridge		1	11	1	45	0
2	19/07/82	Pakistan	Old Trafford	1		11	3	30	1

No	Date	Opposition	Venue	Bat	C		Bowling		
3	26/01/83	Australia	Sydney	3		3.3	0	11	3
4	29/01/83	New Zealand	Adelaide			6	0	49	0
5	30/01/83	Australia	Adelaide			10	0	40	1
6	17/10/87	Sri Lanka	Peshawar		1	10	1	31	2
7	20/10/87	Pakistan	Karachi	4*		10	1	40	0
8	26/10/87	West Indies	Jaipur		1	10	0	46	2
9	30/10/87	Sri Lanka	Poona			10	0	57	3
10	05/11/87	India	Bombay			9.3	1	52	4
11	08/11/87	Australia	Calcutta			10	1	48	2
12	18/11/87	Pakistan	Lahore			9	1	44	2
13	20/11/87	Pakistan	Karachi			9	0	45	0
14	15/10/89	Sri Lanka	Delhi			10	1	34	1
15	19/10/89	Australia	Hyderabad			2	0	17	0
16	22/10/89	Pakistan	Cuttack			4	0	13	1
17	25/10/89	India	Kanpur			10	0	51	1
18	27/10/89	West Indies	Gwalior	1*	1	7	0	44	0
19	14/02/90	West Indies	Port of Spain			9	0	41	1
20	17/02/90	West Indies	Port of Spain						
21	03/03/90	West Indies	Kingston			10	0	31	3
22	07/03/90	West Indies	Georgetown	0*		10	1	33	1
23	15/03/90	West Indies	Georgetown	3*		10	1	37	1
24	03/04/90	West Indies	Bridgetown			9	0	32	1
25	23/05/90	New Zealand	Headingley			11	0	51	0
26	25/05/90	New Zealand	The Oval			11	2	34	0
27	18/07/90	India	Headingley	3		11	0	36	0
28	20/07/90	India	Trent Bridge	0		11	1	53	2
29	01/12/90	New Zealand	Adelaide	3		8	0	51	1
30	13/12/90	New Zealand	Sydney	8*	1	10	1	34	2
31	16/12/90	Australia	Brisbane	3*		10	0	57	0
32	01/01/91	Australia	Sydney	1		10	0	57	1
33	09/02/91	New Zealand	Christchurch			10	0	50	1

Batting & Fielding
Mat	Inns	N/O	Runs	H/S	Avg	100s	50s	Cat
33	12	6	30	8*	5.00	0	0	5

Bowling
Overs	Mds	Runs	Wkts	Avg	Best	5WI	E/R
292	16	1294	37	34.97	4-52	0	4.43

MIKE HENDRICK

Full Name: Michael Hendrick
Born: 22/10/48 - Darley Dale, Derbyshire
Right-arm fast medium bowler - Right-hand lower order batsman

No	Date	Opposition	Venue	Bat	C		Bowling		
1	05/09/73	West Indies	Headingley	1		11	4	27	1
2	08/03/75	New Zealand	Dunedin	1		*2	0	9	0
3	09/03/75	New Zealand	Wellington			*4	0	21	1
4	26/08/76	West Indies	Scarborough		1	9	3	38	1
5	28/08/76	West Indies	Lord's	0*		9	2	34	2
6	30/08/76	West Indies	Edgbaston	1*	1	10	0	45	2
7	23/12/77	Pakistan	Sahiwal			*7	0	50	1
8	15/07/78	New Zealand	Scarborough	2*		11	1	35	2
9	13/01/79	Australia	Sydney			*1	1	0	0
10	24/01/79	Australia	Melbourne			*8	1	25	4
11	04/02/79	Australia	Melbourne			*8	0	47	1

282 England - The Complete One-Day International Record

12	07/02/79	Australia	Melbourne	0*		*6	0	32	0
13	09/06/79	Australia	Lord's		1	12	2	24	0
14	13/06/79	Canada	Old Trafford			8	4	5	1
15	16/06/79	Pakistan	Headingley	1*	1	12	6	15	4
16	20/06/79	New Zealand	Old Trafford			12	0	55	3
17	23/06/79	West Indies	Lord's	0	1	12	2	50	2
18	20/08/80	Australia	The Oval			11	3	31	5
19	22/08/80	Australia	Edgbaston			10	0	54	3
20	04/06/81	Australia	Lord's			11	2	32	0
21	06/06/81	Australia	Edgbaston	0		11	2	21	1
22	08/06/81	Australia	Headingley	0		11	3	31	1

Batting & Fielding

Mat	Inns	N/O	Runs	H/S	Avg	100s	50s	Cat
22	10	5	6	2*	1.20	0	0	5

Bowling

Overs	Mds	Runs	Wkts	Avg	Best	5WI	E/R
208	36	681	35	19.45	5-31	1	3.27

GRAEME HICK

Full Name: Graeme Ashley Hick
Born: 23/05/66 - Salisbury, Rhodesia
Right-hand middle order batsman - Off break bowler

No	Date	Opposition	Venue	Bat	C	Bowling			
1	23/05/91	West Indies	Edgbaston	14					
2	25/05/91	West Indies	Old Trafford	29					
3	27/05/91	West Indies	Lord's	86*					
4	11/01/92	New Zealand	Auckland	23	2	6	0	29	0
5	12/02/92	New Zealand	Dunedin	7					
6	15/02/92	New Zealand	Christchurch	18	1				
7	22/02/92	India	Perth	5	1				
8	27/02/92	West Indies	Melbourne	54	1				
9	01/03/92	Pakistan	Adelaide		1				
10	05/03/92	Australia	Sydney	7*					
11	09/03/92	Sri Lanka	Ballarat	41					
12	12/03/92	South Africa	Melbourne	1	1	8.2	0	44	2
13	15/03/92	New Zealand	Wellington	56		6	0	26	0
14	18/03/92	Zimbabwe	Albury	0					
15	22/03/92	South Africa	Sydney	83	1				
16	25/03/92	Pakistan	Melbourne	17					
17	20/05/92	Pakistan	Lord's	3	2	3.2	0	7	2
18	22/05/92	Pakistan	The Oval	71*		1	0	8	0
19	20/08/92	Pakistan	Trent Bridge	63	1				
20	22/08/92	Pakistan	Lord's	8					
21	24/08/92	Pakistan	Old Trafford	42*					
22	18/01/93	India	Jaipur	13					
23	21/01/93	India	Chandigarh	56					
24	26/02/93	India	Bangalore	56	3				
25	01/03/93	India	Jamshedpur	1					
26	04/03/93	India	Gwalior	18	2	2	0	18	0
27	05/03/93	India	Gwalior	105*	1				
28	10/03/93	Sri Lanka	Colombo (2)	31	1				
29	20/03/93	Sri Lanka	Moratuwa	36		6.2	1	36	0
30	19/05/93	Australia	Old Trafford	85		1	0	6	0
31	21/05/93	Australia	Edgbaston	2					
32	23/05/93	Australia	Lord's	7	3		0	17	0

33	16/02/94	West Indies	Bridgetown	47					
34	26/02/94	West Indies	Kingston	31	1	7	0	32	2
35	02/03/94	West Indies	Arnos Vale	32		3	0	18	0
36	05/03/94	West Indies	Port of Spain	10	1	4	0	33	0
37	06/03/94	West Indies	Port of Spain	47*					
38	19/05/94	New Zealand	Edgbaston	18	2	7	0	31	2
39	25/08/94	South Africa	Edgbaston	81		5	1	19	0
40	27/08/94	South Africa	Old Trafford	0		3	0	14	0
41	06/12/94	Australia	Sydney	6	2	10	0	44	1
42	15/12/94	Zimbabwe	Sydney	64		2	0	8	0
43	07/01/95	Zimbabwe	Brisbane	8	1	7	1	29	1
44	10/01/95	Australia	Melbourne	91		10	1	41	3

Batting & Fielding

Mat	Inns	N/O	Runs	H/S	Avg	100s	50s	Cat
44	43	6	1473	105*	39.81	1	12	25

Bowling

Overs	Mds	Runs	Wkts	Avg	Best	5WI	E/R
95	4	460	13	35.38	3-41	0	4.84

GEOFF HUMPAGE

Full Name: Geoffrey William Humpage
Born: 24/04/54 - Sparkhill, Birmingham
Right-hand middle order batsman - Wicket-keeper

No	Date	Opposition	Venue	Bat	C
1	04/06/81	Australia	Lord's		
2	06/06/81	Australia	Edgbaston	5	1
3	08/06/81	Australia	Headingley	6	1

Batting & Fielding

Mat	Inns	N/O	Runs	H/S	Avg	100s	50s	Cat
3	2	0	11	6	5.50	0	0	2

NASSER HUSSAIN

Full Name: Nasser Hussain
Born: 28/03/68 - Madras, India
Right-hand middle order batsman

No	Date	Opposition	Venue	Bat	C
1	30/10/89	Pakistan	Nagpur	2	
2	03/04/90	West Indies	Bridgetown	15*	1
3	26/02/94	West Indies	Kingston	10	
4	02/03/94	West Indies	Arnos Vale	16	1

Batting & Fielding

Mat	Inns	N/O	Runs	H/S	Avg	100s	50s	Cat
4	4	1	43	16	14.33	0	0	2

ALAN IGGLESDEN

Full Name: Alan Paul Igglesden
Born: 08/10/64 - Farnborough, Kent
Right-arm fast medium bowler - Right-hand lower order batsman

No	Date	Opposition	Venue	Bat	C	Bowling		
1	16/02/94	West Indies	Bridgetown		1	8	2	12	2
2	26/02/94	West Indies	Kingston	2*		7	1	29	0
3	02/03/94	West Indies	Arnos Vale	18		10	1	65	0
4	05/03/94	West Indies	Port of Spain	0		3	0	16	0

Batting & Fielding

Mat	Inns	N/O	Runs	H/S	Avg	100s	50s	Cat
4	3	1	20	18	10.00	0	0	1

Bowling

Overs	Mds	Runs	Wkts	Avg	Best	5WI	E/R
28	4	122	2	61.00	2-12	0	4.35

RAY ILLINGWORTH

Full Name: Raymond Illingworth CBE
Born: 08/06/32 - Pudsey, Yorkshire
Off break bowler - Right-hand middle order batsman

No	Date	Opposition	Venue	Bat	C	Bowling		
1	05/01/71	Australia	Melbourne	1		*8	1	50	3
2	18/07/73	New Zealand	Swansea		1	11	1	34	1
3	20/07/73	New Zealand	Old Trafford	4					

Batting & Fielding

Mat	Inns	N/O	Runs	H/S	Avg	100s	50s	Cat
3	2	0	5	4	2.50	0	0	1

Bowling

Overs	Mds	Runs	Wkts	Avg	Best	5WI	E/R
21.4	2	84	4	21.00	3-50	0	3.87

RICHARD ILLINGWORTH

Full Name: Richard Keith Illingworth
Born: 23/08/63 - Greengates, Bradford, Yorkshire
Left-arm slow bowler - Right-hand lower order batsman

No	Date	Opposition	Venue	Bat	C	Bowling		
1	23/05/91	West Indies	Edgbaston	9*	1	10	1	20	1
2	25/05/91	West Indies	Old Trafford		1	11	1	42	0
3	27/05/91	West Indies	Lord's		2	11	1	53	2
4	12/02/92	New Zealand	Dunedin			9	1	33	1
5	15/02/92	New Zealand	Christchurch			8	0	38	1
6	09/03/92	Sri Lanka	Ballarat		1	10	0	32	2
7	12/03/92	South Africa	Melbourne			10	0	43	0

No	Date	Opposition	Venue	Bat	C		Bowling		
8	15/03/92	New Zealand	Wellington	2*		9	1	46	0
9	18/03/92	Zimbabwe	Albury	11	1	9.1	0	33	3
10	22/03/92	South Africa	Sydney			10	1	46	2
11	25/03/92	Pakistan	Melbourne	14	1	10	0	50	1
12	20/05/92	Pakistan	Lord's			11	0	36	1
13	22/05/92	Pakistan	The Oval		1	11	0	58	2
14	20/08/92	Pakistan	Trent Bridge			11	1	34	3
15	22/08/92	Pakistan	Lord's	4		10	0	43	1
16	24/08/92	Pakistan	Old Trafford			11	0	59	0
17	19/05/93	Australia	Old Trafford	12		11	0	48	3
18	23/05/93	Australia	Lord's	9		10	0	46	1

Batting & Fielding

Mat	Inns	N/O	Runs	H/S	Avg	100s	50s	Cat
18	7	2	61	14	12.20	0	0	8

Bowling

Overs	Mds	Runs	Wkts	Avg	Best	5WI	E/R
182.1	7	760	24	31.66	3-33	0	4.17

ROBIN JACKMAN

Full Name: Robin David Jackman
Born: 13/08/45 - Simla, India
Right-arm fast medium bowler - Right-hand lower order batsman

No	Date	Opposition	Venue	Bat	C		Bowling		
1	13/07/74	India	Headingley			11	0	44	2
2	15/07/74	India	The Oval			11	1	41	3
3	28/08/76	West Indies	Lord's	14		10	1	50	0
4	20/08/80	Australia	The Oval			11	0	46	1
5	22/08/80	Australia	Edgbaston	6		11	1	45	0
6	04/06/81	Australia	Lord's			11	1	27	1
7	06/06/81	Australia	Edgbaston	2		11	0	47	1
8	08/06/81	Australia	Headingley	14	1	11	1	48	1
9	26/01/83	Australia	Sydney	0		10	1	41	3
10	29/01/83	New Zealand	Adelaide			10	1	49	2
11	30/01/83	Australia	Adelaide		1	10	3	36	2
12	05/02/83	New Zealand	Perth	0*	1	2	0	16	0
13	19/02/83	New Zealand	Auckland	4	1	8.3	0	38	0
14	23/02/83	New Zealand	Wellington	9		10	2	38	1
15	26/02/83	New Zealand	Christchurch	5		8	1	32	2

Batting & Fielding

Mat	Inns	N/O	Runs	H/S	Avg	100s	50s	Cat
15	9	1	54	14	6.75	0	0	4

Bowling

Overs	Mds	Runs	Wkts	Avg	Best	5WI	E/R
145.3	13	598	19	31.47	3-41	0	4.10

JOHN JAMESON

Full Name: John Alexander Jameson
Born: 30/06/41 - Byculla, Bombay, India
Right-hand opening batsman - Right-arm medium or Off break bowler

No	Date	Opposition	Venue	Bat	C	Bowling			
1	07/09/73	West Indies	The Oval	28					
2	07/06/75	India	Lord's	21		2	1	3	0
3	11/06/75	New Zealand	Trent Bridge	11					

Batting & Fielding

Mat	Inns	N/O	Runs	H/S	Avg	100s	50s	Cat
3	3	0	60	28	20.00	0	0	0

Bowling

Overs	Mds	Runs	Wkts	Avg	Best	5WI	E/R
2	1	3	0	-	-	0	1.50

PAUL JARVIS

Full Name: Paul William Jarvis
Born: 29/06/65 - Redcar, Yorkshire
Right-arm fast medium bowler - Right-hand lower order batsman

No	Date	Opposition	Venue	Bat	C	Bowling			
1	04/02/88	Australia	Melbourne			10	0	42	0
2	09/03/88	New Zealand	Dunedin			10	2	34	1
3	12/03/88	New Zealand	Christchurch			9	0	33	0
4	16/03/88	New Zealand	Napier	5*		9.3	1	45	1
5	19/03/88	New Zealand	Auckland	0		9.2	1	33	4
6	18/01/93	India	Jaipur			10	0	49	2
7	21/01/93	India	Chandigarh		1	10	1	43	1
8	26/02/93	India	Bangalore	1		8.4	1	35	5
9	01/03/93	India	Jamshedpur			5	0	40	2
10	04/03/93	India	Gwalior	0		10	0	43	2
11	05/03/93	India	Gwalior			10	0	39	3
12	10/03/93	Sri Lanka	Colombo (2)	16*		9	0	57	1
13	20/03/93	Sri Lanka	Moratuwa	4		4	0	22	0
14	19/05/93	Australia	Old Trafford	2		11	0	55	1
15	21/05/93	Australia	Edgbaston			10	1	51	1
16	23/05/93	Australia	Lord's	3		11	1	51	0

Batting & Fielding

Mat	Inns	N/O	Runs	H/S	Avg	100s	50s	Cat
16	8	2	31	16*	5.16	0	0	1

Bowling

Overs	Mds	Runs	Wkts	Avg	Best	5WI	E/R
146.3	8	672	24	28.00	5-35	1	4.58

TREVOR JESTY

Full Name: Trevor Edward Jesty
Born: 02/06/48 - Gosport, Hampshire
Right-hand middle order batsman - Right-arm medium bowler

No	Date	Opposition	Venue	Bat	C	Bowling			
1	11/01/83	Australia	Sydney	12		6	0	23	1
2	13/01/83	New Zealand	Melbourne	5		3	0	11	0
3	15/01/83	New Zealand	Brisbane	4*	2				
4	16/01/83	Australia	Brisbane	0	1	1	0	7	0
5	23/01/83	Australia	Melbourne	1*					
6	26/01/83	Australia	Sydney	30					
7	29/01/83	New Zealand	Adelaide	52*	1	8	0	52	0
8	30/01/83	Australia	Adelaide	22*	1				
9	05/02/83	New Zealand	Perth	0					
10	19/02/83	New Zealand	Auckland	1					

Batting & Fielding

Mat	Inns	N/O	Runs	H/S	Avg	100s	50s	Cat
10	10	4	127	52*	21.16	0	1	5

Bowling

Overs	Mds	Runs	Wkts	Avg	Best	5WI	E/R
18	0	93	1	93.00	1-23	0	5.16

ALAN KNOTT

Full Name: Alan Philip Eric Knott
Born: 09/04/46 - Belvedere, Kent
Right-hand middle order batsman - Wicket-keeper

No	Date	Opposition	Venue	Bat	C/S
1	05/01/71	Australia	Melbourne	24	2+1
2	24/08/72	Australia	Old Trafford		
3	26/08/72	Australia	Lord's	50	3
4	28/08/72	Australia	Edgbaston	6	
5	18/07/73	New Zealand	Swansea		4
6	20/07/73	New Zealand	Old Trafford	12	
7	13/07/74	India	Headingley	15*	
8	15/07/74	India	The Oval		2
9	31/08/74	Pakistan	Trent Bridge		
10	01/01/75	Australia	Melbourne	2*	
11	07/06/75	India	Lord's		1
12	11/06/75	New Zealand	Trent Bridge		
13	14/06/75	East Africa	Edgbaston	18*	
14	18/06/75	Australia	Headingley	0	
15	26/08/76	West Indies	Scarborough	16	
16	28/08/76	West Indies	Lord's	22	
17	30/08/76	West Indies	Edgbaston	10	
18	02/06/77	Australia	Old Trafford	21*	2
19	04/06/77	Australia	Edgbaston	0	1
20	06/06/77	Australia	The Oval	4	

Batting & Fielding

Mat	Inns	N/O	Runs	H/S	Avg	100s	50s	Cat	St
20	14	4	200	50	20.00	0	1	15	1

ALLAN LAMB

Full Name: Allan Joseph Lamb
Born: 20/06/54 - Langebaanweg, Cape Province, South Africa
Right-hand middle order batsman - Right-arm medium bowler

No	Date	Opposition	Venue	Bat	C	Bowling
1	02/06/82	India	Headingley	35*		
2	04/06/82	India	The Oval	99		
3	17/07/82	Pakistan	Trent Bridge	118		
4	19/07/82	Pakistan	Old Trafford	27		
5	11/01/83	Australia	Sydney	49		
6	13/01/83	New Zealand	Melbourne	15		
7	15/01/83	New Zealand	Brisbane	13		
8	16/01/83	Australia	Brisbane	19		
9	20/01/83	New Zealand	Sydney	108*	1	
10	23/01/83	Australia	Melbourne	94		
11	26/01/83	Australia	Sydney	0	1	
12	29/01/83	New Zealand	Adelaide	19		
13	30/01/83	Australia	Adelaide	2	1	
14	05/02/83	New Zealand	Perth	7		
15	19/02/83	New Zealand	Auckland	0	1	
16	23/02/83	New Zealand	Wellington	7		
17	26/02/83	New Zealand	Christchurch	37		
18	09/06/83	New Zealand	The Oval	102	2	
19	11/06/83	Sri Lanka	Taunton	53	2	
20	13/06/83	Pakistan	Lord's	48*		
21	15/06/83	New Zealand	Edgbaston	8		
22	18/06/83	Pakistan	Old Trafford	38*		
23	20/06/83	Sri Lanka	Headingley		2	
24	22/06/83	India	Old Trafford	29		
25	18/02/84	New Zealand	Christchurch	43		
26	22/02/84	New Zealand	Wellington	6		
27	25/02/84	New Zealand	Auckland	97*		
28	09/03/84	Pakistan	Lahore	57		
29	26/03/84	Pakistan	Karachi	19		
30	31/05/84	West Indies	Old Trafford	75		
31	02/06/84	West Indies	Trent Bridge	11		
32	04/06/84	West Indies	Lord's	0		
33	05/12/84	India	Poona	3		
34	27/12/84	India	Cuttack	28		
35	20/01/85	India	Bangalore	59*		
36	23/01/85	India	Nagpur	30		
37	27/01/85	India	Chandigarh	33*		
38	17/02/85	Australia	Melbourne	53		
39	26/02/85	India	Sydney	13	1	
40	02/03/85	Pakistan	Melbourne	81		
41	30/05/85	Australia	Old Trafford	0		
42	01/06/85	Australia	Edgbaston	25		
43	03/06/85	Australia	Lord's	9*		
44	18/02/86	West Indies	Kingston	30		
45	04/03/86	West Indies	Port of Spain	16		
46	19/03/86	West Indies	Bridgetown	18	1	
47	31/03/86	West Indies	Port of Spain	16		
48	24/05/86	India	The Oval	0		
49	26/05/86	India	Old Trafford	45		
50	16/07/86	New Zealand	Headingley	33		
51	18/07/86	New Zealand	Old Trafford	28		
52	01/01/87	Australia	Perth	66		
53	03/01/87	West Indies	Perth	71		

Players   289

54	05/01/87	Pakistan	Perth	32					
55	07/01/87	Pakistan	Perth	47					
56	17/01/87	West Indies	Brisbane	22	1				
57	18/01/87	Australia	Brisbane	6					
58	22/01/87	Australia	Sydney	77*					
59	24/01/87	West Indies	Adelaide	33*	1				
60	26/01/87	Australia	Adelaide	8	1				
61	30/01/87	West Indies	Melbourne	0					
62	01/02/87	Australia	Melbourne	11	1				
63	03/02/87	West Indies	Devonport	36					
64	08/02/87	Australia	Melbourne	15*					
65	11/02/87	Australia	Sydney	35					
66	21/05/87	Pakistan	The Oval	61	1				
67	23/05/87	Pakistan	Trent Bridge	26					
68	25/05/87	Pakistan	Edgbaston	14					
69	09/10/87	West Indies	Gujranwala	67*					
70	12/10/87	Pakistan	Rawalpindi	30					
71	17/10/87	Sri Lanka	Peshawar	76		1	0	3	0
72	20/10/87	Pakistan	Karachi	9					
73	26/10/87	West Indies	Jaipur	40					
74	30/10/87	Sri Lanka	Poona		1				
75	05/11/87	India	Bombay	32*	1				
76	08/11/87	Australia	Calcutta	45					
77	19/05/88	West Indies	Edgbaston	11	2				
78	21/05/88	West Indies	Headingley	2					
79	23/05/88	West Indies	Lord's	30*					
80	04/09/88	Sri Lanka	The Oval	66					
81	25/05/89	Australia	Old Trafford	35					
82	27/05/89	Australia	Trent Bridge	100*					
83	29/05/89	Australia	Lord's	0					
84	15/10/89	Sri Lanka	Delhi	52	1				
85	19/10/89	Australia	Hyderabad	23	1				
86	22/10/89	Pakistan	Cuttack	42	1				
87	25/10/89	India	Kanpur	91					
88	27/10/89	West Indies	Gwalior	0					
89	30/10/89	Pakistan	Nagpur	6	1				
90	14/02/90	West Indies	Port of Spain						
91	17/02/90	West Indies	Port of Spain						
92	03/03/90	West Indies	Kingston	66					
93	07/03/90	West Indies	Georgetown	22					
94	15/03/90	West Indies	Georgetown	9					
95	03/04/90	West Indies	Bridgetown	55*					
96	23/05/90	New Zealand	Headingley	18	1				
97	25/05/90	New Zealand	The Oval	4					
98	18/07/90	India	Headingley	56					
99	20/07/90	India	Trent Bridge	3					
100	01/12/90	New Zealand	Adelaide	49					
101	07/12/90	New Zealand	Perth	20	1				
102	09/12/90	Australia	Perth	3					
103	13/12/90	New Zealand	Sydney	72	1				
104	15/12/90	New Zealand	Brisbane	10					
105	16/12/90	Australia	Brisbane	35					
106	09/02/91	New Zealand	Christchurch	61					
107	13/02/91	New Zealand	Wellington	33					
108	16/02/91	New Zealand	Auckland	42	2				
109	23/05/91	West Indies	Edgbaston	18					
110	25/05/91	West Indies	Old Trafford	62					
111	11/01/92	New Zealand	Auckland	12					
112	12/02/92	New Zealand	Dunedin	40					
113	15/02/92	New Zealand	Christchurch	25					
114	15/03/92	New Zealand	Wellington	12					
115	18/03/92	Zimbabwe	Albury	17	1				

116	22/03/92	South Africa	Sydney	19	
117	25/03/92	Pakistan	Melbourne	31	
118	20/05/92	Pakistan	Lord's	60	
119	22/05/92	Pakistan	The Oval	11	
120	20/08/92	Pakistan	Trent Bridge	16	
121	22/08/92	Pakistan	Lord's	55	
122	24/08/92	Pakistan	Old Trafford	2	

Batting & Fielding

Mat	Inns	N/O	Runs	H/S	Avg	100s	50s	Cat
122	118	16	4010	118	39.31	4	26	31

Bowling

Overs	Mds	Runs	Wkts	Avg	Best	5WI	E/R
1	0	3	0	-	-	0	3.00

WAYNE LARKINS

Full Name: Wayne Larkins
Born: 22/11/53 - Roxton, Bedfordshire
Right-hand opening batsman - Right-arm medium bowler

No	Date	Opposition	Venue	Bat	C	Bowling			
1	20/06/79	New Zealand	Old Trafford	7					
2	23/06/79	West Indies	Lord's	0		2	0	21	0
3	14/01/80	Australia	Sydney	5	1				
4	16/01/80	West Indies	Adelaide	24					
5	20/01/80	West Indies	Melbourne	34	1				
6	22/01/80	West Indies	Sydney	14					
7	15/10/89	Sri Lanka	Delhi	19					
8	19/10/89	Australia	Hyderabad	124					
9	22/10/89	Pakistan	Cuttack	0					
10	25/10/89	India	Kanpur	42	1				
11	27/10/89	West Indies	Gwalior	29					
12	30/10/89	Pakistan	Nagpur	25					
13	14/02/90	West Indies	Port of Spain	2					
14	17/02/90	West Indies	Port of Spain						
15	03/03/90	West Indies	Kingston	33					
16	07/03/90	West Indies	Georgetown	34					
17	15/03/90	West Indies	Georgetown	1					
18	03/04/90	West Indies	Bridgetown	34	1				
19	07/12/90	New Zealand	Perth	44	1				
20	09/12/90	Australia	Perth	38		.3	0	1	0
21	13/12/90	New Zealand	Sydney	8					
22	15/12/90	New Zealand	Brisbane	15					
23	16/12/90	Australia	Brisbane	19	1				
24	01/01/91	Australia	Sydney	40	1				
25	10/01/91	Australia	Melbourne	0	1				

Batting & Fielding

Mat	Inns	N/O	Runs	H/S	Avg	100s	50s	Cat
25	24	0	591	124	24.62	1	0	8

Bowling

Overs	Mds	Runs	Wkts	Avg	Best	5WI	E/R
2.3	0	22	0	-	-	0	8.80

DAVID LAWRENCE

Full Name: David Valentine Lawrence
Born: 28/01/64 - Gloucester
Right-arm fast bowler - Right-hand lower order batsman

No	Date	Opposition	Venue	Bat	C	Bowling
1	27/05/91	West Indies	Lord's			11 1 67 4

Batting & Fielding

Mat	Inns	N/O	Runs	H/S	Avg	100s	50s	Cat
1	0	0	0	-	-	0	0	0

Bowling

Overs	Mds	Runs	Wkts	Avg	Best	5WI	E/R
11	1	67	4	16.75	4-67	0	6.09

JOHN LEVER

Full Name: John Kenneth Lever MBE
Born: 24/02/49 - Stepney, London
Left-arm fast medium bowler - Right-hand lower order batsman

No	Date	Opposition	Venue	Bat	C	Bowling
1	26/08/76	West Indies	Scarborough			9 1 38 0
2	30/08/76	West Indies	Edgbaston	1		10 1 57 2
3	02/06/77	Australia	Old Trafford	1		10 1 45 2
4	04/06/77	Australia	Edgbaston	27*		11 2 29 4
5	06/06/77	Australia	The Oval	2		10 0 43 1
6	30/12/77	Pakistan	Sialkot		1	*6 1 18 3
7	13/01/78	Pakistan	Lahore	0		*7 1 25 2
8	26/05/78	Pakistan	The Oval			7 1 17 0
9	15/07/78	New Zealand	Scarborough	5*		11 2 25 0
10	17/07/78	New Zealand	Old Trafford			7 0 28 1
11	13/01/79	Australia	Sydney			*3 0 8 0
12	24/01/79	Australia	Melbourne			*5 2 7 0
13	04/02/79	Australia	Melbourne			*7 1 51 3
14	07/02/79	Australia	Melbourne	1		*5 0 15 1
15	14/01/80	Australia	Sydney			9 1 11 2
16	16/01/80	West Indies	Adelaide	11		10 1 54 0
17	28/05/80	West Indies	Headingley	6	2	11 3 36 1
18	30/05/80	West Indies	Lord's	0*	2	7 1 23 0
19	25/11/81	India	Ahmedabad		1	10 0 46 0
20	20/12/81	India	Jullundur			7 0 31 0
21	27/01/82	India	Cuttack			10 0 55 0
22	14/02/82	Sri Lanka	Colombo	2*		9 0 51 2

Batting & Fielding

Mat	Inns	N/O	Runs	H/S	Avg	100s	50s	Cat
22	11	4	56	27*	8.00	0	0	6

Bowling

Overs	Mds	Runs	Wkts	Avg	Best	5WI	E/R
192	19	713	24	29.70	4-29	0	3.71

PETER LEVER

Full Name: Peter Lever
Born: 17/09/40 - Todmorden, Yorkshire
Right-arm fast medium bowler - Right-hand lower order batsman

No	Date	Opposition	Venue	Bat	C	Bowling		
1	05/01/71	Australia	Melbourne	4*		*5.6	0	30	0
2	20/07/73	New Zealand	Old Trafford					
3	31/08/74	Pakistan	Trent Bridge			10	0	58	1
4	03/09/74	Pakistan	Edgbaston	8*		4	0	22	0
5	01/01/75	Australia	Melbourne		1	*5	0	24	1
6	09/03/75	New Zealand	Wellington			*6.6	0	35	4
7	07/06/75	India	Lord's		1	10	0	16	1
8	11/06/75	New Zealand	Trent Bridge			12	0	37	1
9	14/06/75	East Africa	Edgbaston			12	3	32	3
10	18/06/75	Australia	Headingley	5		2	0	7	0

Batting & Fielding

Mat	Inns	N/O	Runs	H/S	Avg	100s	50s	Cat
10	3	2	17	8*	17.00	0	0	2

Bowling

Overs	Mds	Runs	Wkts	Avg	Best	5WI	E/R
73.2	3	261	11	23.72	4-35	0	3.55

CHRIS LEWIS

Full Name: Clairmonte Christopher Lewis
Born: 14/02/68 - Georgetown, Guyana
Right-arm fast medium bowler - Right-hand middle order batsman

No	Date	Opposition	Venue	Bat	C	Bowling		
1	14/02/90	West Indies	Port of Spain		1	7	1	30	1
2	17/02/90	West Indies	Port of Spain					
3	03/04/90	West Indies	Bridgetown			5	0	35	0
4	23/05/90	New Zealand	Headingley			11	0	54	3
5	25/05/90	New Zealand	The Oval			11	1	51	1
6	18/07/90	India	Headingley	6		10	0	58	2
7	20/07/90	India	Trent Bridge	7		10	0	54	1
8	01/12/90	New Zealand	Adelaide	6		8	0	39	0
9	07/12/90	New Zealand	Perth	0	1	9.2	1	26	3
10	09/12/90	Australia	Perth	2	2	8	1	36	0
11	13/12/90	New Zealand	Sydney	4		9.1	0	35	4
12	15/12/90	New Zealand	Brisbane	3		9.3	1	31	0
13	23/05/91	West Indies	Edgbaston	0	2	11	3	41	1
14	25/05/91	West Indies	Old Trafford			11	0	62	3
15	11/01/92	New Zealand	Auckland			8	0	33	2
16	12/02/92	New Zealand	Dunedin	18		9	0	32	1
17	15/02/92	New Zealand	Christchurch	0		6	1	21	1
18	22/02/92	India	Perth	10		9.2	0	36	0
19	27/02/92	West Indies	Melbourne			8.2	1	30	3
20	01/03/92	Pakistan	Adelaide					
21	05/03/92	Australia	Sydney		1	10	2	28	0
22	09/03/92	Sri Lanka	Ballarat	20*	1	8	0	30	4
23	12/03/92	South Africa	Melbourne	33				
24	15/03/92	New Zealand	Wellington	0				

No	Date	Opposition	Venue	Bat						
25	22/03/92	South Africa	Sydney	18*	2	5	0	38	0
26	25/03/92	Pakistan	Melbourne	0		10	2	52	0
27	20/05/92	Pakistan	Lord's	6*		8	1	35	0
28	22/05/92	Pakistan	The Oval		1	8	0	47	2
29	20/08/92	Pakistan	Trent Bridge	1*	1	8	2	24	1
30	22/08/92	Pakistan	Lord's	1		10	0	49	0
31	18/01/93	India	Jaipur	8*		9	0	26	1
32	21/01/93	India	Chandigarh	16*		10	0	47	1
33	26/02/93	India	Bangalore	19		10	0	32	1
34	01/03/93	India	Jamshedpur	25		5	0	25	1
35	04/03/93	India	Gwalior	4		10	0	56	0
36	05/03/93	India	Gwalior	3*		10	1	51	2
37	10/03/93	Sri Lanka	Colombo (2)	16		9	0	40	1
38	20/03/93	Sri Lanka	Moratuwa	8		7	1	13	0
39	19/05/93	Australia	Old Trafford	4	2	11	1	54	3
40	21/05/93	Australia	Edgbaston	13*		10.3	0	61	2
41	16/02/94	West Indies	Bridgetown	6*		8	2	18	3
42	26/02/94	West Indies	Kingston	0		9	0	48	0
43	02/03/94	West Indies	Arnos Vale	2	1	9	0	67	0
44	05/03/94	West Indies	Port of Spain	4		9.4	1	59	3
45	06/03/94	West Indies	Port of Spain	16*	1	10	0	35	4
46	19/05/94	New Zealand	Edgbaston	19	2	9.5	2	20	3
47	25/08/94	South Africa	Edgbaston			8	0	32	3
48	27/08/94	South Africa	Old Trafford	17*	2	9	0	44	0

Batting & Fielding

Mat	Inns	N/O	Runs	H/S	Avg	100s	50s	Cat
48	36	11	315	33	12.60	0	0	20

Bowling

Overs	Mds	Runs	Wkts	Avg	Best	5WI	E/R
391.4	25	1735	61	28.44	4-30	0	4.42

ANDY LLOYD

Full Name: Timothy Andrew Lloyd
Born: 05/11/56 - Oswestry, Shropshire
Left-hand middle order batsman - Right-arm medium bowler

No	Date	Opposition	Venue	Bat	C
1	31/05/84	West Indies	Old Trafford	15	
2	02/06/84	West Indies	Trent Bridge	49	
3	04/06/84	West Indies	Lord's	37	

Batting & Fielding

Mat	Inns	N/O	Runs	H/S	Avg	100s	50s	Cat
3	3	0	101	49	33.66	0	0	0

DAVID LLOYD

Full Name: David Lloyd
Born: 18/03/47 - Accrington, Lancashire
Left-hand opening/middle order batsman - Left-arm slow bowler

No	Date	Opposition	Venue	Bat	C	Bowling
1	07/09/73	West Indies	The Oval	8		
2	13/07/74	India	Headingley	34	1	
3	15/07/74	India	The Oval	39	1	
4	31/08/74	Pakistan	Trent Bridge	116*		
5	03/09/74	Pakistan	Edgbaston	4	1	
6	01/01/75	Australia	Melbourne	49		
7	26/05/78	Pakistan	The Oval	34		2 1 3 1
8	28/05/80	West Indies	Headingley	1		

Batting & Fielding

Mat	Inns	N/O	Runs	H/S	Avg	100s	50s	Cat
8	8	1	285	116*	40.71	1	0	3

Bowling

Overs	Mds	Runs	Wkts	Avg	Best	5WI	E/R
2	1	3	1	3.00	1-3	0	1.50

JAMES LOVE

Full Name: James Derek Love
Born: 22/04/55 - Headingley, Leeds, Yorkshire
Right-hand middle order batsman - Right-arm medium bowler

No	Date	Opposition	Venue	Bat	C
1	04/06/81	Australia	Lord's	15	
2	06/06/81	Australia	Edgbaston	43	1
3	08/06/81	Australia	Headingley	3	

Batting & Fielding

Mat	Inns	N/O	Runs	H/S	Avg	100s	50s	Cat
3	3	0	61	43	20.33	0	0	1

BRIAN LUCKHURST

Full Name: Brian William Luckhurst
Born: 05/02/39 - Sittingbourne, Kent
Right-hand opening batsman - Left-arm slow bowler

No	Date	Opposition	Venue	Bat	C
1	01/01/75	Australia	Melbourne	14	
2	08/03/75	New Zealand	Dunedin	0	
3	09/03/75	New Zealand	Wellington	1	

Batting & Fielding

Mat	Inns	N/O	Runs	H/S	Avg	100s	50s	Cat
3	3	0	15	14	5.00	0	0	0

MONTE LYNCH

Full Name: Monte Alan Lynch
Born: 21/05/58 - Georgetown, British Guiana
Right-hand middle order batsman - Off break bowler

No	Date	Opposition	Venue	Bat	C
1	19/05/88	West Indies	Edgbaston	0	
2	21/05/88	West Indies	Headingley	2	1
3	23/05/88	West Indies	Lord's	6	

Batting & Fielding

Mat	Inns	N/O	Runs	H/S	Avg	100s	50s	Cat
3	3	0	8	6	2.66	0	0	1

DEVON MALCOLM

Full Name: Devon Eugene Malcolm
Born: 22/02/63 - Kingston, Jamaica
Right-arm fast bowler - Right-hand lower order batsman

No	Date	Opposition	Venue	Bat	C	Bowling			
1	25/05/90	New Zealand	The Oval			11	5	19	2
2	18/07/90	India	Headingley	4		11	0	57	1
3	01/12/90	New Zealand	Adelaide	3*		9	0	39	2
4	15/12/90	New Zealand	Brisbane			8	0	56	1
5	26/02/93	India	Bangalore	0*		9	1	47	2
6	01/03/93	India	Jamshedpur			6	0	17	1
7	04/03/93	India	Gwalior	0		10	0	40	3
8	05/03/93	India	Gwalior			8	0	56	0
9	10/03/93	Sri Lanka	Colombo (2)	2		7	1	32	1
10	16/02/94	West Indies	Bridgetown		1	8.4	1	41	3

Batting & Fielding

Mat	Inns	N/O	Runs	H/S	Avg	100s	50s	Cat
10	5	2	9	4	3.00	0	0	1

Bowling

Overs	Mds	Runs	Wkts	Avg	Best	5WI	E/R
87.4	8	404	16	25.25	3-40	0	4.60

VIC MARKS

Full Name: Victor James Marks
Born: 25/06/55 - Middle Chinnock, Somerset
Off break bowler - Right-hand middle order batsman

No	Date	Opposition	Venue	Bat	C	Bowling			
1	30/05/80	West Indies	Lord's	9		11	1	44	2
2	11/01/83	Australia	Sydney	7*	1	10	1	27	2
3	13/01/83	New Zealand	Melbourne	5		9	0	47	1
4	15/01/83	New Zealand	Brisbane			10	2	30	3
5	16/01/83	Australia	Brisbane	3	1	10	0	46	0
6	20/01/83	New Zealand	Sydney			10	0	49	1

7	26/01/83	Australia	Sydney	22		6	0	12	2
8	29/01/83	New Zealand	Adelaide			7	1	28	0
9	30/01/83	Australia	Adelaide	10*		10	1	38	1
10	05/02/83	New Zealand	Perth	2					
11	19/02/83	New Zealand	Auckland	23*		10	1	30	0
12	23/02/83	New Zealand	Wellington	27		7	0	34	0
13	26/02/83	New Zealand	Christchurch	1	1	10	2	31	2
14	09/06/83	New Zealand	The Oval			12	1	39	2
15	11/06/83	Sri Lanka	Taunton	5		12	3	39	5
16	13/06/83	Pakistan	Lord's			12	1	33	1
17	15/06/83	New Zealand	Edgbaston	5		12	1	34	1
18	18/06/83	Pakistan	Old Trafford		1	12	0	45	2
19	20/06/83	Sri Lanka	Headingley		1	6	2	18	2
20	22/06/83	India	Old Trafford	8		12	1	38	0
21	18/02/84	New Zealand	Christchurch	28		10	1	33	2
22	22/02/84	New Zealand	Wellington		1	10	3	20	5
23	25/02/84	New Zealand	Auckland	3	1	10	1	27	1
24	09/03/84	Pakistan	Lahore	2		8	1	32	1
25	26/03/84	Pakistan	Karachi			8	1	22	0
26	05/12/84	India	Poona	31		10	0	48	0
27	27/12/84	India	Cuttack	44		8	0	50	3
28	20/01/85	India	Bangalore	17		10	1	35	3
29	23/01/85	India	Nagpur	4		6	0	32	0
30	27/01/85	India	Chandigarh	2					
31	17/02/85	Australia	Melbourne	24		7.2	0	33	1
32	26/02/85	India	Sydney	2	1	10	0	57	0
33	02/03/85	Pakistan	Melbourne	1		10	2	25	1
34	04/09/88	Sri Lanka	The Oval			11	0	59	0

Batting & Fielding

Mat	Inns	N/O	Runs	H/S	Avg	100s	50s	Cat
34	24	3	285	44	13.57	0	0	8

Bowling

Overs	Mds	Runs	Wkts	Avg	Best	5WI	E/R
306.2	28	1135	44	25.79	5-20	2	3.70

MATTHEW MAYNARD

Full Name: Matthew Peter Maynard
Born: 21/03/66 - Oldham, Lancashire
Right-hand middle order batsman - Right-arm medium bowler

No	Date	Opposition	Venue	Bat	C
1	16/02/94	West Indies	Bridgetown	22*	1
2	26/02/94	West Indies	Kingston	22	
3	02/03/94	West Indies	Arnos Vale	6	
4	05/03/94	West Indies	Port of Spain	8	
5	06/03/94	West Indies	Port of Spain	1	

Batting & Fielding

Mat	Inns	N/O	Runs	H/S	Avg	100s	50s	Cat
5	5	1	59	22*	14.75	0	0	1

GEOFF MILLER

Full Name: Geoffrey Miller
Born: 08/09/52 - Chesterfield, Derbyshire
Off break bowler - Right-hand middle order batsman

No	Date	Opposition	Venue	Bat	C		Bowling	
1	06/06/77	Australia	The Oval	4		5	0	24	0
2	23/12/77	Pakistan	Sahiwal	0*		*7	0	46	1
3	30/12/77	Pakistan	Sialkot	16		*6	1	43	1
4	24/05/78	Pakistan	Old Trafford	0					
5	26/05/78	Pakistan	The Oval	0		11	3	24	2
6	15/07/78	New Zealand	Scarborough	2		1	0	6	0
7	17/07/78	New Zealand	Old Trafford			11	4	27	2
8	13/06/79	Canada	Old Trafford			2	1	1	0
9	28/11/79	West Indies	Sydney	4		10	0	33	1
10	02/06/82	India	Headingley			10	0	29	0
11	04/06/82	India	The Oval	0		11	3	27	3
12	17/07/82	Pakistan	Trent Bridge			11	1	36	0
13	19/07/82	Pakistan	Old Trafford	26		11	1	56	2
14	11/01/83	Australia	Sydney	2		10	0	28	3
15	13/01/83	New Zealand	Melbourne	2	1	10	0	46	0
16	15/01/83	New Zealand	Brisbane			10	1	42	0
17	16/01/83	Australia	Brisbane	4		6	0	25	0
18	20/01/83	New Zealand	Sydney		2	10	0	51	1
19	23/01/83	Australia	Melbourne	1		8	0	42	0
20	19/02/83	New Zealand	Auckland	3		10	0	33	1
21	23/02/83	New Zealand	Wellington	46		10	0	51	1
22	26/02/83	New Zealand	Christchurch	7		7	1	32	1
23	31/05/84	West Indies	Old Trafford	7		11	1	32	3
24	02/06/84	West Indies	Trent Bridge	3*		10	2	44	2
25	04/06/84	West Indies	Lord's	10		9	1	35	1

Batting & Fielding

Mat	Inns	N/O	Runs	H/S	Avg	100s	50s	Cat
25	18	2	136	46	8.50	0	0	4

Bowling

Overs	Mds	Runs	Wkts	Avg	Best	5WI	E/R
211.2	20	813	25	32.52	3-27	0	3.84

JOHN MORRIS

Full Name: John Edward Morris
Born: 01/04/64 - Crewe, Cheshire
Right-hand middle order batsman - Right-arm medium bowler

No	Date	Opposition	Venue	Bat	C
1	01/12/90	New Zealand	Adelaide	63*	
2	07/12/90	New Zealand	Perth	31	
3	09/12/90	Australia	Perth	7	
4	13/12/90	New Zealand	Sydney	19	1
5	15/12/90	New Zealand	Brisbane	16	
6	16/12/90	Australia	Brisbane	13	1
7	01/01/91	Australia	Sydney	8	
8	10/01/91	Australia	Melbourne	10	

Batting & Fielding

Mat	Inns	N/O	Runs	H/S	Avg	100s	50s	Cat
8	8	1	167	63*	23.85	0	1	2

MARTYN MOXON

Full Name: Martyn Douglas Moxon
Born: 04/05/60 - Stairfoot, Barnsley, Yorkshire
Right-hand opening batsman - Right-arm medium bowler

No	Date	Opposition	Venue	Bat	C
1	23/01/85	India	Nagpur	70	
2	26/02/85	India	Sydney	48	
3	02/03/85	Pakistan	Melbourne	3	2
4	24/03/85	Australia	Sharjah	0	2
5	26/03/85	Pakistan	Sharjah	11	
6	09/03/88	New Zealand	Dunedin	6	1
7	12/03/88	New Zealand	Christchurch	17	
8	19/03/88	New Zealand	Auckland	19	

Batting & Fielding

Mat	Inns	N/O	Runs	H/S	Avg	100s	50s	Cat
8	8	0	174	70	21.75	0	1	5

CHRIS OLD

Full Name: Christopher Middleton Old
Born: 22/12/48 - Middlesbrough, Yorkshire
Right-arm fast medium bowler - Left-hand lower order batsman

No	Date	Opposition	Venue	Bat	C	Bowling		
1	05/09/73	West Indies	Headingley	4	1	11	1	43	3
2	07/09/73	West Indies	The Oval	21		10	0	52	0
3	13/07/74	India	Headingley	5*		10.5	0	43	3
4	15/07/74	India	The Oval			9.3	0	36	3
5	31/08/74	Pakistan	Trent Bridge	39	1	10	0	65	0
6	03/09/74	Pakistan	Edgbaston	0		5	0	25	0
7	01/01/75	Australia	Melbourne	12		*8	0	57	4
8	08/03/75	New Zealand	Dunedin	27					
9	09/03/75	New Zealand	Wellington			*6	0	32	1
10	07/06/75	India	Lord's	51*		12	4	26	1
11	11/06/75	New Zealand	Trent Bridge	20*	1	12	2	29	2
12	14/06/75	East Africa	Edgbaston	18		1.3	0	2	1
13	18/06/75	Australia	Headingley	0		7	2	29	3
14	02/06/77	Australia	Old Trafford	25		11	3	30	1
15	04/06/77	Australia	Edgbaston	35	2	7	2	15	1
16	06/06/77	Australia	The Oval	20		10.2	0	56	2
17	23/12/77	Pakistan	Sahiwal	1		*7	0	49	0
18	13/01/78	Pakistan	Lahore	4		*7	0	35	1
19	24/05/78	Pakistan	Old Trafford	6*		7	4	6	2
20	26/05/78	Pakistan	The Oval	25*	1	11	1	26	2
21	13/01/79	Australia	Sydney			*3.2	1	5	1
22	04/02/79	Australia	Melbourne	16*	1	*8	1	31	1
23	09/06/79	Australia	Lord's			12	2	33	1
24	13/06/79	Canada	Old Trafford			10	5	8	4
25	16/06/79	Pakistan	Headingley	2		12	2	28	1
26	20/06/79	New Zealand	Old Trafford	0		12	1	33	1
27	23/06/79	West Indies	Lord's	0	1	12	0	55	2
28	28/05/80	West Indies	Headingley	4		11	4	12	2
29	30/05/80	West Indies	Lord's			11	1	43	1

30	20/08/80	Australia	The Oval			9	0	43	0
31	22/08/80	Australia	Edgbaston	2*		11	2	44	0
32	04/02/81	West Indies	Arnos Vale	1		5	4	8	1

Batting & Fielding

Mat	Inns	N/O	Runs	H/S	Avg	100s	50s	Cat
32	25	7	338	51*	18.77	0	1	8

Bowling

Overs	Mds	Runs	Wkts	Avg	Best	5WI	E/R
292.3	42	999	45	22.20	4-8	0	3.41

PAT POCOCK

Full Name: Patrick Ian Pocock
Born: 24/09/46 - Bangor, Caernarvonshire
Off break bowler - Right-hand lower order batsman

No	Date	Opposition	Venue	Bat	C	Bowling			
1	26/03/85	Pakistan	Sharjah	4		10	1	20	0

Batting & Fielding

Mat	Inns	N/O	Runs	H/S	Avg	100s	50s	Cat
1	1	0	4	4	4.00	0	0	0

Bowling

Overs	Mds	Runs	Wkts	Avg	Best	5WI	E/R
10	1	20	0	-	-	0	2.00

DEREK PRINGLE

Full Name: Derek Raymond Pringle
Born: 18/09/58 - Nairobi, Kenya
Right-arm medium bowler - Right-hand middle order batsman

No	Date	Opposition	Venue	Bat	C	Bowling			
1	17/07/82	Pakistan	Trent Bridge			11	1	50	2
2	19/07/82	Pakistan	Old Trafford	34*		11	0	43	2
3	23/01/83	Australia	Melbourne			7	0	47	0
4	23/02/83	New Zealand	Wellington	11		7	0	57	0
5	31/05/84	West Indies	Old Trafford	6	1	11	0	64	0
6	02/06/84	West Indies	Trent Bridge	2*	2	10	3	21	3
7	04/06/84	West Indies	Lord's	8		8	0	38	1
8	24/03/85	Australia	Sharjah	4	1	10	0	49	2
9	26/03/85	Pakistan	Sharjah	13	1	7	1	32	2
10	24/05/86	India	The Oval	28		8.2	4	20	0
11	26/05/86	India	Old Trafford	49*		11	0	49	0
12	16/07/86	New Zealand	Headingley	28		9	0	42	0
13	18/07/86	New Zealand	Old Trafford	0*	1	10	2	63	1
14	09/10/87	West Indies	Gujranwala	12		10	0	83	0
15	12/10/87	Pakistan	Rawalpindi	8		10	0	54	0
16	17/10/87	Sri Lanka	Peshawar			4	0	11	1
17	19/05/88	West Indies	Edgbaston	23*		11	5	26	1
18	21/05/88	West Indies	Headingley	39		11	0	30	3
19	23/05/88	West Indies	Lord's			11	4	27	1

20	04/09/88	Sri Lanka	The Oval	19*	1	11	0	46	1
21	25/05/89	Australia	Old Trafford	9		8	2	19	1
22	27/05/89	Australia	Trent Bridge	25*		11	1	38	1
23	29/05/89	Australia	Lord's	0		10.3	0	50	1
24	19/10/89	Australia	Hyderabad			10	3	42	0
25	30/10/89	Pakistan	Nagpur	21*		5	0	33	0
26	23/05/90	New Zealand	Headingley	30*		7	0	45	0
27	23/05/91	West Indies	Edgbaston	1		7	0	22	0
28	25/05/91	West Indies	Old Trafford		1	11	2	52	2
29	27/05/91	West Indies	Lord's			9	0	56	0
30	11/01/92	New Zealand	Auckland			6	1	32	2
31	12/02/92	New Zealand	Dunedin	14*		10	2	31	1
32	15/02/92	New Zealand	Christchurch	5		6	2	11	2
33	22/02/92	India	Perth	1		10	0	53	0
34	27/02/92	West Indies	Melbourne		1	7	3	16	0
35	01/03/92	Pakistan	Adelaide		1	8.2	5	8	3
36	05/03/92	Australia	Sydney			9	1	24	1
37	09/03/92	Sri Lanka	Ballarat	0*		7	1	27	0
38	12/03/92	South Africa	Melbourne	1		9	2	34	0
39	15/03/92	New Zealand	Wellington	10		6.2	1	34	0
40	25/03/92	Pakistan	Melbourne	18*		10	2	22	3
41	20/05/92	Pakistan	Lord's		1	11	1	42	4
42	22/05/92	Pakistan	The Oval			9	1	35	2
43	19/05/93	Australia	Old Trafford	6		10	3	36	0
44	21/05/93	Australia	Edgbaston			11	0	63	1

Batting & Fielding
Mat	Inns	N/O	Runs	H/S	Avg	100s	50s	Cat
44	30	12	425	49*	23.61	0	0	11

Bowling
Overs	Mds	Runs	Wkts	Avg	Best	5WI	E/R
396.3	53	1677	44	38.11	4-42	0	4.22

NEAL RADFORD

Full Name: Neal Victor Radford
Born: 07/06/57 - Luanshya, Northern Rhodesia
Right-arm fast medium bowler - Right hand lower order batsman

No	Date	Opposition	Venue	Bat	C	Bowling			
1	04/02/88	Australia	Melbourne	0*		10	0	61	0
2	09/03/88	New Zealand	Dunedin			10	0	47	1
3	12/03/88	New Zealand	Christchurch			9	0	30	0
4	16/03/88	New Zealand	Napier	0		8	0	31	0
5	19/03/88	New Zealand	Auckland	0*	2	10	2	32	1
6	23/05/88	West Indies	Lord's			11	2	29	0

Batting & Fielding
Mat	Inns	N/O	Runs	H/S	Avg	100s	50s	Cat
6	3	2	0	0	0.00	0	0	2

Bowling
Overs	Mds	Runs	Wkts	Avg	Best	5WI	E/R
58	4	230	2	115.00	1-32	0	3.96

CLIVE RADLEY

Full Name: Clive Thornton Radley
Born: 13/05/44 - Hertford
Right-hand middle order batsman - Leg break bowler

No	Date	Opposition	Venue	Bat	C
1	24/05/78	Pakistan	Old Trafford	79	
2	26/05/78	Pakistan	The Oval	13	
3	15/07/78	New Zealand	Scarborough	41	
4	17/07/78	New Zealand	Old Trafford	117*	

Batting & Fielding

Mat	Inns	N/O	Runs	H/S	Avg	100s	50s	Cat
4	4	1	250	117*	83.33	1	1	0

MARK RAMPRAKASH

Full Name: Mark Ravin Ramprakash
Born: 05/09/69 - Bushey, Hertfordshire
Right-hand middle order batsman - Off break bowler

No	Date	Opposition	Venue	Bat	C
1	25/05/91	West Indies	Old Trafford	6*	
2	27/05/91	West Indies	Lord's	0*	
3	05/03/94	West Indies	Port of Spain	31	1
4	06/03/94	West Indies	Port of Spain	10	2

Batting & Fielding

Mat	Inns	N/O	Runs	H/S	Avg	100s	50s	Cat
4	4	2	47	31	23.50	0	0	3

DEREK RANDALL

Full Name: Derek William Randall
Born: 24/02/51 - Retford, Nottinghamshire
Right-hand middle order batsman - Right-arm medium bowler

No	Date	Opposition	Venue	Bat	C	Bowling
1	28/08/76	West Indies	Lord's	88	2	
2	30/08/76	West Indies	Edgbaston	39		
3	02/06/77	Australia	Old Trafford	19	1	
4	04/06/77	Australia	Edgbaston	0		
5	06/06/77	Australia	The Oval	6	1	
6	23/12/77	Pakistan	Sahiwal	35	1	
7	30/12/77	Pakistan	Sialkot	51*	1	
8	13/01/78	Pakistan	Lahore	32		
9	17/07/78	New Zealand	Old Trafford	41	2	
10	13/01/79	Australia	Sydney			
11	24/01/79	Australia	Melbourne	12	1	
12	04/02/79	Australia	Melbourne	4		
13	07/02/79	Australia	Melbourne	0		
14	09/06/79	Australia	Lord's	1		

No	Date	Opposition	Venue	Bat	C	Bowling		
15	13/06/79	Canada	Old Trafford	5				
16	16/06/79	Pakistan	Headingley	1				
17	20/06/79	New Zealand	Old Trafford	42*				
18	23/06/79	West Indies	Lord's	15	1			
19	28/11/79	West Indies	Sydney	49	1			
20	08/12/79	Australia	Melbourne	28	1			
21	11/12/79	Australia	Sydney	42	1	.2 0 2 1		
22	23/12/79	West Indies	Brisbane	0				
23	26/12/79	Australia	Sydney	1				
24	14/01/80	Australia	Sydney	0	2			
25	16/01/80	West Indies	Adelaide	16				
26	02/06/82	India	Headingley					
27	04/06/82	India	The Oval	24				
28	17/07/82	Pakistan	Trent Bridge					
29	19/07/82	Pakistan	Old Trafford	6	1			
30	11/01/83	Australia	Sydney	5	1			
31	13/01/83	New Zealand	Melbourne	8	2			
32	15/01/83	New Zealand	Brisbane	34	1			
33	16/01/83	Australia	Brisbane	57				
34	20/01/83	New Zealand	Sydney		1			
35	23/01/83	Australia	Melbourne	51*				
36	26/01/83	Australia	Sydney	47	1			
37	29/01/83	New Zealand	Adelaide	31				
38	30/01/83	Australia	Adelaide	49	1			
39	05/02/83	New Zealand	Perth	12				
40	19/02/83	New Zealand	Auckland	30				
41	23/02/83	New Zealand	Wellington	16				
42	26/02/83	New Zealand	Christchurch	2				
43	18/02/84	New Zealand	Christchurch	70				
44	22/02/84	New Zealand	Wellington	25*	1			
45	25/02/84	New Zealand	Auckland	11				
46	09/03/84	Pakistan	Lahore	16				
47	26/03/84	Pakistan	Karachi	19*				
48	04/06/84	West Indies	Lord's	8	1			
49	24/03/85	Australia	Sharjah	19				

Batting & Fielding

Mat	Inns	N/O	Runs	H/S	Avg	100s	50s	Cat
49	45	5	1067	88	26.67	0	5	25

Bowling

Overs	Mds	Runs	Wkts	Avg	Best	5WI	E/R
0.2	0	2	1	2.00	1-2	0	6.00

DERMOT REEVE

Full Name: Dermot Alexander Reeve
Born: 02/04/63 - Kowloon, Hong Kong
Right-arm medium bowler - Right-hand middle order batsman

No	Date	Opposition	Venue	Bat	C	Bowling		
1	27/05/91	West Indies	Lord's			11	1	43	0
2	11/01/92	New Zealand	Auckland			10	3	20	3
3	12/02/92	New Zealand	Dunedin	31*		8	1	19	1
4	15/02/92	New Zealand	Christchurch	2*	1	5	0	26	1
5	22/02/92	India	Perth	8*		6	0	38	3
6	27/02/92	West Indies	Melbourne		1	10	1	23	1
7	01/03/92	Pakistan	Adelaide		3	5	3	2	1

8	05/03/92	Australia	Sydney			1	0	3	1
9	09/03/92	Sri Lanka	Ballarat		1	4	0	14	2
10	12/03/92	South Africa	Melbourne	10		2.4	0	15	0
11	15/03/92	New Zealand	Wellington	21*		3	0	9	0
12	22/03/92	South Africa	Sydney	25*					
13	25/03/92	Pakistan	Melbourne	15		3	0	22	0
14	22/08/92	Pakistan	Lord's	6*		10	1	31	1
15	24/08/92	Pakistan	Old Trafford			11	1	57	1
16	18/01/93	India	Jaipur	2		10	0	37	0
17	21/01/93	India	Chandigarh	33*	2	6.1	0	33	1
18	26/02/93	India	Bangalore	13*		6	0	25	0
19	01/03/93	India	Jamshedpur	17*		6	0	32	0
20	04/03/93	India	Gwalior	3		6	0	37	0
21	05/03/93	India	Gwalior		2	8.4	0	64	0
22	10/03/93	Sri Lanka	Colombo (2)	16	1	9	1	47	1
23	20/03/93	Sri Lanka	Moratuwa	21		5	0	24	0
24	23/05/93	Australia	Lord's	2		11	1	50	1
25	19/05/94	New Zealand	Edgbaston	16		4	0	15	0

Batting & Fielding
Mat	Inns	N/O	Runs	H/S	Avg	100s	50s	Cat
25	17	9	241	33*	30.12	0	0	11

Bowling
Overs	Mds	Runs	Wkts	Avg	Best	5WI	E/R
161.3	13	686	18	38.11	3-20	0	4.24

STEVE RHODES

Full Name: Steven John Rhodes
Born: 17/06/64 - Dirk Hill, Bradford, Yorkshire
Right-hand middle order batsman - Wicket-keeper

No	Date	Opposition	Venue	Bat	C/S
1	25/05/89	Australia	Old Trafford	8	2
2	27/05/89	Australia	Trent Bridge		1
3	29/05/89	Australia	Lord's	1*	
4	19/05/94	New Zealand	Edgbaston	12	
5	25/08/94	South Africa	Edgbaston	0*	1
6	27/08/94	South Africa	Old Trafford	56	+1
7	06/12/94	Australia	Sydney	8	
8	07/01/95	Zimbabwe	Brisbane	20	3+1
9	10/01/95	Australia	Melbourne	2	2

Batting & Fielding
Mat	Inns	N/O	Runs	H/S	Avg	100s	50s	Cat	St
9	8	2	107	56	17.83	0	1	9	2

'JACK' RICHARDS

Full Name: Clifton James Richards
Born: 10/08/58 - Penzance, Cornwall
Right-hand middle/lower order batsman - Wicket-keeper

304   *England - The Complete One-Day International Record*

No	Date	Opposition	Venue	Bat	C/S
1	25/11/81	India	Ahmedabad		
2	20/12/81	India	Jullundur	0	
3	13/02/82	Sri Lanka	Colombo	3	1
4	16/07/86	New Zealand	Headingley	8	1
5	18/07/86	New Zealand	Old Trafford		
6	01/01/87	Australia	Perth	4	1
7	03/01/87	West Indies	Perth	50	1
8	05/01/87	Pakistan	Perth	0	
9	07/01/87	Pakistan	Perth	7*	1
10	17/01/87	West Indies	Brisbane		2
11	18/01/87	Australia	Brisbane	7	
12	22/01/87	Australia	Sydney	3	1+1
13	24/01/87	West Indies	Adelaide	18	
14	26/01/87	Australia	Adelaide	2	2
15	30/01/87	West Indies	Melbourne	8	1
16	02/04/87	India	Sharjah	14*	
17	07/04/87	Pakistan	Sharjah		3
18	09/04/87	Australia	Sharjah		
19	21/05/87	Pakistan	The Oval		
20	23/05/87	Pakistan	Trent Bridge	0	
21	25/05/87	Pakistan	Edgbaston	16	2
22	04/02/88	Australia	Melbourne	14*	

Batting & Fielding

Mat	Inns	N/O	Runs	H/S	Avg	100s	50s	Cat	St
22	16	3	154	50	11.84	0	1	16	1

TIM ROBINSON

Full Name: Robert Timothy Robinson
Born: 21/11/58 - Skegby, Sutton-in-Ashfield, Nottinghamshire
Right-hand opening/middle order batsman

No	Date	Opposition	Venue	Bat	C
1	05/12/84	India	Poona	15	
2	27/12/84	India	Cuttack	1	
3	20/01/85	India	Bangalore	2	
4	24/03/85	Australia	Sharjah	37	
5	26/03/85	Pakistan	Sharjah	9	2
6	01/06/85	Australia	Edgbaston	26	
7	03/06/85	Australia	Lord's	7	
8	18/02/86	West Indies	Kingston	0	
9	19/03/86	West Indies	Bridgetown	23	
10	31/03/86	West Indies	Port of Spain	55	
11	02/04/87	India	Sharjah	34	1
12	07/04/87	Pakistan	Sharjah	83	
13	09/04/87	Australia	Sharjah	5	1
14	09/10/87	West Indies	Gujranwala	12	
15	12/10/87	Pakistan	Rawalpindi	33	1
16	20/10/87	Pakistan	Karachi	16	
17	26/10/87	West Indies	Jaipur	13	
18	30/10/87	Sri Lanka	Poona	55	
19	05/11/87	India	Bombay	13	
20	08/11/87	Australia	Calcutta	0	
21	04/02/88	Australia	Melbourne	35	
22	09/03/88	New Zealand	Dunedin	17	

23	12/03/88	New Zealand	Christchurch	44	
24	16/03/88	New Zealand	Napier	36	1
25	19/03/88	New Zealand	Auckland	13	
26	04/09/88	Sri Lanka	The Oval	13	

Batting & Fielding

Mat	Inns	N/O	Runs	H/S	Avg	100s	50s	Cat
26	26	0	597	83	22.96	0	3	6

GRAHAM ROOPE

Full Name: Graham Richard James Roope
Born: 12/07/46 - Fareham, Hampshire
Right-hand middle order batsman - Right-arm medium bowler

No	Date	Opposition	Venue	Bat	C
1	18/07/73	New Zealand	Swansea	0	1
2	20/07/73	New Zealand	Old Trafford	44	
3	23/12/77	Pakistan	Sahiwal	29	
4	30/12/77	Pakistan	Sialkot	7	
5	13/01/78	Pakistan	Lahore	37	
6	24/05/78	Pakistan	Old Trafford	10	1
7	26/05/78	Pakistan	The Oval	35	
8	15/07/78	New Zealand	Scarborough	11	

Batting & Fielding

Mat	Inns	N/O	Runs	H/S	Avg	100s	50s	Cat
8	8	0	173	44	21.62	0	0	2

BRIAN ROSE

Full Name: Brian Charles Rose
Born: 04/06/50 - Dartford, Kent
Left-hand opening batsman - Left-arm medium bowler

No	Date	Opposition	Venue	Bat	C
1	23/12/77	Pakistan	Sahiwal	54	
2	30/12/77	Pakistan	Sialkot	45	1

Batting & Fielding

Mat	Inns	N/O	Runs	H/S	Avg	100s	50s	Cat
2	2	0	99	54	49.50	0	1	1

'JACK' RUSSELL

Full Name: Robert Charles Russell
Born: 15/08/63 - Stroud, Gloucestershire
Left-hand middle/lower order batsman - Wicket-keeper

No	Date	Opposition	Venue	Bat	C/S
1	22/11/87	Pakistan	Peshawar	2*	3
2	04/09/88	Sri Lanka	The Oval		
3	15/10/89	Sri Lanka	Delhi	10*	1
4	19/10/89	Australia	Hyderabad		
5	22/10/89	Pakistan	Cuttack	7*	1+1
6	25/10/89	India	Kanpur	10*	1+1
7	27/10/89	West Indies	Gwalior	8*	
8	14/02/90	West Indies	Port of Spain		1
9	17/02/90	West Indies	Port of Spain		
10	03/03/90	West Indies	Kingston	2	1
11	07/03/90	West Indies	Georgetown	28	1
12	15/03/90	West Indies	Georgetown	19	
13	03/04/90	West Indies	Bridgetown		1
14	23/05/90	New Zealand	Headingley	13	1+1
15	25/05/90	New Zealand	The Oval	47*	1
16	18/07/90	India	Headingley	14	
17	20/07/90	India	Trent Bridge	50	+1
18	01/12/90	New Zealand	Adelaide	7	2
19	07/12/90	New Zealand	Perth	5	3
20	09/12/90	Australia	Perth	13	1
21	09/02/91	New Zealand	Christchurch	10	2
22	13/02/91	New Zealand	Wellington	2	2+1
23	16/02/91	New Zealand	Auckland	13	
24	23/05/91	West Indies	Edgbaston	1	2
25	25/05/91	West Indies	Old Trafford		1
26	27/05/91	West Indies	Lord's		1

Batting & Fielding

Mat	Inns	N/O	Runs	H/S	Avg	100s	50s	Cat	St
26	19	6	261	50	20.07	0	1	26	5

IAN SALISBURY

Full Name: Ian David Kenneth Salisbury
Born: 21/01/70 - Northampton
Leg break and googly bowler - Right-hand lower order batsman

No	Date	Opposition	Venue	Bat	C	Bowling			
1	21/01/93	India	Chandigarh			8	1	42	0
2	20/03/93	Sri Lanka	Moratuwa	2*	1	4	0	36	2
3	05/03/94	West Indies	Port of Spain	5		9	0	58	0
4	06/03/94	West Indies	Port of Spain			10	0	41	3

Batting & Fielding

Mat	Inns	N/O	Runs	H/S	Avg	100s	50s	Cat
4	2	1	7	5	7.00	0	0	1

Bowling

Overs	Mds	Runs	Wkts	Avg	Best	5WI	E/R
31	1	177	5	35.40	3-41	0	5.70

KEN SHUTTLEWORTH

Full Name: Kenneth Shuttleworth
Born: 13/11/44 - St Helens, Lancashire
Right-arm fast bowler - Right-hand lower order batsman

No	Date	Opposition	Venue	Bat	C		Bowling		
1	05/01/71	Australia	Melbourne	7	1	*7	0	29	1

Batting & Fielding

Mat	Inns	N/O	Runs	H/S	Avg	100s	50s	Cat
1	1	0	7	7	7.00	0	0	1

Bowling

Overs	Mds	Runs	Wkts	Avg	Best	5WI	E/R
9.2	0	29	1	29.00	1-29	0	3.10

WILF SLACK

Full Name: Wilfred Norris Slack
Born: 12/12/54 - Troumaca, St Vincent
Died: 15/01/89 - Banjul, The Gambia
Left-hand opening batsman - Right-arm medium bowler

No	Date	Opposition	Venue	Bat	C
1	04/03/86	West Indies	Port of Spain	34	
2	19/03/86	West Indies	Bridgetown	9	

Batting & Fielding

Mat	Inns	N/O	Runs	H/S	Avg	100s	50s	Cat
2	2	0	43	34	21.50	0	0	0

GLADSTONE SMALL

Full Name: Gladstone Cleophas Small
Born: 18/10/61 - Brighton, St George, Barbados
Right-arm fast medium bowler - Right-hand lower order batsman

No	Date	Opposition	Venue	Bat	C		Bowling		
1	01/01/87	Australia	Perth			9	0	62	1
2	03/01/87	West Indies	Perth	8*		10	1	37	2
3	05/01/87	Pakistan	Perth			10	0	41	0
4	07/01/87	Pakistan	Perth			10	0	28	3
5	17/01/87	West Indies	Brisbane			10	1	29	1
6	18/01/87	Australia	Brisbane	2		10	0	57	1
7	24/01/87	West Indies	Adelaide			10	1	46	1
8	26/01/87	Australia	Adelaide	2		10	0	42	0
9	30/01/87	West Indies	Melbourne	1*		10	3	16	0
10	01/02/87	Australia	Melbourne	4		10	0	49	1
11	03/02/87	West Indies	Devonport	6*		10	0	35	1
12	07/04/87	Pakistan	Sharjah			10	2	25	0
13	09/04/87	Australia	Sharjah			9	1	23	1

308 England - The Complete One Day International Record

No	Date	Opposition	Venue	Bat	C	Bowling		
14	09/10/87	West Indies	Gujranwala			10	0	45	1
15	12/10/87	Pakistan	Rawalpindi	0		10	1	47	2
16	17/10/87	Sri Lanka	Peshawar			7	0	27	0
17	20/10/87	Pakistan	Karachi	0		9	0	63	0
18	26/10/87	West Indies	Jaipur			10	0	61	1
19	30/10/87	Sri Lanka	Poona			10	1	33	1
20	05/11/87	India	Bombay			6	0	22	1
21	08/11/87	Australia	Calcutta	3*		6	0	33	0
22	19/05/88	West Indies	Edgbaston			11	0	31	4
23	21/05/88	West Indies	Headingley	7*		9	2	11	2
24	23/05/88	West Indies	Lord's			10	1	34	0
25	04/09/88	Sri Lanka	The Oval			11	1	44	3
26	15/10/89	Sri Lanka	Delhi			6	0	26	0
27	19/10/89	Australia	Hyderabad			10	0	55	1
28	22/10/89	Pakistan	Cuttack	0*		8	2	29	1
29	25/10/89	India	Kanpur	0*		10	0	44	1
30	27/10/89	West Indies	Gwalior	4		10	0	39	3
31	30/10/89	Pakistan	Nagpur			5.3	0	30	1
32	14/02/90	West Indies	Port of Spain			10	1	41	2
33	17/02/90	West Indies	Port of Spain			3	1	7	0
34	03/03/90	West Indies	Kingston	0	1	9	0	37	2
35	07/03/90	West Indies	Georgetown	18*		9.2	1	43	0
36	15/03/90	West Indies	Georgetown	0		7	0	32	1
37	03/04/90	West Indies	Bridgetown			9	1	29	3
38	23/05/90	New Zealand	Headingley			11	1	43	1
39	25/05/90	New Zealand	The Oval		1	11	0	59	1
40	20/07/90	India	Trent Bridge	4		10	0	73	1
41	01/12/90	New Zealand	Adelaide	5		7	1	25	2
42	07/12/90	New Zealand	Perth	9*	1	10	1	30	2
43	09/12/90	Australia	Perth	5		4.3	0	14	1
44	01/01/91	Australia	Sydney	15	2	10	1	43	0
45	10/01/91	Australia	Melbourne	0	1	10	2	50	1
46	16/02/91	New Zealand	Auckland	0		10	2	51	0
47	15/02/92	New Zealand	Christchurch			8	0	46	1
48	01/03/92	Pakistan	Adelaide			10	1	29	2
49	12/03/92	South Africa	Melbourne			2	0	14	0
50	15/03/92	New Zealand	Wellington			4	0	13	0
51	18/03/92	Zimbabwe	Albury	5		9	1	20	1
52	22/03/92	South Africa	Sydney			10	1	51	2
53	20/08/92	Pakistan	Trent Bridge		1	5.1	0	28	1

Batting & Fielding

Mat	Inns	N/O	Runs	H/S	Avg	100s	50s	Cat
53	24	9	98	18*	6.53	0	0	7

Bowling

Overs	Mds	Runs	Wkts	Avg	Best	5WI	E/R
465.3	33	1942	58	33.48	4-31	0	4.17

CHRIS SMITH

Full Name: Christopher Lyall Smith
Born: 15/10/58 - Durban, South Africa
Right-hand opening batsman - Off break bowler

No	Date	Opposition	Venue	Bat	C	Bowling
1	18/02/84	New Zealand	Christchurch	17		
2	22/02/84	New Zealand	Wellington	70		

| 3 | 25/02/84 | New Zealand | Auckland | 5 | | 3 | 0 | 20 | 0 |
| 4 | 26/03/84 | Pakistan | Karachi | 17 | | 3 | 0 | 8 | 2 |

Batting & Fielding

Mat	Inns	N/O	Runs	H/S	Avg	100s	50s	Cat
4	4	0	109	70	27.25	0	1	0

Bowling

Overs	Mds	Runs	Wkts	Avg	Best	5WI	E/R
6	0	28	2	14.00	2-8	0	4.66

DAVID SMITH

Full Name: David Mark Smith
Born: 09/01/56 - Balham, London
Left-hand middle order batsman - Right-arm medium bowler

No	Date	Opposition	Venue	Bat	C
1	04/03/86	West Indies	Port of Spain	10*	
2	03/04/90	West Indies	Bridgetown	5	

Batting & Fielding

Mat	Inns	N/O	Runs	H/S	Avg	100s	50s	Cat
2	2	1	15	10*	15.00	0	0	0

MICHAEL SMITH

Full Name: Michael John Smith
Born: 04/01/42 - Enfield, Middlesex
Right-hand opening batsman - Left-arm slow bowler

No	Date	Opposition	Venue	Bat	C
1	05/09/73	West Indies	Headingley	31	
2	07/09/73	West Indies	The Oval	19	
3	15/07/74	India	The Oval	6	1
4	31/08/74	Pakistan	Trent Bridge	14	
5	03/09/74	Pakistan	Edgbaston	0	

Batting & Fielding

Mat	Inns	N/O	Runs	H/S	Avg	100s	50s	Cat
5	5	0	70	31	14.00	0	0	1

ROBIN SMITH

Full Name: Robin Arnold Smith
Born: 13/09/63 - Durban, South Africa
Right-hand middle order batsman - Off break bowler

No	Date	Opposition	Venue	Bat	C
1	04/09/88	Sri Lanka	The Oval	9	

310   England - The Complete One Day International Record

2	25/05/89	Australia	Old Trafford	35	1
3	27/05/89	Australia	Trent Bridge	3	
4	29/05/89	Australia	Lord's	21	
5	15/10/89	Sri Lanka	Delhi	81*	
6	19/10/89	Australia	Hyderabad	24*	
7	22/10/89	Pakistan	Cuttack	19	
8	25/10/89	India	Kanpur	0	
9	27/10/89	West Indies	Gwalior	65	1
10	30/10/89	Pakistan	Nagpur	55	1
11	14/02/90	West Indies	Port of Spain	6*	1
12	15/02/90	West Indies	Port of Spain		
13	03/03/90	West Indies	Kingston	43	2
14	07/03/90	West Indies	Georgetown	18	
15	15/03/90	West Indies	Georgetown	1	
16	03/04/90	West Indies	Bridgetown	69	1
17	23/05/90	New Zealand	Headingley	128	
18	25/05/90	New Zealand	The Oval	5	2
19	18/07/90	India	Headingley	6	
20	20/07/90	India	Trent Bridge	103	
21	01/12/90	New Zealand	Adelaide	8	
22	07/12/90	New Zealand	Perth	0	
23	09/12/90	Australia	Perth	37	
24	13/12/90	New Zealand	Sydney	4	1
25	15/12/90	New Zealand	Brisbane	41	
26	16/12/90	Australia	Brisbane	6	
27	01/01/91	Australia	Sydney	1	
28	10/01/91	Australia	Melbourne	7	
29	09/02/91	New Zealand	Christchurch	65	1
30	13/02/91	New Zealand	Wellington	38	1
31	16/02/91	New Zealand	Auckland	35	
32	11/01/92	New Zealand	Auckland	61*	
33	12/02/92	New Zealand	Dunedin	17	
34	15/02/92	New Zealand	Christchurch	85	1
35	22/02/92	India	Perth	91	
36	27/02/92	West Indies	Melbourne	8	
37	01/03/92	Pakistan	Adelaide	5*	
38	05/03/92	Australia	Sydney	30*	
39	09/03/92	Sri Lanka	Ballarat	19	1
40	12/03/92	South Africa	Melbourne	0	2
41	15/03/92	New Zealand	Wellington	38	
42	18/03/92	Zimbabwe	Albury	2	
43	20/05/92	Pakistan	Lord's	85	1
44	22/05/92	Pakistan	The Oval	7	
45	20/08/92	Pakistan	Trent Bridge	77	
46	22/08/92	Pakistan	Lord's	4	
47	24/08/92	Pakistan	Old Trafford	85*	1
48	18/01/93	India	Jaipur	16	
49	21/01/93	India	Chandigarh	42	
50	26/02/93	India	Bangalore	29	
51	01/03/93	India	Jamshedpur	17	
52	04/03/93	India	Gwalior	129	
53	05/03/93	India	Gwalior	72	
54	10/03/93	Sri Lanka	Colombo (2)	3	
55	20/03/93	Sri Lanka	Moratuwa	31	
56	19/05/93	Australia	Old Trafford	9	
57	21/05/93	Australia	Edgbaston	167*	
58	23/05/93	Australia	Lord's	6	
59	16/02/94	West Indies	Bridgetown	12	1
60	26/02/94	West Indies	Kingston	56	1
61	02/03/94	West Indies	Arnos Vale	18	2
62	05/03/94	West Indies	Port of Spain	45	
63	06/03/94	West Indies	Port of Spain	4	1

| 64 | 19/05/94 | New Zealand | Edgbaston | 15 | | | | |

Batting & Fielding

Mat	Inns	N/O	Runs	H/S	Avg	100s	50s	Cat
64	63	8	2218	167*	40.32	4	13	23

JOHN SNOW

Full Name: John Augustine Snow
Born: 13/10/41 - Peopleton, Worcestershire
Right-arm fast medium bowler - Right-hand lower order batsman

No	Date	Opposition	Venue	Bat	C	Bowling		
1	05/01/71	Australia	Melbourne	2	*8	0	38	0
2	24/08/72	Australia	Old Trafford		11	1	33	1
3	26/08/72	Australia	Lord's	5*	11	2	35	3
4	28/08/72	Australia	Edgbaston	0*	11	0	29	0
5	18/07/73	New Zealand	Swansea		1	10	0	32	4
6	20/07/73	New Zealand	Old Trafford					
7	07/06/75	India	Lord's		12	2	24	0
8	14/06/75	East Africa	Edgbaston		12	6	11	4
9	18/06/75	Australia	Headingley	2	12	0	30	2

Batting & Fielding

Mat	Inns	N/O	Runs	H/S	Avg	100s	50s	Cat
9	4	2	9	5*	4.50	0	0	1

Bowling

Overs	Mds	Runs	Wkts	Avg	Best	5WI	E/R
89.4	11	232	14	16.57	4-11	0	2.58

DAVID STEELE

Full Name: David Stanley Steele
Born: 29/09/41 - Bradeley, Staffordshire
Right-hand middle order batsman - Left-arm slow bowler

No	Date	Opposition	Venue	Bat	C	Bowling		
1	26/08/76	West Indies	Scarborough	8	1	0	9	0

Batting & Fielding

Mat	Inns	N/O	Runs	H/S	Avg	100s	50s	Cat
1	1	0	8	8	8.00	0	0	0

Bowling

Overs	Mds	Runs	Wkts	Avg	Best	5WI	E/R
1	0	9	0	-	-	0	9.00

312 England - The Complete One Day International Record

GRAHAM STEVENSON

Full Name: Graham Barry Stevenson
Born: 16/12/55 - Ackworth, Yorkshire
Right-arm medium bowler - Right-hand lower order batsman

No	Date	Opposition	Venue	Bat	C	Bowling			
1	14/01/80	Australia	Sydney	28*		9.4	0	33	4
2	16/01/80	West Indies	Adelaide	1		8	1	53	1
3	04/02/81	West Indies	Arnos Vale	6*	1	8.2	2	18	2
4	26/02/81	West Indies	Berbice	8*	1	6	0	21	0

Batting & Fielding

Mat	Inns	N/O	Runs	H/S	Avg	100s	50s	Cat
4	4	3	43	28*	43.00	0	0	2

Bowling

Overs	Mds	Runs	Wkts	Avg	Best	5WI	E/R
32	3	125	7	17.85	4-33	0	3.90

ALEC STEWART

Full Name: Alec James Stewart
Born: 08/04/63 - Merton, Surrey
Right-hand opening/middle order batsman - Wicket-keeper

No	Date	Opposition	Venue	Bat	C/S
1	15/10/89	Sri Lanka	Delhi	4	1
2	19/10/89	Australia	Hyderabad	4*	
3	22/10/89	Pakistan	Cuttack	31	
4	25/10/89	India	Kanpur	61	
5	27/10/89	West Indies	Gwalior	20	1
6	30/10/89	Pakistan	Nagpur	0	
7	14/02/90	West Indies	Port of Spain		2
8	17/02/90	West Indies	Port of Spain		
9	03/03/90	West Indies	Kingston	0	
10	07/03/90	West Indies	Georgetown	0	
11	15/03/90	West Indies	Georgetown	13	
12	23/05/90	New Zealand	Headingley	33	1
13	25/05/90	New Zealand	The Oval	28	
14	07/12/90	New Zealand	Perth	29*	
15	09/12/90	Australia	Perth	41	
16	13/12/90	New Zealand	Sydney	42	2
17	15/12/90	New Zealand	Brisbane	30*	1
18	16/12/90	Australia	Brisbane	40	
19	01/01/91	Australia	Sydney	18	1
20	10/01/91	Australia	Melbourne	55	2
21	09/02/91	New Zealand	Christchurch	40	
22	13/02/91	New Zealand	Wellington	5	
23	16/02/91	New Zealand	Auckland	3	
24	11/01/92	New Zealand	Auckland		2
25	12/02/92	New Zealand	Dunedin	0	1
26	15/02/92	New Zealand	Christchurch	13	1
27	22/02/92	India	Perth	13	2
28	27/02/92	West Indies	Melbourne	0*	1
29	01/03/92	Pakistan	Adelaide		3
30	05/03/92	Australia	Sydney		
31	09/03/92	Sri Lanka	Ballarat	59	1

No	Date	Opposition	Venue	Bat	C			
32	12/03/92	South Africa	Melbourne	77				
33	15/03/92	New Zealand	Wellington	41				
34	18/03/92	Zimbabwe	Albury	29	+1			
35	22/03/92	South Africa	Sydney	33				
36	25/03/92	Pakistan	Melbourne	7	1			
37	20/05/92	Pakistan	Lord's	50	2+1			
38	22/05/92	Pakistan	The Oval	103				
39	20/08/92	Pakistan	Trent Bridge	34	1+1			
40	22/08/92	Pakistan	Lord's	0	2			
41	24/08/92	Pakistan	Old Trafford	51				
42	18/01/93	India	Jaipur	91				
43	21/01/93	India	Chandigarh	7				
44	26/02/93	India	Bangalore	14	1			
45	04/03/93	India	Gwalior	33	1			
46	05/03/93	India	Gwalior	11				
47	10/03/93	Sri Lanka	Colombo	5	1			
48	20/03/93	Sri Lanka	Moratuwa	14	1			
49	19/05/93	Australia	Old Trafford	22	1			
50	21/05/93	Australia	Edgbaston	0	1			
51	23/05/93	Australia	Lord's	74	3			
52	16/02/94	West Indies	Bridgetown	11				
53	26/02/94	West Indies	Kingston	66	+1			
54	02/03/94	West Indies	Arnos Vale	13	1			
55	05/03/94	West Indies	Port of Spain	2	1			
56	06/03/94	West Indies	Port of Spain	53	2			
57	19/05/94	New Zealand	Edgbaston	24	2			
58	25/08/94	South Africa	Edgbaston	32				
59	27/08/94	South Africa	Old Trafford	11				
60	06/12/94	Australia	Sydney	48				
61	15/12/94	Zimbabwe	Sydney	29	4			

Batting & Fielding

Mat	Inns	N/O	Runs	H/S	Avg	100s	50s	Cat	St
61	56	4	1567	103	30.13	1	10	47	4

CHRIS TAVARE

Full Name: Christopher James Tavare
Born: 27/10/54 - Orpington, Kent
Right-hand opening/middle order batsman - Off break bowler

No	Date	Opposition	Venue	Bat	C	Bowling			
1	28/05/80	West Indies	Headingley	82*	1				
2	30/05/80	West Indies	Lord's	5					
3	27/01/82	India	Cuttack	11					
4	14/02/82	Sri Lanka	Colombo	5					
5	02/06/82	India	Headingley	66	2				
6	04/06/82	India	The Oval	27		2	0	3	0
7	17/07/82	Pakistan	Trent Bridge	48					
8	19/07/82	Pakistan	Old Trafford	16					
9	11/01/83	Australia	Sydney	6					
10	13/01/83	New Zealand	Melbourne	16					
11	15/01/83	New Zealand	Brisbane	24					
12	20/01/83	New Zealand	Sydney	83*					
13	23/01/83	Australia	Melbourne	20					
14	26/01/83	Australia	Sydney	14					
15	29/01/83	New Zealand	Adelaide	16					
16	30/01/83	Australia	Adelaide	18					

17	05/02/83	New Zealand	Perth	0	1
18	19/02/83	New Zealand	Auckland	11	
19	23/02/83	New Zealand	Wellington	32	
20	26/02/83	New Zealand	Christchurch	4	
21	09/06/83	New Zealand	The Oval	45	
22	11/06/83	Sri Lanka	Taunton	32	1
23	13/06/83	Pakistan	Lord's	8	1
24	15/06/83	New Zealand	Edgbaston	18	
25	18/06/83	Pakistan	Old Trafford	58	
26	20/06/83	Sri Lanka	Headingley	19	
27	22/06/83	India	Old Trafford	32	
28	09/03/84	Pakistan	Lahore	4	1
29	26/03/84	Pakistan	Karachi		

Batting & Fielding

Mat	Inns	N/O	Runs	H/S	Avg	100s	50s	Cat
29	28	2	720	83*	27.69	0	4	7

Bowling

Overs	Mds	Runs	Wkts	Avg	Best	5WI	E/R
2	0	3	0	-	-	0	1.50

BOB TAYLOR

Full Name: Robert William Taylor MBE
Born: 17/07/41 - Stoke-on-Trent, Staffordshire
Right-hand lower order batsman - Wicket-keeper

No	Date	Opposition	Venue	Bat	C/S
1	05/09/73	West Indies	Headingley	8	2+1
2	07/09/73	West Indies	The Oval	3	1
3	03/09/74	Pakistan	Edgbaston	26*	
4	08/03/75	New Zealand	Dunedin	23*	
5	09/03/75	New Zealand	Wellington		1
6	30/12/77	Pakistan	Sialkot		2
7	13/01/78	Pakistan	Lahore	12	+1
8	24/05/78	Pakistan	Old Trafford		1
9	26/05/78	Pakistan	The Oval		1+1
10	15/07/78	New Zealand	Scarborough	0	2+1
11	17/07/78	New Zealand	Old Trafford		1+1
12	09/06/79	Australia	Lord's		1
13	13/06/79	Canada	Old Trafford		
14	16/06/79	Pakistan	Headingley	20*	2
15	20/06/79	New Zealand	Old Trafford	12	
16	23/06/79	West Indies	Lord's	0	1
17	27/01/82	India	Cuttack	2*	+1
18	14/02/82	Sri Lanka	Colombo	3	2
19	02/06/82	India	Headingley		4
20	04/06/82	India	The Oval	3*	1
21	17/07/82	Pakistan	Trent Bridge		
22	19/07/82	Pakistan	Old Trafford	1*	
23	11/01/83	Australia	Sydney	2	2
24	13/01/83	New Zealand	Melbourne	5*	
25	18/02/84	New Zealand	Christchurch	2	2
26	22/02/84	New Zealand	Wellington		
27	25/02/84	New Zealand	Auckland	8	

Batting & Fielding

Mat	Inns	N/O	Runs	H/S	Avg	100s	50s	Cat	St
27	17	7	130	26*	13.00	0	0	26	6

LES TAYLOR

Full Name: Leslie Brian Taylor
Born: 25/10/53 - Earl Shilton, Leicestershire
Right-arm fast medium bowler - Right-hand lower order batsman

No	Date	Opposition	Venue	Bat	C	Bowling
1	18/02/86	West Indies	Kingston			7 2 17 0
2	24/05/86	India	The Oval	1*		7 1 30 0

Batting & Fielding

Mat	Inns	N/O	Runs	H/S	Avg	100s	50s	Cat
2	1	1	1	1*	-	0	0	0

Bowling

Overs	Mds	Runs	Wkts	Avg	Best	5WI	E/R
14	3	47	0	-	-	0	3.35

PAUL TAYLOR

Full Name: Jonathan Paul Taylor
Born: 08/08/64 - Ashby-de-la-Zouch, Leicestershire
Left-arm fast medium bowler - Left-hand lower order batsman

No	Date	Opposition	Venue	Bat	C	Bowling
1	20/03/93	Sri Lanka	Moratuwa	1	3	0 20 0

Batting & Fielding

Mat	Inns	N/O	Runs	H/S	Avg	100s	50s	Cat
1	1	0	1	1	1.00	0	0	0

Bowling

Overs	Mds	Runs	Wkts	Avg	Best	5WI	E/R
3	0	20	0	-	-	0	6.66

GREG THOMAS

Full Name: John Gregory Thomas
Born: 12/08/60 - Trebanos, Glamorgan
Right-arm fast bowler - Right-hand lower order batsman

No	Date	Opposition	Venue	Bat	C	Bowling
1	18/02/86	West Indies	Kingston	0*		8 1 35 1
2	19/03/86	West Indies	Bridgetown	0		7 1 50 0
3	25/05/87	Pakistan	Edgbaston	1*		11 0 59 2

Batting & Fielding

Mat	Inns	N/O	Runs	H/S	Avg	100s	50s	Cat
3	3	2	1	1*	1.00	0	0	0

Bowling

Overs	Mds	Runs	Wkts	Avg	Best	5WI	E/R
26	2	144	3	48.00	2-59	0	5.53

GRAHAM THORPE

Full Name: Graham Paul Thorpe
Born: 01/08/69 - Farnham, Surrey
Left-hand middle order batsman - Right-arm medium bowler

No	Date	Opposition	Venue	Bat	C
1	19/05/93	Australia	Old Trafford	31	1
2	21/05/93	Australia	Edgbaston	36	
3	23/05/93	Australia	Lord's	22	
4	16/02/94	West Indies	Bridgetown	4	3
5	25/08/94	South Africa	Edgbaston	26	1
6	27/08/94	South Africa	Old Trafford	55	
7	06/12/94	Australia	Sydney	21	
8	15/12/94	Zimbabwe	Sydney	0	
9	07/01/95	Zimbabwe	Brisbane	89	
10	10/01/95	Australia	Melbourne	8	

Batting & Fielding

Mat	Inns	N/O	Runs	H/S	Avg	100s	50s	Cat
10	10	0	292	89	29.20	0	2	5

FRED TITMUS

Full Name: Frederick John Titmus MBE
Born: 24/11/32 - Kentish Town, London
Off break bowler - Right-hand middle order batsman

No	Date	Opposition	Venue	Bat	C	Bowling			
1	08/03/75	New Zealand	Dunedin	11					
2	09/03/75	New Zealand	Wellington		1	*7	0	53	3

Batting & Fielding

Mat	Inns	N/O	Runs	H/S	Avg	100s	50s	Cat
2	1	0	11	11	11.00	0	0	1

Bowling

Overs	Mds	Runs	Wkts	Avg	Best	5WI	E/R
9.2	0	53	3	17.66	3-53	0	5.67

ROGER TOLCHARD

Full Name: Roger William Tolchard
Born: 15/06/46 - Torquay, Devon
Right-hand middle order batsman - Wicket-keeper

No	Date	Opposition	Venue	Bat	C
1	13/01/79	Australia	Sydney		1

Batting & Fielding

Mat	Inns	N/O	Runs	H/S	Avg	100s	50s	Cat
1	0	0	0	-	-	0	0	1

PHIL TUFNELL

Full Name: Philip Clive Roderick Tufnell
Born: 29/04/66 - Barnet, Hertfordshire
Left-arm slow bowler - Right-hand lower order batsman

No	Date	Opposition	Venue	Bat	C	Bowling			
1	07/12/90	New Zealand	Perth			10	1	31	1
2	09/12/90	Australia	Perth			10	1	49	1
3	13/12/90	New Zealand	Sydney	2		10	1	27	0
4	15/12/90	New Zealand	Brisbane			10	0	43	1
5	16/12/90	Australia	Brisbane		2	10	0	43	0
6	01/01/91	Australia	Sydney	0*		10	2	40	3
7	10/01/91	Australia	Melbourne	5*		3	0	23	0
8	13/02/91	New Zealand	Wellington	0*	1	10	0	45	2
9	16/02/91	New Zealand	Auckland	3*		10	1	46	1
10	11/01/92	New Zealand	Auckland			10	3	17	0
11	12/02/92	New Zealand	Dunedin			8	0	31	0
12	22/02/92	India	Perth	3*		4	0	25	0
13	27/02/92	West Indies	Melbourne			5	0	20	0
14	05/03/92	Australia	Sydney			9	0	52	1
15	18/03/92	Zimbabwe	Albury	0*		10	2	36	2
16	16/02/94	West Indies	Bridgetown			8	0	32	1
17	26/02/94	West Indies	Kingston	2*		4	0	22	0
18	02/03/94	West Indies	Arnos Vale	0*		9	0	52	2
19	15/12/94	Zimbabwe	Sydney	0*		10	0	43	0

Batting & Fielding

Mat	Inns	N/O	Runs	H/S	Avg	100s	50s	Cat
19	10	9	15	5*	15.00	0	0	3

Bowling

Overs	Mds	Runs	Wkts	Avg	Best	5WI	E/R
160	11	677	15	45.13	3-40	0	4.23

SHAUN UDAL

Full Name: Shaun David Udal
Born: 18/03/69 - Cove, Farnborough, Hampshire
Off break bowler - Right-hand lower order batsman

No	Date	Opposition	Venue	Bat	C	Bowling			
1	19/05/94	New Zealand	Edgbaston	3*		11	0	39	2
2	25/08/94	South Africa	Edgbaston			11	0	34	0
3	27/08/94	South Africa	Old Trafford			11	2	17	1
4	06/12/94	Australia	Sydney	4		10	1	37	2
5	15/12/94	Zimbabwe	Sydney	10		8	0	31	0
6	07/01/95	Zimbabwe	Brisbane	11*		8	0	41	2
7	10/01/95	Australia	Melbourne	2*	1	9	1	43	1

Batting & Fielding

Mat	Inns	N/O	Runs	H/S	Avg	100s	50s	Cat
7	5	3	30	11*	15.00	0	0	1

Bowling

Overs	Mds	Runs	Wkts	Avg	Best	5WI	E/R
68	4	242	8	30.25	2-37	0	3.55

DEREK UNDERWOOD

Full Name: Derek Leslie Underwood MBE
Born: 08/06/45 - Bromley, Kent
Left-arm slow/medium bowler - Right-hand lower order batsman

No	Date	Opposition	Venue	Bat	C	Bowling		
1	18/07/73	New Zealand	Swansea			11	3	29	1
2	05/09/73	West Indies	Headingley	1*		11	2	30	3
3	07/09/73	West Indies	The Oval	1*		7	0	26	0
4	15/07/74	India	The Oval			11	0	36	1
5	31/08/74	Pakistan	Trent Bridge			8	1	32	1
6	03/09/74	Pakistan	Edgbaston	17		3	0	16	1
7	01/01/75	Australia	Melbourne	1*		*6	0	20	0
8	08/03/75	New Zealand	Dunedin	2					
9	11/06/75	New Zealand	Trent Bridge		2	12	2	30	2
10	14/06/75	East Africa	Edgbaston			10	5	11	0
11	26/08/76	West Indies	Scarborough	14		9	1	35	1
12	28/08/76	West Indies	Lord's	2	1	10	0	27	3
13	30/08/76	West Indies	Edgbaston	6		3	0	28	1
14	02/06/77	Australia	Old Trafford	0*		11	1	29	3
15	04/06/77	Australia	Edgbaston	0					
16	06/06/77	Australia	The Oval	5		11	2	21	1
17	28/11/79	West Indies	Sydney			10	0	44	4
18	08/12/79	Australia	Melbourne			10	0	49	1
19	11/12/79	Australia	Sydney			6	1	29	0
20	23/12/79	West Indies	Brisbane		1	9	0	43	0
21	26/12/79	Australia	Sydney			10	2	36	0
22	25/11/81	India	Ahmedabad		1	10	3	18	2
23	20/12/81	India	Jullundur			7	1	26	1
24	27/01/82	India	Cuttack			10	0	48	3
25	13/02/82	Sri Lanka	Colombo	4	1	7	0	34	2
26	14/02/82	Sri Lanka	Colombo	0		9	0	37	1

Batting & Fielding

Mat	Inns	N/O	Runs	H/S	Avg	100s	50s	Cat
26	13	4	53	17	5.88	0	0	6

Bowling

Overs	Mds	Runs	Wkts	Avg	Best	5WI	E/R
213	24	734	32	22.93	4-44	0	3.44

STEVE WATKIN

Full Name: Steven Llewellyn Watkin
Born: 15/09/64 - Duffryn Rhondda, Maesteg, Glamorgan
Right-arm fast medium bowler - Right-hand lower order batsman

No	Date	Opposition	Venue	Bat	C	Bowling		
1	16/02/94	West Indies	Bridgetown			8	1	27	1
2	26/02/94	West Indies	Kingston	0		9.5	1	49	4
3	02/03/94	West Indies	Arnos Vale	4		9	0	61	2
4	06/03/94	West Indies	Port of Spain			10	0	56	0

Batting & Fielding

Mat	Inns	N/O	Runs	H/S	Avg	100s	50s	Cat
4	2	0	4	4	2.00	0	0	0

Bowling

Overs	Mds	Runs	Wkts	Avg	Best	5WI	E/R
36.5	2	193	7	27.57	4-49	0	5.23

COLIN WELLS

Full Name: Colin Mark Wells
Born: 03/03/60 - Newhaven, Sussex
Right-hand middle order batsman - Right-arm medium bowler

No	Date	Opposition	Venue	Bat	C
1	24/03/85	Australia	Sharjah	17	
2	26/03/85	Pakistan	Sharjah	5	

Batting & Fielding

Mat	Inns	N/O	Runs	H/S	Avg	100s	50s	Cat
2	2	0	22	17	11.00	0	0	0

JAMES WHITAKER

Full Name: John James Whitaker
Born: 05/05/62 - Skipton, Yorkshire
Right-hand middle order batsman

No	Date	Opposition	Venue	Bat	C
1	02/04/87	India	Sharjah	4	1
2	07/04/87	Pakistan	Sharjah	44*	

Batting & Fielding

Mat	Inns	N/O	Runs	H/S	Avg	100s	50s	Cat
2	2	1	48	44*	48.00	0	0	1

CRAIG WHITE

Full Name: Craig White
Born: 16/12/69 - Morley, Yorkshire
Right-hand middle order batsman - Right-arm medium bowler

No	Date	Opposition	Venue	Bat	C	Bowling		
1	06/12/94	Australia	Sydney	0		5	0	22	0

Batting & Fielding

Mat	Inns	N/O	Runs	H/S	Avg	100s	50s	Cat
1	1	0	0	0	0.00	0	0	0

Bowling

Overs	Mds	Runs	Wkts	Avg	Best	5WI	E/R
5	0	22	0	-	-	0	4.40

320   England - The Complete One-Day International Record

PETER WILLEY

Full Name: Peter Willey
Born: 06/12/49 - Sedgefield, Co Durham
Right-hand middle order batsman - Off break bowler

No	Date	Opposition	Venue	Bat	C	Bowling			
1	02/06/77	Australia	Old Trafford	1		11	1	29	0
2	04/06/77	Australia	Edgbaston	6					
3	28/11/79	West Indies	Sydney	58*		8	0	29	0
4	08/12/79	Australia	Melbourne	37	1	8	0	33	3
5	11/12/79	Australia	Sydney	64		5	0	18	2
6	23/12/79	West Indies	Brisbane	34		6	0	39	0
7	26/12/79	Australia	Sydney	51					
8	14/01/80	Australia	Sydney	0		10	0	35	1
9	16/01/80	West Indies	Adelaide	5		10	1	37	1
10	20/01/80	West Indies	Melbourne	51		10	0	48	0
11	22/01/80	West Indies	Sydney	3		10	2	35	1
12	28/05/80	West Indies	Headingley	7		4	0	12	0
13	30/05/80	West Indies	Lord's	56		5	0	18	0
14	20/08/80	Australia	The Oval	2	1	8	0	34	0
15	04/02/81	West Indies	Arnos Vale	0	1	10	1	29	1
16	26/02/81	West Indies	Berbice	21		9	0	23	0
17	04/06/81	Australia	Lord's			6	1	26	0
18	06/06/81	Australia	Edgbaston	37		6	0	36	0
19	08/06/81	Australia	Headingley	42					
20	30/05/85	Australia	Old Trafford	12		9	1	31	1
21	01/06/85	Australia	Edgbaston	0	1	11	1	38	1
22	03/06/85	Australia	Lord's			10	1	44	1
23	18/02/86	West Indies	Kingston	26		6.5	0	25	1
24	04/03/86	West Indies	Port of Spain	10		3	0	19	0
25	19/03/86	West Indies	Bridgetown	9		6	0	21	0
26	31/03/86	West Indies	Port of Spain	6					

Batting & Fielding

Mat	Inns	N/O	Runs	H/S	Avg	100s	50s	Cat
26	24	1	538	64	23.39	0	5	4

Bowling

Overs	Mds	Runs	Wkts	Avg	Best	5WI	E/R
171.5	9	659	13	50.69	3-33	0	3.83

BOB WILLIS

Full Name: Robert George Dylan Willis MBE
Born: 30/05/49 - Sunderland, Co Durham
Right-arm fast bowler - Right-hand lower order batsman

No	Date	Opposition	Venue	Bat	C	Bowling			
1	05/09/73	West Indies	Headingley	5*		10	2	29	2
2	07/09/73	West Indies	The Oval	4*		10.2	0	55	0
3	31/08/74	Pakistan	Trent Bridge		1	10	2	34	1
4	02/06/77	Australia	Old Trafford			8	2	16	1
5	04/06/77	Australia	Edgbaston	7		6	1	14	2
6	06/06/77	Australia	The Oval	0*		11	0	49	2
7	24/05/78	Pakistan	Old Trafford			11	5	15	4

8	26/05/78	Pakistan	The Oval		1	9	1	25	0
9	15/07/78	New Zealand	Scarborough			11	1	35	1
10	17/07/78	New Zealand	Old Trafford			9	5	21	1
11	24/01/79	Australia	Melbourne		2	*8	4	15	1
12	04/02/79	Australia	Melbourne			*8	1	21	1
13	07/02/79	Australia	Melbourne	2		*5	2	16	2
14	09/06/79	Australia	Lord's			11	2	20	1
15	13/06/79	Canada	Old Trafford			10.3	3	11	4
16	16/06/79	Pakistan	Headingley	24		11	2	37	1
17	20/06/79	New Zealand	Old Trafford	1*		12	1	41	1
18	28/11/79	West Indies	Sydney		1	6	0	35	2
19	08/12/79	Australia	Melbourne			7	0	28	0
20	11/12/79	Australia	Sydney			10	1	32	2
21	23/12/79	West Indies	Brisbane			10	2	27	0
22	26/12/79	Australia	Sydney			10	1	38	1
23	20/01/80	West Indies	Melbourne			10	1	51	1
24	22/01/80	West Indies	Sydney			10	0	35	0
25	30/05/80	West Indies	Lord's		2	10	1	25	2
26	04/06/81	Australia	Lord's			11	0	56	2
27	06/06/81	Australia	Edgbaston	1*	1	11	3	41	1
28	08/06/81	Australia	Headingley	2*		11	1	35	2
29	25/11/81	India	Ahmedabad			9	3	17	1
30	20/12/81	India	Jullundur		1	7.3	2	41	0
31	27/01/82	India	Cuttack		1	6	1	29	0
32	13/02/82	Sri Lanka	Colombo	2*		9	1	32	2
33	14/02/82	Sri Lanka	Colombo	0		9	1	26	0
34	02/06/82	India	Headingley			11	0	32	2
35	04/06/82	India	The Oval		1	7	2	10	1
36	17/07/82	Pakistan	Trent Bridge		2	11	1	46	0
37	19/07/82	Pakistan	Old Trafford			8	0	36	1
38	11/01/83	Australia	Sydney	0		6.4	1	20	1
39	13/01/83	New Zealand	Melbourne		1	8	1	29	2
40	15/01/83	New Zealand	Brisbane			9.2	1	30	2
41	16/01/83	Australia	Brisbane	7*		7	1	31	0
42	20/01/83	New Zealand	Sydney		1	9	0	23	4
43	23/01/83	Australia	Melbourne			6.4	1	29	0
44	26/01/83	Australia	Sydney	5*	1	6	1	23	1
45	29/01/83	New Zealand	Adelaide		1	9.5	2	43	1
46	30/01/83	Australia	Adelaide			10	1	40	1
47	05/02/83	New Zealand	Perth			8.3	1	28	2
48	19/02/83	New Zealand	Auckland	1*		10	1	39	1
49	23/02/83	New Zealand	Wellington	2*		9	0	54	2
50	26/02/83	New Zealand	Christchurch	6		10	1	35	0
51	09/06/83	New Zealand	The Oval			7	2	9	2
52	11/06/83	Sri Lanka	Taunton		1	11	3	43	0
53	13/06/83	Pakistan	Lord's			12	4	24	2
54	15/06/83	New Zealand	Edgbaston	0		12	1	42	4
55	18/06/83	Pakistan	Old Trafford		2	12	3	37	1
56	20/06/83	Sri Lanka	Headingley			9	4	9	1
57	22/06/83	India	Old Trafford	0	1	10.4	2	42	1
58	18/02/84	New Zealand	Christchurch			6.1	1	18	2
59	22/02/84	New Zealand	Wellington			9	4	17	0
60	25/02/84	New Zealand	Auckland	7*		10	1	36	1
61	09/03/84	Pakistan	Lahore			7.4	1	25	1
62	31/05/84	West Indies	Old Trafford	1*	1	11	2	38	1
63	02/06/84	West Indies	Trent Bridge			9.3	0	26	2
64	04/06/84	West Indies	Lord's	6*		10.5	2	52	0

Batting & Fielding

Mat	Inns	N/O	Runs	H/S	Avg	100s	50s	Cat
64	22	14	83	24	10.37	0	0	22

Bowling
Overs	Mds	Runs	Wkts	Avg	Best	5WI	E/R
599.1	97	1968	80	24.60	4-11	0	3.28

BARRY WOOD

Full Name: Barry Wood
Born: 26/12/42 - Ossett, Yorkshire
Right-hand opening batsman - Right-arm medium bowler

No	Date	Opposition	Venue	Bat	C	Bowling			
1	28/08/72	Australia	Edgbaston	19	2	6	0	20	2
2	08/03/75	New Zealand	Dunedin	33					
3	09/03/75	New Zealand	Wellington	14*	1	*6	0	41	0
4	07/06/75	India	Lord's			5	2	4	0
5	14/06/75	East Africa	Edgbaston	77		7	3	10	0
6	18/06/75	Australia	Headingley	6					
7	26/08/76	West Indies	Scarborough	0		8	2	29	1
8	28/08/76	West Indies	Lord's	4	1	3	0	13	1
9	30/08/76	West Indies	Edgbaston	34	1				
10	24/05/78	Pakistan	Old Trafford	26	1	11	3	25	2
11	26/05/78	Pakistan	The Oval	8		4	0	14	2
12	02/06/82	India	Headingley	78*		7	2	17	0
13	04/06/82	India	The Oval	15		11	0	51	1

Batting & Fielding
Mat	Inns	N/O	Runs	H/S	Avg	100s	50s	Cat
13	12	2	314	78*	31.40	0	2	6

Bowling
Overs	Mds	Runs	Wkts	Avg	Best	5WI	E/R
70	12	224	9	24.88	2-14	0	3.20

BOB WOOLMER

Full Name: Robert Andrew Woolmer
Born: 14/05/48 - Kanpur, India
Right-hand opening/middle order batsman - Right-arm medium bowler

No	Date	Opposition	Venue	Bat	C	Bowling			
1	24/08/72	Australia	Old Trafford			10	1	33	3
2	26/08/72	Australia	Lord's	9		9.3	1	47	1
3	28/08/72	Australia	Edgbaston	0	1	11	1	50	1
4	13/07/74	India	Headingley		1	11	0	62	2
5	26/08/76	West Indies	Scarborough	3		2	0	16	0
6	28/08/76	West Indies	Lord's	9	1	10	0	52	2

Batting & Fielding
Mat	Inns	N/O	Runs	H/S	Avg	100s	50s	Cat
6	4	0	21	9	5.25	0	0	3

Bowling
Overs	Mds	Runs	Wkts	Avg	Best	5WI	E/R
53.3	3	260	9	28.88	3-33	0	4.85

ONE-DAY INTERNATIONAL RECORDS

1971-1995

ONE DAY INTERNATIONAL VENUES 1971-1995

First Match

England and Wales
Old Trafford	Manchester	24/08/72
Lord's	London	26/08/72
Edgbaston	Birmingham	28/08/72
St Helen's	Swansea (Wales)	18/07/73
Headingley	Leeds	05/09/73
The Oval	London	07/09/73
Trent Bridge	Nottingham	31/08/74
Scarborough Cricket Ground	Scarborough	26/08/76
County Ground	Taunton	11/06/83

Australia
Melbourne Cricket Ground	Melbourne	05/01/71
Sydney Cricket Ground	Sydney	13/01/79
Woolloongabba	Brisbane	23/12/79
Adelaide Oval	Adelaide	16/01/80
WACA Ground	Perth	05/02/83
Devonport Oval	Devonport	03/02/87
Eastern Oval	Ballarat	09/03/92
Lavington Oval	Albury	18/03/92

India
Sardar Patel Stadium	Ahmedabad	25/11/81
Burlton Park	Jullundur	20/12/81
Barabati Stadium	Cuttack	27/01/82
Nehru Stadium	Poona	05/12/84
Chinnaswamy Stadium	Bangalore	20/01/85
Vidarbha CA Ground	Nagpur	23/01/85
Sector 16 Stadium	Chandigarh	27/01/85
Sawai Mansingh Stadium	Jaipur	26/10/87
Wankhede Stadium	Bombay	05/11/87
Eden Gardens	Calcutta	08/11/87
Feroz Shah Kotla	Delhi	15/10/89
Lal Bahadur Stadium	Hyderabad	19/10/89
Green Park, Modi Stadium	Kanpur	25/10/89
Roop Singh Stadium	Gwalior	27/10/89
Keenan Stadium	Jamshedpur	01/03/93

New Zealand
Carisbrook	Dunedin	08/03/75
Basin Reserve	Wellington	09/03/75
Eden Park	Auckland	19/02/83
Lancaster Park	Christchurch	26/02/83
McLean Park	Napier	16/03/88

Pakistan
Sahiwal Stadium	Sahiwal	23/12/77
Jinnah Park	Sialkot	30/12/77
Gaddafi Stadium	Lahore	13/01/78
National Stadium	Karachi	26/03/84
Municipal Stadium	Gujranwala	09/10/87
Pindi Club Ground	Rawalpindi	12/10/87
Shahi Bagh Stadium	Peshawar	17/10/87

Sri Lanka
Sinhalese Sports Club	Colombo	13/02/82
Khettarama Stadium	Colombo (2)	10/03/93
Tyronne Fernando Stadium	Moratuwa	20/03/93

United Arab Emirates
Sharjah CA Stadium	Sharjah	24/03/85

West Indies
Arnos Vale	Arnos Vale, St Vincent	04/02/81
Albion Sports Complex	Berbice, Guyana	26/02/81
Sabina Park	Kingston, Jamaica	18/02/86

Queens Park Oval	Port-of-Spain, Trinidad	04/03/86
Kensington Oval	Bridgetown, Barbados	19/03/86
Bourda	Georgetown, Guyana	07/03/90

RESULTS PER VENUE

	Mat	Won	Lost	Tied	Aban	% Won
Melbourne Cricket Ground	20	7	13	0	0	35.00
Old Trafford	19	14	4	0	1	77.77
Sydney Cricket Ground	18	11	6	0	1	64.70
Lord's	16	9	7	0	0	56.25
Edgbaston	15	9	6	0	0	60.00
Headingley	12	6	6	0	0	50.00
The Oval	12	9	3	0	0	75.00
Trent Bridge	8	4	3	1	0	50.00
WACA Ground	8	6	2	0	0	75.00
Woolloongabba	8	3	5	0	0	37.50
Adelaide Oval	7	2	4	0	1	33.33
Queens Park Oval	6	2	2	0	2	50.00
Basin Reserve	5	1	3	0	1	25.00
Eden Park	5	1	4	0	0	20.00
Lancaster Park	5	4	1	0	0	80.00
Sharjah CA Stadium	5	2	3	0	0	40.00
Barabati Stadium	3	2	1	0	0	66.66
Roop Singh Stadium	3	0	3	0	0	00.00
Carisbrook	3	2	0	0	1	100.00
Gaddafi Stadium	3	1	2	0	0	33.33
Kensington Oval	3	1	2	0	0	33.33
National Stadium	3	2	1	0	0	66.66
Sabina Park	3	0	3	0	0	00.00
Arnos Vale	2	0	2	0	0	00.00
Bourda	2	0	2	0	0	00.00
Chinnaswamy Stadium	2	2	0	0	0	100.00
Nehru Stadium	2	2	0	0	0	100.00
Sawai Mansingh Stadium	2	2	0	0	0	100.00
Shahi Bagh Stadium	2	2	0	0	0	100.00
Sinhalese Sports Club	2	1	1	0	0	50.00
Scarborough Cricket Ground	2	1	1	0	0	50.00
Sector 16 Stadium	2	1	1	0	0	50.00
Vidarbha CA Ground	2	0	2	0	0	00.00
Albion Sports Complex	1	0	1	0	0	00.00
Lavington Oval	1	0	1	0	0	00.00
Burlton Park	1	0	1	0	0	00.00
County Ground	1	1	0	0	0	100.00
Devonport Oval	1	1	0	0	0	100.00
Eastern Oval	1	1	0	0	0	100.00
Eden Gardens	1	0	1	0	0	00.00
Feroz Shah Kotla	1	1	0	0	0	100.00
Green Park, Modi Stadium	1	0	1	0	0	00.00
Jinnah Park	1	1	0	0	0	100.00
Keenan Stadium	1	1	0	0	0	100.00
Khettarama Stadium	1	0	1	0	0	00.00
Lal Bahadur Stadium	1	1	0	0	0	100.00
McLean Park	1	0	1	0	0	00.00
Municipal Stadium	1	1	0	0	0	100.00
Pindi Club Ground	1	0	1	0	0	00.00
Sahiwal Stadium	1	1	0	0	0	100.00
Sardar Patel Stadium	1	1	0	0	0	100.00
St Helen's	1	1	0	0	0	100.00
Tyronne Fernando Stadium	1	0	1	0	0	00.00
Wankhede Stadium	1	1	0	0	0	100.00
TOTAL	**231**	**121**	**102**	**1**	**7**	**54.01**

Percentages do not include abandoned matches

ONE-DAY INTERNATIONAL RESULTS 1971-1995

No	Date	Opposition	Venue	Result
1*	05/01/71	Australia	Melbourne	Australia won by 5 wkts

Prudential Trophy

2	24/08/72	Australia	Old Trafford	England won by 6 wkts
3	26/08/72	Australia	Lord's	Australia won by 5 wkts
4	28/08/72	Australia	Edgbaston	England won by 2 wkts

Prudential Trophy

5	18/07/73	New Zealand	Swansea	England won by 7 wkts
6	20/07/73	New Zealand	Old Trafford	Match Abandoned

Prudential Trophy

7	05/09/73	West Indies	Headingley	England won by 1 wkt
8	07/09/73	West Indies	The Oval	West Indies won by 8 wkts

Prudential Trophy

9	13/07/74	India	Headingley	England won by 4 wkts
10	15/07/74	India	The Oval	England won by 6 wkts

Prudential Trophy

11	31/08/74	Pakistan	Trent Bridge	Pakistan won by 7 wkts
12	03/09/74	Pakistan	Edgbaston	Pakistan won by 8 wkts
13*	01/01/75	Australia	Melbourne	England won by 3 wkts
14*	08/03/75	New Zealand	Dunedin	Match Abandoned
15*	09/03/75	New Zealand	Wellington	Match Abandoned

Prudential World Cup

16	07/06/75	India	Lord's	England won by 202 runs
17	11/06/75	New Zealand	Trent Bridge	England won by 80 runs
18	14/06/75	East Africa	Edgbaston	England won by 196 runs
19	18/06/75	Australia	Headingley	Australia won by 4 wkts

Prudential Trophy

20	26/08/76	West Indies	Scarborough	West Indies won by 6 wkts
21	28/08/76	West Indies	Lord's	West Indies won by 36 runs
22	30/08/76	West Indies	Edgbaston	West Indies won by 50 runs

Prudential Trophy

23	02/06/77	Australia	Old Trafford	England won by 2 wkts
24	04/06/77	Australia	Edgbaston	England won by 101 runs
25	06/06/77	Australia	The Oval	Australia won by 2 wkts
26*	23/12/77	Pakistan	Sahiwal	England won by 3 wkts
27*	30/12/77	Pakistan	Sialkot	England won by 6 wkts
28*	13/01/78	Pakistan	Lahore	Pakistan won by 36 runs

Prudential Trophy

29	24/05/78	Pakistan	Old Trafford	England won by 132 runs
30	26/05/78	Pakistan	The Oval	England won by 94 runs

Prudential Trophy

31	15/07/78	New Zealand	Scarborough	England won by 19 runs
32	17/07/78	New Zealand	Old Trafford	England won by 126 runs

Benson & Hedges Cup

33*	13/01/79	Australia	Sydney	Match Abandoned

One-Day International Records 327

34*	24/01/79	Australia	Melbourne	England won by 7 wkts
35*	04/02/79	Australia	Melbourne	Australia won by 4 wkts
36*	07/02/79	Australia	Melbourne	Australia won by 6 wkts

Prudential World Cup

37	09/06/79	Australia	Lord's	England won by 6 wkts
38	13/06/79	Canada	Old Trafford	England won by 8 wkts
39	16/06/79	Pakistan	Headingley	England won by 14 runs
40	20/06/79	New Zealand	Old Trafford	England won by 9 runs
41	23/06/79	West Indies	Lord's	West Indies won by 92 runs

Benson & Hedges World Series Cup

42	28/11/79	West Indies	Sydney	England won by 2 runs
43	08/12/79	Australia	Melbourne	England won by 3 wkts
44	11/12/79	Australia	Sydney	England won by 72 runs
45	23/12/79	West Indies	Brisbane	West Indies won by 9 wkts
46	26/12/79	Australia	Sydney	England won by 4 wkts
47	14/01/80	Australia	Sydney	England won by 2 wkts
48	16/01/80	West Indies	Adelaide	West Indies won by 107 runs
49	20/01/80	West Indies	Melbourne	West Indies won by 2 runs
50	22/01/80	West Indies	Sydney	West Indies won by 8 wkts

Prudential Trophy

51	28/05/80	West Indies	Headingley	West Indies won by 24 runs
52	30/05/80	West Indies	Lord's	England won by 3 wkts

Prudential Trophy

53	20/08/80	Australia	The Oval	England won by 23 runs
54	22/08/80	Australia	Edgbaston	England won by 47 runs
55	04/02/81	West Indies	Arnos Vale	West Indies won by 2 runs
56	26/02/81	West Indies	Berbice	West Indies won by 6 wkts

Prudential Trophy

57	04/06/81	Australia	Lord's	England won by 6 wkts
58	06/06/81	Australia	Edgbaston	Australia won by 2 runs
59	08/06/81	Australia	Headingley	Australia won by 71 runs

Wills Series

60	25/11/81	India	Ahmedabad	England won by 5 wkts
61	20/12/81	India	Jullundur	India won by 6 wkts
62	27/01/82	India	Cuttack	India won by 5 wkts
63	13/02/82	Sri Lanka	Colombo	England won by 5 runs
64	14/02/82	Sri Lanka	Colombo	Sri Lanka won by 3 runs

Prudential Trophy

65	02/06/82	India	Headingley	England won by 9 wkts
66	04/06/82	India	The Oval	England won by 114 runs

Prudential Trophy

67	17/07/82	Pakistan	Trent Bridge	England won by 7 wkts
68	19/07/82	Pakistan	Old Trafford	England won by 73 runs

Benson & Hedges World Series Cup

69	11/01/83	Australia	Sydney	Australia won by 31 runs
70	13/01/83	New Zealand	Melbourne	New Zealand won by 2 runs
71	15/01/83	New Zealand	Brisbane	England won by 54 runs
72	16/01/83	Australia	Brisbane	Australia won by 7 wkts
73	20/01/83	New Zealand	Sydney	England won by 8 wkts

74	23/01/83	Australia	Melbourne	Australia won by 5 wkts
75	26/01/83	Australia	Sydney	England won by 98 runs
76	29/01/83	New Zealand	Adelaide	New Zealand won by 4 wkts
77	30/01/83	Australia	Adelaide	England won by 14 runs
78	05/02/83	New Zealand	Perth	New Zealand won by 7 wkts

Rothmans Cup

79	19/02/83	New Zealand	Auckland	New Zealand won by 6 wkts
80	23/02/83	New Zealand	Wellington	New Zealand won by 103 runs
81	26/02/83	New Zealand	Christchurch	New Zealand won by 84 runs

Prudential World Cup

82	09/06/83	New Zealand	The Oval	England won by 106 runs
83	11/06/83	Sri Lanka	Taunton	England won by 47 runs
84	13/06/83	Pakistan	Lord's	England won by 8 wkts
85	15/06/83	New Zealand	Edgbaston	New Zealand won by 2 wkts
86	18/06/83	Pakistan	Old Trafford	England won by 7 wkts
87	20/06/83	Sri Lanka	Headingley	England won by 9 wkts
88	22/06/83	India	Old Trafford	India won by 6 wkts

Rothmans Cup

89	18/02/84	New Zealand	Christchurch	England won by 54 runs
90	22/02/84	New Zealand	Wellington	England won by 6 wkts
91	25/02/84	New Zealand	Auckland	New Zealand won by 7 wkts

Wills Series

92	09/03/84	Pakistan	Lahore	Pakistan won by 6 wkts
93	26/03/84	Pakistan	Karachi	England won by 6 wkts

Texaco Trophy

94	31/05/84	West Indies	Old Trafford	West Indies won by 104 runs
95	02/06/84	West Indies	Trent Bridge	England won by 3 wkts
96	04/06/84	West Indies	Lord's	West Indies won by 8 wkts
97	05/12/84	India	Poona	England won by 4 wkts
98	27/12/84	India	Cuttack	England won on FSR
99	20/01/85	India	Bangalore	England won by 3 wkts
100	23/01/85	India	Nagpur	India won by 3 wkts
101	27/01/85	India	Chandigarh	England won by 7 runs

Benson & Hedges World Championship

102	17/02/85	Australia	Melbourne	Australia won by 7 wkts
103	26/02/85	India	Sydney	India won by 86 runs
104	02/03/85	Pakistan	Melbourne	Pakistan won by 67 runs

Rothmans Four-Nations Trophy

105	24/03/85	Australia	Sharjah	Australia won by 2 wkts
106	26/03/85	Pakistan	Sharjah	Pakistan won by 43 runs

Texaco Trophy

107	30/05/85	Australia	Old Trafford	Australia won by 3 wkts
108	01/06/85	Australia	Edgbaston	Australia won by 4 wkts
109	03/06/85	Australia	Lord's	England won by 8 wkts
110	18/02/86	West Indies	Kingston	West Indies won by 6 wkts
111	04/03/86	West Indies	Port of Spain	England won by 5 wkts
112	19/03/86	West Indies	Bridgetown	West Indies won by 135 runs
113	31/03/86	West Indies	Port of Spain	West Indies won by 8 wkts

Texaco Trophy

114	24/05/86	India	The Oval	India won by 9 wkts
115	26/05/86	India	Old Trafford	England won by 5 wkts

Texaco Trophy

116	16/07/86	New Zealand	Headingley	New Zealand won by 47 runs
117	18/07/86	New Zealand	Old Trafford	England won by 6 wkts

Benson & Hedges Challenge

118	01/01/87	Australia	Perth	England won by 37 runs
119	03/01/87	West Indies	Perth	England won by 19 runs
120	05/01/87	Pakistan	Perth	England won by 3 wkts
121	07/01/87	Pakistan	Perth	England won by 5 wkts

Benson & Hedges World Series Cup

122	17/01/87	West Indies	Brisbane	England won by 6 wkts
123	18/01/87	Australia	Brisbane	Australia won by 11 runs
124	22/01/87	Australia	Sydney	England won by 3 wkts
125	24/01/87	West Indies	Adelaide	England won by 89 runs
126	26/01/87	Australia	Adelaide	Australia won by 33 runs
127	30/01/87	West Indies	Melbourne	West Indies won by 6 wkts
128	01/02/87	Australia	Melbourne	Australia won by 109 runs
129	03/02/87	West Indies	Devonport	England won by 29 runs
130	08/02/87	Australia	Melbourne	England won by 6 wkts
131	11/02/87	Australia	Sydney	England won by 8 runs

Four Nations Tournament

132	02/04/87	India	Sharjah	India won by 3 wkts
133	07/04/87	Pakistan	Sharjah	England won by 5 wkts
134	09/04/87	Australia	Sharjah	England won by 11 runs

Texaco Trophy

135	21/05/87	Pakistan	The Oval	England won by 7 wkts
136	23/05/87	Pakistan	Trent Bridge	Pakistan won by 6 wkts
137	25/05/87	Pakistan	Edgbaston	England won by 1 wkt

Reliance World Cup

138	09/10/87	West Indies	Gujranwala	England won by 2 wkts
139	12/10/87	Pakistan	Rawalpindi	Pakistan won by 18 runs
140	17/10/87	Sri Lanka	Peshawar	England won on FSR
141	20/10/87	Pakistan	Karachi	Pakistan won by 7 wkts
142	26/10/87	West Indies	Jaipur	England won by 34 runs
143	30/10/87	Sri Lanka	Poona	England won by 8 wkts
144	05/11/87	India	Bombay	England won by 35 runs
145	08/11/87	Australia	Calcutta	Australia won by 7 runs
146	18/11/87	Pakistan	Lahore	England won by 2 wkts
147	20/11/87	Pakistan	Karachi	England won by 23 runs
148	22/11/87	Pakistan	Peshawar	England won by 98 runs

Australian Bicentennial match

149	04/02/88	Australia	Melbourne	Australia won by 22 runs

Rothmans Cup

150	09/03/88	New Zealand	Dunedin	England won by 5 wkts
151	12/03/88	New Zealand	Christchurch	England won by 6 wkts
152	16/03/88	New Zealand	Napier	New Zealand won by 7 wkts
153	19/03/88	New Zealand	Auckland	New Zealand won by 4 wkts

Texaco Trophy
154	19/05/88	West Indies	Edgbaston	England won by 6 wkts
155	21/05/88	West Indies	Headingley	England won by 47 runs
156	23/05/88	West Indies	Lord's	England won by 7 wkts

Texaco Trophy
157	04/09/88	Sri Lanka	The Oval	England won by 5 wkts

Texaco Trophy
158	25/05/89	Australia	Old Trafford	England won by 95 runs
159	27/05/89	Australia	Trent Bridge	Match Tied
160	29/05/89	Australia	Lord's	Australia won by 6 wkts

Nehru Cup
161	15/10/89	Sri Lanka	Delhi	England won by 5 wkts
162	19/10/89	Australia	Hyderabad	England won by 7 wkts
163	22/10/89	Pakistan	Cuttack	England won by 4 wkts
164	25/10/89	India	Kanpur	India won by 6 wkts
165	27/10/89	West Indies	Gwalior	West Indies won by 26 runs
166	30/10/89	Pakistan	Nagpur	Pakistan won by 6 wkts

Cable & Wireless Series
167	14/02/90	West Indies	Port of Spain	Match Abandoned
168	17/02/90	West Indies	Port of Spain	Match Abandoned
169	03/03/90	West Indies	Kingston	West Indies won by 3 wkts
170	07/03/90	West Indies	Georgetown	West Indies won by 6 wkts
171	15/03/90	West Indies	Georgetown	West Indies won by 7 wkts
172	03/04/90	West Indies	Bridgetown	West Indies won by 4 wkts

Texaco Trophy
173	23/05/90	New Zealand	Headingley	New Zealand won by 4 wkts
174	25/05/90	New Zealand	The Oval	England won by 6 wkts

Texaco Trophy
175	18/07/90	India	Headingley	India won by 6 wkts
176	20/07/90	India	Trent Bridge	India won by 5 wkts

Benson & Hedges World Series Cup
177	01/12/90	New Zealand	Adelaide	New Zealand won by 7 runs
178	07/12/90	New Zealand	Perth	England won by 4 wkts
179	09/12/90	Australia	Perth	Australia won by 6 wkts
180	13/12/90	New Zealand	Sydney	England won by 33 runs
181	15/12/90	New Zealand	Brisbane	New Zealand won by 8 wkts
182	16/12/90	Australia	Brisbane	Australia won by 37 runs
183	01/01/91	Australia	Sydney	Australia won by 68 runs
184	10/01/91	Australia	Melbourne	Australia won by 3 runs

Bank of New Zealand Series
185	09/02/91	New Zealand	Christchurch	England won by 14 runs
186	13/02/91	New Zealand	Wellington	New Zealand won by 9 runs
187	16/02/91	New Zealand	Auckland	New Zealand won by 7 runs

Texaco Trophy
188	23/05/91	West Indies	Edgbaston	England won by 1 wkt
189	25/05/91	West Indies	Old Trafford	England won by 9 runs
190	27/05/91	West Indies	Lord's	England won by 7 wkts

Bank of New Zealand Series
191	11/01/92	New Zealand	Auckland	England won by 7 wkts
192	12/02/92	New Zealand	Dunedin	England won by 3 wkts

193	15/02/92	New Zealand	Christchurch	England won by 71 runs

Benson & Hedges World Cup

194	22/02/92	India	Perth	England won by 9 runs
195	27/02/92	West Indies	Melbourne	England won by 6 wkts
196	01/03/92	Pakistan	Adelaide	Match Abandoned
197	05/03/92	Australia	Sydney	England won by 8 wkts
198	09/03/92	Sri Lanka	Ballarat	England won by 106 runs
199	12/03/92	South Africa	Melbourne	England won by 3 wkts
200	15/03/92	New Zealand	Wellington	New Zealand won by 7 wkts
201	18/03/92	Zimbabwe	Albury	Zimbabwe won by 9 runs
202	22/03/92	South Africa	Sydney	England won by 19 runs
203	25/03/92	Pakistan	Melbourne	Pakistan won by 22 runs

Texaco Trophy

204	20/05/92	Pakistan	Lord's	England won by 79 runs
205	22/05/92	Pakistan	The Oval	England won by 39 runs
206	20/08/92	Pakistan	Trent Bridge	England won by 198 runs
207	22/08/92	Pakistan	Lord's	Pakistan won by 3 runs
208	24/08/92	Pakistan	Old Trafford	England won by 6 wkts

Charminar Challenge Series

209	18/01/93	India	Jaipur	England won by 4 wkts
210	21/01/93	India	Chandigarh	India won by 5 wkts
211	26/02/93	India	Bangalore	England won by 48 runs
212	01/03/93	India	Jamshedpur	England won by 6 wkts
213	04/03/93	India	Gwalior	India won by 3 wkts
214	05/03/93	India	Gwalior	India won by 4 wkts
215	10/03/93	Sri Lanka	Colombo (2)	Sri Lanka won by 80 runs
216	20/03/93	Sri Lanka	Moratuwa	Sri Lanka won by 8 wkts

Texaco Trophy

217	19/05/93	Australia	Old Trafford	Australia won by 4 runs
218	21/05/93	Australia	Edgbaston	Australia won by 6 wkts
219	23/05/93	Australia	Lord's	Australia won by 19 runs

Cable & Wireless Series

220	16/02/94	West Indies	Bridgetown	England won by 61 runs
221	26/02/94	West Indies	Kingston	West Indies won by 3 wkts
222	02/03/94	West Indies	Arnos Vale	West Indies won by 165 runs
223	05/03/94	West Indies	Port of Spain	West Indies won by 72 runs
224	06/03/94	West Indies	Port of Spain	England won by 5 wkts

Texaco Trophy

225	19/05/94	New Zealand	Edgbaston	England won by 42 runs

Texaco Trophy

226	25/08/94	South Africa	Edgbaston	England won by 6 wkts
227	27/08/94	South Africa	Old Trafford	England won by 4 wkts

Benson & Hedges World Series Cup

228	06/12/94	Australia	Sydney	Australia won by 28 runs
229	15/12/94	Zimbabwe	Sydney	Zimbabwe won by 13 runs
230	07/01/95	Zimbabwe	Brisbane	England won by 26 runs
231	10/01/95	Australia	Melbourne	England won by 37 runs

* denotes 8-ball overs

SUMMARY OF RESULTS

	Matches	Won	Lost	Tied	Aban	% Won
Australia	57	26	29	1	1	46.42
Canada	1	1	0	0	0	100.00
East Africa	1	1	0	0	0	100.00
India	29	16	13	0	0	55.17
New Zealand	41	21	17	0	3	55.26
Pakistan	36	23	12	0	1	65.71
South Africa	4	4	0	0	0	100.00
Sri Lanka	11	8	3	0	0	72.72
West Indies	48	20	26	0	2	43.47
Zimbabwe	3	1	2	0	0	33.33
TOTAL	231	121	102	1	7	54.01

Percentages do not include abandoned matches

WORLD CUP 1975-1992

1975 Prudential World Cup
Hosts: England
Winners: West Indies
Runners-up: Australia
Semi-finalists: England and New Zealand

Matches

07/06/75	India	Lord's	England won by 202 runs
11/06/75	New Zealand	Trent Bridge	England won by 80 runs
14/06/75	East Africa	Edgbaston	England won by 196 runs
18/06/75	Australia	Headingley	Australia won by 4 wkts

Most runs: D.L. Amiss 243
Highest score: D.L. Amiss 137
100s: 2   (D.L. Amiss & K.W.R. Fletcher)
Most wickets: C.M. Old 7
Best bowling: J.A. Snow 4-11
Most dismissals: A.P.E. Knott 1 (1+0)
Most catches: D.L. Underwood 2
Captain: M.H. Denness

1979 Prudential World Cup
Hosts: England
Winners: West Indies
Runners-up: England
Semi-finalists: New Zealand & Pakistan

Matches

09/06/79	Australia	Lord's	England won by 6 wkts
13/06/79	Canada	Old Trafford	England won by 8 wkts
16/06/79	Pakistan	Headingley	England won by 14 runs
20/06/79	New Zealand	Old Trafford	England won by 9 runs
23/06/79	West Indies	Lord's	West Indies won by 92 runs

Most runs: G.A. Gooch 210
Highest score: G.A. Gooch 71
100s: None
Most wickets: M. Hendrick 10
Best bowling: C.M. Old 4-8
Most dismissals: R.W. Taylor 4 (4+0)
Most catches: J.M. Brearley 4
Captain: J.M. Brearley

1983 Prudential World Cup
Hosts: England
Winners: India
Runners-up: West Indies
Semi-finalists: England and Pakistan

Matches

09/06/83	New Zealand	The Oval	England won by 106 runs
11/06/83	Sri Lanka	Taunton	England won by 47 runs
13/06/83	Pakistan	Lord's	England won by 8 wkts
15/06/83	New Zealand	Edgbaston	New Zealand won by 2 wkts
18/06/83	Pakistan	Old Trafford	England won by 7 wkts
20/06/83	Sri Lanka	Headingley	England won by 9 wkts
22/06/83	India	Old Trafford	India won by 6 wkts

Most runs: D.I. Gower 384
Highest score: D.I. Gower 130
100s: 2   (D.I. Gower & A.J. Lamb)
Most wickets: V.J. Marks 13
Best bowling: V.J. Marks 5-39
Most dismissals: I.J. Gould 12 (11+1)
Most catches: A.J. Lamb 6
Captain: R.G.D. Willis

1987 Reliance World Cup
Hosts: India & Pakistan
Winners: Australia
Runners-up: England
Semi-finalists: Pakistan and India

Matches

09/10/87	West Indies	Gujranwala	England won by 2 wkts
12/10/87	Pakistan	Rawalpindi	Pakistan won by 18 runs
17/10/87	Sri Lanka	Peshawar	England won on FSR
20/10/87	Pakistan	Karachi	Pakistan won by 7 wkts
26/10/87	West Indies	Jaipur	England won by 34 runs
30/10/87	Sri Lanka	Poona	England won by 8 wkts
05/11/87	India	Bombay	England won by 35 runs
08/11/87	Australia	Calcutta	Australia won by 7 runs

Most runs: G.A. Gooch 471
Highest score: G.A. Gooch 115
100s: 1 (G.A. Gooch)
Most wickets: E.E. Hemmings 13
Best bowling: E.E. Hemmings 4-52
Most dismissals: P.R. Downton 9 (8+1)
Most catches: C.W.J. Athey 4
Captain: M.W. Gatting

1992 Benson & Hedges World Cup
Hosts: Australia & New Zealand
Winners: Pakistan
Runners-up: England
Semi-finalists: New Zealand and South Africa

Matches

22/02/92	India	Perth	England won by 9 runs
27/02/92	West Indies	Melbourne	England won by 6 wkts
01/03/92	Pakistan	Adelaide	Match Abandoned
05/03/92	Australia	Sydney	England won by 8 wkts
09/03/92	Sri Lanka	Ballarat	England won by 106 runs
12/03/92	South Africa	Melbourne	England won by 3 wkts
15/03/92	New Zealand	Wellington	New Zealand won by 7 wkts
18/03/92	Zimbabwe	Albury	Zimbabwe won by 9 runs
22/03/92	South Africa	Sydney	England won by 19 runs
25/03/92	Pakistan	Melbourne	Pakistan won by 22 runs

Most runs: N.H. Fairbrother 285
Highest score: R.A. Smith 91
100s: None
Most wickets: I.T. Botham 16

Best bowling: C.C. Lewis 4-30
Most dismissals: A.J. Stewart 8+1
Most catches: N.H. Fairbrother 6
Captain: G.A. Gooch (A.J. Stewart)

RECORD AGAINST EACH COUNTRY

	Mat	Won	Lost	Tied	Aban	% Won
Australia	4	2	2	0	0	50.00
Canada	1	1	0	0	0	100.00
East Africa	1	1	0	0	0	100.00
India	4	3	1	0	0	75.00
New Zealand	5	3	2	0	0	60.00
Pakistan	7	3	3	0	1	50.00
South Africa	2	2	0	0	0	100.00
Sri Lanka	5	5	0	0	0	100.00
West Indies	4	3	1	0	0	75.00
Zimbabwe	1	0	1	0	0	00.00
TOTAL	34	23	10	0	1	69.69

Percentages do not include abandoned matches

TOURNAMENT RECORDS 1975-1992

Highest total: 334-4 v India 1975
Lowest total: 93 v Australia 1975
Greatest victory (runs): 202 runs v India 1975
Greatest victory (wickets): 9 wkts v Sri Lanka 1983
Narrowest victory (runs): 9 runs v New Zealand 1979 & India 1992
Narrowest victory (wickets): 2 wkts v West Indies 1987
Most wins in an individual tournament: 6 - 1992
Most defeats in an individual tournament: 3 - 1987 & 1992
Most Appearances: 22 - I.T. Botham
Most Runs: 897 - G.A. Gooch
Highest Score: 137 - D.L. Amiss
Most 100s: 1 - D.L. Amiss, K.W.R. Fletcher, A.J. Lamb, D.I. Gower, G.A. Gooch
Most 50s: 8 - G.A. Gooch
Highest partnership: 176 v India 1975 (D.L. Amiss & K.W.R. Fletcher)
Most Wickets: 30 - I.T. Botham
Best bowling: 5-39 - V.J. Marks
Most 5 wkt innings: 1 - V.J. Marks
Most dismissals: 12 (11+1) - I.J. Gould
Most catches: 10 - I.T. Botham
Most appearances as captain: 8 - M.W. Gatting 1987 & G.A. Gooch 1992

PRUDENTIAL AND TEXACO TROPHY SERIES 1972-1994

Year	Opposition	Mat	Won	Lost	Tied	Aban
Prudential Trophy						
1972	Australia	3	2	1	0	0
1973	New Zealand	2	1	0	0	1
1973	West Indies*	2	1	1	0	0
1974	India	2	2	0	0	0
1974	Pakistan	2	0	2	0	0
1976	West Indies	3	0	3	0	0
1977	Australia	3	2	1	0	0
1978	Pakistan	2	2	0	0	0
1978	New Zealand	2	2	0	0	0
1980	West Indies*	2	1	1	0	0
1980	Australia	2	2	0	0	0
1981	Australia	3	1	2	0	0
1982	India	2	2	0	0	0
1982	Pakistan	2	2	0	0	0
Texaco Trophy						
1984	West Indies	3	1	2	0	0
1985	Australia	3	1	2	0	0
1986	India*	2	1	1	0	0
1986	New Zealand*	2	1	1	0	0
1987	Pakistan	3	2	1	0	0
1988	West Indies	3	3	0	0	0
1988	Sri Lanka	1	1	0	0	0
1989	Australia+	3	1	1	1	0
1990	New Zealand	2	1	1	0	0
1990	India	2	0	2	0	0
1991	West Indies	3	3	0	0	0
1992	Pakistan	5	4	1	0	0
1993	Australia	3	0	3	0	0
1994	New Zealand	1	1	0	0	0
1994	South Africa	2	2	0	0	0

+ England won on faster scoring rate
* England lost on faster scoring rate

RECORD AGAINST EACH COUNTRY

	Mat	Won	Lost	Tied	Aban	% Won
Australia	20	9	10	1	0	45.00
India	8	5	3	0	0	62.50
New Zealand	9	6	2	0	1	75.00
Pakistan	14	10	4	0	0	71.42
South Africa	2	2	0	0	0	100.00
Sri Lanka	1	1	0	0	0	100.00
West Indies	16	9	7	0	0	56.25
TOTAL	**70**	**42**	**26**	**1**	**1**	**60.86**

Percentages do not include abandoned matches

BENSON & HEDGES WORLD SERIES CUP 1979-1995

Winners: 1986/87
Runners-up: 1979/80

Year	Opposition	Mat	Won	Lost	Tied	Aban
79/80	West Indies	5	1	4	0	0
79/80	Australia	4	4	0	0	0
82/83	Australia	5	2	3	0	0
82/83	New Zealand	5	2	3	0	0
86/87	West Indies	4	3	1	0	0
86/87	Australia	6	3	3	0	0
90/91	New Zealand	4	2	2	0	0
90/91	Australia	4	0	4	0	0
94/95	Australia	2	1	1	0	0
94/95	Zimbabwe	2	1	1	0	0
94/95	Australia A	2	1	1	0	0

RECORD AGAINST EACH COUNTRY

	Mat	Won	Lost	Tied	Aban	% Won
Australia	21	10	11	0	0	47.61
Australia A	2	1	1	0	0	50.00
New Zealand	9	4	5	0	0	44.44
West Indies	9	4	5	0	0	44.44
Zimbabwe	2	1	1	0	0	50.00
TOTAL	43	20	23	0	0	46.51

The two matches against Australia A are not recognised as official one-day Internationals

HIGHEST TOTALS

Score	Overs	RPO	Opposition	Venue	Date
363 - 7*	55	6.60	Pakistan	Trent Bridge	20/08/92
334 - 4	60	5.56	India	Lord's	07/06/75
333 - 9	60	5.55	Sri Lanka	Taunton	11/06/83
322 - 6	60	5.36	New Zealand	The Oval	09/06/83
320 - 8	55	5.81	Australia	Edgbaston	22/08/80
302 - 5	55	5.49	Pakistan	The Oval	22/05/92
296 - 4	50	5.92	Sri Lanka	Peshawar	17/10/87
296 - 5	50	5.92	New Zealand	Adelaide	29/01/83
295 - 6	55	5.36	New Zealand	Headingley	23/05/90
295 - 8	55	5.36	Pakistan	Old Trafford	19/07/82
290 - 5	60	4.83	East Africa	Edgbaston	14/06/75
286 - 4	53.4	5.32	New Zealand	Old Trafford	18/07/86
281	55	5.10	India	Trent Bridge	20/07/90
280 - 6	50	5.60	Sri Lanka	Ballarat	09/03/92
278 - 5	55	5.05	New Zealand	Old Trafford	17/07/78
278 - 6	55	5.05	Pakistan	Lord's	20/05/92
278 - 7	54.3	5.10	Australia	Lord's	29/05/89
277 - 5	55	5.03	Australia	Edgbaston	21/05/93
276 - 9	55	5.01	India	The Oval	04/06/82
272 - 6	49	5.55	Australia	Perth	01/01/87
270 - 4	55	4.90	West Indies	Old Trafford	25/05/91
269 - 5	50	5.38	West Indies	Jaipur	26/10/87
267 - 6	50	5.34	New Zealand	Brisbane	15/01/83
266 - 6	51.1	5.19	India	Headingley	13/07/74
266 - 6	60	4.43	New Zealand	Trent Bridge	11/06/75
265 - 3	46.1	5.74	West Indies	Lord's	27/05/91
265 - 4	48	5.52	India	Gwalior	05/03/93
264 - 7	49	5.38	Australia	Sydney	11/12/79
263 - 6	44	5.97	Pakistan	Karachi	20/11/87
257 - 2	49	5.24	Australia	Lord's	03/06/85
256 - 5	53.5	4.75	India	Old Trafford	26/05/86
256	50	5.12	India	Gwalior	04/03/93
255 - 4	43.4	5.84	Pakistan	Old Trafford	24/08/92
255 - 7	50	5.10	India	Kanpur	25/10/89
255 - 7	40	6.37	New Zealand	Christchurch	15/02/92
254 - 6	50	5.08	India	Bombay	05/11/87
254	54.5	4.63	Australia	Old Trafford	19/05/93
253 - 8	50	5.06	West Indies	Kingston	26/02/94
252 - 3	47.1	5.34	Pakistan	Trent Bridge	17/07/82
252 - 6	50	5.04	West Indies	Adelaide	24/01/87
252 - 6	45	5.60	South Africa	Sydney	22/03/92
250 - 9	50	5.00	Australia	Brisbane	18/01/87

* World Record

LOWEST COMPLETED INNINGS

Score	Overs	RPO	Opposition	Venue	Date
81 - 9	35	2.31	Pakistan	Edgbaston	03/09/74
88 - 7	23	3.82	New Zealand	Perth	05/02/83
93	36.2	2.55	Australia	Headingley	18/06/75

94	31.7 *	2.21	Australia	Melbourne	07/02/79
114	39	2.92	West Indies	Bridgetown	19/03/86
121	15	8.06	India	Chandigarh	27/01/85
122	31.6 *	2.88	Pakistan	Lahore	13/01/78
125	48.2	2.58	West Indies	Arnos Vale	04/02/81
125	49.1	2.54	Zimbabwe	Albury	18/03/92
127	40.1	3.16	New Zealand	Christchurch	26/02/83
132	48.2	2.73	Pakistan	Sharjah	26/03/85
136	34.1 *	2.98	New Zealand	Dunedin	08/03/75
137	47.2	2.89	West Indies	Berbice	26/02/81
139	42.5	3.24	West Indies	Adelaide	16/01/80
139	47.3	2.92	Australia	Melbourne	01/02/87
145 - 8	46	3.15	West Indies	Kingston	18/02/86
146	24.2	6.00	Pakistan	Melbourne	02/03/85
147	48.2	3.04	West Indies	Melbourne	30/01/87
148 - 9	50	2.96	West Indies	Arnos Vale	02/03/94
149	41.1	3.62	Australia	Sydney	11/01/83
149	41.4	3.57	India	Sydney	26/02/85

HIGHEST TOTALS AGAINST ENGLAND

Score	Overs	RPO	Opposition	Venue	Date
313 - 6	50	6.26	West Indies	Arnos Vale	02/03/94
298 - 6	54.5	5.43	New Zealand	Headingley	23/05/90
297 - 6	48.5	6.08	New Zealand	Adelaide	29/01/83
295 - 6	50	5.90	New Zealand	Wellington	23/02/83
286 - 9	60	4.76	West Indies	Lord's	23/06/79
286	58	4.93	Sri Lanka	Taunton	11/06/83
284 - 5	55	5.16	New Zealand	Old Trafford	18/07/86
283 - 5	50	5.66	Australia	Brisbane	16/12/90
282 - 5	53	5.32	India	Trent Bridge	20/07/90
280 - 4	53.3	5.23	Australia	Edgbaston	21/05/93
279 - 4	54.3	5.11	Australia	Lord's	29/05/89
273 - 5	55	4.96	Australia	Edgbaston	22/08/80
272 - 9	55	4.94	West Indies	Old Trafford	31/05/84
267 - 6	46.4	5.72	India	Gwalior	05/03/93
265 - 5	50	5.30	West Indies	Gwalior	27/10/89
265 - 7	45.4	5.80	West Indies	Port of Spain	05/03/94
265	53.5	4.92	India	Headingley	13/07/74
264 - 9	55	4.80	West Indies	Lord's	27/05/91
263	50.5	5.17	Pakistan	The Oval	22/05/92
261 - 4	50	5.22	Australia	Brisbane	18/01/87
261 - 8	55	4.74	West Indies	Old Trafford	25/05/91
259 - 4	48.1	5.37	India	Kanpur	25/10/89
258 - 9	55	4.69	Australia	Old Trafford	19/05/93
257 - 7	48	5.35	India	Gwalior	04/03/93
254 - 5	55	4.61	Australia	Lord's	03/06/85
254 - 5	55	4.61	Pakistan	Old Trafford	24/08/92
254 - 6	55	4.61	India	Old Trafford	26/05/86
253 - 5	50	5.06	Australia	Calcutta	08/11/87
252 - 5	49	5.14	India	Cuttack	27/12/84
250 - 5	47	5.31	Sri Lanka	Colombo	10/03/93
250 - 6	55	4.54	Pakistan	Trent Bridge	17/07/82
250 - 9	50	5.00	West Indies	Port of Spain	06/03/94

LOWEST COMPLETED INNINGS AGAINST ENGLAND

Score	Overs	RPO	Opposition	Venue	Date
45	40.3	1.11	Canada	Old Trafford	13/06/79
70	25.2	2.76	Australia	Edgbaston	04/06/77
74	40.2	1.83	Pakistan	Adelaide	01/03/92
85	47	1.80	Pakistan	Old Trafford	24/05/78
94	52.3	1.79	East Africa	Edgbaston	14/06/75
101	33.5 *	2.25	Australia	Melbourne	24/01/79
109	27.3	3.96	Australia	Sydney	26/01/83
114 - 5	15	7.60	India	Chandigarh	27/01/85
127	47.2	2.68	West Indies	Arnos Vale	04/02/81
132 - 3	60	2.20	India	Lord's	07/06/75
134	42.1	3.17	New Zealand	Christchurch	18/02/84
134	46.1	2.90	Zimbabwe	Albury	18/03/92
135	47.1	2.86	New Zealand	Wellington	22/02/84
136	50.4	2.68	Sri Lanka	Headingley	20/06/83
136	47.1	2.88	Australia	Old Trafford	25/05/89
137 - 7*	26	5.26	India	Jamshedpur	01/03/93
138	31.5	4.33	Pakistan	Peshawar	22/11/87
139	46.3	2.98	West Indies	Headingley	21/05/88
141	40.4	3.46	West Indies	Bridgetown	16/02/94
148	48	3.08	West Indies	Devonport	03/02/87
148 - 9	50	2.96	Pakistan	Cuttack	22/10/89

* denotes 8-ball overs

GREATEST VICTORIES

Runs	Opposition	Venue	Date
202 runs	India	Lord's	07/06/75
198 runs	Pakistan	Trent Bridge	20/08/92
196 runs	East Africa	Edgbaston	14/06/75
132 runs	Pakistan	Old Trafford	24/05/78
126 runs	New Zealand	Old Trafford	17/07/78
114 runs	India	The Oval	04/06/82
106 runs	New Zealand	The Oval	09/06/83
106 runs	Sri Lanka	Ballarat	09/03/92
101 runs	Australia	Edgbaston	04/06/77
98 runs	Australia	Sydney	26/01/83
98 runs	Pakistan	Peshawar	22/11/87
95 runs	Australia	Old Trafford	25/05/89
94 runs	Pakistan	The Oval	26/05/78
89 runs	West Indies	Adelaide	24/01/87
80 runs	New Zealand	Trent Bridge	11/06/75
79 runs	Pakistan	Lord's	20/05/92
73 runs	Pakistan	Old Trafford	19/07/82
72 runs	Australia	Sydney	11/12/79
71 runs	New Zealand	Christchurch	15/02/92
61 runs	West Indies	Bridgetown	16/02/94
54 runs	New Zealand	Brisbane	15/01/83
54 runs	New Zealand	Christchurch	18/02/84

Wickets

9 wkts	India	Headingley	02/06/82
9 wkts	Sri Lanka	Headingley	20/06/83
8 wkts	Canada	Old Trafford	13/06/79
8 wkts	New Zealand	Sydney	20/01/83
8 wkts	Pakistan	Lord's	13/06/83
8 wkts	Australia	Lord's	03/06/85
8 wkts	Sri Lanka	Poona	30/10/87
8 wkts	Australia	Sydney	05/03/92
7 wkts	New Zealand	Swansea	18/07/73
7 wkts	Australia	Melbourne	24/01/79
7 wkts	Pakistan	Trent Bridge	17/07/82
7 wkts	Pakistan	Old Trafford	18/06/83
7 wkts	Pakistan	The Oval	21/05/87
7 wkts	West Indies	Lord's	23/05/88
7 wkts	Australia	Hyderabad	19/10/89
7 wkts	West Indies	Lord's	27/05/91
7 wkts	New Zealand	Auckland	11/01/92

NARROWEST VICTORIES

One wicket victories

Opposition	Venue	Date	10th Wkt
West Indies	Headingley	05/09/73	6*
Pakistan	Edgbaston	25/05/87	8*
West Indies	Edgbaston	23/05/91	23*

Two wicket victories

			9th Wkt
Australia	Edgbaston	28/08/72	8*
Australia	Old Trafford	02/06/77	5*
Australia	Sydney	14/01/80	35*
West Indies	Gujranwala	09/10/87	37*
Pakistan	Lahore	18/11/87	27*

Victories by less than 20 runs

2 runs	West Indies	Sydney	28/11/79
5 runs	Sri Lanka	Colombo	13/02/82
7 runs	India	Chandigarh	27/01/85
8 runs	Australia	Sydney	11/02/87
9 runs	New Zealand	Old Trafford	20/06/79
9 runs	West Indies	Old Trafford	25/05/91
9 runs	India	Perth	22/02/92
11 runs	Australia	Sharjah	09/04/87
14 runs	Pakistan	Headingley	16/06/79
14 runs	Australia	Adelaide	30/01/83
14 runs	New Zealand	Christchurch	09/02/91
19 runs	New Zealand	Scarborough	15/07/78
19 runs	West Indies	Perth	03/01/87
19 runs	South Africa	Sydney	22/03/92

Tied match

Australia	Trent Bridge	27/05/89

HEAVIEST DEFEATS

Runs	Opposition	Venue	Date
165 runs	West Indies	Arnos Vale	02/03/94
135 runs	West Indies	Bridgetown	19/03/86
109 runs	Australia	Melbourne	01/02/87
107 runs	West Indies	Adelaide	16/01/80
104 runs	West Indies	Old Trafford	31/05/84
103 runs	New Zealand	Wellington	23/02/83
92 runs	West Indies	Lord's	23/06/79
86 runs	India	Sydney	26/02/85
84 runs	New Zealand	Christchurch	26/02/83
80 runs	Sri Lanka	Colombo	10/03/93
72 runs	West Indies	Port of Spain	05/03/94
71 runs	Australia	Headingley	08/06/81
68 runs	Australia	Sydney	01/01/91
67 runs	Pakistan	Melbourne	02/03/85
50 runs	West Indies	Edgbaston	30/08/76

Wickets	Opposition	Venue	Date
9 wkts	West Indies	Brisbane	23/12/79
9 wkts	India	The Oval	24/05/86
8 wkts	West Indies	The Oval	07/09/73
8 wkts	Pakistan	Edgbaston	03/09/74
8 wkts	West Indies	Sydney	22/01/80
8 wkts	West Indies	Lord's	04/06/84
8 wkts	West Indies	Port of Spain	31/03/86
8 wkts	New Zealand	Brisbane	15/12/90
8 wkts	Sri Lanka	Moratuwa	20/03/93

NARROWEST DEFEATS

Two wicket defeats

Opposition	Venue	Date	9th Wkt
Australia	The Oval	06/06/77	9*
New Zealand	Edgbaston	15/06/83	7*
Australia	Sharjah	24/03/85	10*

Defeats by less than 20 runs

Runs	Opposition	Venue	Date
2 runs	West Indies	Melbourne	20/01/80
2 runs	West Indies	Arnos Vale	04/02/81
2 runs	Australia	Edgbaston	06/06/81
2 runs	New Zealand	Melbourne	13/01/83
3 runs	Sri Lanka	Colombo	14/02/82
3 runs	Australia	Melbourne	10/01/91
3 runs	Pakistan	Lord's	22/08/92
4 runs	Australia	Old Trafford	19/05/93
7 runs	Australia	Calcutta	08/11/87
7 runs	New Zealand	Adelaide	01/12/90
7 runs	New Zealand	Auckland	16/02/91
9 runs	New Zealand	Wellington	13/02/91
9 runs	Zimbabwe	Albury	18/03/92
11 runs	Australia	Brisbane	18/01/87
13 runs	Zimbabwe	Sydney	15/12/94
18 runs	Pakistan	Rawalpindi	12/10/87
19 runs	Australia	Lord's	23/05/93

TOTAL APPEARANCES

Player	Mat	Aus	Can	EA	Ind	NZ	Pak	SA	SL	WI	Zim
G.A. Gooch	125	32	1	0	17	16	16	1	7	32	3
A.J. Lamb	122	23	0	0	15	28	22	1	6	26	1
I.T. Botham	116	33	1	0	7	19	23	2	5	25	1
D.I. Gower	114	32	1	0	16	24	15	0	4	22	0
M.W. Gatting	92	21	0	0	18	11	19	0	8	15	0
P.A.J. DeFreitas	91	19	0	0	12	12	19	4	5	17	3
R.A. Smith	64	12	0	0	10	14	8	1	5	13	1
R.G.D. Willis	64	18	1	0	6	16	9	0	4	10	0
J.E. Emburey	61	15	0	0	5	6	11	0	5	19	0
A.J. Stewart	61	10	0	0	7	13	9	4	4	12	2
G.C. Small	53	10	0	0	3	7	9	2	4	17	1
D.W. Randall	49	18	1	0	2	13	8	0	0	7	0
N.A. Foster	48	10	0	0	7	5	13	0	2	11	0
C.C. Lewis	48	4	0	0	9	11	6	4	3	11	0
N.H. Fairbrother	44	7	0	0	8	5	11	4	3	4	2
G.A. Hick	44	6	0	0	7	5	7	4	3	9	3
D.R. Pringle	44	9	0	0	3	8	9	1	3	11	0
G. Boycott	36	17	1	0	2	3	4	0	0	9	0
G.R. Dilley	36	9	0	0	5	4	6	0	1	11	0
B.C. Broad	34	9	0	0	1	4	10	0	1	9	0
V.J. Marks	34	5	0	0	7	13	5	0	3	1	0
E.E. Hemmings	33	6	0	0	4	6	6	0	3	8	0
C.M. Old	32	10	1	1	3	4	7	0	0	6	0
C.W.J. Athey	31	11	0	0	1	2	9	0	2	6	0
A.R.C. Fraser	31	6	0	0	3	8	2	0	1	10	1
P.H. Edmonds	29	9	0	0	8	2	7	0	0	3	0
C.J. Tavare	29	4	0	0	4	10	6	0	3	2	0
P.R. Downton	28	5	0	0	8	0	4	0	2	9	0
R.W. Taylor	27	2	1	0	3	9	8	0	1	3	0
G. Fowler	26	3	0	0	9	3	6	0	2	3	0
R.T. Robinson	26	6	0	0	5	4	4	0	2	5	0
R.C. Russell	26	2	0	0	3	7	2	0	2	10	0
D.L. Underwood	26	7	0	1	4	3	2	0	2	7	0
P. Willey	26	13	0	0	0	0	0	0	0	13	0
J.M. Brearley	25	12	1	0	0	3	3	0	0	6	0
W. Larkins	25	6	0	0	1	4	2	0	1	11	0
G. Miller	25	4	1	0	2	8	6	0	0	4	0
D.A. Reeve	25	2	0	0	7	5	4	2	3	2	0
K.W.R. Fletcher	24	6	0	1	6	5	2	0	2	2	0
D.J. Capel	23	3	0	0	2	4	6	0	1	7	0
N.G. Cowans	23	7	0	0	5	8	2	0	1	0	0
M.A. Atherton	22	3	0	0	2	5	0	2	0	8	2
A.W. Greig	22	8	0	1	3	4	2	0	0	4	0
M. Hendrick	22	10	1	0	0	4	2	0	0	5	0
J.K. Lever	22	8	0	0	3	2	3	0	1	5	0
C.J. Richards	22	6	0	0	3	2	6	0	1	4	0
D.L. Bairstow	21	9	0	0	0	0	0	0	0	12	0
A.P.E. Knott	20	9	0	1	3	3	1	0	0	3	0
P.C.R. Tufnell	19	5	0	0	1	7	0	0	0	4	2
D.L. Amiss	18	8	0	1	2	4	0	0	0	3	0

344 England - The Complete One-Day International Record

I.J. Gould	18	4	0	0	1	9	2	0	2	0	0
R.K. Illingworth	18	2	0	0	0	3	6	2	1	3	1
P.W. Jarvis	16	4	0	0	6	4	0	0	2	0	0
R.D. Jackman	15	7	0	0	2	5	0	0	0	1	0
G.G. Arnold	14	5	0	0	3	4	1	0	0	1	0
R.M. Ellison	14	2	0	0	7	1	2	0	0	2	0
P.J.W. Allott	13	3	0	0	3	2	2	0	3	0	0
B.N. French	13	4	0	0	1	4	3	0	0	1	0
B. Wood	13	2	0	1	3	2	2	0	0	3	0
M.H. Denness	12	2	0	1	3	2	2	0	0	2	0
T.E. Jesty	10	5	0	0	0	5	0	0	0	0	0
P. Lever	10	3	0	1	1	3	2	0	0	0	0
D.E. Malcolm	10	0	0	0	5	3	0	0	1	1	0
G.P. Thorpe	10	5	0	0	0	0	0	2	0	1	2
S.J. Rhodes	9	5	0	0	0	1	0	2	0	0	1
J.A. Snow	9	5	0	1	1	2	0	0	0	0	0
D. Lloyd	8	1	0	0	2	0	3	0	0	2	0
J.E. Morris	8	4	0	0	0	4	0	0	0	0	0
M.D. Moxon	8	1	0	0	2	3	2	0	0	0	0
G.R.J. Roope	8	0	0	0	0	3	5	0	0	0	0
M.P. Bicknell	7	3	0	0	0	4	0	0	0	0	0
J.H. Edrich	7	1	0	0	2	2	2	0	0	0	0
D. Gough	7	2	0	0	0	1	0	2	0	0	2
S.D. Udal	7	2	0	0	0	1	0	2	0	0	2
G.D. Barlow	6	3	0	0	0	0	0	0	0	3	0
G. Cook	6	1	0	0	3	0	0	0	2	0	0
F.C. Hayes	6	1	0	1	0	3	0	0	0	1	0
N.V. Radford	6	1	0	0	0	4	0	0	0	1	0
R.A. Woolmer	6	3	0	0	1	0	0	0	0	2	0
A.R. Caddick	5	3	0	0	0	0	0	0	0	2	0
D.G. Cork	5	2	0	0	0	0	1	2	0	0	0
M.P. Maynard	5	0	0	0	0	0	0	0	0	5	0
M.J. Smith	5	0	0	0	1	0	2	0	0	2	0
R.J. Bailey	4	1	0	0	0	0	1	0	1	1	0
B.L. D'Oliveira	4	4	0	0	0	0	0	0	0	0	0
N. Hussain	4	0	0	0	0	0	1	0	0	3	0
A.P. Igglesden	4	0	0	0	0	0	0	0	0	4	0
C.T. Radley	4	0	0	0	0	2	2	0	0	0	0
M.R. Ramprakash	4	0	0	0	0	0	0	0	0	4	0
I.D.K. Salisbury	4	0	0	0	1	0	0	0	1	2	0
C.L. Smith	4	0	0	0	0	3	1	0	0	0	0
G.B. Stevenson	4	1	0	0	0	0	0	0	0	3	0
S.L. Watkin	4	0	0	0	0	0	0	0	0	4	0
J.P. Agnew	3	1	0	0	2	0	0	0	0	0	0
R.J. Blakey	3	0	0	0	2	0	1	0	0	0	0
R.O. Butcher	3	1	0	0	0	0	0	0	0	2	0
D.B. Close	3	3	0	0	0	0	0	0	0	0	0
N.G.B. Cook	3	0	0	0	0	0	3	0	0	0	0
C.S. Cowdrey	3	1	0	0	2	0	0	0	0	0	0
J.P. Crawley	3	1	0	0	0	0	0	0	0	0	2
J.H. Hampshire	3	3	0	0	0	0	0	0	0	0	0
G.W. Humpage	3	3	0	0	0	0	0	0	0	0	0
R. Illingworth	3	1	0	0	0	2	0	0	0	0	0

J.A. Jameson	3	0	0	0	1	1	0	0	0	1	0
T.A. Lloyd	3	0	0	0	0	0	0	0	0	3	0
J.D. Love	3	3	0	0	0	0	0	0	0	0	0
B.W. Luckhurst	3	1	0	0	0	2	0	0	0	0	0
M.A. Lynch	3	0	0	0	0	0	0	0	0	3	0
J.G. Thomas	3	0	0	0	0	0	1	0	0	2	0
J.E. Benjamin	2	1	0	0	0	0	0	0	0	0	1
G.A. Cope	2	0	0	0	0	0	2	0	0	0	0
N.G. Gifford	2	1	0	0	0	0	1	0	0	0	0
B.C. Rose	2	0	0	0	0	0	2	0	0	0	0
W.N. Slack	2	0	0	0	0	0	0	0	0	2	0
D.M. Smith	2	0	0	0	0	0	0	0	0	2	0
L.B. Taylor	2	0	0	0	1	0	0	0	0	1	0
F.J. Titmus	2	0	0	0	0	2	0	0	0	0	0
C.M. Wells	2	1	0	0	0	0	1	0	0	0	0
J.J. Whitaker	2	0	0	0	1	0	1	0	0	0	0
K.J. Barnett	1	0	0	0	0	0	0	0	1	0	0
M.R. Benson	1	0	0	0	0	1	0	0	0	0	0
A.R. Butcher	1	1	0	0	0	0	0	0	0	0	0
M.C. Cowdrey	1	1	0	0	0	0	0	0	0	0	0
D.V. Lawrence	1	0	0	0	0	0	0	0	0	1	0
P. Pocock	1	0	0	0	0	0	1	0	0	0	0
K. Shuttleworth	1	1	0	0	0	0	0	0	0	0	0
D.S. Steele	1	0	0	0	0	0	0	0	0	1	0
J.P. Taylor	1	0	0	0	0	0	0	0	1	0	0
R.W. Tolchard	1	1	0	0	0	0	0	0	0	0	0
C. White	1	1	0	0	0	0	0	0	0	0	0

LEADING RUN SCORERS

	Mat	Inn	No	Runs	HS	Avg	100	50
G.A. Gooch	125	122	6	4290	142	36.98	8	23
A.J. Lamb	122	118	16	4010	118	39.31	4	26
D.I. Gower	114	111	8	3170	158	30.77	7	12
R.A. Smith	64	63	8	2218	167*	40.32	4	13
I.T. Botham	116	106	15	2113	79	23.21	0	9
M.W. Gatting	92	88	17	2095	115*	29.50	1	9
A.J. Stewart	61	56	4	1567	103	30.13	1	10
B.C. Broad	34	34	0	1361	106	40.02	1	11
G.A. Hick	44	43	6	1473	105*	39.81	1	12
N.H. Fairbrother	44	42	9	1268	113	38.42	1	9
G. Boycott	36	34	4	1082	105	36.06	1	9
D.W. Randall	49	45	5	1067	88	26.67	0	5
D.L. Amiss	18	18	0	859	137	47.72	4	1
C.W.J. Athey	31	30	3	848	142*	31.40	2	4
K.W.R. Fletcher	24	22	3	757	131	39.84	1	5
G. Fowler	26	26	2	744	81*	31.00	0	4
C.J. Tavare	29	28	2	720	83*	27.69	0	4
R.T. Robinson	26	26	0	597	83	22.96	0	3
W. Larkins	25	24	0	591	124	24.62	1	0
M.A. Atherton	22	22	2	841	86	42.05	0	7
P. Willey	26	24	1	538	64	23.39	0	5
P.A.J. DeFreitas	91	59	23	551	49*	15.30	0	0
J.M. Brearley	25	24	3	510	78	24.28	0	3
J.E. Emburey	61	45	10	501	34	14.31	0	0

HIGHEST INDIVIDUAL SCORES

Centuries

167*	R.A. Smith	Australia	Edgbaston	21/05/93
158	D.I. Gower	New Zealand	Brisbane	15/01/83
142*	C.W.J. Athey	New Zealand	Old Trafford	18/07/86
142	G.A. Gooch	Pakistan	Karachi	20/11/87
137	D.L. Amiss	India	Lord's	07/06/75
136	G.A. Gooch	Australia	Lord's	29/05/89
131	K.W.R. Fletcher	New Zealand	Trent Bridge	11/06/75
130	D.I. Gower	Sri Lanka	Taunton	11/06/83
129*	G.A. Gooch	West Indies	Port of Spain	04/03/86
129	R.A. Smith	India	Gwalior	04/03/93
128	R.A. Smith	New Zealand	Headingley	23/05/90
124	W. Larkins	Australia	Hyderabad	19/10/89
122	D.I. Gower	New Zealand	Melbourne	13/01/83
118	A.J. Lamb	Pakistan	Trent Bridge	17/07/82
117*	C.T. Radley	New Zealand	Old Trafford	17/07/78
117*	G.A. Gooch	Australia	Lord's	03/06/85
116*	D. Lloyd	Pakistan	Trent Bridge	31/08/74
115*	M.W. Gatting	India	Poona	05/12/84
115	G.A. Gooch	Australia	Edgbaston	01/06/85
115	G.A. Gooch	India	Bombay	05/11/87
114*	D.I. Gower	Pakistan	The Oval	26/05/78
113	N.H. Fairbrother	West Indies	Lord's	27/05/91
112*	G.A. Gooch	New Zealand	The Oval	25/05/90
111	C.W.J. Athey	Australia	Brisbane	18/01/87
109	D.I. Gower	New Zealand	Adelaide	29/01/83
108*	A.J. Lamb	New Zealand	Sydney	20/01/83
108	D.L. Amiss	Australia	The Oval	06/06/77
108	G.A. Gooch	Australia	Edgbaston	22/08/80
106	B.C. Broad	New Zealand	Napier	16/03/88
105*	G.A. Hick	India	Gwalior	05/03/93
105	G. Boycott	Australia	Sydney	11/12/79
103	D.L. Amiss	Australia	Old Trafford	24/08/72
103	R.A. Smith	India	Trent Bridge	20/07/90
103	A.J. Stewart	Pakistan	The Oval	22/05/92
102	A.J. Lamb	New Zealand	The Oval	09/06/83
102	D.I. Gower	Australia	Lord's	03/06/85
101*	D.I. Gower	Australia	Melbourne	04/02/79
100*	A.J. Lamb	Australia	Trent Bridge	27/05/89
100	D.L. Amiss	New Zealand	Swansea	18/07/73

Most Centuries (39)

G.A. Gooch	8		N.H. Fairbrother	1
D.I. Gower	7		K.W.R. Fletcher	1
D.L. Amiss	4		M.W. Gatting	1
A.J. Lamb	4		G.A. Hick	1
R.A. Smith	4		W. Larkins	1
C.W.J. Athey	2		D. Lloyd	1
G. Boycott	1		C.T. Radley	1
B.C. Broad	1		A.J. Stewart	1

Fifties

99	G. Boycott	Australia	The Oval	20/08/80
99	A.J. Lamb	India	The Oval	04/06/82
99	B.C. Broad	Pakistan	The Oval	21/05/87
97*	A.J. Lamb	New Zealand	Auckland	25/02/84
97	B.C. Broad	Pakistan	Perth	05/01/87

348   *England - The Complete One-Day International Record*

96	M.W. Gatting	Australia	Edgbaston	06/06/81
94	G.A. Gooch	New Zealand	Scarborough	15/07/78
94	A.J. Lamb	Australia	Melbourne	23/01/83
92*	D.I. Gower	New Zealand	Edgbaston	15/06/83
92	G.A. Gooch	West Indies	Jaipur	26/10/87
91	G.A. Gooch	New Zealand	Old Trafford	18/07/86
91	A.J. Lamb	India	Kanpur	25/10/89
91	R.A. Smith	India	Perth	22/02/92
91	A.J. Stewart	India	Jaipur	18/01/93
91	G.A. Hick	Australia	Melbourne	10/01/95
90	J.H. Edrich	India	Headingley	13/07/74
89	G.P. Thorpe	Zimbabwe	Brisbane	07/01/95
88	D.L. Amiss	East Africa	Edgbaston	14/06/75
88	D.W. Randall	West Indies	Lord's	28/08/76
86*	G. Boycott	Australia	Sydney	26/12/79
86*	G.A. Hick	West Indies	Lord's	27/05/91
86	G.A. Gooch	Australia	Sharjah	09/04/87
86	C.W.J. Athey	Pakistan	Karachi	20/10/87
86	M.A. Atherton	West Indies	Bridgetown	16/02/94
85*	R.A. Smith	Pakistan	Old Trafford	24/08/92
85	R.A. Smith	New Zealand	Christchurch	15/02/92
85	R.A. Smith	Pakistan	Lord's	26/05/92
85	G.A. Hick	Australia	Old Trafford	19/05/93
84	D.I. Gower	New Zealand	Auckland	19/02/83
84	G.A. Gooch	Sri Lanka	Peshawar	17/10/87
84	K.J. Barnett	Sri Lanka	The Oval	04/09/88
83*	C.J. Tavare	New Zealand	Sydney	20/01/83
83	R.T. Robinson	Pakistan	Sharjah	07/04/87
83	G.A. Hick	South Africa	Sydney	22/03/92
82*	C.J. Tavare	West Indies	Headingley	28/05/80
82*	M.W. Gatting	West Indies	Edgbaston	19/05/88
82	J.H. Edrich	Australia	Melbourne	05/01/71
81*	G. Fowler	Sri Lanka	Headingley	20/06/83
81*	R.A. Smith	Sri Lanka	Delhi	15/10/89
81	A.J. Lamb	Pakistan	Melbourne	02/03/85
81	D.I. Gower	India	Old Trafford	26/05/86
81	M.A. Atherton	New Zealand	Edgbaston	19/05/94
81	G.A. Hick	South Arica	Edgbaston	25/08/94
80*	G.D. Barlow	West Indies	Scarborough	26/08/76
79	C.T. Radley	Pakistan	Old Trafford	24/05/78
79	I.T. Botham	New Zealand	Christchurch	15/02/92
78*	B. Wood	India	Headingley	02/06/82
78*	G. Fowler	Pakistan	Lord's	13/06/83
78	J.M. Brearley	Australia	The Oval	06/06/77
78	G. Boycott	Australia	Edgbaston	22/08/80
77*	A.J. Lamb	Australia	Sydney	22/01/87
77	B. Wood	East Africa	Edgbaston	14/06/75
77	D.I. Gower	Australia	Adelaide	30/01/83
77	A.J. Stewart	South Africa	Melbourne	12/03/92
77	R.A. Smith	Pakistan	Trent Bridge	20/08/92
76	D.I. Gower	India	The Oval	04/06/82
76	M.W. Gatting	Pakistan	Old Trafford	19/07/82
76	B.C. Broad	Australia	Perth	01/01/87
76	B.C. Broad	West Indies	Devonport	03/02/87
76	A.J. Lamb	Sri Lanka	Peshawar	17/10/87
75*	G. Boycott	Australia	Lord's	04/06/81
75*	N.H. Fairbrother	South Africa	Melbourne	12/03/92

One-Day International Records 349

75	A.J. Lamb	West Indies	Old Trafford	31/05/84
74	G.A. Gooch	Sri Lanka	Colombo	14/02/82
74	M.A. Atherton	West Indies	Old Trafford	25/05/91
74	A.J. Stewart	Australia	Lord's	23/05/93
72	I.T. Botham	Australia	Old Trafford	30/05/85
72	A.J. Lamb	New Zealand	Sydney	13/12/90
72	R.A. Smith	India	Gwalior	05/03/93
71*	M.W. Gatting	India	Jullundur	20/12/81
71*	G.A. Hick	Pakistan	The Oval	22/05/92
71	G.A. Gooch	New Zealand	Old Trafford	20/06/79
71	A.J. Lamb	West Indies	Perth	03/01/87
71	I.T. Botham	Australia	Melbourne	08/02/87
70	G. Boycott	West Indies	Lord's	30/05/80
70	D.W. Randall	New Zealand	Christchurch	18/02/84
70	C.L. Smith	New Zealand	Wellington	22/02/84
70	M.D. Moxon	India	Nagpur	23/01/85
69*	M.A. Atherton	West Indies	Edgbaston	23/05/91
69	G.A. Gooch	Australia	Sydney	14/01/80
69	K.W.R. Fletcher	India	Cuttack	27/01/82
69	G. Fowler	New Zealand	Edgbaston	15/06/83
69	G. Fowler	Pakistan	Old Trafford	18/06/83
69	R.A. Smith	West Indies	Bridgetown	03/04/90
68	K.W.R. Fletcher	India	Lord's	07/06/75
68	G. Boycott	Australia	Melbourne	08/12/79
68	G. Boycott	West Indies	Brisbane	23/12/79
68	I.T. Botham	Australia	Perth	01/01/87
67*	A.J. Lamb	West Indies	Gujranwala	09/10/87
66	M.H. Denness	West Indies	Headingley	05/09/73
66	C.J. Tavare	India	Headingley	02/06/82
66	A.J. Lamb	Australia	Perth	01/01/87
66	B.C. Broad	Pakistan	Peshawar	22/11/87
66	A.J. Lamb	Sri Lanka	The Oval	04/09/88
66	A.J. Lamb	West Indies	Kingston	03/03/90
66	A.J. Stewart	West Indies	Kingston	26/02/94
65	I.T. Botham	New Zealand	Adelaide	29/01/83
65	B.C. Broad	Pakistan	Sharjah	07/04/87
65	R.A. Smith	West Indies	Gwalior	27/10/89
65	R.A. Smith	New Zealand	Christchurch	09/02/91
65	G.A. Gooch	West Indies	Melbourne	27/02/92
64	J.M. Brearley	West Indies	Lord's	23/06/79
64	P. Willey	Australia	Sydney	11/12/79
64	G.A. Gooch	Sri Lanka	Colombo	13/02/82
64	C.W.J. Athey	West Indies	Adelaide	24/01/87
64	G.A. Hick	Zimbabwe	Sydney	15/12/94
63*	J.E. Morris	New Zealand	Adelaide	01/12/90
63	K.W.R. Fletcher	West Indies	The Oval	07/09/73
63	G. Boycott	West Indies	Sydney	22/01/80
63	N.H. Fairbrother	Sri Lanka	Ballarat	09/03/92
63	N.H. Fairbrother	Pakistan	The Oval	22/05/92
63	G.A. Hick	Pakistan	Trent Bridge	20/08/92
62	A.J. Lamb	West Indies	Old Trafford	25/05/91
62	N.H. Fairbrother	Pakistan	Melbourne	25/03/92
62	N.H. Fairbrother	Pakistan	Trent Bridge	20/08/92
61*	R.A. Smith	New Zealand	Auckland	11/01/92
61	A.J. Lamb	Pakistan	The Oval	21/05/87
61	G.A. Gooch	Sri Lanka	Poona	30/10/87
61	D.I. Gower	Australia	Lord's	29/05/89
61	A.J. Stewart	India	Kanpur	25/10/89

350 *England - The Complete One-Day International Record*

61	A.J. Lamb	New Zealand	Christchurch	09/02/91
60	K.W.R. Fletcher	Australia	Old Trafford	24/08/72
60	I.T. Botham	West Indies	Arnos Vale	04/02/81
60	I.T. Botham	Sri Lanka	Colombo	13/02/82
60	M.W. Gatting	Pakistan	Karachi	20/10/87
60	A.J. Lamb	Pakistan	Lord's	26/05/92
60	M.A. Atherton	Australia	Sydney	06/12/94
59*	A.J. Lamb	India	Bangalore	20/01/85
59	D.I. Gower	West Indies	Brisbane	23/12/79
59	M.W. Gatting	India	Cuttack	27/12/84
59	G.A. Gooch	West Indies	Gwalior	27/10/89
59	M.A. Atherton	India	Trent Bridge	20/07/90
59	A.J. Stewart	Sri Lanka	Ballarat	09/03/92
59	N.H. Fairbrother	Australia	Old Trafford	19/05/93
58*	P. Willey	West Indies	Sydney	28/11/79
58	C.J. Tavare	Pakistan	Old Trafford	18/06/83
58	M.W. Gatting	Sri Lanka	Peshawar	17/10/87
58	C.W.J. Athey	Australia	Calcutta	08/11/87
58	G.A. Gooch	Australia	Sydney	05/03/92
57	G. Boycott	West Indies	Lord's	23/06/79
57	D.W. Randall	Australia	Brisbane	16/01/83
57	A.J. Lamb	Pakistan	Lahore	09/03/84
57	G.A. Gooch	Australia	Old Trafford	30/05/85
57	B.C. Broad	India	Sharjah	02/04/87
57	G.A. Gooch	Pakistan	Peshawar	22/11/87
56	P. Willey	West Indies	Lord's	30/05/80
56	M.W. Gatting	India	Bombay	05/11/87
56	B.C. Broad	New Zealand	Christchurch	12/03/88
56	G.A. Gooch	Australia	Hyderabad	19/10/89
56	A.J. Lamb	India	Headingley	18/07/90
56	G.A. Hick	New Zealand	Wellington	15/03/92
56	G.A. Hick	India	Chandigarh	21/01/93
56	G.A. Hick	India	Bangalore	26/02/93
56	R.A. Smith	West Indies	Kingston	26/02/94
56	S.J. Rhodes	South Africa	Old Trafford	27/08/94
55*	K.W.R. Fletcher	India	The Oval	15/07/74
55*	A.J. Lamb	West Indies	Bridgetown	03/04/90
55	R.T. Robinson	West Indies	Port of Spain	31/03/86
55	B.C. Broad	West Indies	Adelaide	24/01/87
55	R.T. Robinson	Sri Lanka	Poona	30/10/87
55	R.A. Smith	Pakistan	Nagpur	30/10/89
55	G.A. Gooch	New Zealand	Headingley	23/05/90
55	A.J. Stewart	Australia	Melbourne	10/01/91
55	A.J. Lamb	Pakistan	Lord's	22/08/92
55	G.P. Thorpe	South Africa	Old Trafford	27/08/94
54	B.C. Rose	Pakistan	Sahiwal	23/12/77
54	G.A. Gooch	Australia	The Oval	20/08/80
54	N.H. Fairbrother	New Zealand	Auckland	19/03/88
54	G.A. Gooch	West Indies	Old Trafford	25/05/91
54	G.A. Hick	West Indies	Melbourne	27/02/92
53*	N.H. Fairbrother	India	Jamshedpur	01/03/93
53	G.A. Gooch	Australia	Lord's	09/06/79
53	J.M. Brearley	New Zealand	Old Trafford	20/06/79
53	G.A. Gooch	Australia	Lord's	04/06/81
53	D.I. Gower	India	Jullundur	20/12/81
53	D.I. Gower	New Zealand	Christchurch	26/02/83
53	A.J. Lamb	Sri Lanka	Taunton	11/06/83
53	A.J. Lamb	Australia	Melbourne	17/02/85

53	B.C. Broad	Australia	Sydney	11/02/87
53	M.W. Gatting	Pakistan	Peshawar	22/11/87
53	I.T. Botham	Australia	Sydney	05/03/92
53	A.J. Stewart	West Indies	Port of Spain	06/03/94
52*	T.E. Jesty	New Zealand	Adelaide	29/01/83
52	F.C. Hayes	East Africa	Edgbaston	14/06/75
52	R.O. Butcher	Australia	Edgbaston	22/08/80
52	I.T. Botham	India	Cuttack	27/01/82
52	B.C. Broad	Pakistan	Trent Bridge	23/05/87
52	G.A. Gooch	Australia	Old Trafford	25/05/89
52	A.J. Lamb	Sri Lanka	Delhi	15/10/89
51*	C.M. Old	India	Lord's	07/06/75
51*	D.W. Randall	Pakistan	Sialkot	30/12/77
51*	D.W. Randall	Australia	Melbourne	23/01/83
51	P. Willey	Australia	Sydney	26/12/79
51	P. Willey	West Indies	Melbourne	20/01/80
51	C.W.J. Athey	Australia	Edgbaston	22/08/80
51	G.A. Gooch	India	Perth	22/02/92
51	A.J. Stewart	Pakistan	Old Trafford	24/08/92
51	M.A. Atherton	West Indies	Port of Spain	06/03/94
50*	D.J. Capel	Pakistan	Karachi	20/11/87
50*	N.H. Fairbrother	New Zealand	Dunedin	09/03/88
50	A.P.E. Knott	Australia	Lord's	26/08/72
50	D.I. Gower	New Zealand	Old Trafford	17/07/78
50	C.J. Richards	West Indies	Perth	03/01/87
50	D.I. Gower	Australia	Sydney	22/01/87
50	D.I. Gower	India	Headingley	18/07/90
50	R.C. Russell	India	Trent Bridge	20/07/90
50	A.J. Stewart	Pakistan	Lord's	26/05/92

Most Fifties (207)

A.J. Lamb	26		G.P. Thorpe	2
G.A. Gooch	23		B. Wood	2
R.A. Smith	13		D.L. Amiss	1
D.I. Gower	12		G.D. Barlow	1
G.A. Hick	12		K.J. Barnett	1
B.C. Broad	11		R.O. Butcher	1
A.J. Stewart	10		D.J. Capel	1
I.T. Botham	9		M.H. Denness	1
G. Boycott	9		F.C. Hayes	1
N.H. Fairbrother	9		T.E. Jesty	1
M.W. Gatting	9		A.P.E. Knott	1
M.A. Atherton	7		J.E. Morris	1
K.W.R. Fletcher	5		M.D. Moxon	1
D.W. Randall	5		C.M. Old	1
P. Willey	5		C.T. Radley	1
C.W.J. Athey	4		S.J. Rhodes	1
G. Fowler	4		C.J. Richards	1
C.J. Tavare	4		B.C. Rose	1
J.M. Brearley	3		R.C. Russell	1
R.T. Robinson	3		C.L. Smith	1
J.H. Edrich	2			

HIGHEST PARTNERSHIPS FOR EACH WICKET

Wkt	Runs	Opposition	Venue	Date	Batsmen
1st	193	New Zealand	Old Trafford	18/07/86	G.A. Gooch/C.W.J. Athey
2nd	202	Australia	Lord's	03/06/85	G.A. Gooch/D.I. Gower
3rd	213	West Indies	Lord's	27/05/91	G.A. Hick/N.H. Fairbrother
4th	139	Australia	Melbourne	23/01/83	A.J. Lamb/D.W. Randall
5th	142	Australia	Edgbaston	21/05/93	R.A Smith/G.P. Thorpe
6th	98	Sri Lanka	Taunton	11/06/83	D.I. Gower/I.J. Gould
7th	86*	India	Poona	05/12/84	M.W. Gatting/P.R. Downton
8th	55	West Indies	Lord's	28/08/76	D.W. Randall/A.P.E. Knott
	55	Australia	Edgbaston	04/06/77	C.M. Old/J.K. Lever
9th	47	West Indies	Old Trafford	31/05/84	A.J. Lamb/N.A. Foster
10th	43*	Australia	Melbourne	10/01/91	A.R.C. Fraser/P.C.R. Tufnell

TOTAL HIGHEST PARTNERSHIPS

Runs	Wkt	Opposition	Venue	Date	Batsmen
213	3rd	West Indies	Lord's	27/05/91	G.A. Hick/N.H. Fairbrother
202	2nd	Australia	Lord's	03/06/85	G.A. Gooch/D.I. Gower
193	1st	New Zealand	Old Trafford	18/07/86	G.A. Gooch/C.W.J. Athey
190*	3rd	New Zealand	Sydney	20/01/83	C.J. Tavare/A.J. Lamb
185	1st	Australia	Hyderabad	19/10/89	G.A. Gooch/W. Larkins
176	2nd	India	Lord's	07/06/75	D.L. Amiss/K.W.R. Fletcher
161	1st	Australia	The Oval	06/06/77	D.L. Amiss/J.M. Brearley
159	3rd	India	The Oval	04/06/82	A.J. Lamb/D.I. Gower
158	1st	East Africa	Edgbaston	14/06/75	B. Wood/D.L. Amiss
156	1st	West Indies	Old Trafford	25/05/91	G.A. Gooch/M.A. Atherton
154	1st	Australia	Edgbaston	22/08/80	G.A. Gooch/G. Boycott
142	5th	Australia	Edgbaston	21/05/93	R.A. Smith/G.P. Thorpe
140	2nd	Pakistan	Sharjah	07/04/87	B.C. Broad/R.T. Robinson
139	4th	Australia	Melbourne	23/01/83	A.J. Lamb/D.W. Randall
135	1st	West Indies	Lord's	30/05/80	P. Willey/G. Boycott
135	3rd	Pakistan	Karachi	20/10/87	C.W.J. Athey/M.W. Gatting
133	1st	India	Headingley	02/06/82	B. Wood/C.J. Tavare
130	4th	India	Kanpur	25/10/89	A.J. Lamb/A.J. Stewart
129	1st	West Indies	Lord's	23/06/79	J.M. Brearley/G. Boycott
129	3rd	Pakistan	Trent Bridge	20/08/92	R.A. Smith/N.H. Fairbrother
127	4th	Australia	Old Trafford	19/05/93	G.A. Hick/N.H. Fairbrother
125	2nd	Australia	Old Trafford	24/08/72	D.L. Amiss/K.W.R. Fletcher
123	2nd	Pakistan	The Oval	21/05/87	B.C. Broad/A.J. Lamb
123	1st	Sri Lanka	Poona	30/10/87	G.A. Gooch/R.T. Robinson
123	1st	Australia	Lord's	29/05/89	G.A. Gooch/D.I. Gower
121	1st	West Indies	Adelaide	24/01/87	B.C. Broad/C.W.J. Athey
118	2nd	Australia	Sydney	11/12/79	G. Boycott/P. Willey
118	1st	Australia	Sharjah	09/04/87	G.A. Gooch/B.C. Broad
118	3rd	Sri Lanka	The Oval	04/09/88	K.J. Barnett/A.J. Lamb
117	3rd	India	Bombay	05/11/87	G.A. Gooch/M.W. Gatting
116	4th	Australia	Old Trafford	30/05/85	G.A. Gooch/I.T. Botham
116	2nd	India	Gwalior	05/03/93	R.A. Smith/G.A. Hick
115	4th	New Zealand	The Oval	09/06/83	A.J. Lamb/M.W. Gatting
115	1st	Pakistan	Old Trafford	18/06/83	G. Fowler/C.J. Tavare
115	3rd	India	Old Trafford	26/05/86	D.I. Gower/A.J. Lamb
113	5th	New Zealand	Brisbane	15/01/83	D.I. Gower/D.W. Randall
113	2nd	New Zealand	Headingley	23/05/90	G.A. Gooch/R.A. Smith
112	1st	West Indies	Kingston	26/02/94	M.A. Atherton/A.J. Stewart
111	2nd	New Zealand	Scarborough	15/07/78	G.A. Gooch/C.T. Radley
111	2nd	Australia	Sydney	26/12/79	G. Boycott/P. Willey
111	4th	India	Trent Bridge	20/07/90	M.A. Atherton/R.A. Smith
110	5th	India	Jullundur	20/12/81	D.I. Gower/M.W. Gatting
110	2nd	India	Perth	22/02/92	G.A. Gooch/R.A. Smith
109*	5th	New Zealand	The Oval	25/05/90	G.A. Gooch/R.C. Russell
109	1st	Sri Lanka	Colombo	14/02/82	G.A. Gooch/G. Cook

109	4th	Pakistan	Karachi	20/11/87	G.A. Gooch/D.J. Capel
108	3rd	Australia	Lord's	09/06/79	J.M. Brearley/G.A. Gooch
108	1st	Australia	The Oval	20/08/80	G.A. Gooch/G. Boycott
107	2nd	Pakistan	Trent Bridge	17/07/82	C.J. Tavare/A.J. Lamb
107	1st	Australia	Sydney	05/03/92	G.A. Gooch/I.T. Botham
106*	3rd	Pakistan	Lord's	13/06/83	G. Fowler/A.J. Lamb
106	4th	Australia	Adelaide	30/01/83	D.I. Gower/D.W. Randall
106	4th	Australia	Perth	01/01/87	A.J. Lamb/I.T. Botham
105	4th	Pakistan	The Oval	26/05/78	D.I. Gower/G.R.J. Roope
105	3rd	New Zealand	Old Trafford	17/07/78	C.T. Radley/D.I. Gower
104	1st	Pakistan	Perth	05/01/87	B.C. Broad/C.W.J. Athey
103	3rd	Pakistan	Trent Bridge	31/08/74	D. Lloyd/M.H. Denness
103	3rd	Sri Lanka	Delhi	15/10/89	R.A. Smith/A.J. Lamb
102	3rd	Pakistan	Trent Bridge	17/07/82	A.J. Lamb/M.W. Gatting
102	3rd	West Indies	Old Trafford	25/05/91	M.A. Atherton/A.J. Lamb
101	1st	Pakistan	Peshawar	22/11/87	G.A. Gooch/B.C. Broad
101	1st	India	Gwalior	04/03/93	R.A. Smith/A.J. Stewart
100	1st	Australia	Sydney	06/12/94	M.A. Atherton/A.J. Stewart

LEADING WICKET TAKERS

Name	Overs	Mds	Runs	Wkts	Avg	B/B	5WI	E/R
I.T.Botham	1045.1	109	4139	145	28.54	4-31	0	3.96
P.A.J.DeFreitas	848.1	105	3284	104	31.57	4-35	0	3.87
R.G.D.Willis	599.1	97	1968	80	24.60	4-11	0	3.28
J.E.Emburey	570.5	39	2346	76	30.86	4-37	0	4.10
C.C.Lewis	391.4	25	1735	61	28.44	4-30	0	4.42
N.A.Foster	437.5	25	1836	59	31.11	3-20	0	4.19
G.C.Small	465.3	33	1942	58	33.48	4-31	0	4.17
G.R.Dilley	340.3	33	1291	48	26.89	4-23	0	3.79
C.M.Old	292.3	42	999	45	22.20	4-8	0	3.41
V.J.Marks	306.2	28	1135	44	25.79	5-20	2	3.70
D.R.Pringle	396.3	53	1677	44	38.11	4-42	0	4.22
E.E.Hemmings	292	16	1294	37	34.97	4-52	0	4.43
G.A.Gooch	344.2	26	1516	36	42.11	3-19	0	4.40
M.Hendrick	208	36	681	35	19.45	5-31	1	3.27
D.L.Underwood	213	24	734	32	22.93	4-44	0	3.44
A.R.C.Fraser	291.4	39	1069	35	30.54	4-22	0	3.66
P.H.Edmonds	255.4	19	965	26	37.11	3-39	0	3.77
G.Miller	211.2	20	813	25	32.52	3-27	0	3.84
R.K.Illingworth	182.1	7	760	24	31.66	3-33	0	4.17
P.W.Jarvis	146.3	8	672	24	28.00	5-35	1	4.58
J.K.Lever	192	19	713	24	29.70	4-29	0	3.71
N.G.Cowans	213.4	17	913	23	39.69	3-44	0	4.27

BEST BOWLING

5 Wicket Innings

5-20	V.J. Marks	New Zealand	Wellington	22/02/84
5-31	M. Hendrick	Australia	The Oval	20/08/80
5-35	P.W. Jarvis	India	Bangalore	26/02/93
5-39	V.J. Marks	Sri Lanka	Taunton	11/06/83
5-44	D. Gough	Zimbabwe	Sydney	15/12/94

Most 5 Wicket Innings (5)

V.J. Marks	2		M. Hendrick	1
D. Gough	1		P.W. Jarvis	1

4 Wicket Innings

4-8	C.M. Old	Canada	Old Trafford	13/06/79
4-11	J.A. Snow	East Africa	Edgbaston	14/06/75
4-11	R.G.D. Willis	Canada	Old Trafford	13/06/79
4-15	R.G.D. Willis	Pakistan	Old Trafford	24/05/78
4-15	M. Hendrick	Pakistan	Headingley	16/06/79
4-22	A.R.C. Fraser	Australia	Melbourne	10/01/95
4-23	R.G.D. Willis	New Zealand	Sydney	20/01/83
4-23	N. Gifford	Pakistan	Sharjah	26/03/85
4-23	G.R. Dilley	West Indies	Brisbane	17/01/87
4-25	M. Hendrick	Australia	Melbourne	24/01/79
4-27	G.G. Arnold	Australia	Edgbaston	28/08/72
4-29	J.K. Lever	Australia	Edgbaston	04/06/77
4-30	C.C. Lewis	Sri Lanka	Ballarat	09/03/92
4-31	G.C. Small	West Indies	Edgbaston	19/05/88
4-31	I.T. Botham	Australia	Sydney	05/03/92
4-32	J.A. Snow	New Zealand	Swansea	18/07/73
4-33	G.B. Stevenson	Australia	Sydney	14/01/80
4-33	P.W. Jarvis	New Zealand	Auckland	19/03/88
4-35	P. Lever	New Zealand	Wellington	09/03/75
4-35	P.A.J. DeFreitas	Australia	Adelaide	26/01/87
4-35	C.C. Lewis	New Zealand	Sydney	13/12/90
4-35	C.C. Lewis	West Indies	Port of Spain	06/03/94
4-37	J.E. Emburey	West Indies	Adelaide	24/01/87
4-39	J.E. Emburey	New Zealand	Dunedin	09/03/88
4-42	R.G.D. Willis	New Zealand	Edgbaston	15/06/83
4-42	D.R. Pringle	Pakistan	Lord's	26/05/92
4-44	D.L. Underwood	West Indies	Sydney	28/11/79
4-45	A.W. Greig	New Zealand	Trent Bridge	11/06/75
4-45	G.R. Dilley	Sri Lanka	Taunton	11/06/83
4-45	I.T. Botham	West Indies	Edgbaston	23/05/91
4-46	G.R. Dilley	West Indies	Perth	03/01/87
4-49	S.L. Watkin	West Indies	Kingston	26/02/94
4-52	E.E. Hemmings	India	Bombay	05/11/87
4-56	I.T. Botham	India	Headingley	02/06/82
4-57	C.M. Old	Australia	Melbourne	01/01/75
4-67	D.V. Lawrence	West Indies	Lord's	27/05/91

Most 4 Wicket Innings (36)

R.G.D. Willis	4		A.W. Greig	1
I.T. Botham	3		E.E. Hemmings	1
G.R. Dilley	3		P.W. Jarvis	1
C.C. Lewis	3		D.V. Lawrence	1
J.E. Emburey	2		J.K. Lever	1
M. Hendrick	2		P. Lever	1
C.M. Old	2		D.R. Pringle	1
J.A. Snow	2		G.C. Small	1

356   England - The Complete One-Day International Record

G.G. Arnold	1		G.B. Stevenson	1
P.A.J. DeFreitas	1		D.L. Underwood	1
A.R.C. Fraser	1		S.L. Watkin	1
N. Gifford	1			

3 Wicket Innings

3-8	D.R. Pringle	Pakistan	Adelaide	01/03/92
3-11	E.E. Hemmings	Australia	Sydney	26/01/83
3-15	P.A.J. DeFreitas	West Indies	Adelaide	24/01/87
3-16	I.T. Botham	Australia	Melbourne	24/01/79
3-17	J.E. Emburey	Pakistan	Lahore	18/11/87
3-18	J.K. Lever	Pakistan	Sialkot	30/12/77
3-18	C.C. Lewis	West Indies	Bridgetown	16/02/94
3-19	G.A. Gooch	Pakistan	Cuttack	22/10/89
3-20	N.A. Foster	Pakistan	Peshawar	22/11/87
3-20	D.A. Reeve	New Zealand	Auckland	11/01/92
3-20	C.C. Lewis	New Zealand	Edgbaston	19/05/94
3-21	D.R. Pringle	West Indies	Trent Bridge	02/06/84
3-22	A.R.C. Fraser	New Zealand	Wellington	13/02/91
3-22	D.R. Pringle	Pakistan	Melbourne	25/03/92
3-23	I.T. Botham	Zimbabwe	Albury	18/03/92
3-26	J.E. Emburey	West Indies	Devonport	03/02/87
3-26	I.T. Botham	Australia	Sydney	11/02/87
3-26	C.C. Lewis	New Zealand	Perth	07/12/90
3-27	D.L. Underwood	West Indies	Lord's	28/08/76
3-27	G. Miller	India	The Oval	04/06/82
3-28	G.G. Arnold	New Zealand	Swansea	18/07/73
3-28	G. Miller	Australia	Sydney	11/01/83
3-28	G.C. Small	Pakistan	Perth	07/01/87
3-28	P.A.J. DeFreitas	West Indies	Jaipur	26/10/87
3-28	A.R.C. Fraser	Australia	Sydney	01/01/91
3-29	C.M. Old	Australia	Headingley	18/06/75
3-29	D.L. Underwood	Australia	Old Trafford	02/06/77
3-29	I.T. Botham	Australia	Brisbane	16/01/83
3-29	I.T. Botham	Pakistan	Perth	07/01/87
3-29	N.A. Foster	Pakistan	Edgbaston	25/05/87
3-29	N.A. Foster	Australia	Old Trafford	25/05/89
3-29	G.C. Small	West Indies	Bridgetown	03/04/90
3-30	D.L. Underwood	West Indies	Headingley	05/09/73
3-30	V.J. Marks	New Zealand	Brisbane	15/01/83
3-30	D.R. Pringle	West Indies	Headingley	21/05/88
3-30	C.C. Lewis	West Indies	Melbourne	27/02/92
3-31	J.E. Emburey	Australia	Old Trafford	25/05/89
3-31	E.E. Hemmings	West Indies	Kingston	03/03/90
3-31	A.R.C. Fraser	West Indies	Port of Spain	05/03/94
3-32	P. Lever	East Africa	Edgbaston	14/06/75
3-32	M.W. Gatting	Pakistan	Karachi	26/03/84
3-32	G. Miller	West Indies	Old Trafford	31/05/84
3-32	G.R. Dilley	Australia	Melbourne	08/02/87
3-32	C.C. Lewis	South Africa	Edgbaston	25/08/94
3-33	R.A. Woolmer	Australia	Old Trafford	24/08/72
3-33	P. Willey	Australia	Melbourne	08/12/79
3-33	I.T. Botham	West Indies	Melbourne	20/01/80
3-33	I.T. Botham	West Indies	Devonport	03/02/87
3-33	R.K. Illingworth	Zimbabwe	Albury	18/03/92
3-33	P.A.J. DeFreitas	Pakistan	Trent Bridge	20/08/92
3-34	P.A.J. DeFreitas	West Indies	Melbourne	27/02/92
3-34	R.K. Illingworth	Pakistan	Trent Bridge	20/08/92
3-35	J.A. Snow	Australia	Lord's	26/08/72

One-Day International Records 357

3-35	V.J. Marks	India	Bangalore	20/01/85
3-35	J.E. Emburey	West Indies	Brisbane	17/01/87
3-36	C.M. Old	India	The Oval	15/07/74
3-38	J.P. Agnew	India	Nagpur	23/01/85
3-38	J.E. Emburey	India	Sharjah	02/04/87
3-38	D.J. Capel	Pakistan	Sharjah	07/04/87
3-38	J.E. Emburey	New Zealand	Christchurch	12/03/88
3-38	P.A.J. DeFreitas	Sri Lanka	Delhi	15/10/89
3-38	D.A. Reeve	India	Perth	22/02/92
3-38	P.A.J. DeFreitas	South Africa	Edgbaston	25/08/94
3-39	I.T. Botham	Pakistan	Sahiwal	23/12/77
3-39	P.H. Edmonds	New Zealand	Old Trafford	17/07/78
3-39	N.A. Foster	West Indies	Bridgetown	19/03/86
3-39	G.C. Small	West Indies	Gwalior	27/10/89
3-39	P.W. Jarvis	India	Gwalior	05/03/93
3-39	A.R. Caddick	Australia	Lord's	23/05/93
3-40	I.T. Botham	New Zealand	Melbourne	13/01/83
3-40	P.C.R. Tufnell	Australia	Sydney	01/01/91
3-40	D.E. Malcolm	India	Gwalior	04/03/93
3-41	R.D. Jackman	India	The Oval	15/07/74
3-41	R.D. Jackman	Australia	Sydney	26/01/83
3-41	P.J.W. Allott	Sri Lanka	Headingley	20/06/83
3-41	D.E. Malcolm	West Indies	Bridgetown	16/02/94
3-41	I.D.K. Salisbury	West Indies	Port of Spain	06/03/94
3-41	G.A. Hick	Australia	Melbourne	10/01/95
3-42	R.M. Ellison	Pakistan	Melbourne	02/03/85
3-42	P.A.J. DeFreitas	Australia	Perth	01/01/87
3-42	J.E. Emburey	Australia	Sydney	22/01/87
3-42	P.A.J. DeFreitas	Pakistan	Rawalpindi	12/10/87
3-43	C.M. Old	West Indies	Headingley	05/09/73
3-43	C.M. Old	India	Headingley	13/07/74
3-43	R.M. Ellison	New Zealand	Headingley	16/07/86
3-44	N.A. Foster	India	Poona	05/12/84
3-44	N.G. Cowans	India	Nagpur	23/01/85
3-44	G.C. Small	Sri Lanka	The Oval	04/09/88
3-47	I.T. Botham	New Zealand	Brisbane	15/01/83
3-47	N.A. Foster	India	Bombay	05/11/87
3-48	D.L. Underwood	India	Cuttack	27/01/82
3-48	R.K. Illingworth	Australia	Old Trafford	19/05/93
3-49	D.G. Cork	South Africa	Old Trafford	27/08/94
3-50	R. Illingworth	Australia	Melbourne	05/01/71
3-50	V.J. Marks	India	Cuttack	27/12/84
3-51	J.K. Lever	Australia	Melbourne	04/02/79
3-53	F.J. Titmus	New Zealand	Wellington	09/03/75
3-53	N.A. Foster	West Indies	Gujranwala	09/10/87
3-54	M. Hendrick	Australia	Edgbaston	22/08/80
3-54	C.C. Lewis	New Zealand	Headingley	23/05/90
3-54	C.C. Lewis	Australia	Old Trafford	19/05/93
3-55	M. Hendrick	New Zealand	Old Trafford	20/06/79
3-55	M.P. Bicknell	New Zealand	Christchurch	09/02/91
3-57	I.T. Botham	Pakistan	Trent Bridge	17/07/82
3-57	E.E. Hemmings	Sri Lanka	Poona	30/10/87
3-57	P.A.J. DeFreitas	Australia	Brisbane	16/12/90
3-59	N.G. Cowans	India	Sydney	26/02/85
3-59	M.W. Gatting	Australia	Melbourne	01/02/87
3-59	C.C. Lewis	West Indies	Port of Spain	05/03/94
3-62	C.C. Lewis	West Indies	Old Trafford	25/05/91

Most 3 Wicket Innings (110)

I.T. Botham	11	D.A. Reeve	2
P.A.J. DeFreitas	9	J.P. Agnew	1
C.C. Lewis	9	P.J.W. Allott	1
J.E. Emburey	7	G.G. Arnold	1
N.A. Foster	7	M.P. Bicknell	1
D.R. Pringle	4	A.R. Caddick	1
C.M. Old	4	D.J. Capel	1
D.L. Underwood	4	D.G. Cork	1
G.C. Small	4	G.R. Dilley	1
A.R.C. Fraser	3	P.H. Edmonds	1
E.E. Hemmings	3	G.A. Gooch	1
R.K. Illingworth	3	G.A. Hick	1
V.J. Marks	3	R. Illingworth	1
G. Miller	3	P.W. Jarvis	1
N.G. Cowans	2	P. Lever	1
R.M. Ellison	2	I.D.K. Salisbury	1
M.W. Gatting	2	J.A. Snow	1
M. Hendrick	2	F.J. Titmus	1
R.D. Jackman	2	P.C.R. Tufnell	1
J.K. Lever	2	P. Willey	1
D.E. Malcolm	2	R.A. Woolmer	1

MOST CAREER DISMISSALS

Name	Mat	Cat	St	Total	DPM
A.J. Stewart*	38	37	4	41	1.07
R.W. Taylor	27	26	6	32	1.18
R.C. Russell	26	26	5	31	1.19
P.R. Downton	28	26	3	29	1.03
D.L. Bairstow	21	17	4	21	1.00
I.J. Gould	18	15	3	18	1.00
C.J. Richards	22	16	1	17	0.77
B.N. French	13	13	3	16	1.23
A.P.E. Knott	20	15	1	16	0.80
S.J. Rhodes	9	9	2	11	1.22

* Also took 10 catches in 23 matches when not keeping wicket

MOST DISMISSALS IN A MATCH

Dis	C/S	Player	Opposition	Venue	Date
4	4+0	A.P.E. Knott	New Zealand	Swansea	18/07/73
4	4+0	R.W. Taylor	India	Headingley	02/06/82
4	4+0	P.R. Downton	West Indies	Headingley	21/05/88
4	4+0	A.J. Stewart	Zimbabwe	Sydney	15/12/94
4	3+1	S. Rhodes	Zimbabwe	Brisbane	07/01/95
3	2+1	A.P.E. Knott	Australia	Melbourne	05/01/71
3	3+0	A.P.E. Knott	Australia	Lord's	26/08/72
3	2+1	R.W. Taylor	West Indies	Headingley	05/09/73
3	2+1	R.W. Taylor	New Zealand	Scarborough	15/07/78
3	2+1	D.L. Bairstow	Australia	Sydney	11/12/79
3	2+1	D.L. Bairstow	Australia	Sydney	14/01/80
3	3+0	D.L. Bairstow	West Indies	Melbourne	20/01/80
3	2+1	I.J. Gould	New Zealand	Brisbane	15/01/83
3	3+0	I.J. Gould	Pakistan	Lord's	13/06/83
3	1+2	G. Fowler	Pakistan	Karachi	26/03/84
3	2+1	P.R. Downton	West Indies	Kingston	18/02/86
3	3+0	B.N. French	West Indies	Devonport	03/02/87
3	3+0	C.J. Richards	Pakistan	Sharjah	07/04/87
3	3+0	P.R. Downton	West Indies	Jaipur	26/10/87
3	3+0	R.C. Russell	Pakistan	Peshawar	22/11/87
3	3+0	R.C. Russell	New Zealand	Perth	07/12/90
3	2+1	R.C. Russell	New Zealand	Wellington	13/02/91
3	3+0	A.J. Stewart	Pakistan	Adelaide	01/03/92
3	2+1	A.J. Stewart	Pakistan	Lord's	20/05/92
3	3+0	A.J. Stewart	Australia	Lord's	23/05/93

MOST CAREER CATCHES

					Opposition				
Player	Cat	Aus	Can	Ind	NZ	Pak	SA	SL	WI	Zim
G.A. Gooch	45	14	0	9	4	6	0	4	7	1
D.I. Gower	44	10	0	6	11	8	0	3	6	0
I.T. Botham	36	5	1	4	8	7	0	3	8	0
A.J. Lamb	31	5	0	2	9	3	0	6	5	1
P.A.J. DeFreitas	25	5	0	2	2	2	1	2	10	1
G.A. Hick	25	2	0	7	5	4	2	1	3	1
D.W. Randall	25	10	0	0	7	3	0	0	5	0
R.A. Smith	23	1	0	0	6	3	2	1	10	0
M.W. Gatting	22	7	0	4	1	5	0	2	3	0
R.G.D. Willis	22	4	0	4	3	6	0	1	4	0
C.C. Lewis	20	5	0	0	3	2	4	1	5	0
J.E. Emburey	19	8	0	1	0	1	0	2	7	0
N.H. Fairbrother	19	5	0	2	1	3	0	1	4	3
C.W.J. Athey	16	7	0	1	0	5	0	0	3	0
J.M. Brearley	12	7	0	0	1	2	0	0	2	0
N.A. Foster	12	1	0	0	3	3	0	1	4	0
D.R. Pringle	11	1	0	0	1	3	0	1	5	0
D.A. Reeve	11	0	0	4	1	3	0	2	1	0
B.C. Broad	10	2	0	0	2	3	0	1	2	0

MOST CATCHES IN A MATCH

Cat	Player	Opposition	Venue	Date
3	A.W. Greig	West Indies	Headingley	05/09/73
3	G. Boycott	Pakistan	Lahore	13/01/78
3	D.I. Gower	Pakistan	Perth	07/01/87
3	C.W.J. Athey	Australia	Sydney	22/01/87
3	D.A. Reeve	Pakistan	Adelaide	01/03/92
3	G.A. Hick	India	Bangalore	26/02/93
3	N.H. Fairbrother	Australia	Old Trafford	19/05/93
3	G.P. Thorpe	West Indies	Bridgetown	16/02/94

BEST ALL-ROUND PERFORMANCES IN A MATCH

Fifty runs and four wickets

53 & 4-31	I.T. Botham	Australia	Sydney	05/03/92

Fifty runs and three wickets

91 & 3-41	G.A. Hick	Australia	Melbourne	10/01/95

Forty runs and three wickets

49* & 3-57	P.A.J. DeFreitas	Australia	Brisbane	16/12/90
44 & 3-50	V.J. Marks	India	Cuttack	27/12/84
41 & 3-40	I.T. Botham	New Zealand	Melbourne	13/01/83

Fifty runs and two wickets

94 & 2-29	G.A. Gooch	New Zealand	Scarborough	15/07/78
60 & 2-45	I.T. Botham	Sri Lanka	Colombo	13/02/82
65 & 2-61	I.T. Botham	New Zealand	Adelaide	29/01/83
64 & 2-18	P. Willey	Australia	Sydney	11/12/79
59 & 2-49	M.W. Gatting	India	Cuttack	27/12/84
55 & 2-23	G.A. Gooch	New Zealand	Headingley	23/05/90

Hundred runs and one wicket

117* & 1-46	G.A. Gooch	Australia	Lord's	03/06/85
108 & 1-16	G.A. Gooch	Australia	Edgbaston	22/08/80

Four Wickets and 25 runs

4-29 & 27*	J.K. Lever	Australia	Edgbaston	04/06/77
4-33 & 28*	G.B. Stevenson	Australia	Sydney	14/01/80
4-45 & 29	G.R. Dilley	Sri Lanka	Taunton	11/06/83

Fifty runs and three catches

59 & 3	N.H. Fairbrother	Australia	Old Trafford	19/05/93
56 & 3	G.A. Hick	India	Bangalore	26/02/93

Three wickets and two catches

3-16 & 2	I.T. Botham	Australia	Melbourne	24/01/79
3-20 & 2	C.C. Lewis	New Zealand	Edgbaston	19/05/94
3-21 & 2	D.R. Pringle	West Indies	Trent Bridge	02/06/84
3-26 & 2	J.E. Emburey	West Indies	Devonport	03/02/87
3-54 & 2	C.C. Lewis	Australia	Old Trafford	19/05/93

Fifty runs and three dismissals

74 & 3 (3+0)	A.J. Stewart	Australia	Lord's	23/05/93
50 & 3 (3+0)	A.P.E. Knott	Australia	Lord's	26/08/72
50 & 3 (2+1)	A.J. Stewart	Pakistan	Lord's	20/05/92

Thirty runs and four dismissals

30 & 4 (4+0)	P.R. Downton	West Indies	Headingley	21/05/88

BEST CAREER ALL-ROUND PERFORMANCES

2000 runs and 100 wickets
2113 & 145   I.T. Botham

500 runs and 100 wickets
551 & 104   P.A.J. DeFreitas

500 runs and 50 wickets
501 & 76   J.E. Emburey

4000 runs and 30 wickets
4290 & 36   G.A. Gooch

400 runs and 40 wickets
425 & 44   D.R. Pringle

300 runs and 50 wickets
315 & 61   C.C. Lewis

300 runs and 40 wickets
338 & 45   C.M. Old

250 runs and 40 wickets
285 & 44   V.J. Marks

1500 runs and 50 dismissals
1567 & 51 (47+4) A.J. Stewart

250 runs and 30 dismissals
261 & 31 (26+5) R.C. Russell

CAPTAINCY RECORDS

	Mat	Won	Lost	Tied	Aban	% Won
G.A. Gooch	50	24	23	0	3	51.06
M.W. Gatting	37	26	11	0	0	70.27
R.G.D. Willis	29	16	13	0	0	55.17
J.M. Brearley	25	15	9	0	1	62.50
D.I. Gower	24	10	13	1	0	41.66
M.H. Denness	12	7	4	0	1	63.63
I.T. Botham	9	4	5	0	0	44.44
M.A. Atherton	12	7	5	0	0	58.33
A.J. Stewart	6	2	4	0	0	33.33
K.W.R. Fletcher	5	2	3	0	0	40.00
J.E. Emburey	4	2	2	0	0	50.00
D.B. Close	3	2	1	0	0	66.66
R. Illingworth	3	1	1	0	1	50.00
A.J. Lamb	4	1	3	0	0	25.00
G. Boycott	2	2	0	0	0	100.00
N. Gifford	2	0	2	0	0	0.00
A.W. Greig	2	0	2	0	0	0.00
J.H. Edrich	1	0	0	0	1	0.00
A.P.E. Knott	1	0	1	0	0	0.00
TOTAL	**231**	**121**	**102**	**1**	**7**	**54.01**

Percentages do not include abandoned matches

WORLD ONE-DAY INTERNATIONAL RECORDS

1971-1995

MOST APPEARANCES

Opposition

Player	Team	Mat	Aus	Ban	Can	Eng	Ind	NZ	Pak	SA	SL	UAE	WI	Zim
A.R. Border	Aus	273	-	1	1	43	38	52	34	15	23	0	61	5
D.L. Haynes	WI	238	64	0	0	35	36	13	65	8	14	0	-	3
Javed Miandad	Pak	228	35	1	1	26	34	23	-	3	35	0	64	6
Kapil Dev	Ind	224	41	2	0	23	-	29	32	13	33	0	42	9
Salim Malik	Pak	207	24	1	0	21	28	31	-	11	40	1	45	5
R.B. Richardson	WI	202	45	0	0	32	31	11	59	8	14	0	-	2
M. Azharuddin	Ind	189	30	2	0	18	-	25	27	13	29	1	36	8
I.V.A. Richards	WI	187	54	0	0	36	31	12	41	0	11	0	-	2
Wasim Akram	Pak	183	26	2	0	20	26	16	-	9	31	1	46	6
S.R. Waugh	Aus	178	-	1	0	23	28	38	25	18	13	0	29	3
Imran Khan	Pak	175	29	1	1	20	29	12	-	1	32	0	49	1
D.C. Boon	Aus	175	-	1	0	21	28	38	19	19	16	0	28	5
P.J.L. Dujon	WI	169	47	0	0	26	31	9	44	0	10	0	-	2
D.M. Jones	Aus	164	-	1	0	20	21	27	21	13	17	0	41	3
Ramiz Raja	Pak	159	18	2	0	21	19	15	-	3	27	0	51	3
A.L. Logie	WI	158	41	0	0	16	24	11	49	4	11	0	-	2
A. Ranatunga	SL	157	21	2	0	9	31	24	42	7	-	0	15	6
R.J. Shastri	Ind	150	31	0	0	18	-	11	29	6	18	0	32	5
J.G. Wright	NZ	149	42	1	0	30	21	-	18	0	24	0	11	2
P.A. de Silva	SL	149	20	3	0	7	29	20	42	7	-	0	15	6
K. Srikkanth	Ind	146	28	1	0	15	-	15	26	3	19	0	34	5
M.D. Crowe	NZ	139	35	1	0	24	13	-	26	3	21	0	11	5
M.D. Marshall	WI	136	40	0	0	26	21	3	37	1	6	0	-	2
C.A. Walsh	WI	135	17	0	0	25	27	7	41	3	15	0	41	0

LEADING RUN SCORERS

Player	Team	Mat	Inn	No	Runs	HS	Avg	100	50
D.L. Haynes	WI	238	237	28	8648	152*	41.37	17	57
Javed Miandad	Pak	228	215	40	7327	119*	41.86	8	50
I.V.A. Richards	WI	187	167	24	6721	189*	47.00	11	45
A.R. Border	Aus	273	252	39	6524	127*	30.62	3	39
D.M. Jones	Aus	164	161	25	6068	145	44.61	7	46
D.C. Boon	Aus	175	171	14	5738	122	36.54	5	36
R.B. Richardson	WI	202	195	27	5641	122	33.57	5	41
Salim Malik	Pak	207	187	27	5246	102	32.78	5	33
M. Azharuddin	Ind	189	176	34	5162	108*	36.35	3	28
C.G. Greenidge	WI	128	127	13	5134	133*	45.03	11	31
Ramiz Raja	Pak	159	158	11	4915	119*	33.43	8	29
M.D. Crowe	NZ	139	136	17	4517	105*	37.95	3	33
A. Ranatunga	SL	157	150	28	4366	101*	35.78	1	30
G.R. Marsh	Aus	117	115	6	4357	126	39.97	9	22
G.A. Gooch	Eng	125	122	6	4290	142	36.98	8	23
P.A. de Silva	SL	149	145	14	4226	107*	32.25	3	31
K. Srikkanth	Ind	146	145	4	4092	123	29.02	4	27
A.J. Lamb	Eng	122	118	16	4010	118	39.31	4	26

HIGHEST INDIVIDUAL SCORES

189*	I.V.A. Richards	WI v Eng	Old Trafford	31/05/84
181	I.V.A. Richards	WI v SL	Karachi	13/10/87
175*	Kapil Dev	Ind v Zim	Tunbridge Wells	18/06/83
171*	G.M. Turner	NZ v EA	Edgbaston	07/06/75
169*	D.J. Callaghan	SA v NZ	Verwoerdburg	11/12/94
167*	R.A. Smith	Eng v Aus	Edgbaston	21/05/93
158	D.I. Gower	Eng v NZ	Brisbane	15/01/83
153*	I.V.A. Richards	WI v Aus	Melbourne	09/12/79
153	B.C. Lara	WI v Pak	Sharjah	05/11/93
152*	D.L. Haynes	WI v Ind	Georgetown	21/03/89
149	I.V.A. Richards	WI v Ind	Jamshedpur	07/12/83
148	D.L. Haynes	WI v Aus	St John's	22/02/78
146*	D.L. Haynes	WI v NZ	Berbice	14/04/85
145	D.M. Jones	Aus v Eng	Brisbane	16/12/90
142*	C.W.J. Athey	Eng v NZ	Old Trafford	18/07/86
142*	D.L. Haynes	WI v Pak	Port of Spain	18/03/88
142	G.A. Gooch	Eng v Pak	Karachi	20/11/87
141	D.L. Houghton	Zim v NZ	Hyderabad	10/10/87
140	G.M. Turner	NZ v SL	Auckland	20/03/83
140	S.T. Jayasuriya	SL v NZ	Bloemfonte	08/12/94

HIGHEST PARTNERSHIPS FOR EACH WICKET

Wkt	Runs	Countries	Venue	Date	Batsmen
1st	212	Aus v Ind	Jaipur	07/09/86	G.R. Marsh/D.C. Boon
2nd	263	Pak v NZ	Sharjah	20/04/94	Aamir Sohail/Inzamam-ul-Haq
3rd	224	Aus v SL	Adelaide	28/01/85	D.M. Jones/A.R. Border
4th	173	Aus v Pak	Perth	02/01/87	D.M. Jones/S.R. Waugh
5th	152	WI v SL	Brisbane	12/01/85	I.V.A. Richards/C.H. Lloyd
6th	154	WI v Pak	Sharjah	21/10/91	R.B. Richardson/P.J.L. Dujon
7th	115	WI v Pak	Gujranwala	04/11/86	P.J.L. Dujon/M.D. Marshall
8th	119	Aus v SA	Port Elizabeth	04/04/94	P.R. Reiffel/S.K. Warne
9th	126*	Ind v Zim	Tunbridge Wells	18/06/83	Kapil Dev/S.M.H. Kirmani
10th	106*	WI v Eng	Old Trafford	31/05/84	I.V.A. Richards/M.A. Holding

TOTAL HIGHEST PARTNERSHIPS

Runs	Wkt	Opposition	Venue	Date	Batsmen
263	2nd	Pak v NZ	Sharjah	20/04/94	Aamir Sohail/Inzamam-ul-Haq
224*	3rd	Aus v SL	Adelaide	28/01/85	D.M. Jones/A.R. Border
221	2nd	WI v Ind	Jamshedpur	07/12/83	C.G. Greenidge/I.V.A. Richards
213	3rd	Eng v WI	Lord's	27/05/91	G.A. Hick/N.H. Fairbrother
212	1st	Aus v Ind	Jaipur	07/09/86	G.R. Marsh/D.C. Boon
206	3rd	Pak v Ban	Chittagong	29/10/88	Moin-ul-Atiq/Ijaz Ahmed
205	2nd	WI v Aus	Melbourne	09/12/79	D.L. Haynes/I.V.A. Richards
205	2nd	Pak v Ind	Multan	17/12/82	Mohsin Khan/Zaheer Abbas
204	2nd	Pak v SL	Rawalpindi	19/01/92	Inzamam-ul-Haq/Salim Malik
204	1st	Pak v SL	Sharjah	04/02/93	Saeed Anwar/Ramiz Raja
202	2nd	Eng v Aus	Lord's	03/06/85	G.A. Gooch/D.I. Gower
202	1st	Pak v SL	Adelaide	17/02/90	Ramiz Raja/Saeed Anwar

Partnerships by three batsmen after one retired hurt

221*	1st	WI v Pak	Melbourne	23/02/92	D.L. Haynes/(B.C. Lara)/ R.B. Richardson
200	3rd	Pak v Ind	Sharjah	25/10/91	(Zahid Fazal)/Salim Malik/ Imran Khan

LEADING WICKET TAKERS

Player	Team	Overs	Mds	Runs	Wkts	Avg	B/B	5WI	E/R
Wasim Akram	Pak	1577.3	124	5992	263	22.78	5-15	5	3.79
Kapil Dev	Ind	1867	235	6946	253	27.45	5-43	1	3.72
C.J. McDermott	Aus	1144.3	94	4625	184	25.13	5-44	1	4.04
Imran Khan	Pak	1243.3	123	4845	182	26.62	6-14	1	3.89
Waqar Younis	Pak	871.5	66	3800	176	21.59	6-26	7	4.35
S.R. Waugh	Aus	1199.3	49	5290	159	33.27	4-33	0	4.41
R.J. Hadlee	NZ	1030.2	185	3408	158	21.56	5-25	5	3.30
M.D. Marshall	WI	1195.5	122	4233	157	26.96	4-18	0	3.53
C.E.L. Ambrose	WI	952.5	126	3325	152	21.87	5-17	4	3.48
C.A. Walsh	WI	1190.4	110	4542	148	30.68	5-1	1	3.81
J. Garner	WI	888.2	141	2752	146	18.84	5-31	3	3.09
I.T. Botham	Eng	1045.1	109	4139	145	28.54	4-31	0	3.96
M.A. Holding	WI	912.1	99	3034	142	21.36	5-26	1	3.32
M. Prabhakar	Ind	944.1	74	3924	142	27.63	5-35	1	4.15
E.J. Chatfield	NZ	1010.5	155	3621	140	25.86	5-34	1	3.58
Abdul Qadir	Pak	850	54	3443	132	26.08	5-44	2	4.05
R.J. Shastri	Ind	1102.1	56	4650	129	36.04	5-15	1	4.21
I.V.A. Richards	WI	940.4	26	4227	118	35.82	6-41	2	4.49
C.L. Hooper	WI	839.4	23	3618	116	31.18	4-34	0	4.30
M.C. Snedden	NZ	753.1	70	3235	114	28.37	4-34	0	4.29
Aqib Javed	Pak	879.4	68	3582	113	31.69	7-37	1	4.07
Mudassar Nazar	Pak	809.1	43	3432	111	30.91	5-28	1	4.24
S.P. O'Donnell	Aus	725	49	3102	108	28.72	5-13	1	4.27
J. Srinath	Ind	611.5	47	2613	106	24.65	5-24	2	4.27
P.A.J. DeFreitas	Eng	848.1	105	3284	104	31.57	4-35	0	3.87
D.K. Lillee	Aus	598.5	80	2145	103	20.82	5-34	1	3.58

BEST BOWLING

7-37	Aqib Javed	Pak v Ind	Sharjah	25/10/91
7-51	W.W. Davis	WI v Aus	Headingley	11/06/83
6-12	A.R. Kumble	Ind v WI	Calcutta	27/11/93
6-14	G.J. Gilmour	Aus v Eng	Headingley	18/06/75
6-14	Imran Khan	Pak v Ind	Sharjah	22/03/85
6-15	C.E.H. Croft	WI v Eng	Arnos Vale	04/02/81
6-26	Waqar Younis	Pak v SL	Sharjah	29/04/90
6-29	B.P. Patterson	WI v Ind	Nagpur	08/12/87
6-29	S.T. Jayasuriya	SL v Eng	Moratuwa	20/03/93
6-30	Waqar Younis	Pak v NZ	Auckland	13/03/94
6-39	K.H. Macleay	Aus v Ind	Trent Bridge	13/06/83
6-41	I.V.A. Richards	WI v Ind	Delhi	23/10/89
6-50	A.H. Gray	WI v Aus	Port of Spain	09/03/91
5-1	C.A. Walsh	WI v SL	Sharjah	03/12/86
5-11	Waqar Younis	Pak v NZ	Peshawar	04/11/90
5-13	S.P. O'Donnell	Aus v NZ	Christchurch	04/03/90
5-15	G.S. Chappell	Aus v Ind	Sydney	08/01/81
5-15	R.J. Shastri	Ind v Aus	Perth	08/12/91
5-15	Wasim Akram	Pak v Zim	Karachi	24/12/93

MOST CAREER DISMISSALS

Player	Team	Mat	Cat	St	Total	DPM
P.J.L. Dujon	WI	169	183	21	204	1.20
I.A. Healy	Aus	122	146	26	172	1.40
R.W. Marsh	Aus	92	120	4	124	1.34
Salim Yousuf	Pak	86	81	22	103	1.19
D.J. Richardson	SA	68	82	12	94	1.38
K.S. More	Ind	94	63	27	90	0.95
I.D.S. Smith	NZ	98	81	5	86	0.87
Rashid Latif	Pak	65	60	18	78	1.20
Wasim Bari	Ind	51	52	10	62	1.21
H.P. Tillekeratne	SL	97	52	5	57	0.58

MOST CAREER CATCHES

Opposition

Player	Team	Cat	Aus	Ban	Eng	Ind	NZ	Pak	SA	SL	WI	Zim
A.R. Border	Aus	127	-	0	14	17	33	18	4	12	26	3
I.V.A. Richards	WI	101	20	0	11	27	6	27	0	8	-	2
M. Azharuddin	Ind	77	8	1	15	-	10	15	4	8	12	4
Kapil Dev	Ind	71	16	1	5	-	14	9	2	10	11	3
R.B. Richardson	WI	70	9	0	15	13	5	21	2	4	-	1
Javed Miandad	Pak	70	10	0	12	11	6	-	1	12	14	2
R.S. Mahanama	SL	66	8	1	1	14	6	19	9	-	6	2
Salim Malik	Pak	65	5	0	3	8	21	-	3	12	12	1
M.D. Crowe	NZ	64	23	0	12	5	-	9	1	9	0	5
S.R. Waugh	Aus	62	-	0	5	8	13	8	6	3	17	2
C.L. Hooper	WI	61	11	0	1	14	2	27	2	4	-	0
A.L. Logie	WI	61	16	0	4	10	8	21	1	1	-	0
D.L. Haynes	WI	59	16	0	6	14	1	12	3	5	-	2
D.M. Jones	Aus	54	-	1	5	14	14	3	3	5	8	1
J.G. Wright	NZ	51	17	1	11	8	-	3	0	10	1	0